DANCE OF THE ELEPHANT WALK OF THE DRAGON

Also by the author

Never Too Big To Fail: The Collapse of IL&FS and its Ten Trillion-Rupee Maze

DANCE OF THE ELEPHANT WALK OF THE DRAGON

HOW **INDIA** AND **CHINA** ARE **RESHAPING** THE **WORLD** IN DIFFERENT WAYS

Sandeep Hasurkar

RUPA

First published by
Rupa Publications India Pvt. Ltd 2024
7/16, Ansari Road, Daryaganj
New Delhi 110002

Sales centres:
Bengaluru Chennai
Hyderabad Jaipur Kathmandu
Kolkata Mumbai Prayagraj

P-ISBN: 978-93-6156-459-8
E-ISBN: 978-93-6156-574-8

First impression 2024

10 9 8 7 6 5 4 3 2 1

The moral right of the author has been asserted.

Printed in India

To my parents, for the advice they gave me,
and I now give to my children

———∞∞∞———

विद्या ददाति विनयं विनयाद्याति पात्रताम् ।
पात्रत्वाद्धनमाप्नोति धनाद्धर्म ततः सुखम् ॥

[*Knowledge imparts politeness and good behaviour, which in turn gives worthiness. From that worthiness one earns wealth. That wealth leads to the path of virtue which in turn gives happiness.*]

'You have brains in your head.
You have feet in your shoes.
You can steer yourself any direction you choose.'

—Dr Seuss, *Oh, the Places You'll Go!*

Contents

Introduction   *xi*

PART ONE: THE BACKGROUND

1. Geography: The Destiny of Nations   3
2. Culture: Shaping Identities   11
3. History and Political Economy: The Past in the Present   28

PART TWO: THREE DETERMINANTS OF REFORM

4. Leadership   43
5. Federalism   52
6. Institutions and the Legal Framework   59

PART THREE: THE DRIVERS OF GROWTH

7. The First Yang: Agricultural Land Reforms and Markets   73
8. The Second Yang: Special Economic Zones   89
9. The Third Yang: Real Estate and Urbanization   109
10. The Fourth Yang: Policy and Infrastructure   137
11. The Fifth Yang: Entrepreneurship   146

PART FOUR: THE COSTS OF GROWTH

12. The First Yin: Debt   163
13. The Second Yin: Corruption   176

14. The Third Yin: Geopolitics   190

15. The Fourth Yin: Demographics   219

16. The Fifth Yin: Environment   229

PART FIVE: THE AUTHORITARIAN DRAGON AND
THE DEMOCRATIC ELEPHANT

17. Understanding the Differential   247

18. Influence of Culture   251

19. Democracy with Indian Characteristics   257

20. Institutional Reforms   263

21. Local Government   269

22. Land and Agricultural Market Reforms   273

In Conclusion: Parrots and Tea Leaves   276

Endnotes   286

Bibliography   304

Index   313

Introduction

It's the Dragon.

Since its inception as a novel 'socialist market economy' under Deng Xiaoping in 1978, the world has marvelled at China's remarkable rise—speculating about its underlying causes and worrying about its stability and sustainability. Yet, China is today the world's second-largest economy (the largest in terms of purchasing power parity [PPP]), the 'factory of the world' and one of the largest global consumer markets. Over the last four decades, the Chinese economy has doubled every eight years, consistently achieving nearly 10 per cent annual growth and confounding experts and laypeople alike. This meteoric rise is unprecedented in world history. Former Australian Prime Minister (PM) Kevin Rudd described it as 'the English Industrial Revolution and the global information revolution combusting simultaneously and compressed into not 300 years, but 30'.[1]

China's growth trajectory has sparked widespread concern around the world with significant geopolitical and security implications as the existing global structure grapples with the rapid emergence of an increasingly dominant and rising power. Its newfound status as an economic hegemon is widely perceived as the driving force behind its current geopolitical assertiveness. Its flagship Belt and Road Initiative (BRI), a global infrastructure development outreach programme with construction and debt financing that initially spanned trade routes and countries of the ancient Silk Road but has since expanded, demonstrates its intent to broaden its spheres of influence and reclaim what it deems as its rightful place in world affairs. However, from Ecuador to Uganda, Zambia and Sri Lanka, the initiative has faced accusations of poor quality, crippling debt and unsustainable projects. Recent trade wars and geopolitical shifts triggered by this intent have also influenced multinational defence alliances, such as the Quadrilateral Security Dialogue (QSD; more commonly Quad) and AUKUS[2], in response to the growing economic and military influence of *Zhongguo*—the Middle Kingdom[3] as China historically identifies itself.

Politicians, bureaucrats and policymakers in the government, along with academics and ordinary citizens have all attempted to learn more about and comprehend the incredible economic phenomenon of the rise of a poor nation with a per capita income lower than that of many sub-Saharan African countries in 1962. The nation lost an estimated 30 million of its citizens to famine caused by one of the world's most devastating man-made disasters ever.[4] Yet, in less than 60 years, it has transformed into the richest nation in the world.[5]

China's economic progress is not only astounding but also difficult to grasp for the scale of its achievements. It has the most successful special economic zones (SEZs) in the world, with giant manufacturing facilities that produce goods ranging from ordinary safety pins to luxury BMW cars. China is home to eight of the world's 15 tallest buildings.[6] It has constructed massive multipurpose power plants, including the world's largest power station—the Three Gorges Dam—which has an installed capacity of 22,500 MW.[7] Magnetic levitation trains with cutting-edge technology have just made their debut in Qingdao, with the world's fastest magnetic levitation train reaching speeds of 600 km/hr.[8] China has large and fast transport expressways (its highway network of 149,600 km is the longest in the world[9]) and extensive railways (its railway network of over 100,000 km is the second longest in the world[10]). It has pioneered cross-country, inter-basin water diversion projects. Water supply from the Danjiangkou Reservoir in Central China travels 1,432 km through canals and pipelines, including across the Yellow River by burrowing beneath it, and arrives at its water treatment plants in Beijing 15 days later. This South-to-North Water Diversion Project is, unsurprisingly, the longest water transfer project in the world.[11]

China has also built the Jiaozhou Bay Bridge, which connects the eastern coastal city of Qingdao to its suburb of Huangdao and spans 42.4 km, making it the world's longest over-sea bridge. In comparison, this bridge could easily span the English Channel, which is 32 km wide at its narrowest point.[12] Furthermore, China produced and utilized more cement between 2011 and 2013 than the United States (US) did throughout the entire twentieth century.[13] A Chinese company built a 30-storey skyscraper in just 15 days in 2011. Three years later, another Chinese company accomplished an even more astonishing feat by constructing a 57-storey skyscraper in 19 days.[14] Evidently, imperial scale and speed are inherent features of the Chinese psyche, lying dormant since the days of Shi Huangdi's Great Wall[15] in 215 BCE which has now reawakened. However, the costs to the environment, population, social stability and inequalities resulting from this single-minded pursuit of economic growth have been enormous and unprecedented, and have been the recent focus of attention of policymakers in China.

But the entire enterprise of building China by the Communist Party of China (CPC) under the banner of what Deng Xiaoping's modern China's ideologue called 'socialism with Chinese characteristics'[16] has surprisingly worked against conventional economic theory, wisdom and experience. In fact, despite many sceptics and pundits predicting failure and collapse of China over the past four decades, the approach has proven remarkably successful. However, recent events like the Evergrande real estate company debt crisis, a slowing economy in an increasingly hostile geopolitical environment and the growing issues in real estate and other sectors that have fuelled growth for many years, serve as timely reminders that all may not be well behind the inscrutable and Sphinx-like facade of the CPC-led monolith economy. The moving parts of this economy are not visible or disclosed, hindering comprehensive assessments by observers.

China and India are subcontinent-sized Asian neighbours separated by the world's highest mountain range—the Himalayas. The great rivers that flow from the mighty Himalayas and the Tibetan Plateau have shaped much of their civilization, history, culture, environment and economy. They also house around 36 per cent (nearly two of every five persons) of the population on Earth.[17] As a result, both countries are critical to the future of global economic growth, climate change and politics in what has been dubbed the 'Asian Century' by some commentators. As the country has grown, the Indian government has kept a close eye on China's policies.

On the infrastructure front, India has undertaken development initiatives ranging from the successful Golden Quadrilateral and National Highway programme launched in 1998 to the SEZs in 2000; from the Sagarmala project launched in 2003 to the Indian rivers interlinking project and the Delhi–Mumbai Industrial Corridor launched in 2005. Similar initiatives have been undertaken in policies encouraging private and foreign investment participation and fiscal incentives in the energy, telecom, cluster manufacturing and other infrastructure sectors. However, a few of these initiatives intended to act as economic force multipliers to accelerate economic growth have not yielded results as expected.

This has been a moot point for policymakers, since India, too, began its economic liberalization in 1991. Both countries' per capita gross domestic products (GDPs) were comparable in 1991 (China: $333 [approx. ₹24,975 at current exchange rates] to India: $304 [approx. ₹22,725]). In fact, in 1991, India had a higher per capita GDP in terms of PPP—the ability to purchase a defined basket of goods in their respective markets using local currencies.[18]

By 2020, less than 30 years later, China's per capita GDP had risen to $10,409, while India's had only risen to $1,913—a difference of more than five times. Even in terms of per capita GDP on PPP, China increased to $17,209, while India was at $6,518 with a nearly threefold difference.[19] This geometric progression differential between the two economies is best illustrated by the fact that the increment of growth in China's GDP has been greater than the entire Indian economy for every two-year period between 2008 and 2014. For example, China's GDP grew from $8.5 trillion in 2012 to $10.5 trillion in 2014. By comparison, India's total GDP was $1.8 trillion in 2012, which grew to $2 trillion in 2014.[20]

Both India and China operated under command economies with socialist or communist characteristics that were opening up to market economics and seeking foreign investment and export-led growth. However, a significant disparity emerged between them. What caused such a large disparity? Were wrong multiplier-drivers picked? Are the policies, results and consequences of China's choices unique to its national, political and institutional context? Most importantly, what lessons can India garner from it for its own development journey?

Another pressing concern for economic and foreign policymakers in recent years has been India's massive and growing trade deficit (imports minus exports). In 2000–01, India's imports from China stood at $1.5 billion, while exports totalled to only $0.83 billion, resulting in a modest trade deficit of $0.67 billion. This trade deficit has now surged to a staggering $101 billion (2022). This is the largest deficit with any nation and constitutes the bulk of India's overall trade deficit. India's imports from China are now at $119 billion, while its exports languish at $18 billion, a difference of more than six times.[21]

The components of trade have also been a source of serious concern. According to some analysts, primary commodities account for a sizeable portion of India's exports to China, its largest trading partner, whereas China primarily exports manufactured goods to India. This, they argue, is reminiscent of India's colonial past[22], when Britain fuelled its industries by using India as a source of raw materials and a captive market for its finished goods.

China is also viewed with increasing suspicion and hostility in India due to the heightened military belligerence resulting in border clashes and loss of life along the unresolved 3,488-km border[23], a longstanding dispute dating back to the Sino-Indian War of 1962. As the two neighbouring countries navigate their intertwined yet conflicted journey towards an 'Asian Century', India's interest in understanding China as a nation and political entity—its economy, policies, geopolitics, institutions and culture—has grown.

There has been a significant amount of literature published on both India and China over the years. There is, however, little material for the general reader who wants to understand the Indo-China stories, their evolution over the last 30 years, the origins of Chinese economic miracle, its components, context, environment, risks and, most importantly, potential long-term outcomes. In the minds of many, the question of what, how and why did China do differently (the 'China Question') remains unanswered.

In the absence of informed public debate, some have simplistically and incorrectly, attributed China's higher economic growth to its single-party authoritarian structure rather than India's multi-party democracy, along with its system of institutional checks and balances. Recent apparent failures and contradictions in Western democracy and markets have also sparked a fierce global debate over whether the 'Beijing Consensus' model of national political and economic development is superior to the 'Washington Consensus' model. It is a highly contentious viewpoint that China has attempted to promote and evangelize in Africa, Asia and a number of developing countries in the Global South.

These concerns are summarized by three critical questions that must be addressed. The first question is 'what are the factors that have led to China's explosive growth, outpacing India over the 30-year period between 1991 to 2021?' The second question is 'to what extent can China's higher economic growth over this period be attributed to its authoritarian structure of governance, or is India's growth slower due to its democratic structure of checks and balances?' The third and perhaps the most important question, in the time-honoured fortune telling traditions of card drawing parrots in India and reading tea leaves in China is 'what are the lessons learned, and what insight does it give to potential economic growth for India and China over the next 30 years?'

This book sets out to address that gap.

My journey to write this book, too, is of three decades—as a participant and contributor in India's economic liberalization process, in some of the previously mentioned national policies and projects while also tracking the trajectory of China's reform and opening-up policies in trade, finance and infrastructure. In 1993, I was part of a team that advised the Government of India on the eight fast-track power projects as the country opened up the power sector to foreign investment. In the same year, I led the initial public offering of the first public sector bank to list on stock exchanges after nationalization. I was also involved in the country's first housing mortgage securitization and other market-facing innovations as financial sector reforms got underway.

Over the subsequent decades, I was involved with reforms and initiatives related to SEZs, waterways, interlinking of rivers, roads, maritime, power and other infrastructure. The span of my work ranged from helping formulate concept and assessment studies on potential projects of national importance for government consideration, advising and assisting governments with infrastructure policies and public–private partnership frameworks and drafting documents; to structuring, financing, raising funds, implementing and operating pioneering infrastructure projects, particularly in the renewable and bioenergy sectors. I, therefore, believe that I have both the 'bird's eye' view of policy and reform, and the 'worm's eye' view of its implementation and operation on ground to burnish my credentials for undertaking this study. In fact, I had originally envisaged that I would research this subject as the thesis for my doctoral programme and even enrolled at IIT Bombay for the same. I, however, came to the conclusion that a book for the general reader would serve a larger purpose and reach a wider audience too, who, like me, may have an unaddressed curiosity on the Indo-China economic growth stories. The book, however, draws extensively from academic research and seeks to maintain its rigour and cross references throughout its narrative.

My primary research on China's and India's economic performance led me to the conclusion that the answer to these questions lay not only in the immediate and visible domains of modern economics and finance but also in a comprehensive and multidisciplinary approach to understand their respective backgrounds and contexts. More research followed on the histories, philosophies, geographies, sociologies, anthropologies, cultures, political economies, laws and institutions of the two countries. I have spent the last 24 months immersed in these subjects, conducting extensive research to find answers to these questions.

So, why this book? The volume of published material on China is, to put it mildly, enormous. China is likely the most researched country in the world. The majority of this literature, however, is written by academics. Even though it is well-researched and thoroughly analysed for the most part, it only answers the specific part of their research question. This siloed approach in place of an interdisciplinary one, in my opinion, leaves a large gap in which a unified story and the 'big picture'—one that may perhaps better explain the topic and help connect dots for the general reader, who is interested in the subject but does not want to wade through multiple academic research papers and books to find answers—goes unidentified and unarticulated. To the best of my knowledge, the Indo-China economic comparison in this 'zoomed out' context has also gone unaddressed.

This is exactly what the book aims to do—put together a jigsaw puzzle of oddly shaped pieces viewed through the lens of various disciplines to help tell these two stories better. In doing so, it relies extensively on academic research, but draws conclusions that are uniquely its own. Looking at the past would be a tedious pastime if it didn't suggest or even hint at possible futures. As a result, the book also examines the current states of both the Chinese and Indian economies, the current geopolitical situation and potential scenarios for how these stories may unfold in the future.

The book is divided into five sections: The Background; Three Determinants of Reform; The Drivers of Growth—the Yang; The Costs of Growth—the Yin; Authoritarian Dragon and Democratic Elephant. These sections are then followed by the conclusion—Parrots and Tea Leaves.

A country's economy is more than just a map of its economic and political policies. To gain a better understanding, it must be examined against a backdrop of many colours, complexities and interactions. History, geography, culture, language, philosophy, sociology and anthropology are all primary colours that make up the white light of economic growth. The first part of the book, titled 'The Background', consists of three chapters—'Geography: The Destiny of Nations', 'Culture: Shaping Identities and History' and 'Political Economy: The Past in the Present'—that use broad brushstrokes to paint a background.

The second part, 'Three Determinants of Reform', identifies and explains three key factors—leadership, federalism and institutions and legal framework—in the context of India and China.

In the third and fourth part of the book, the drivers and costs—the yang and yin of growth in China and India—are compared and contrasted. It is divided into five chapters each that examine the dynamic unity and duality of this economic growth through the lens of 'yin and yang', a philosophical concept with shared roots in both nations—in India, as the cosmic 'tantra' forces of male and female elements—dwelling in the interaction of energies of equal but opposing forces that create the balanced sum or the equilibrated whole.

The five yang—agricultural land reforms and markets, SEZs, real estate and urbanization, policy and infrastructure and entrepreneurship—investigate each of the growth drivers in the context of China and India's reforms and growth stories. The five yin—debt, corruption, geopolitics, demographics and environment—examine the comparative costs, challenges and consequences of India's and China's growth policies and processes.

'Authoritarian Dragon and Democratic Elephant', the fifth part of the book, summarizes the findings from the preceding research and extensive analysis. It comes to the conclusion, based on the evidence presented, that the difference between India and China in economic growth from 1991 to 2021 is the result of a complex interaction of individually identified leadership, along with institutional, historical and cultural factors, and not the basic 'authoritarianism vs democracy' arguments as some have suggested. It also identifies issues that must be addressed in order for India to realize its full potential in the upcoming decades.

The book's conclusion, 'Parrots and Tea Leaves', builds on the previous section by highlighting opportunities and threats to the economic growth of both India and China in the context of their past and present, rapidly changing geopolitics, transforming global economic and financial frameworks and emerging networks of cooperation. It concludes that, due to its democratic processes and system of checks and balances, India is likely to experience higher and more stable growth over the next two decades, even as it implements administrative and institutional reforms to improve governance and the delivery of public goods and prosperity to its citizens. China, on the other hand, is dealing with long-standing issues and imbalances that pose significant challenges to its stability and growth.

Aside from state and institutional capacities, government models and other differentiators, two root threads that emerged from the research that run through the narrative are those of leadership and land.

Since the establishment of the People's Republic of China in 1949, five men have principally shaped the CPC and the nation. Deng Xiaoping, who succeeded Mao Zedong as paramount leader, is widely recognized as the architect of 'reform and opening-up' and modern China, wielding power and influence from 1978 onwards. While he formally stepped down from party and government positions in 1989, his pervasive influence and informal authority over the party and the nation continued. This influence was also evident during the tumultuous phase when, following the Tiananmen Square protests in 1989 and the subsequent crackdown, party hardliners threatened to derail reforms. This phase also saw him coming out of retirement where he undertook his famous 'Southern Tour' which shifted the battle decisively in favour of the reform process. By the time of his death in 1997, reforms were deeply entrenched and irreversible in both the CPC and the nation. Since then, his successors have followed the path set by Deng: consolidating the gains, continuing with the reforms process and responding to opportunities like the World Trade Organization accession in 2001 that gave China access to global markets. The rise to power of Xi Jinping in 2012 and his elevation to paramount leader since, represents a continuity of leadership that has enabled China to take long-term perspectives and decisions in its reform process.

In contrast, India has had 15 PMs since 1947, with only six serving a full term or more. In the 75 years since Independence, the prime ministership has been held by a member of a single political family for 38 years. More importantly, no grassroots level politician with an electoral majority in Parliament has held the position of PM after Indira Gandhi in 1984, until a majority government led by PM Narendra Modi was elected in 2014. For nearly 25 critical years, from 1991—when Indian economic liberalization began following a crisis—until 2014, the pace and depth of reforms were hampered by a lack of political capital and direction that only a government with an electoral majority mandate can bring. As a result, India's reforms were limited to 'shallow reforms', plucking low hanging fruits by bringing changes to policy and through gazette notifications in sectors like international trade, foreign exchange rates, banking and finance, industrial policy, and so on, leaving foundational but sensitive reforms with political implications (like land and agriculture) untouched. The increased institutional contestation for executive policy and governance space towards the end of this period also resulted in an unholy mess that collapsed under the confusion, allegations and recriminations it generated. It directly led to a change and the formation of a government with a majority mandate and political leadership at its helm after 30 years, following which, reforms and implementation on the ground have picked up visible pace.

The other root narrative shaping the economic growth stories of both countries is land. Four of the five identified yang growth drivers are related to the history, availability, ownership and monetization of land. Indeed, the roots and most important branches of the so-called 'Chinese economic miracle' are in land.

Land has always been at the heart of China's policies. State ownership of all land in China, undertaken in the failed collectivization and commune experiment in the late 1950s, enabled the household responsibility system 'contract farming' in the late 1970s, which improved agricultural productivity and enabled the creation of national agricultural produce markets. Due to state ownership, local governments were able to offer large tracts of land to foreign investors in the 1980s for the establishment of SEZs. Local governments were able to repurpose state-owned land away from rural agriculture and monetize it by selling building rights to real estate developers beginning in the 1990s, resulting in the greatest urbanization in human history.

The massive real estate and infrastructure construction that has fuelled China's economy, particularly since 2008, has been financed in large part by the establishment of private rights ownership and a real estate market in China for the first time since the CPC took power in 1949. The subsequent transfer of Chinese households' historically high savings as payment for this private rights-owned real estate built on government-owned land has triggered one of the largest monetization and valuations in global financial history. China's real estate market has grown from zero in 1994 to $52 trillion in 2019. Real estate accounts for 29 per cent of China's GDP. China is now at a record 64 per cent urbanization rate, up from barely 30 per cent in 1994, as its cities have grown rapidly. According to some estimates, the real estate sector accounts for nearly 70 to 80 per cent of household wealth in China. The Chinese real estate market is now one of the most important sectors of the global economy. It is twice the size of the US and four times the size of China's GDP. The enormous financial firepower that the monetization of land urbanization rights has provided local and provincial governments in a communist state that had no private property until recently, and was only recently opening up as a market economy cannot be overstated. Since the 1990s, it has been a source of unchecked and unquestioned funds that have helped the local governments fund budgets and infrastructure expenditures, and it is also a cause of many of the current issues that China is dealing with.

On the other hand, India has had limited success with land policies since Independence. A complicated system of political interest groups has kept subsidies in place and stopped the reforms in the agricultural sector that are needed to create market-driven farming at profitable prices over time. Also, land holdings that are getting smaller and more scattered, as well as the purchase of project land, have been controversial for a long time. Over the years, these have made it much harder for governments to carry out their SEZ policies, large infrastructure projects and urbanization plans. Even though different governments have tried to pass laws that set up processes and provide generous compensation for land acquisition, it is still an emotional and political issue.

In the same way, four of the five yin challenges to China's growth—debt, environment, geopolitics and demographics—can be traced back to land. Local government financing vehicles (LGFVs) were set up randomly and without oversight to turn state-owned land into cash. This led to a complex pyramid structure of government, institutional and private debt that is now linked to rising real estate prices and a construction and infrastructure boom. This expansion, however, is losing steam, despite the government's desperate efforts to keep it going by announcing new infrastructure spending as housing prices fall and real estate firms fail. The LGFVs have also been a source of endemic corruption in China, with their ruthless and unquestioned takeover of rural land with paltry compensation to those tilling it while selling land construction rights to private builders at high prices. The resulting inequalities and rural–urban divide have significantly contributed to 'zero tolerance for corruption' and the 'common prosperity' programmes becoming keystones of President Xi Jinping's agenda. Local governments' unchecked greed to monetize and urbanize has also raised serious concerns about the shrinking agricultural land available for food cultivation and long-term food security—a critical concern in a country that has seen famines and starvation in its history. It has resulted in the Red Line Policy for land use, which defines the minimum amount of arable land required for cultivation and prohibits local governments from repurposing it. It is also concerning that increasing tracts of arable land are being degraded as a result of intensive exploitation and the use of chemical fertilizers to improve productivity—a factor that, together with China's environmental challenges and growing climate change extremes of floods, droughts and adverse weather conditions, poses a significant risk to its future. Similarly, while other land concerns are absent, land degradation is a major concern in India, particularly in its 'food bowl' northern states, due to distorted cropping patterns and unsustainable agricultural practices. As both countries enter the next chapter of their respective economic histories, how they deal with the unique yin-yang of opportunities and challenges will determine their future trajectories.

This brings us back to the Dragon.

The cultural symbol of the 'dragon' and what it means to different cultures exemplifies the issue of viewing not only an individual economy but an entire civilization through a lens that is completely alien to not only its context but the very norms that underpin its existence.

The dragon is widely revered in China. It is the mythical progenitor of Liu Bang, the commoner founder of the Han dynasty (from which China's ethnic majority Han population descended), who claimed that his mother conceived him after dreaming of a dragon.[24] Since then, the dragon has served as a symbol of China, both imperial and communist. The dragon's symbolism in Chinese mythology dates back even further, and it has almost always been viewed positively. Associated with life-giving rains and water sources, its particular significance in China's perennially flood- or drought-affected agricultural history can only be imagined. It is regarded as the most auspicious year sign in the Chinese zodiac, and was worn on the robes of its emperors, depicted in the most precious metals from gold jewellery to jade figurines, and with countless references in Chinese literature and the performing arts. The dragon was ubiquitous in ancient China and remains so in the Chinese psyche today.[25] It has also been used by the state and popular culture in modern communist China to reinforce a common sinicized identity among minority (non-Han) ethnic groups.[26]

In contrast, the dragon has been depicted in various negative ways in Western culture, beginning with Greek and Roman times as the Gryphon, Hydra, Typhon and Cetus.[27] It is a widespread perception that continues in popular Western imagination today, as evil, winged, horned, fire-breathing oppressors who were battled and heroically slayed by Christian knights and saints during Europe's Middle Ages. The popular story of the titular saint (303 CE) who killed a dragon that terrorized villagers while rescuing a beautiful princess is narrated in the legend of Saint George and the Dragon.[28]

In Indian mythology and popular folklore, the closest approximation of the dragon are the Nagas, a semi-divine race that can be both benevolent or dangerous[29] and interestingly, live either underwater or near water sources and act as its protectors.[30] Vasuki, the serpent King who adorns Lord Shiva's neck, guards the Nagamani jewel and was the rope for the *Samudra Manthan*—the churning of the ocean in search of Amrit. He is also one of the eight great dragon kings in Chinese mythology, a journey that took place during the spread of Buddhism from India to China.

The paleontological origins of dragon legends in various cultures may have scientific roots in common. However, the fact that the dragon is viewed so differently and has such radically different meanings in three distinct civilizations (albeit with greater cultural affinity between China and India due to geographical proximity and exchange of religious and philosophical thought between the two Asian neighbours), highlights human perception's limited ability to step outside of its individual, worldview-shaping cultural influences to understand another culture. However, unless an effort is also made to understand the roots of Chinese civilization, culture and state, the trees of economics and related disciplines may be missed.

This is a cultural lens that the reader may want to keep in mind when they read the book to take a fresh look at commonly held and assumed-to-be-universal first principles assumptions as they look at the different parts of the India and China stories.

Writing this book has been a long, and often difficult, process. When I embarked on this venture a couple of years ago, I was surprised to find that little had been written on the Indo-China post-reform economic growth stories for the general reader, and almost none through a multi-dimensional lens of people, culture, politics and institutions. As I moved forward, I understood why. While the canvas is vast and the stories are compelling and worth narrating, they are fraught with multiple lines of fractured opinion. These lines run not only across maps of geography but also landscapes of culture, society, politics and history. All directions of the compass—east or west, north or south, are unfortunately polarized. And books become gladiatorial arenas of justification rather than a refuge for quiet reflection, polite debate and disagreement. There are many who have helped write this book—recommending reading and reference material, engaging in discussions, helping shape perspectives, reviewing drafts and making suggestions. These have included guides and friends from the world of academia, policy think tanks, geopolitics, finance, banking and economics, journalism, publishing and more. To each of them, I owe a deep and personal debt of gratitude. This book would not have been written if it had not been for you. I do not wish to impose any burden of public acknowledgment. All opinions, views, conclusions or mistakes made in this book are mine, and mine alone. Finally, I would like to thank my family for their unwavering encouragement and support.

I sincerely hope you find this book as fascinating and enjoyable to read as I did while researching and writing it.

Part One

The Background

1

Geography:
The Destiny of Nations

There is no getting around geography. The complexities of a country's culture, civilization, history and economic activity are shaped by an unseen and often ignored geographical genetic code. It defines today's national boundaries, geopolitics and economies, just as it has for millennia in human history. 'What makes a nation in the beginning is a good piece of geography,' said renowned American poet Robert Frost.

India and China, in particular, have been shaped by their geographies in ways that only few other nations in history have. They are Asian neighbours but are separated by the towering Himalayan ranges that arc across the Indian subcontinent from east to north, ending in the jumbled mass of the Karakoram and Pir Panjal ranges. It is an impassable geographical feature that has kept trade and interaction between the two civilizations to a bare minimum because of their independent river valley origins.

The Himalayas have also played an important role in one of the critical determinants of these two nations' linked destinies—water. The Indian monsoon and the vast river systems of India owe their existence to these mountains which block the passage of rain clouds, corralling them into annual seasonal rains over the subcontinent. Agriculture and the density of human population would not have thrived without the water brought to the Indian subcontinent by the Himalayas.

Similarly, as the Himalayas slope away towards Eastern China, the high-altitude, barren and sparsely populated Tibetan Plateau—the 'roof of the world'—lies in the rain shadow of the Himalayas. Tibet is also the source of six of Asia's largest rivers, including the Indus, which gave rise to one of the earliest prehistoric civilizations of India; the Yellow River, which gave rise to Chinese agriculture; and the Yangtze River.

China is the world's third-largest country, with an area of nearly 9.6 million sq. km. It is also the world's second-most populous country now, with a population of approximately 1.4 billion people, with its eastern region (also known as 'core' China) being the most concentrated. Hu Huanyong, a Chinese population geographer, devised a 'geo-demographic demarcation line'—the Heihe–Tengchong Line (also known as the Hu Line)—in 1935. He demonstrated that a line could be drawn across the China map from Heihe in the northeast to Tengchong in the southwest, dividing it roughly in half. Only 6 per cent of China's population lives in the west of the Hu line (in a 43 per cent area), while 94 per cent lives in the eastern side of it.

In 1908, geographer Zhang Xiangwen had come up with the geographic Qinling–Huaihe (QH) Line, drawn from the Qinling mountains in the east to the Huai River in the west, which divides this populated eastern half of China into North and South China. It is also, in many ways, the cultural and economic boundary between North and South China. South China has a humid climate, grows more rice and has more hilly terrain as compared to the North, which has plains, cultivates mostly wheat and has temperate weather with snow in the winters. The Yellow River in northern China and the Yangtze River in southern China are the world's two longest river systems, rising on the Tibetan Plateau in the east and flowing into the China Sea in the west. They are defining geographical features and lifelines in these regions.

The southeastern part of China, as defined by the Hu and QH lines, is one of the most densely populated areas on the planet. It also has a GDP that is nearly double of the northeastern region.

Since the late 1970s, Chinese economic miracle—particularly its light manufacturing exports-led coastal SEZs, port cities, rapid urbanization and real estate boom, massive infrastructure development in rapid transport and energy consumption—has primarily been the story of this densely populated Cantonese-speaking southeast China (as compared to the heavy industry-dominated, Mandarin-speaking northeast). It has also been a key engine of its high and continued decadal economic growth.

Much of China's economic history has been shaped by geographical factors. To support an ever-growing population over generations, it has required intensive cultivation techniques for its marginal and subsistence-level fragmented farm holdings, including small terraces carved from hills. Because of the scarcity of arable land and the need for higher productivity, it has necessitated the careful nurturing of nutrients in agricultural land, including the use of night soil (not so long ago) prior to the introduction of manufactured fertilizers. It has also required ingenuity and public infrastructure projects to build irrigation and flood control systems on its rivers that date back to its ancient past.

Centralized public infrastructure projects have been a notable and consistent feature of Chinese civilization. The Great Wall of China, the most popular of these projects, was started in 221 BCE under the first Emperor to keep the northern 'barbarians'—mostly Mongol and other pastoral tribes—out of agricultural and sedentary 'civilized' China. The Grand Canal, another one of these public infrastructure projects, is less well-known, but is perhaps more effective and long-lasting in its impact. Its construction began around 486 BCE (predating the Great Wall) and was built in sections over a thousand years, reaching its current contours around 618 CE. It enabled the connection of the Yellow River in North China to the Yangtze River in the South, making grain transportation from the agricultural South to political and military power centres in the North easier and cheaper. Indeed, the change it brought about in the widespread use of water transportation was critical in China's imperial history and civilization, allowing the reunification of North and South China. Even by modern standards, the Grand Canal is an engineering marvel. It is 1,776 km long and has a maximum elevation of 42 m in the Shandong mountains. Ships, however, have easily navigated the elevation since the invention of the pound lock by engineer Qiao Weiyue during the Song dynasty's reign in the tenth century. With maintenance and modifications, it remains the world's largest man-made waterway system.

Besides, efforts over millennia to create its land boundaries and harness its rivers through infrastructure projects, natural port harbours on its southern coastline (like Guangzhou, Shanghai and Hong Kong and the extensive Pearl River Delta) have encouraged maritime trade since its ancient past well into modern times, including the extraterritorial 'treaty ports' controlled by foreign powers during its 'century of humiliation'. This was the period between 1839 and 1949 when China's government lost control over large portions of its territory at the hands of foreigners. In fact, many of the policies that have driven the Chinese economy's rapid and consistent growth since reform and opening-up are not new, but rather a modern continuation of the same historical forces shaped by its geography.

China's treaty ports and its light goods manufacturing hinterlands of the nineteenth century are reflected in its modern manufacturing export-led SEZs. Its historic Grand Canal is now just a part (the eastern route) of the even more ambitious and modern South–North Water Transfer Project, which aims to transfer a staggering 45 billion cubic metres of water from the water surplus Yangtze River basin to the arid and industrial North via the central and western routes. It is, incidentally, also one of the most expensive infrastructure projects in the world with an aim to be completed in 2050.

China now seeks to replicate a similar 'transfer' infrastructure model for its public works in the field of energy generation and transmission, in addition to harnessing the waters of the Yangtze River for hydroelectricity through its massive 22.5 GW Three Gorges Dam in Central China—the world's largest power plant, also serving for flood control and navigation—and the 16 GW Baihetan Dam in Southwestern China. Plagued by severe environmental issues and extensive air and water pollution in the heavily populated East China, it is working on developing renewable energy projects to the west of the Hu line, to be evacuated through west to east Ultra High Voltage Direct Current (UHVDC) transmission line corridors.[1] Its Desert

Project, located in West China, envisages an initial capacity of 100 GW of wind and solar capacity (to go up to 400 GW), half of which is expected to be commissioned by 2025.[2]

Since 2000, China has started to build a transfer infrastructure for its densely populated areas by constructing the world's longest and fastest mass rapid transit intra and intercity rail systems, allowing for rapid urbanization. The construction of these transit systems and 17 (10 million-plus) megacities has further facilitated the migration of large segments of its population from marginal, agriculture-dependent rural areas to newly created and rapidly expanding value-added manufacturing and services-oriented cities. It has also enabled the government to fund continued high rates of economic growth by capitalizing on the resulting real estate boom and the significant growth multiplier of these construction activities.

In comparison, India is the seventh largest country in the world and the most populous nation with approximately 1.4 billion people, overtaking China in 2022, with an area of approximately 3.28 million sq. km. India's land area is roughly one-third of China's,[3] but it is more appropriately comparable with the populated area in the east of China's Hu line, which is approximately 4 million sq. km.[4] There is no comparable demographic or geographic Hu Line in India with a distinct distribution of population. However, there is a higher concentration of population in the fertile Gangetic alluvial plains to the north and east (nearly 40 per cent of India's population live in the states of Uttar Pradesh, Bihar and West Bengal), that curve in an arc parallel to the Himalayan ranges and down to the Sundarbans delta as the Ganga flows into the Bay of Bengal. The other dominant feature of the Indian subcontinent is the Deccan Plateau, which lies to the south and west of the Gangetic river system (and the Indus basin). The Vindhya Range, which runs west to east, along the Narmada and Mahanadi, has traditionally marked the border between North India's predominantly Hindi-speaking plains and central highlands, and South India's multilingual Deccan Plateau. The relatively arid Deccan Plateau, bounded on the west by the Western Ghats, slopes gently eastwards and is regularly interspersed by the three major river systems (the Krishna, Godavari and Kaveri) which flow from west to east before fanning out into fertile deltas.

Throughout the subcontinent's long history of mostly monsoon-dependent, spatially dispersed agriculture and cultivation in broad and fertile river valleys, the pressures of population, intensive cultivation and environment have never quite reached the levels seen in China. The geography of the subcontinent has had a varied and decentralized impact on the economy and its development. While large kingdoms dominated the plains of North India, the South saw many independent regional kingdoms and cultures emerge with the ebb and flow of time. Also, unlike imperial (culturally Han-dominated) China through much of its medieval history, North and South India were never under a single state or ruler (including British India) at any point of time in history until the formation of the Union of India in 1947.

With few natural ports and an insular culture, sea trade was limited, with the North mostly trading through the port of Surat, while the Malabar Coast's southwest region has carried on a lucrative international trade through West Asia since ancient times. South India's extensive trade and cultural influence in the near and far east reached its peak during the reign of the Cholas in the eleventh century, through maritime trade, conquest and cultural exchange. Cultural and economic influence in kingdoms such as Cambodia, Indonesia and Vietnam (which came under Chinese imperial hegemonic influence in later years), however, waned over time, largely due to new cultural and religious taboo. It wasn't until the British in colonial India established and expanded the ports of Madras, Calcutta and Bombay (now Chennai, Kolkata and Mumbai, respectively)—to systematically exploit India's potential for raw materials, and as a market for its own manufactured goods—that maritime trade came back into focus.

However, unlike China's treaty ports, there was little development of manufacturing and exports in the port hinterland, aside from processing of agricultural raw material such as cotton textiles, jute and tea. India's pre-Independence geographical administration, whether as princely India or British-ruled India, was geared solely towards colonial exploitation. The debilitating and long-term effects of this well-organized exploitation of its agriculture and population were especially severe in North and East India. In modern India, the biggest cities are still the British-built port cities and the medieval and colonial capital city of Delhi.

The two biggest infrastructure projects in India, before its independence in 1947, were the Grand Trunk Road and the Indian Railways. The Grand Trunk Road, built as the *Uttarapatha* by Chandragupta Maurya in the third century BCE and restored and improved during the medieval period by Sher Shah Suri (1486–1545), ran across the entire northern plains from Kabul in modern-day Afghanistan to the Bangladesh–Myanmar border, covering a distance of approximately 2,400 km. It was critical in tying the northern plains of the subcontinent as a common political and administrative unit for marching armies, trade, empire, culture and ideas for most of their history. The Indian railway network, on the other hand, was built during British rule to serve colonial interests of transporting raw materials from the subcontinent's interiors for export through its port cities, and delivering British-manufactured imports to interior markets.

As both countries set out to achieve economic growth, their paths to prosperity were shaped by geographical realities. In China's case, policies have capitalized on its geographically rooted historical past, reviving old networks of treaty ports and its diaspora through its coastal SEZs for manufacturing exports, subsequently linking it to rapid urbanization and a real estate boom in the hinterland of its prosperous port-cities. It has used its waterways for both transportation and power generation, launching massive infrastructure projects in clean energy and evacuation from its sparsely populated western regions.

In India, there have been, at times, individual projects and policies that have seemed similar to China's, rather than unique opportunities building a comprehensive investment story based on India's traditional history and strengths. Some of these have had limited success. A stalled manufacturing SEZ policy, limited ability to leverage its large diaspora for investments, incomplete and poorly integrated rapid urban transport systems with no forward and backward linkages to real estate, poorly conceptualized plans for interlinking rivers, abandoned or stalled agricultural and land reforms, green energy generation and transmission corridors without distribution sector reforms—the list of challenges that India's liberalization and development have faced is a long one.

While some of these challenges can be attributed to the differences between how a democracy and a totalitarian government work, there has also been a lack of originality in identifying India's specific strengths, finding solutions to its problems and having limited political capital, will to implement them and building on these in a systematic and integrated way over the decades. These factors have also played a significant role in the disparity in economic outcomes between the two countries.

2

Culture: Shaping Identities

U nderstanding the economic narratives of nations necessitates, at the very least, a cursory familiarity with their culture. It plays a pivotal role in shaping the national identities in terms of language and beliefs, social structure, individual behaviour, public perspective, private goals and the policies employed in economic affairs.

Culture is a broad and nebulous concept that is difficult to define. Language, however, serves as a vital repository and transmitter of civilization and culture that serves as an excellent starting point. A language's keywords and phrases frequently reflect a distinct nuance of cultural and social programming and behaviour. This is especially true in older societies, where stylized meaning has been embedded in keywords, phrases and concepts over time. When translated to a different language, the cultural attitudes and values reflected in the language frequently gets lost or their original meaning gets altered. Studying these translated languages in their original context, on the other hand, provides insight into the thought processes of a nation's identity and culture.

For the purpose of discussing India and China's economies in this book, six keywords or concepts were chosen from among many that qualified to provide a sense of some root cultural aspects of China, as well as its parallel context in India. The treatment of these two civilizations' fundamental cultural aspects in the context of their modern nation state objectives has also been discussed.

Hanzi

Hanzi is the Chinese system of writing with ideographs or 'Chinese characters'. China has many spoken dialects, each vastly different from the other across its various regions, ranging from Mandarin dialects in the North to Cantonese dialects in the South. Throughout its long history, China, however, has used a single writing system. This unique writing system, which began in a pictorial form over 3,000 years ago, now has over 47,000 characters, though only 3,500 to 4,000 of them are used in everyday language in modern-day China. Its role in shaping the unitary Chinese identity seen today is as important as the spiritual and religious teachings of its philosophers and the political power of its emperors. Every character represents a syllable or word, and each word is made up of one, two, three or more characters. Unlike English's Roman letters, China's uniformly styled ideograms are pictures of things, ideas and sounds. This means that they are 'alive' with meanings that go all the way back to the beginning of Chinese civilization. Since the meanings of the pictographs were universal, they were absorbed into the cultures of all of China's ethnic groups, regardless of dialect or language.

Throughout its vast territories and long history, all educated Chinese used the same script and could read whatever was written. Furthermore, as the characters directly symbolized the elements and concepts constituting the Chinese understanding of the cosmos, along with the people and the social, political and spiritual context in which they lived, the Hanzi evolved into a living repository of mainstream Chinese culture. It served as the primary vehicle through which culture was transmitted from one educated generation to the next, a feature that other living civilizations' written scripts lacked. Up until the mid or late nineteenth century, China's upper classes spent years memorizing, reading and learning how to write thousands of Hanzi.

According to journalist and author Boye Lafayette De Mente, learning to read and draw the over 3,000 characters, with its multiple strokes done in the right way and the right order, has had an enormous impact not only on the physical and manual dexterity required but also on how they are conditioned to recognize forms and relationships, to think about things and also to do things in a precise, methodical manner. The Hanzi has shaped the character and personality of the Chinese over millennia and has given China a deep sense of cultural and civilizational coherence. It, however, also posed the biggest challenge when they encountered the West and its different world views and ways of society and business. De Mente writes:

> Both the spoken form and the written form of the language held the people of China and their culture firmly in their grip until near the end of the 20th century—binding them to beliefs and behavior that were totally incompatible with a capitalistic, consumer oriented, democratic society. The imperatives of thinking and acting differently to cope with the demands of capitalism and consumerism were, in fact, one of the primary reasons why the culture of younger generations of Chinese changed so rapidly, including creating their own slang and way of using the language.[1]

However, as China's rise as a global power continues, challenging the post-Cold War American hegemony, a key barrier to the evangelization of its brand of economics and geopolitics is the gap not only in language but also in culture. As Lee Kuan Yew, the widely respected former PM of Singapore, said in respect to China's rise in the future and its ability for cross-cultural exchange and emigration essential for its growth, in a similar context of the US as a cross-cultural and emigration destination:

> Chinese is a very difficult language to learn—monosyllabic and tonal. One can learn conversational Chinese after a few years, but it is very difficult to be able to read quickly. I do not know if China will be able to overcome the language barrier and the attendant difficulty in recruiting outside talent unless it makes English the dominant language, as Singapore has. Children there learn Chinese first. Then they learn English. They might go to the U.S. as a teenager and become fluent, but they have 4,000 years of Chinese epigrams in their head.[2]

It is a unitary and primarily Han cultural identity that has facilitated the sinicization of China's territories, particularly the expansion of its borders to include Inner Mongolia, Tibet and Xinjiang during the rule of the Qing dynasty (1644–1912) and since. Jing Tsu, professor of comparative literature and east asian languages and literatures at Yale University, in her book *Kingdom of Characters: The Language Revolution That Made China Modern*, describes the enormous challenge of bringing the language to the masses in education and modernizing such a complex language, whose written form has remained largely unchanged since it was first standardized nearly 2,200 years ago: 'For the majority of the population, to people like Wang, (Wang Zhao, an early pioneer for reforming Chinese to the Mandarin phonetic alphabet over competing alternatives like Cantonese and even Esperanto, in the early decades of the 20th century) a tremendous handicap that prevented the Chinese from progressing'.[3] It was the official adoption and propagation of the much simplified Mandarin phonetic alphabet 'pinyin' that enabled China to have a common, nationwide language of communication and allowed it to progress from a literacy rate of barely 20 per cent in 1949[4], to near universal literacy in 2022.[5]

In India's equally long cultural and civilizational history, beyond the extinct Harappan pictorial script that remains undeciphered, the Brahmi script[6] is commonly accepted as the root script from which all other scripts—including Tamil, Sanskrit, Bengali, Malayalam and other regional scripts—later evolved. Sanskrit and Tamil served a similar, albeit traditional, cultural function as a written script of the literate classes for communication and cultural transmission. Their use was not uniform across the subcontinent's geography, with regional scripts developing and evolving independently, particularly in South and East India. The use of Sanskrit was also restricted by caste and class considerations, with no universal propagation or evangelization permitted. Furthermore, with the onslaught of Islamic invasion and subsequent conquest of India in the thirteenth century, its use as the language of the court or administrative power declined progressively. It was gradually supplanted by Persian, Turki, assimilated Urdu and eventually, Hindustani or Hindi, especially in the northern part of the subcontinent, limiting its scope to Hindu religious thought, philosophy and rituals. These languages and scripts were eventually replaced by the Roman script of the English language, which became the lingua franca of colonial India. British rule in India was also accompanied by the cultural colonialism of language and education, with English becoming the default medium of instruction as well as developing a Western temper and outlook with the adoption of Macaulay's famous *Minute on Education* as official policy in 1835.[7]

The cultural dominance of Western thought, facilitated by the English language, gave rise to a new English-speaking Indian middle class population that gradually became alienated from its indigenous roots. This new middle class initially assisted its colonial rulers, and subsequently led movements for self-rule and independence that arose from those very same Western principles of democracy, law and individual human rights. The widespread usage of English among the aspirational middle class, along with its democratic principles, rule of law and greater cultural affinity with the West than China, has facilitated India's rise and seamless integration in the service sector with the global economy. It is also a cultural affinity that has often driven its geopolitical and alliance choices. In a linguistically organized polity, however, the lack of agreement on a common national language (Hindi and English are the only official languages of the state) has been a persistent source of competitive identity politics and an impediment to shaping a common national communication and education identity. India's literacy rate which was about 12 per cent in 1947[8], is about 78 per cent in 2022.[9]

Jun Jun Chen Chen Fu Fu Zi Zi

Jun Jun Chen Chen Fu Fu Zi Zi or 'Let the ruler rule as he should and the minister be a minister as he should. Let the father act as a father should and the son act as a son should,' said Confucius. Philosophy, religion and the idealized role of the individual in an organized and hierarchical society, with an emperor state at its centre, was shaped in China by the three pillars of Chinese society—Confucianism, Taoism and Buddhism.[10]

Confucius (551–479 BCE) was a philosopher and contemporary of the Buddha in India who is credited with developing the Confucian code of ethics, a codified rule of conduct to guide the ruling elite class. Confucian society was structured around what was perceived to be the cosmic order and the hierarchy of superior-inferior relationships. Parents were superior to children, men were superior to women and rulers were superior to subjects. Each person had a role to play that was defined by authority and conformed to a conventional and defined set of social expectations. According to Confucius, social order (which was paramount in the Confucian worldview and remains so in communist China today) would be maintained if everyone did their part. People were known by their observed behaviour and were thus reliant on the collective opinion and moral judgement of their fellow elites.

A major Confucian principle was that men, by nature, are good; they have an innate moral sense and can be guided in the right direction through their own efforts at self-cultivation and the influence of sages and superior men who have succeeded in putting right conduct ahead of all other considerations. Over centuries, Chinese social standards have been shaped by idealized philosophical characteristics such as defined moral behaviour in upholding a social order, hierarchy, natural equality of men at birth as opposed to any hereditary privilege and individual agency to improve the self through ongoing moral education, self-examination and state guidance. These civilizational social standards have endured and been reflected in China's goal-setting, prioritization of the 'greater good' over the 'individual self', popular mobilization campaigns and its Confucian approach to economics and development even during its period of atheism and rejection of its traditional past. It has continued in its 'socialism with Chinese characteristics' market economy and society.

Confucius also emphasized proper behaviour on the part of the ruler, who gained moral status by setting a good example in accordance with the rules of propriety. This moral prestige gave him influence over the people. According to Confucius, 'The people are like grass, the ruler like the wind' and 'when a prince's personal conduct is correct, his government is effective without the issuing of orders. If his personal conduct is not correct, he may issue orders, but they will not be followed.'

The similarity in philosophy to the Indian subcontinent's concept of *Ram Rajya* (the ruler's moral authority by setting a personal example and thereby influencing the people) and the '*Yatha Raja, Tatha Praja* (as the ruler, so the people)' principle articulated by Chanakya in his famous treatise on moral, economic and statecraft instructions for the ruler, the *Arthashastra*[11], is remarkable and likely not coincidental. It points to the active transmission of ideas and philosophies—including Buddhism—between the two regions.

Taoism (Daoism), on the other hand, was a repository for a variety of animism, alchemy and early medicinal beliefs and practices among the common people and pre-dated elite Confucianism. It emerged as a school of thought through works attributed to Lao Tsu. Taoists argued that the Confucian statement of rules of propriety is actually a reflection of the world's moral disorder. Taoists sought a philosophy of passivity, expressed in the term *wuwei*, which means 'action by inaction' or 'effortlessness', of following one's irrational inner nature and accepting life's experiences without struggle. The 'three teachings' of Confucianism, Taoism and Buddhism that underpin Chinese philosophical thought and which shaped Chinese society over the millennia of its imperial age are likely shaped by Hinduism from the subcontinent. In fact, further shared characteristics of concepts like karma or good deeds; reincarnation or fatalism; Dharma/Dhamma; ancestor worship; and geomancy—feng shui and *vastu shastra*, along with the idea of the family as the central unit in Confucian thought (the *kutumb*) suggest evidence of active philosophical influences of Hinduism.

The communist party is officially atheist and prohibits religious beliefs among its members, though this by all accounts is more in its breach than observance. However, religious observance in China is on the rise. The Chinese constitution (Article 36) states that citizens have the right to religious beliefs and prohibits religious discrimination. According to the World Religion Database 2020, of the total Chinese population, Chinese folk-religionists were estimated at 30.8 per cent, Buddhist at 16.6 per cent, Christian at 7.4 per cent, Ethnic religionist at 4.2 per cent, Muslim at 1.8 per cent and Taoist at 0.4 per cent. The rest were agnostic or atheist.[12] Despite strenuous efforts to break Confucian traditions during Mao's Cultural Revolution, its millennia-old legacy and influence on modern China remain. In recent years, the party has pushed to sinicize religion, and Chinese leadership has reportedly 'expressed hope that China's "traditional cultures" of Confucianism, Buddhism, and Daoism could help curb the country's "moral decline".[13] Confucian thinking and worldviews have continued to be reflected in communist China's geopolitics, its attitude towards nature and environment, and even the party's organization and political structure. 'Maintaining social order' remains a dominant, if not primary, concern of Chinese governance.

Yin-yang

Ying-yang is a principle that underlies not only Chinese culture but also those of Japan and Korea, which are branches of a cultural tree whose roots are in the Middle Kingdom since at least 1,400 BCE. Several of the most basic elements of the Chinese culture—including personal and business relationships—are manifestations of this principle. The terms yin and yang are commonly understood as opposites, such as hot-cold, sweet-sour, male-female and positive-negative from a simplistic, two-dimensional and static Western perspective. This view is, however, an incomplete one. In Chinese culture, the principle of yin and yang is an explanation of the behaviour of all organic and inorganic things in the universe, as well as the invisible energy that infuses the cosmos, incorporating the creation, interaction and extinction of all things in an unending cycle.

The principle postulates that the yin-yang relationships between things and people are not fixed but in a constant state of flux, and that they wax and wane in inverse proportions. The objective is to keep all yin-yang relationships in harmony. The most important key to understand this principle in the Chinese cultural context, according to De Mente, is that, harmony does not mean equality in relationships. It only means that the relationships are on a level that is acceptable or bearable to the parties concerned—whether or not they like them, or how disadvantageous they might be. The Chinese yin-yang view of human relations is situational, a view that is not arising from the sense of 'fair' as prevalent in the Western cultural sense, but a realistic appreciation that in nature, absolute equality exists only in relative terms and only for very short periods of time. It is a perspective that modern China brings to its personal, social, business and geopolitical interactions, influencing decisions and policymaking—including economic thinking—at all levels of its society and government.

There are no exact parallels to be found of yin-yang in the Indian cultural context, though its philosophical roots find resonance in Hindu philosophical thought of *advaita* (singularity) and *dvaita* (dualism), of dualistic monism in Shiva-Shakti[14], or even the linga-yoni of Tantric philosophy and practices.

Zhongguo and Tianxia

Zhongguo and *tianxia* are words that the Chinese have used for millennia to describe the world and China's unique place within it. Zhongguo, which means 'the central state', idiomatically translates to 'Middle Kingdom'. Analogously, tianxia—which translates literally as 'sky beneath' and idiomatically as 'all under heaven', refers to a 'world' or a global system. Throughout ancient times, the Chinese acknowledged the existence of other 'worlds' beyond their borders or areas of cultural influence, such as India, Persia and the Roman Empire. However, they were not considered a part of their world, the Chinese tianxia, of which Zhongguo represents China. In Chinese thought, Zhongguo was also the enlightened kingdom of Confucian thinkers and mandarins who elevated it to a culture of universal values against which it determined who met the civilization's criteria and who did not.

China was bordered by lands inhabited by truculent and raiding nomadic tribes, particularly to its North (against which it built the Great Wall), with whom it had prickly relations of trade, tribute and marriage for millenia—including invasions by the barbaric Mongols and the Manchus. Military conquest and rule over imperial China by non-Han dynasties, however, did not imply the imposition of a foreign culture. China, as Zhongguo, was a cultural construct, deemed superior to all others under its tianxia, leading to the absorption and sinicization of its conquerors and rulers. For over two millennia, China's tianxia was regarded as eternal, and it served as the yardstick for East Asian civilization, which included Japan, Korea, Vietnam and other states with which it shared its borders. The abrupt collapse of this Sinocentric worldview in the late nineteenth century, with losses in the First Opium War and the start of the century of humiliation by foreign powers (discussed in detail later in the book), is a force that continues to dominate the Chinese psyche and influence its economic, political and global strategy and action.[15]

One of the earliest references to the Indian subcontinent's civilizational consciousness as *Bharatavarsha* can be found in the Mahabharata. The famous historian R.C. Majumdar looked at the idea of ancient Bharatavarsha from a political and cultural point of view. According to him, the subcontinent entered an age of imperial unity beginning around 600 BCE, which was marked by the rise of large empires. Multiple kingdoms contested the political chessboard of ancient Bharatavarsha, including the Greeks, Parthians, Sakas and Kushanas. The Mauryan empire's rise to dominance, the subcontinent's unification and Emperor Ashoka's reign, along with the grand conquests achieved through wars and the proselytization drives based on pacifist ideals, played a role in further developing Bharatavarsha's identity. According to Majumdar, ancient Bharatavarsha conceptually marked a terrain of free thoughts; religious consolidation; the rise of an exuberant literature, particularly in classical Sanskrit; the emergence of exquisite artistic traditions; and the maturation of Indian political thought.[16]

Puranic literature describes the spatial and geographical aspect of the subcontinent as the southernmost *varsha*, named Bharata, territorially located between the Himavat and the oceans. The etymological origins of the term 'Bharatavarsha' have been suggested as being derived from the Puranic King Bharata, but perhaps more credibly, from the Bharata tribe extensively referred to in the Mahabharata, the Vedas, the Brahmanas and certain Buddhist texts. The idea of Bharatavarsha, according to historian Rupendra Kumar Chattopadhyaya, was more centred on the various *janapadas*—including the indigenous proto-democracies of ancient India—or rather, the 'spatio-social components of it'. Bharatavarsha, according to Chattopadhyaya, was hence more of a geographically unfrozen space, that was 'part of a cosmography in which, at least in the *Puranic* cosmography and *Puranic* world-scape...narration of creation and royal genealogy (of which *Bharata* genealogy is a segment) are important parts'.[17]

This unity in diversity aspect of the Indian subcontinent's cultural identity tracing back to the janapadas, and the likely source of the 'mother of democracies' argument, has thus been a fundamental element in its social, political, philosophical and institutional development over millennia. It is an identity that has survived debilitating British colonial and cultural rule for nearly two centuries and continues to be the dominant narrative, albeit contested, even today. However, notably, the context of Bharatavarsha has always also been a geographical construct, compared to the cultural 'area of influence' of East Asian tianxia of the Zhongguo. It is a cultural understanding that continues to shape the geopolitics and geoeconomics of both nations even today.

Guanxi and Chaxugeju

Guanxi loosely translates to 'network of personal connections' in English. It has often been portrayed, overused and satirized in a commercial context as a 'necessary requirement' for conducting business in China. The translation, however, does not adequately or completely convey the term's social and cultural meaning and importance. In China's millennia-long civilizational history, which has never been ruled by any Western power, there has never been a concept of 'rule of law' as understood in a Western sense. The Western rule of law evolved over time as a set of jurisprudential principles applied independently and without discrimination in the arbitration of any matter involving the rights of both parties. In the millennial social and jurisprudential evolution of China, there is, however, no mirror concept or principle. With no such 'rights-based' legal protection by an independent organization in a Confucian hierarchical and imperial structure, social norms in then predominantly rural China evolved towards the establishment of a network of mutually beneficial relationships based on trust for personal and business purposes.

In his authoritative work *Xiangtu Zhongguo* (*From the Soil: The Foundations of Chinese Society*), sociologist Fei Xiaotong describes the difference between Western and Chinese societies as:

> [In] the West individuals produce their society by applying an organizational mode of association (*tuantigeju*). People create groups that have clear boundaries. Membership in these groups is unambiguous; everyone knows who is and who is not a member. And the rights and duties of members are clearly delineated. Such groups are organizations, and they, in turn, shape Western society's social structure. These organizations are firms in the economy, the bureaucracies in the government, the universities in the educational system, and the clubs in local society. They are everywhere and serve as devices for framing individualism in modern Western societies. By contrast, people in China create their society by applying the logic of *chaxugeju*... With this mode of association, the society is composed not of discrete organizations, but of overlapping networks of people linked together through differentially categorized social relationships.[18]

In Chinese society, each relationship is, simultaneously both defined (in terms of ritual behaviour) and strictly personal (in that specific actions needed to maintain the relationship are based on norms of reciprocity and as personal obligations of each individual, e.g., child to the parent, wife to the husband, official to the ruler, younger to the older, etc.). Fei uses two metaphors to explain the difference— 'Western society is represented by straws collected to form a haystack, and Chinese society is represented by the ripples flowing out from the splash of a rock thrown into water.'

The personalized yet collective network structure of Chinese society is best explained in an example from 'The Myth of the "Five Human Relations" of Confucius' through a story. According to this story, the wife of Cheng Han-eheng was very insolent to beat her mother-in-law. This was considered such a heinous offence that by way of deterrent punishment, Cheng and his wife were skinned alive in front of his mother. Their skin was displayed at the gates of several towns and their bones were burnt to ashes. The head of the Cheng clan, along with his uncle and two brothers were hanged, while Cheng's grand uncle (who was the oldest of his close relatives) was beheaded. The mother of Cheng's wife was paraded through seven provinces with the phrase 'neglecting her daughter's education' tattooed on her face. Her father received 80 beatings and was exiled 3,000 li away from his home. But it didn't end there. The heads of family in the houses to the left and right of the Cheng house were beaten 80 strokes and banished to Heilongjiang. The educational officer received 60 strokes and was banished from the town. Cheng's nine-month-old child was given a new name and put in the care of the county magistrate. Cheng's land was ordered to be left in waste 'forever', and all this was recorded on a stone stele and rubbings of the inscriptions were distributed throughout the empire.[19]

It is an ancient Chinese story with echoes as recent as the purges of the Cultural Revolution (1966–76) and after. Building, maintaining and expanding an individual's 'circle of trust' was their reputation. Maintaining face or reputation, among people within their network, therefore, became an important characteristic of Chinese culture. An individual will not usually take advantage of someone with whom they have guanxi because if they do, everyone in their network will know, and they will lose face, respect and the connection to their network and the opportunities it provides. It also explains why the Chinese spend more time and effort than Westerners do, in establishing deeper social networks. It is common for people with strong guanxi to lend money to one another or form a group to pursue business opportunities together.[20] Individual trust-based networks of personal connections can also be extended and expanded by granting access of one's network to another. This effectively provides a reputational guarantee or face for another person by leveraging one's personal network guanxi.

Guanxi and its strong trust-based networks were instrumental in identifying and directing Chinese diaspora-led investments into China as it opened up. It also played a crucial role in investor interaction with local, provincial and central government levels and issue resolution. While the importance of guanxi is diminishing as urban China adopts Western cultural mores and norms, it still plays an important role in Chinese personal, social and business lives. Its significance in understanding the opaque processes of the all-powerful CPC and the Chinese state, including the formation of 'opinion', 'consensus' and 'election' of party representatives and leaders, and thus, policy, economic structures and developments in unitarian and totalitarian China cannot be overstated.

There is no cultural or social parallel in the colonial and postcolonial Indian subcontinent, with the exception of village and community-based panchayats, which continue in rural India. The closest in a business context could be community or clan-based networks like the Marwaris, Chettiars, and so on. Personal networks and relationships continue to play an important role in Indian society. However, after two centuries of British colonial rule and the development of an English-speaking and Westernized 'middle class' manning its institutions of governance, the legal and social superstructure of a universal and independent Anglo-Saxon rule of law has been well developed and embedded in India's social, political and economic structures.

Guanzi

The Guanzi (along with the Salt and Iron Debate[21]) are ancient Chinese political economy texts that deal with the role of markets in a nation and the role of state intervention or control, particularly in the nation's transition to a new type of economy. This 'economics with Chinese characteristics' has shaped Chinese political thought and economic policy well into its modern era. The Guanzi was written in the form of dialogues between Duke Huan (685–643 BCE) of Qi and his advisor Guan Zhong (720–645 BCE) during a period of rapid and drastic social change. It was a period marked by the breakdown of the previous regime's institutions of control and production, with agricultural land being taken from landowners and given to peasants, and the emergence of a commodity market economy.

With the invention of coinage and the increased use of currency, long-distance trade flourished, and a class of private merchants arose. Rulers of warring states turned to this merchant class to establish new state control institutions over the economy, particularly the new market forces. The Guanzi enunciated Qing Zhong (Light-Heavy) principles to achieve the goals of strengthening the state and the army (at the heart of which were a powerful monarch and meritocratic bureaucracy to carry out the necessary interventions), and enriching the country and its people was the starting point.

According to the Qing Zhong, objects can only be considered heavy or light in respect to other objects. Similarly, all economic phenomena can only be comprehended in relation to one another. Light commodities are viewed as inessential, while heavy commodities are thought to be necessary for production or human welfare. However, the exact definition of what constitutes a heavy or light commodity is dynamic and depends on various aspects such as the time of year, production methods and market conditions. The job of economic policy is to weigh and balance, using what is deemed to be heavy to counterbalance what is light.

In the words of the Guanzi, 'To use the thing that is "heavy" to shoot at that which is "light," to use the cheap to level down the dear... Hence, the state should not work against the spontaneous forces inherent in the economy, society, and natural environment; it should instead use these forces to first enrich and then govern the people while generating revenue for the state.'[22] The Guanzi recognized that the relative value of goods depends on demand and supply. Rather than focussing on the equilibrium of demand and supply, as is done in neoclassical modern economics, the Guanzi emphasizes investigating the cause of the change.

The price-determining conditions were thought to vary depending on the specific circumstances, and it was proposed that the art of economic governance depended on the fundamental pivot of flexibility. Grain, for example, was considered the most fundamental commodity in the Guanzi. It mentions, 'A man can't eat without grain, grain can't grow without land, land can't do without man, and man can't get rich without labor'. Grain, therefore, was seen as the most crucial commodity and was central to Qing Zhong economic policy. Price stabilization through state intervention in markets has thus been a central and largely unbroken tenet of Chinese economic and political thought and policy from its inception until the end of the imperial era in 1911. This 'economics with Chinese characteristics' influenced the CPC's thinking on economic struggles during its civil war, its postwar economic policies from 1949 onwards, and Chinese economic policy during the 'reform and opening-up' period from 1978 onwards, all under the stewardship of veteran Chen Yun and economist Xue Muqiao.

Some commentators believe it is also the reason how China, with its 'dual circulation' economic reforms, avoided the disastrous consequences of popular Western neoliberal 'Big Bang' reform recommendations by classical economists, which resulted in the implosion of a similarly liberalizing communist Russian economy. It is also worth noting that whether yin-yang or Qing Zhong, China's cultural approach to complex issues such as public policy, is driven by multidimensional relativity rather than unitarism, as is the Western cultural approach.

In the Indian context, Chanakya's *Arthashastra* is the closest parallel to any independently evolved 'economics with Indian characteristics'. Its impact on the Indian political economy has, however, been negligible over the centuries of disruption and colonial rule. Western neoliberal economic thought has been the framework underlying policy prescriptions for India's political economy challenges in modern, post-Independence India.

The keywords and concepts listed above are by no means exhaustive or definitive of the complex cultural identities and traditions of these two ancient civilizations. It is only a limited attempt to give colour to the cultural forces that have shaped (and continue to shape) their societies and choices—hierarchical conformity versus plural individuality, centralized authoritarianism versus federal democracy, conversion versus tolerance, contextual and situational adjudication and rule versus rights-based rule of law. These have also contributed to these nation states' current economic models, policies, outcomes and risks.

3

History and Political Economy: The Past in the Present

The assassination of Dara Shikoh, the eldest son of Shah Jahan and crown prince of the Mughal Empire, at the hands of his brother Aurangzeb on 30 August 1659 in Delhi was a significant moment in Indian history. But how is the assassination of Dara Shikoh, which occurred over 350 years ago, relevant to the Indo-China economic growth stories from 1991 to 2021?

For historians, the multi-hued tapestry of history stretching back into the past offers multiple strands of temptation for 'what if' possibilities. If tugged at these open wormholes in time and space, transporting historians to new and alternate worlds—other tianxia—each with their own path-dependent future. Of course, there is no academic rigour to this type of speculation. There are too many variables at work to determine what the outcomes might have been if the erratic dice of chance had landed differently. Real historical events, on the other hand, continue to impact and shape society, governance and politics even centuries later.

According to most accounts, Dara Shikoh resembled his great grandfather Akbar in terms of secular philosophy and tolerant outlook. He was a Sufi and Vedanta scholar with a unifying approach to religion and rule. His views represented a nascent and syncretic indicization of culture, society, government and religions that were in sharp contrast to the bigoted and intolerant views of his brother, Aurangzeb. However, it was Aurangzeb who succeeded in capturing the Mughal Empire's peacock throne in 1659.

As Supriya Gandhi writes in her book, *The Emperor Who Never Was: Dara Shukoh in Mughal India*, 'The battle for succession between Dara Shukoh and Aurangzeb is an origin myth of the subcontinent's present, seen as a crucial turning point in the progression of South Asian history. But it is not a stable myth. Its tellings and retellings shift and settle into the subcontinent's fault lines of nation and ideology.' There are alternate views as well, which seek to suggest that Aurangzeb was not a bigoted tyrant as he is painted to be. Whatever the truth is, the indisputable fact is that in popular imagination, even in those tracing back to his reign, Aurangzeb was instrumental in gouging wounds of a divide between the subcontinent's two largest communities—a schism that accelerated the fragmentation of the Mughal empire soon after his death, creating favourable conditions for foreign interests, primarily the British East India Company, which went on to establish its own colonial empire.

British rule further exploited this divide for its own purposes through a policy of 'divide and rule', directly leading to the partition of the sub-continent[1], echoes of which continue to resound within India. The British exploited other social and class fault lines too, giving impetus to fragmenting, centrifugal forces of division rather than centripetal impulses of social and cultural unity and national consciousness.

Colonial rule resulted not only in the systematic exploitation of the Indian subcontinent's economic resources but also in the deliberate destruction of weakened indigenous institutions, culture and markets left over from the collapse of a centralized Mughal empire. It actively encouraged social fault lines over social cohesion, creating a new and co-opted middle class with an English education that aided the British in the Western Anglo-Saxon institutional framework created for ruling its Indian colony.

China, on the other hand, has existed as a unified cultural construct of Zhongguo—a civilization marked by centralized and uninterrupted (and predominantly Han) 'core' empire, albeit varying in territorial size over various periods. This civilizational identity as the Middle Kingdom finds its beginning since the days of the First Emperor Shi Huangdi of the Qin dynasty (The 'Dragon Emperor' most famously known for his Terracotta Army and as builder of the original Great Wall) in 221 BCE[2] upto the end of the reign of the last emperor Xuantong of the Qing dynasty (immortalized in an Oscar winning film by Bernardo Bertolucci) in 1912.[3]

China existed as a centrally organized and unitary state (in varying degrees) for nearly three millennia, with 83 dynasties and 559 emperors[4], mostly with an inherent belief in its cultural superiority and nationhood. It still does so in many ways as a modern communist state in continuation of its imperial and cultural past.

China, like the Indian subcontinent, experienced invasions that resulted in the establishment of their own ruling dynasties—notably, the Mongol Yuan (1279)[5] and Manchu Qing (1644)[6] in China, and the Timurid Mughals in India (1526)[7]. Unlike in the Indian subcontinent, however, all empire builders of different ethnicities were absorbed into imperial China's existing institutions and culture. As the *Britannica* notes: 'Under the Qing (1644–1912), the territory of the empire grew to treble its size under the preceding Ming dynasty (1368–1644), the population grew from some 150 million to 450 million, many of the non-Chinese minorities within the empire were Sinicized, and an integrated national economy was established.'[8] According to China's 2020 census, Han Chinese made up 91.11 per cent of the population, while ethnic minorities made up 8.89 per cent.[9]

To return to the story of Dara Shikoh's assassination as a wormhole in Indian history, while the seeds of the Mughal Empire's demise were being sown with Aurangzeb's ascension to the throne in 1659, another great empire was rising to its east. It was this empire that shaped the current contours and territorial boundaries of the modern nation state of Zhongguo China as well as its geopolitics.

The Qing dynasty ruled the largest empire China has ever known. It more than doubled the size of the Ming empire (which it displaced in 1644) and tripled its own population. The Qing empire included not only people who identified as 'Chinese' but also people who had never been a part of a Chinese dynastic state before. This included:

Tibetans, Uighur Muslims, certain groups of Mongols, Burmese and Tais along the southwestern frontier, indigenous populations of Taiwan, and other newly colonized areas both on the frontiers and in interior highlands, and also the people from Manchuria who occupied the Qing throne itself and would come to be known as 'Manchus.' This enormous territory, or at least the vast bulk of it, and this huge and continuously growing population, with all its attendant tensions, would be bequeathed to its successor states, the Republic of China and the People's Republic of China.[10]

During the early Qing period, China flourished, becoming the largest and most powerful Eurasian empire with one of the world's most efficient economies. However, after 1830, China slipped into a deep crisis. Klaus Muhlhahn speaks of this saying:

> […] Large rebellions, coupled with Western and Japanese imperialism, further weakened the government. China also fell behind the advanced technology of the West. These events and factors marked the era known in China as the 'century of humiliation,' a chapter in the country's history that featured an unrelenting series of wars, occupations, and revolutions… China would display remarkable resilience, however, after 1870. It suffered the era of imperialism, but managed to survive it better than most parts of the world, in that it stayed largely intact and was able to lay the foundations for future development.[11]

The century of humiliation (1839–1949) had a profound effect on China's collective psyche. The repeated defeats at the hands of foreign forces sparked a churn in Chinese politics and society, with many rejecting tradition and old Confucian thought, blaming them for China's inability to modernize or face these threats, and turning to the West for solutions to reclaim China's lost status and centrality in the world. This Westward gaze encompassed religion (Christianity) as well as political ideologies (Marxism). The century of humiliation continues to play an evocative and key role in the psyche and geopolitics of the modern communist nation state. As Mark Tischler writes:

This trauma plays a significant role in Beijing's policies. The Century of Humiliation was made possible by the internal weakening of the *Qing* dynasty due to corruption and rebellions. This in turn explains why maintaining domestic stability is such a crucial part of Beijing's national security policy. At the same time, losing territory to foreign powers [...] has created a never again mentality in China [...] not just a grim lesson of the past, but also a warning [...] China must not only learn from history, but also actively work to prevent a second century of humiliation.[12]

Since the establishment of the People's Republic of China, the memories of the century of humiliation have greatly shaped and continue to shape China's policy, including its economic and geopolitical choices.

This yin-yang of national narratives has unfolded uniquely for each nation over the centuries, shaping their individual, path-dependent trajectories. These narratives have played an important role in forming pieces of the jigsaw puzzle of India and China's economic stories from 1991 to 2021—shaping events, circumstances, contexts and leadership. If China's modern and strict *hukou* system[13] of residency permits (which restricts the mobility of its population) has its origins in the Qing empire, India's current land ownership and administration systems have their origins in Raja Todar Mal's settlement system during the reign of Mughal Emperor Akbar, which were later modified by the colonial British.

Similarly, modern China's concept of its national boundaries includes Mongolia, Tibet, Manchuria and Xinjiang. However, these territories came under Chinese rule, with varying degrees of administrative or nominal control, only during the late seventeenth century Qing dynasty.[14] In fact, Mao regarded parts of Manchuria and Outer Mongolia—constituents of the then-Soviet Union and the Republic of Mongolia—along with Taiwan, as 'unfinished business'.

The ongoing Indo-China border dispute that casts a long shadow on their relations, traces its roots to Qing China and British colonial

India. The CPC construct of 'Greater China' rooted in the maximalist geographical boundaries of the Qing empire, saw the annexation of Xinjiang in 1949 and Tibet in 1950 that were till then largely autonomous regions with intermittent phases of independence.[15] The minority populations of Xinjiang and Tibet became the primary focus of social cohesion and sinicization under CPC rule.[16] The incorporation of these regions brought CPC-ruled China directly to a shared, ill-defined and disputed 3,440 km long border with India.[17] It is a festering and unresolved dispute that led to the Sino-Indian war in 1967, and has seen conflicts and confrontation along the long Himalayan border since.

In contrast, the Indian concept of *Akhand Bharat*, or 'undivided India' is based on a shared and historical cultural geography of the Indian subcontinent that predates its Islamic invasion and subsequent colonization. However, unlike the CPC, which militarily reclaimed most of China's Qing Empire boundaries, religious and social differences in India were accentuated under British colonial rule, resulting in the subcontinent's geographical division along religious lines.

India gained independence from British colonial rule of nearly two centuries on 15 August 1947, after a remarkable peaceful freedom struggle led by Mahatma Gandhi. However, the independence yielded a brutal dismemberment of its cultural identity, social fabric and territories in the form of Partition. A patchwork of 17 British ruled provinces and 562 protectorate states were cajoled and persuaded into the republic Union of India.

China, on the other hand, emerged as a modern nation from the chaos of the World War II in battle, first against the colonizing Japanese and then from the equally brutal Chinese Civil War (1945–1949) between the CPC led by Mao Zedong and the Nationalist Party, Kuomintang, led by Chiang Kai-shek. Under the CPC rule, it became the People's Republic of China, with Chairman Mao as its unquestioned authoritarian leader.

During their struggle to become modern nation states, both China and India turned towards the West for political frameworks.

The CPC was among the first to embrace communism, inspired by the Russian Revolution of 1917. After defeating an authoritarian Kuomintang in an armed civil war struggle, it went on to establish a similar Marxist-Leninist style of authoritarian government. It was initially guided and assisted by the Soviet Union but it broke up with the Russian communists early on. Under Deng Xiaoping's leadership, it further adapted its model of 'communism or socialism with Chinese characteristics' about a decade before the Soviet Union's demise.

On the other hand, under the Indian National Congress (INC), its party of national freedom, India added to the institutions of British legacy it already had. The universal adult franchise with electoral representation to the legislature and the separation of powers between the three pillars of the Indian state—the legislature, executive and judiciary—were two defining features of the Western democracy nation state model adopted by India. It followed the Westminster model of government and Anglo-Saxon law but distinguished itself from the British model by having a written constitution. The umbilical cord of colonial rule, however, was never quite outgrown as evidenced by its continued reliance on Britain for precedents—in its governance, institutions and law—even after decades of independence.

Both Jawaharlal Nehru and Mao Zedong were charismatic and popular leaders who ruled their respective parties and the political scene for decades without facing significant challenges. During this period, they shaped their young countries' political and economic cultures as well as established institutions and policies to achieve party and constitutional socialist goals. When Nehru and Mao took power, they faced similar challenges—widespread poverty; a low-productivity agricultural sector struggling to feed their massive and rapidly growing population; a poor and insufficient industrial base; and a lack of both capital and technology to modernize and expand the economy. Both identified industrialization as the solution, beginning with heavy industry while also working to improve agricultural productivity. Both believed that this could only be accomplished by state-driven investments and allocating scarce national resources in a planned manner, implementing Soviet-style five-year plans for a controlled economy. The only difference in their economic policies lay in the degree of state control, with Mao advocating for total state control and Nehru content with the 'commanding heights' of a 'mixed' economy that left only a small space for a licenced private sector and controlled market forces.

Mao, however, was impatient with the rate of progress and was eager to match and exceed the industrial output of Britain and other Western nations (perhaps mindful of the century of humiliation) in an impossibly short period of time. He imperiously launched the Great Leap Forward (GLF) between 1959 and 1961, shortly after the success of China's first Five-Year Plan. The nation's resources—material, social and human—were all yoked to this massive national task.[18] It was perhaps the largest ever enterprise undertaken since the construction of the Great Wall, as the enormous effort of the entire nation was put behind it. However, the GLF was an unmitigated disaster that resulted in mass famine and starvation deaths. According to estimates, nearly 30 million Chinese citizens died.[19]

As Mao came under political pressure following the failure of the GLF, he launched a purge of his critics, and encouraged a 'revolution from below' in which students, bureaucrats and cadres turned on their superiors in a witch hunt for 'ideological purity'.[20] The Cultural Revolution suppressed potential resistance or questioning of totalitarian centralization in both the party and bureaucracy, erecting a unitary state machine that was highly responsive to signals from the top leadership. It also contributed directly to China's crisis at the time of Mao's death. These two defining events consolidated the communist party-state's absolute and totalitarian control over all resources, including the Chinese people, with authority being vested in a totalitarian leader, echoing Chinese culture's millennia-old imperial 'Mandate of Heaven' for the ruler.

It is in the GLF and the subsequent (and consequent) Cultural Revolution that key features of the new Chinese state and the building blocks of Deng's eventual and cautious reforms of 1978 were embedded, offering lessons that would be carried forward in its spectacular growth. Mass political and social mobilization (through a mix of popular appeals to a 'greater cause', individual self-criticism and improvement, and slogans); decentralization of administration to city and provincial levels; unity of objective across all political and administrative levels of party and state; party and cadre control over the state bureaucracy (most holding both party and administrative positions); consolidation of power and totalitarian control by a central leader; and 'continuous revolution' (albeit now in reforms than in the original Maoist sense)—are all inherent characteristics that continue to live on in the Chinese political economy in 2023.

In contrast, Nehru was a staunch democrat and federalist. Despite his widespread popularity, he used his leadership to strengthen Indian democracy and its institutions. It is notable that in a South Asian environment where most democracies collapsed into totalitarian dictatorships within a few years of independence, India has stood out as its democracy has taken root and strengthened over decades. With its five-year plans and state-led heavy industry investments, his planned economy created a stable, if slow, base of growth. Early emphasis on agricultural research also resulted in the 'Green Revolution' and a much-needed self-sufficiency in food grain production. The 'unity in diversity' aspect of India's democratic and federal polity was enshrined in its Constitution, which detailed individual rights, institutional roles and the framework of the state.

Except for a brief period of totalitarian rule during the Emergency (1975–77), India's political economy has remained democratic and federal. The challenges of electoral politics have often led to competitive short-term messaging rather than coherent long-term strategies, due to the influence of political corruption and crony capitalism. The early idealism and political hegemony of PM Nehru's INC gave way to PM Indira Gandhi's populism in the early 1970s, marked by the slogan of '*Garibi Hatao* (Remove Poverty)' and the rise of a personality cult.

Later, faced with rising social unrest and economic challenges in the country, including an unfavourable judicial verdict on her own election, Indira declared a state of emergency in 1975, suspending all rights, imprisoning Opposition leaders and silencing the media.[21]

However, general elections were called unexpectedly, and her Congress (I) party lost. A short-lived coalition of Opposition parties formed the government, which fell in 1979, paving the way for her return to power. She was, however, assassinated in 1984. Her son, Rajiv Gandhi, a political novice and reluctant politician, came to power in a landslide victory but lost elections in 1989. The short-lived coalition government that came to power soon fell, but in an act of electoral cynicism, not before giving legislative and political teeth to a long-festering social issue by accepting the Mandal Commission recommendations for job reservations for backward classes.[22] In 1991, the coalition government fell apart, and Rajiv Gandhi too, was assassinated.

The underlying forces of social churn in the country continued to roil, fostering interest group bargaining and coalitions for electoral politics.[23] By the late 1980s and early 1990s, India's rising electoral consciousness and assertiveness of its diverse identities had begun to coalesce around historical caste-based groups. It saw the rise of powerful regional leaders in various states, even as national parties' grip on the country's electoral politics weakened.[24] It is a movement that, despite its decline, continues to define Indian politics at both the national and state levels.

The third defining impulse of the Indian political economy that emerged (the first being 'secular', economic status-based 'populism' politics; and the second, fragmentary, caste-based identity or interest groupings as discussed above) was Hindutva nationalism. To much controversy and contestation, Hindutva nationalism posits that the cause of Indian nationalism is rooted in the socio-religious and cultural traditions of the country. Therefore, it seeks to adopt the roles of both social reform and nation-building, with Vedic or Vedanta nationalism as a means to facilitate the emancipation and unification of all sections of Indian society.[25] Hindutva nationalism also emerged as a competing political force through its political manifestation, the Bharatiya Janata Party (BJP) during this period.

The 1990s heralded the era of coalition politics in India. Ironically, India's economic liberalization and market reforms were also initiated during this period in response to a balance of payments crisis. It was not until 2014, 23 years after the reform process began, that a government with an electoral majority was formed in India by the BJP under the leadership of PM Narendra Modi. From 1947 until 1989, the Indian political landscape was dominated by three members of the same Nehru–Gandhi family: Jawaharlal Nehru, Indira Gandhi and Rajiv Gandhi. In contrast, India had eight PMs of coalition governments from 1989 (and, in the case of Dr Manmohan Singh, as a nominee with no effective political authority despite serving two full terms as PM of a Congress-led coalition) until the BJP government came to power in 2014 under PM Modi.

This contrasts with the long tenures in office of empowered Chinese leadership and the long-term direction—for better or worse—that they provided to its political economy over the same period. Only five paramount leaders have helmed the Chinese state since 1949, including Xi Jinping, who came to power in 2012 and is consolidating power in a way not seen since Mao. Xi Jinping is the third generation in power from the civil war (after Hu Jintao) and the first from the generation born after the nation state's founding in 1949. He is also, somewhat controversially and with long-term implications for future succession, from among those who are referred to as 'princelings'—children of elite senior officials who have risen up the ranks to positions of power.

A key and persistent feature of China's authoritarian leadership in politics, economics and society has been its theory of 'perpetual revolution' as enunciated by Mao. According to Mao:

> Our revolution is like fighting a war. After winning one battle, we must immediately put forward new tasks. In this way, we can maintain the revolutionary enthusiasm of the cadres and the masses, and diminish their self satisfaction, since they have no time to be satisfied with themselves even if they wanted to; new tasks keep pressing in, and everyone devotes his mind to the question of how to fulfil the new tasks.[26]

Critics describe it as an effective strategy of mass distraction through the discovery of grand tasks and new enemies in order to keep the enormous authoritarian-directed machine of the CPC and the masses engaged in a strenuous lock-step effort to prevent questioning of wrong policy choices and obvious failures of monumental proportions, as well as turning against the leadership elite. It was a classic playbook that would be once again used to great effect by the successor who most resembles Mao's stature in the Chinese communist pantheon, Xi Jinping, well into the modern times.

The Chinese political space is the CPC which is also effectively the China state (there are, for appearance's sake, eight other nominal 'democratic' parties that function under the CPC's 'guidance' in 'multiparty cooperation'[27]). It operates along a single centripetal and hierarchical vector of the centralized and authoritarian leader and the Politburo Standing Committee, in whom all effective political and executive power is vested. The Indian political space is determined by parties aligned along three centrifugal vectors—populism and personality based politics; caste and regional based groups; and the nationalist, Hindutva movement—each pulling in different directions, and their influences rising and ebbing in the changing tide along with the nation's electoral fortunes.

During the coalition era in India, multiple political forces and interest groups diluted the intent, effectiveness and implementation of the reform programmes' opportunities. This contrasted with Chinese leaders' relatively longer tenures and authority, as well as the consistency of policy intent, experimentation, speed and implementation in the Chinese economy during the same period.

The Indian political economy during 1989 to 2014 served primarily as the greatest common denominator of disparate interest groups. It was hampered by a lack of political will and capital which was required to push through critical reforms. In the absence of a strong central political force, other institutional mechanisms asserted themselves, causing policy to be pulled in different directions. India's decentralized institutional structure, with its built-in checks and balances to prevent political power concentration, played a role. The various parties and coalitions that ruled India's various states had their own policies on subjects within their constitutional powers. The independent judiciary, professional bureaucracy and free media in India—all had different perspectives on the legitimacy, process and pace of the reforms. While the democratic process considered all points of view, the lack of a strong central political force to forge a consensus among the many powerful domestic institutions and interest groups resulted in the loss of fleeting global market opportunities and the speed required to capitalize on them.

Multicultural diversity versus monocultural unitary, centrifugal versus centripetal forces, non-violence versus war, democracy versus communism, continuity versus disruption, long-term stability and social consensus versus short-term growth risks and imposed views highlight the swirl of yin and yang through the contrasting histories of the two nations.

Forces of time, circumstance and the randomness of events over history's arc also shape individual nations. It is important to note, though, that these threads of history, beliefs, society, ethnography and culture cannot capture or do justice to the vast canvases of China and India as modern nation states. They only offer a limited context for better understanding some of the historical, social and cultural forces that have shaped both societies and nations; the role these have played, and will continue to play in the economic trajectories of the two countries.

Part Two

Three Determinants of Reform

4

Leadership

If only one element in the comparative narrative of China and India could be chosen, one that clearly set China on a different trajectory of economic growth, it would be Deng Xiaoping's rise to power.

In our sweeping and traditional view of history, we tend to focus on events, circumstances, policies and environment, tracing resultant outcomes over a period of time. This approach, however, ignores the role of the personality, character and capabilities of rare individuals who, from time to time, rise to power and shape the future of their nations. Those who have led freedom struggles and served as founding fathers of their countries, such as George Washington, Mahatma Gandhi, Mao Zedong and Nelson Mandela, have traditionally played this role. It is uncommon for a leader to have the same impact at the time of a great challenge, and also nearly three decades after a country's independence.

China, after the death of Chairman Mao Zedong, was on the cusp of disaster. The highly charismatic and popular 'Great Helmsman' had been responsible for the victory of the Communist Party of China (CPC) and the founding of the modern nation state in 1949, and had ruled unchallenged (purging all opposition, real or suspected) for nearly three decades. He had also brought China—through the economic, political and social disasters of the Great Leap Forward (GLF) and the Cultural Revolution—to near collapse. Deeply paranoid, Mao's first chosen successor President and Party Vice Chairman Liu Shaoqi died in 1969 under house arrest and without medical care, while his wife languished in prison after being purged in 1966. His second, Marshal Lin Biao, died in a plane crash in 1971 while fleeing to the former Soviet Union after an alleged failed coup attempt.

Deng Xiaoping was a prominent party leader (who was once considered Lin Biao's main rival to succeed Mao from among the next generation leadership) and a close associate of the fallen Liu Shaoqi. He too had been purged in 1966, but after a long house arrest, during which he and his wife were isolated and their children sent away, he was sent to work in a factory in 1969, where he remained till he was rehabilitated and brought back in 1973. The four years of exile were a period of great difficulty. Politically ostracized and personally humiliated, Deng's family was also persecuted by the Red Guards, with his eldest son ending up paralysed. Brought back by Zhou Enlai with the approval of Mao as a knowledgeable and competent leader in foreign affairs as China was warming up to the United States (US), Deng allied with Zhou to bring about whatever policy reforms he could while Mao's paranoia about Zhou grew.

Mao gradually elevated Deng to prominence, in part to counterbalance Zhou, but he was increasingly targeted by the infamous 'Gang of Four', led by Mao's wife Jiang Qing, who was wary of his growing power. Concerned about his posthumous reputation in a post-Mao China led by Deng, and the possibility of Deng abandoning Mao's legacy, an ailing Mao put pressure on Deng to accept the Cultural Revolution. Deng, however, refused to yield. This led to an orchestrated attempt to rein him in politically. However, when Zhou died in early 1976, the shabby treatment meted out at his funeral sparked an unsettling outpouring of public sentiment in Zhou's and his protégé, Deng's favour. This resulted in Deng's removal from all positions of power in April 1976.

A new leader, Hua Guofeng, was anointed as Mao's successor. However, before Hua could consolidate significant power, Mao died in September 1976, throwing the country and the CPC into an existential turmoil. The party leadership coalesced around the removal and arrest of the widely unpopular Gang of Four—responsible for the disaster of the extremist Cultural Revolution—and the rehabilitation (the fourth of his long career) of the reformist and pragmatic Deng Xiaoping. Deng returned to the party and government in July 1977 to assist Hua with specific 'back office' or 'key' mission tasks such as education, science and technology, but their power to influence was unequal from the start.

While the relatively unknown and next generation Hua held primary formal positions in both the party and government, he could not compare with Deng's stature, respect and networks as one of the original heroes of the Revolution, as well as his long and brilliant career as a leader of the military, party and government. Even as the two continued to work together, the balance of power naturally gravitated to Deng. His pragmatic 'practice is the sole criteria for judging truth' and the launch of his 'reform and opening-up' policies were formalized by the CPC in December 1978.

Deng's governance was in stark contrast to Mao's personality cult. Deng remained in the background; even his formal titles were limited to modest positions like vice-chairman of the party and vice premier (in government), though he retained the powerful position of chairman of the Central Military Commission. Despite this, he was able to acquire and effectively control key levers of power.

So, how did Deng Xiaoping govern?

Ezra Vogel suggests that he did so by 'fully utilizing his reputation and moving boldly to create a well-run system capable of building a strong, prosperous country. If Mao were like an emperor above the clouds, reading history and novels and issuing edicts, Deng was more like a commanding general, checking carefully to see that his battle plans were properly staffed and implemented.'[1]

Deng's renowned statement—'It doesn't matter if the cat is black or white, as long as it catches mice'[2] (first said by him in the 1960s)— marked the phased opening-up of the Chinese economy in the early 1980s. Under Deng's leadership, China actively encouraged foreign investments in establishing manufacturing facilities in designated special economic zones (SEZs), and subsequently in other reforms. Deng's reform strategy was distinctly different from Mao's hasty and disastrous GLF. Likely influenced by the pitfalls of the GLF, Deng adopted a cautious approach, or in his words, 'cross the river by feeling the stone'.[3] He preferred a gradual approach, initiating partial reforms in specific regions as an experiment, which were then deepened and widened based on the testing and success of the localized experiments. This incremental approach allowed an idea to be tested and refined in one region before being adopted as a policy in other regions. This 'point to surface' approach became a distinguishing feature of Chinese policymaking in subsequent decades. It played an important role in providing stability and fewer course corrections as China opened up its markets in a complex transition from being a completely state-owned economy.

Deng died in 1997, nearly 20 years after coming to power as the paramount leader, with his reforms well entrenched and largely irreversible with China well on its way to economic prosperity. It is a path that was continued on by his successors, including Xi Jinping. It is only now that some recent policy pivots and new 'Xi Jinping Thought' and 'common prosperity' rhetoric suggest that there may be some revisitation of Deng's path in light of China's new economic and sociopolitical challenges of the twenty-first century.

The Deng era is officially recognized as lasting from 1978 to 1989 when he stepped down from all positions, though his influence lasted until his death in 1997. Deng's economic army was led by his contemporary, the formidable Chen Yun, who was also a member of the Politburo Standing Committee (PSC, the party's most powerful decision-making authority, then consisting of seven members). Chen, having been involved in China's economic policies for more than three-and-a-half decades, and having been assigned responsibility for the management of Northwest China in 1942, even while the war was raging, he laid the groundwork for Deng's reform and opening-up programme. Despite having no formal education beyond elementary school, he was widely regarded as Deng's equal. Deeply influenced by traditional Chinese political economy thought of Guanzi and the Salt and Iron debate (policies which he had used to great effect to control inflation and bring economic order in Northwest China during the years of war) than Western neoliberal economic theory, he reflected their cautious approach rather than a 'Big Bang' reform. His views on gradualism in opening up and the first generation of reforms in the early 1980s were best summed up in what he called the 'bird cage economy'.

According to Chen, it was best to define the 'cage' (the overall plan by the state) and let the 'bird' (the market forces) fly free within the 'cage'. In later years, however, he became critical of the scale of 'reform and opening-up', as in his opinion, there was too much left to 'markets' and receding state planning and intervention. Deng and Chen, the elder party statesmen, were supported by next generation leaders, Hu Yaobang (as head of party) and Zhou Ziyang (as head of government), after the removal of Mao-appointee Hua in 1981.

During this period (1978–97), the 'dual track' reforms were implemented, allowing households as the unitary entity for cultivating agricultural land and retaining or selling agricultural surplus in markets at market prices above the contracted level to the state. A similar 'dual pricing' incentive of selling 'surplus' at market prices above 'contracted production' was extended to the industrial sector's dominant state-owned enterprises (SOEs). The town and village enterprises (TVE) experiment, which unleashed rural and small-town market-oriented entrepreneurship—an intermediate step in creating a market economy—was also carried out, before the policy environment caused their subsequent decline.[4] The key experiments of the SEZs in Guangdong and Fujian, which eventually laid the foundation for China's export-driven economic success, were carried out between 1979 and 1984. In 1994, land use reforms were also implemented to allow for private, urban real estate markets.

During these early years, Deng laid the groundwork for China's future economic growth. While many senior leaders in the CPC had reservations about the reforms' direction, maintaining the party's unity and hegemony in the aftermath of the deeply divisive Cultural Revolution, during which many party leaders and cadres were persecuted, was of paramount importance. Deng was the only leader of stature who could unite both the party and the nation by rehabilitating the persecuted while ensuring public continuity with the Mao Zedong Thought and his political legacy.

Even today, the horrors of the Cultural Revolution continue to haunt the party, reinforcing its hierarchical and centripetal impulses of unity and discipline at all costs, under a pyramidal leadership structure with a paramount leader. It was Deng who instituted constitutional limits on the time that the top leadership could hold official positions, limiting it to 10 years to avoid power concentration and a repeat of the Mao personality cult, which concentrated and accrued power to a single leader and coterie. This practice was followed by all subsequent leadership till it was abolished by Xi Jinping in 2018.

While Deng was the paramount leader, he was also one among the 'Eight Elders/Immortals', a group of eight revolution-era leaders who collectively held power and helped shape the party and China's policies following Mao's death in 1976. The stature and moral authority of Deng and the other seven elders/immortals among the party and the public in China's sociopolitical structure cannot be overemphasized. It was this largely collective authority that enabled difficult grassroots and far-reaching economic reforms to be pushed through in its early years. These were the main reforms that set the stage for the next, smaller steps, taken by the next generation of party and national leaders.

The history of political leadership in India, on the other hand, is a fractured one. Following the death of Prime Minister (PM) Jawaharlal Nehru (1889–1964)—the unquestioned leader of both the ruling party and the government, and with a public and political stature to match—Indian political leadership soon fell into turmoil. The only other person of Nehru's stature, political and moral authority—Sardar Vallabhbhai Patel (1875–1950)—had passed away earlier, within just a few years of India's independence. The Indian National Congress (INC) that the two had led in government soon split, with Jawaharlal Nehru's daughter, Indira Gandhi forming her own Congress (Indira) in 1969. She had been elevated to the post of PM as a compromise candidate of warring factions of party political syndicates. Her personality cult and populist programmes subsumed her party and gave her electoral victories, but culminated in her declaration of Emergency in 1975 in the face of widespread political and social unrest.

India's version of the Cultural Revolution saw the administration run amok under her younger son, Sanjay Gandhi. When elections were called in 1977, she lost. However, she came back to power in 1980. Shortly after, her son and political heir died in a plane crash. Keen to continue a dynastic family legacy, she brought in her elder son, Rajiv Gandhi—a pilot with no political or administrative experience, hoping to groom him as her successor. Her assassination in 1984, however, cut short this process, and Rajiv Gandhi was catapulted to the prime ministership with a landslide electoral majority. Politically inexperienced, administratively unseasoned and surrounded by a coterie of friends and palace retainers, Rajiv Gandhi squandered opportunities for significant reform. Losing power in 1989 amid accusations of corruption by his own former Finance Minister, he was assassinated while campaigning for elections in 1991. His party, however, came to power at the head of an unstable coalition, with P.V. Narasimha Rao as the PM. He was a loyalist politician with no independent political base or political capital. The story of unstable political coalitions and resulting weak leadership would be repeated in multiple elections until 2014.

In China, the contrast could not be starker. Even at the height of his paranoia, Mao was conscious of the need for a competent and experienced leadership succession for the CPC and China, although successive nominees (Liu Shaoqi, Lin Biao) were purged by Mao or rebelled. Deng Xiaoping's rehabilitation in 1973 was a part of this thought process as was Deng's not being expelled from the party by Mao in 1976, despite being removed from all positions of official power. It left the door open for his return under the collective consensus of the party leadership in 1978 as the most competent leader to stabilize the party and China in its hour of crisis. With the generation of revolutionary independence leaders still in power, the rise of the 'princelings' in China—the offspring of these leaders—and the troubling questions of future succession and stability of the CPC and China were still a few decades away.

Tugging at that fickle tapestry of history and its wormhole strands of 'what if' possibilities once more, it can only be speculated whether the trajectory of India's reform process would have been different if it had been undertaken by a leader from the generation of its freedom struggle. Would their political and public stature, as well as moral authority, been able to take the tough decisions and push through reforms in the early years of the Indian republic? Would Sardar Patel have been able to more effectively implement the difficult agricultural land reforms in the grassroots that eventually became hostage to the deeply entrenched and vested political interest groups if he had lived longer? If Indira Gandhi had not been assassinated in 1984, would she have been able and willing to use her towering public stature and political capital to engage with deeper and more fundamental reforms of private participation and collaboration in public enterprises to create champions of industry in then sunrise industries like telecommunications? Would the outcomes of the manufacturing SEZs experiments in India have been different? Could India's reform process have been deeper and more fundamental in nature than the 'shallow reforms' of 'art of the possible' coalition politics it has often been accused of? Could India's trajectory of economic growth have been different?

It is also true that, having followed Mao's footsteps and centralized all authority and power under his unrivalled leadership, with Xi's political thought now enshrined in the party's core, and having been re-elected for a record third time after amending the constitution, China now finds itself (after more than five decades), in a situation where any mistakes made by an authoritarian leader cut off from feedback can result in amplified disaster. The GLF and the Cultural Revolution under Mao's unquestioned leadership set China's development back by decades and brought widespread misery to its people. A 'zero-COVID' policy that resulted in widespread closure of large parts of urban China that caused economic distress and disruption; a show of aggressive posture towards Taiwan and its neighbours leading to realigned geopolitics and rapidly changing military and economic alliances; slowing economic growth; debt and excesses of previous decades coming to roost; corruption; and rising income and wealth inequalities—the challenges that China has been facing are many. The jury is still out on Xi's ability to successfully manage these challenges. China lost disastrously under Mao's leadership, but won under Deng's reform and opening-up. Will history compare Xi's tenure with Mao's era or Deng's success?

India, on the other hand, is now well into the second five year term of an electoral majority government under the undisputed leadership of PM Narendra Modi. First elected in 2014, barring a few initial missteps, the strengths of India's uninterrupted economic journey of over 75 years, under successive governments, has been consolidated and weaknesses worked upon. It has been a consistent feature of Indian democracy that, regardless of the political party in power, India's economic progress has been characterized by broad political consensus and stable growth. It has also been remarkable in India's journey as a nation that, with the exception of a brief interregnum of Emergency, all successive leaders have upheld democratic processes of the people's electoral will as feedback mechanisms, and functioned within the framework of its written constitution and institutions. As a result, while India may not have achieved the singular goal of high economic growth at the expense of everything else, it has also avoided the disasters of social and economic repression and unaddressed policy imbalances that now threaten other authoritarian economies and nations.

5

Federalism

China's political, administrative and governance structures are rooted in Marxist-Leninist totalitarianism—or, more precisely, as 'socialist administration with Chinese characteristics' of imperial China. China has 23 provinces, five autonomous regions, four centrally administered municipalities and two special administrative regions (Hong Kong and Macao are administered under the 'one country, two systems' framework). The remarkable diversity of this structure has its origins in imperial China, as shaped by the experiences of the communist struggle and tempered by the pragmatic compromises of its recent history.

While organized at three levels of local, provincial and central government, China's unique feature is that the CPC is the government. This is an aspect that cannot be emphasized enough. Party cadres can, and mostly do, hold positions in both party and government from the lowest village level to the highest standing committee of the Politburo. In all matters of power and decision-making, the party is the last word, and the party general secretary at the local or provincial level is the final 'boss' rather than the highest corresponding government official. This party-government structure is hierarchical and interconnected, with each level reporting to the next higher level, culminating in the Politburo Standing Committee (PSC).

The structure tolerates no public dissent from the official party line or strategy that flows from the PSC. The career advancement of these party-government officials is dependent on the results they achieve on these directives. The systemic tendencies of bureaucratic inertia and resistance to directives, inherent in any organizational structure, were effectively broken during the terror of the Cultural Revolution and Mao's practice of 'perpetual revolution', which saw widespread attacks and persecution of the middle levels of bureaucratic power by lower level functionaries. During this time, it made the party-government apparatus even more responsive to directives from above.

During the post-Mao period, the centralized structure saw greater decentralization of policymaking to lower levels of the government. China had always followed a delegated 'bird in cage' policy structure that gave provincial and local government leaders broad leeway of decision-making to achieve the leadership's broader strategic objectives. This style of policymaking had its roots in the revolutionary origins of the Communist party's three-decade struggle to come to power (as also in traditional legalist political philosophy of Shang Yang[1] and Han Fei[2], and the economic thought of the Guanzi), which had required an array of creative—proactive as well as evasive—tactics for managing sudden change and uncertainty. This aspect of policymaking became even more prominent during the Deng reform period, with greater delegation to local and provincial governments.

Since 1978, decentralized reform initiatives and local reform experiments that could be expanded into national political programmes have been a unique feature of China's economic growth. China successfully adopted a unique policy experimentation methodology (*zhengce shiyan*) to encourage innovation in a cumbersome, bureaucratic and authoritarian government system.

As Sebastian Heilmann, a leading German political scientist and sinologist describes it, this methodology consists of three steps. First, local 'experimentation points/zones (*shidian/shiyanqu*)' are established. Second, successful 'model experiments (*dianxing shiyan*)' are identified within these pilot experimental projects and expanded 'from point to surface (*you dian dao mian* or *yidian daimian*)' to determine whether the new policy options can be generalized or need to be modified. Third, policies are not included in national legislation until they have been thoroughly tested in a real-world administrative setting, which usually takes several years.

China's SEZs (*jingji tequ*) are the world's most well known examples of such experimentation. Almost without exception, the most important policy reform measures—ranging from rural decollectivization to management reforms in state-owned enterprises and the establishment of stock markets, to reforms in the rural health system—were initiated in decentralized experiments that were subject to selective intervention by CPC and high-level government leaders.

While overarching policy objectives are established centrally, policy instruments are created locally and tested before being implemented throughout the country. In practice, the experimental approach enables new solutions to be identified and tailored to constantly changing requirements during the ongoing search process. This step-by-step policymaking approach has been critical for China's ability to carry out such comprehensive political and institutional changes since the 1980s, despite the many institutional, policy and ideological forces of inertia, without resulting in the party-state's collapse.[3]

India, in contrast, is a federation of states and (presently) has 28 states and eight Union (centrally administered) territories. While the Indian political administrative structure has three levels of governance—local, state and central government, its responsibilities are defined by a constitutional arrangement. Certain subjects are dealt with exclusively by the Union government, others by the state governments and some by the concurrent (joint) list. Separate elections for fixed terms are held at each level of government, from the lowest (village panchayat) to the highest (Parliament).

The fall of the political hegemony of the INC (which began in the late 1960s and early 1970s) and the rise of other political forces, as previously discussed, resulted in the difference of power at each level of government. Due to the diverse range of political goals among the different levels of government controlled by various political parties, each of which caters to its own interest groups and coalitions, policy and strategy fragmentation has become a prominent feature of Indian politics. The coalition era of Indian politics, which began in 1991, was especially vulnerable to these forces. In this environment, the Indian bureaucracy was the only constant source of administrative and governing power.

In contrast to China's party-government system, India's civilian bureaucracy was a holdover from the colonial era. The patwari village officer, the district magistrate, the undersecretaries and secretaries of various ministries in state capitals and finally, the Union ministries in Delhi, comprised a vast administrative apparatus that was initially established to collect taxes and maintain law and order. These bureaucrats wielded considerable power, which was bolstered by the permanent nature of their employment and the cadre of their government service. At the pinnacle of this structure, as is still the case today, was the Indian Administrative Service (IAS), which was made up of officers chosen through the merit-based Union Public Services Commission examination and filled all senior government positions. Officers of the IAS cadre effectively ran the administration across the country, ostensibly implementing policies of the current incumbent government, but in practice exercising great discretion and power, particularly in delaying, diluting and burying initiatives of their political masters in files and red tape. It was mostly made up of well-educated, upright officers with high moral standards who sought to serve the national cause, while being surrounded by the venal and corrupt atmosphere of political power that constant election-inclined politics and its funding fostered. It was also a rule-based administrative system that did not set targets with incentives or punishments and did not encourage initiatives or decision-making, but instead encouraged a preference for safe options, the power of refusal and an inherent inertia towards maintaining the status quo. The cadres were generalists but had an administrative hegemony even over positions requiring specialist knowledge and experience, a feature that further diluted any deeper cooperation or commitment towards reform initiatives.

Some of this attitude on the part of bureaucrats was justified by the fear of the three C's of the Indian administration—the Comptroller and Auditor General of India, the Central Vigilance Commission and the Central Bureau of Investigation. However, its downside for policy reforms was also equally evident.

It is not surprising, then, that the scope and speed of the Indian reform process during the coalition era, beyond the initial backing of P.V. Narasimha Rao's limited political capital in his single five-year tenure, was largely driven by the bureaucracy. The structure of competitive electoral politics in India encouraged a preference for welfare economics over hard policy decisions and structural shifts. Dr Manmohan Singh was a highly regarded economist and bureaucrat who rose to the political position of finance minister during Rao's regime, when the reform process was launched in response to India's precarious financial situation.

His second tenure in power was also as a nominee PM of a political family legacy, leading another unstable coalition from 2004 to 2014. While he was widely respected by the public for his gravitas, knowledge and probity, he lacked political capital and had little control over the Cabinet that he led as the PM. The telecom and coal scams as well as the subsequent judicial intervention, the cloud of suspicion of crony corruption and the crisis of confidence in many other critical sectors, such as roads and power, effectively derailed the reform process and contributed to his government's electoral defeat in 2014.

The authors of Indian reforms were, without exception, bureaucrats. Dr Rakesh Mohan, a Princeton-educated economist who joined the government as an economic advisor after working at the World Bank, wrote infrastructure and industry reforms. Montek Ahluwalia, an Oxford-educated economist, inducted initially as an economic advisor after a long stint at the World Bank, wrote the famous 'M document', which laid out a blueprint of reforms. Jairam Ramesh, a key member of the finance ministry and Planning Commission reforms team, was another Carnegie Mellon- and MIT-educated public policy economist who joined the government after a brief stint at the World Bank. Dr Manmohan Singh, with a doctorate from Oxford, spent many years in the government as an economic technocrat, and also at the World Bank and the International Monetary Fund (IMF). It was thus not surprising that everyone was largely on the same page of neoliberal economics, with standardized World Bank and IMF prescriptions for liberalizing developing economies.

The only reformer in the Manmohan Singh government who had some limited grassroots political experience, was Harvard-educated minister P. Chidambaram. He was, however, seen more at ease in Lutyens' Delhi than in hard selling reforms in the grimy political battles of India's hinterland. Pranab Mukherjee was another such politician in the Manmohan Singh government, without a political base and a reluctant reformer. In hindsight, it is clear that this mostly academic team of nominated politicians, economists and bureaucrats lacked the experienced political leadership and capital required to shape realpolitik policy, give clear direction to the reform process, engage in dialogue and get buy-in from states, the implementing bureaucracy and the general public, all the while taking responsibility for policy outcomes.

As a result, the majority of reforms implemented were low-hanging fruits, such as those that could be implemented through gazette notifications and without too much political opposition or controversy. Some of the reforms implemented included delicencing industries, removing price controls, lowering tariffs and duties, reforming the financial sector (excluding the privatization of public sector banks), establishing new regulatory infrastructure, introducing a new public–private infrastructure policy, ensuring private sector participation in telecommunications, allocating coal blocks and implementing an SEZ policy. Even in those cases, a lack of political capital and a policymaking style based on the 'path of least resistance', with little room for course correction, resulted in suboptimal outcomes.

So, how did authoritarian China manage to create more efficient markets than federal India? According to Gabriella Montinola, Yingyi Qian and Barry Weingast, any government attempting to build and protect markets face a fundamental dilemma—it must not only be strong enough to enforce the legal rights and rules required to maintain the economy but must also be credible in its commitment to honouring such rules. According to them, while decentralization is a fundamental feature of federalism, not all decentralization systems are federal. They identified a different type of federalism in terms of markets—'market-preserving federalism'— which necessitates a set of five conditions for the distribution of authority and responsibilities among different levels of government:

a) There is a hierarchy of governments with delineated spheres of authority (for example, between the national and subnational governments) so that each government is autonomous within its own sphere of authority.

b) Subnational governments have primary authority over the economy within their jurisdictions.

c) The national government has the authority to police the common market and ensure the mobility of goods and factors across subnational government jurisdictions.

d) Revenue sharing among governments is limited and borrowing by governments is constrained so that all governments face hard budget constraints.

e) The allocation of authority and responsibility has an institutionalized degree of durability so that it cannot be altered by the national government either unilaterally or under pressures from subnational governments.[4]

Viewed through this market-preserving federalism framework, it is easier to understand how even institutional processes of diffused and thorny concurrent list 'shared responsibilities' between the Centre and the states, contested devolution of fiscal resources and most importantly, lack of political authority and capital to create, maintain and regulate common markets, have resulted in suboptimal outcomes in the Indian context.

6

Institutions and the Legal Framework

To be fair, enacting effective reforms in the Indian context has been and continues to be a Herculean task. The role and robustness of a nation's institutions and processes determine the effectiveness of the individual, enterprise, public and state. Decision-making, concentration of power, legal and social structures and economic checks and balances, all take place within this institutional framework.

The constitutional structure of India includes multiple institutions with clearly defined separation of powers. The elected legislature creates laws for the country, while the executive—the government—is led by the party with the most seats in the legislature and is in charge of governance and policy formulation. The independent judiciary interprets and adjudicates legal issues. The written constitution also establishes fundamental rights for Indian citizens that are sacred and inviolable against the state and are upheld by an active judiciary.

This institutional structure is represented at the national level by the Parliament, the Government of India and the Supreme Court, and is mirrored at the state and district levels by state legislatures and local councils, as well as high courts and district courts. All of these institutions, each with its own jurisdiction and powers, interact with one another in a complex web of decision-making, policy implementation and adjudication, forming the institutional framework within which the Indian nation state operates.

China, on the other hand, is different. While it has a written constitution as the nominal supreme law (the most recent of which was adopted in 1982 and is subject to revision every five years) and a nominal judiciary, China—the modern nation state—is without a doubt, the CPC. For those from other political cultures or experiences, grasping the enormity or singularity of this concept is difficult, but it is a point worth emphasizing and requires deeper reflection.

To elaborate, there are nearly 90 million party members in China, roughly one-tenth of China's adult population. The party has branches in nearly all of China's 4 million grassroots organizations (villages, townships and urban committees). It has dominated every aspect of life for every resident of the People's Republic of China for over seven decades—at individual, family, social, cultural, economic and political levels. It is also important to note that the People's Liberation Army (PLA) is not a national army in the traditional sense but rather the CPC's army and one of the key levers of power in China. Indeed, one of the key positions for its paramount leader, among others, is chairman of the Central Military Commission. As some observers put it, most nations have a party or parties that form their political framework and governance. China, on the other hand, is a party with a nation, and its primary goal, first and foremost, even to the exclusion of all else, is to keep the party in power. It is, therefore, of utmost importance to understand the nature and organization of the CPC, which is the primary and only institution that matters in China.

China has attempted to create a monolithic (sinicized), hierarchical, organized and obedient society over millennia, with long legalist traditions of realpolitik governance propagated by Shang Yang (390–338 BCE) and Han Fei (280–233 BCE). As a vast country with diverse topography, climate, religion and culture, China has 55 recognized national minorities that occupy 60 per cent of its land[1] (mostly in border states—Tibet, Xinjiang and Manchuria— surrounding its Han core) but account for less than 10 per cent of its population.[2] There are, however, multiple realities that exist beneath the surface of a unitary nation state. While generalizations of CPC policy are difficult, and some local adjustments have been made in the past, the party has always regarded other identities—religious, cultural or political—that could grow to provide an alternative narrative to the party-state as a potential threat. It has responded to these with a mix of repression, suppression, blaming 'outside forces' and increased local investment in the hope of solving the problem through development. In minority and border areas, this has been accompanied by the settlement of Han ethnic majority migrants in the hope that sinicization of these regions will foster obedience to the unitary party-state.[3]

The CPC is a complex organization in terms of both its constitution and hierarchy. It is a Leninist and autocratic institution, guided by directives from the party's highest levels. Despite its long history, the party's power structure and power sharing has not been institutionalized, and the mechanisms of its discussions, operations and decision-making processes remain opaque. The threat has been most evident whenever the question of succession has arisen. Evidentially, whenever its ruling elite have been united on the way forward, it has worked well. However, whenever the elite have been divided (the GLF, the Cultural Revolution, the overthrow of the Gang of Four after Mao's death), a crisis has ensued. This has also led to a great deal of uncertainty, with dramatic shifts accompanying each new succession as the 'will of the majority' shifts, with a new winner emerging from intra-party struggles. Deng Xiaoping, China's reform architect, was purged and rehabilitated four times during his long career. When his father, veteran party leader Xi Zhongxun (and one of the Eight Elders or Immortals) was purged during the Cultural Revolution, Xi Jinping, the current and undisputed paramount leader, was exiled to rural China.

Yet, despite these upheavals and internal regime changes, the party's credo has held fast till now. The CPC continues to believe that an individual will gain more by entrusting his or her choices and freedom to the collective, than by acting on their own. This remains an unchanged axiom even after the introduction and subsequent success of market reforms that have permitted individual choices and wants, but which remains subservient to party-prescribed ideology. There are rigid limits to what people may read, view, write or publish, with extensive and graded censorship. For each interest group, only one party-approved organization is permitted, which will communicate its views to party leadership via a hierarchical structure. Any independent organization will be suppressed and any overt opposition to the CPC's rule will be crushed immediately. The party apparatus' hierarchical communication structure facilitates the formation of 'silos', preventing any coalition of interest groups from forming what could potentially undermine the CPC's ability to exert control.

The party exerts control over its cadres and the masses through its two most powerful departments in charge of organization and propaganda. The department in charge of organization has enormous powers of patronage, as it selects members for manning all key posts. Individual records detailing all personal details and political performance are kept at all local organization departments and workplaces. Those deemed undesirable are weeded out while those who follow the party line are promoted to higher positions of responsibility. The propaganda department of the party promotes 'correct behaviour'. It oversees a large network of research organizations and training schools to inculcate understanding and support of central policies among its cadre, ensuring that there is a near unanimity of public expression of the 'official line'. During times of leadership change, the system allows time for its cadres to adjust to new realities and policies as fresh alignment occurs to the thoughts, policies and directives emanating from the top.

The CPC is organized on Leninist principles, with democratic centralism as its distinguishing feature. The party organization is hierarchical, with the individual subordinate to the organization and the minority subordinate to the party's Central Committee. The party is also organized, at least in theory, around the principle of collective leadership, which is intended to mitigate any tendency toward a dominant leader. This has, however, rarely worked in practice. Only this centralization, according to the party, can ensure the necessary solidarity and unity to carry out its decisions. Individuals can express their opinions all the way up to the Central Committee, but they must follow the party's policy while waiting for a decision. In practice though, personal networks and factions are a reality of politics and are particularly seen at times of succession, with new alignments and changing power equations.

The CPC's Politburo, which has about 25 members, and more importantly its PSC, which has seven members, are at the pinnacle of power.[4] The Politburo is formally elected by the Central Committee—though in practice, the Central Committee is presented with a list of candidates already pre-negotiated by the party elite. The title of 'core leader' is important, however, because not all leaders are given the title. The term core leader in the party's terminology indicates that the person is more than just being the first among equals, though in practice it is often much more. Deng Xiaoping defined and resurrected the concept, referring to Mao as the core of the first generation, and himself as the core of the second generation. Xi Jinping is not only a designated core leader but enjoys a status within the party not seen since Mao. This means, he not only has the deciding vote in the event of a policy impasse, but he can also initiate a policy without consulting other senior party leaders. The core or paramount leader promotes a guiding ideology that the party cadres must follow, and the power of the leader is indicated by the reverence with which these are treated. 'Mao Thought' evolved from the time the party seized power in 1949 till 1978, and was followed by 'Deng Theory', which guided the period of reform. Neither of Deng's successors, Jiang Zemin or Hu Jintao, achieved that eminence until 'Xi Jinping Thought' on 'Socialism with Chinese Characteristics for a New Era' elevated him to the same level as Mao. It is also interesting to note that in the over 70-year history of the party-state, there have been only five leaders, of which three have been 'core' leaders of the CPC.

The CPC's policies are carried out through the Chinese bureaucracy, the state's administrative apparatus that spans all levels of federal, provincial, urban, rural, industrial, agricultural and state-owned financial institutions and enterprises. The bureaucracy in China has a long history, stretching back as far as the beginning of its imperial age and which, according to American professor and politician Kenneth Lieberthal, '…was a profoundly non pluralistic system based squarely on the notions of hierarchy, centralisation, and the state as the propagator of the correct moral framework of society... Even China's concrete administrative system today bears a strong resemblance to its imperial forebear.'[5] Lieberthal calls this modern system, the 'fragmented authoritarianism model'. It was a model that worked during the Mao era, and even more so after any potential political or bureaucratic opposition to the central directive was eliminated in the governance structure that emerged from the turmoil of the Cultural Revolution.

However, as David M. Lampton, professor and director of China and China studies at John Hopkins School of Advanced International Studies, points out, there was a relative decline in the hierarchical command in the first few decades of reform in the post-Mao era under Deng and his successors, with significant delegation of authority downward.[6] There was a greater emphasis on collective leadership within the elite party command, with an increase in the use of market mechanisms through experimentation and delegated authority to provincial and city levels. As the reform agenda was dominated by complex economic and technical issues requiring multiple trade-offs in the context of a collective leadership and bureaucracies of increasing size and technical complexity, there was also a significant increase in the use of bargaining. China under Xi Jinping, however, is seeing a reconcentration of centralized power in the paramount leader not seen since the days of Mao.

So, where does the rule of law fit into this unique Chinese institutional structure of a communist party-state served by an adjunct bureaucracy? In China, law has always had a very different meaning than in countries with an Anglo-Saxon legal tradition. In imperial China, law only applied to obligations to the Emperor, and detailed rules, procedures and penalties were established. The judicial process, which was co-executed within and by the empire's administrative framework, recognized no 'rights' of individuals, institutions or society apart from their obligations to the 'Son of Heaven' and their own Confucian place in the imperial order. The same holds true of the modern nation state of China. It has made some reforms, most notably—the enactment of the constitution and the promulgation of laws in the post-liberalization era. Leaders from Deng Xiaoping onwards have stressed that policies and government actions must be based on the constitution and the law. There has been strong rhetorical support from them too for '*yifa zhiguo*[7] (running the country according to law)'—a concept that has also been described as 'rule *by* law with Chinese characteristics'.

However, there is a significant distinction between the concept of rule 'of' law as understood by Western democracies and rule 'by' law. The rule 'by' law is a derivation of the imperial legal framework, with the ruling party running the country in accordance with the laws that it has drafted. The CPC has never recognized the concept of an independent judiciary. In a national meeting of the *zhengfa* (political and legal cluster) system in 2008, Hu Jintao called upon 'judicial workers' to follow three *zhishang* (foremost priorities): 'the party's enterprise; the people's interest; and the Constitution and the laws'. Even Xi Jinping, while exhorting that 'party organizations of all levels should insist on acting within the parameters of the Constitution and the laws,' noted that cadres must 'unswervingly uphold the party's leadership over *zhengfa* work'.[8]

In contrast, the Indian judicial system is an independent arm of the state established by its written constitution. It is distinct from the state's lawmaking and administrative arms, with its own institutional hierarchy and powers. The Indian Constitution recognizes the citizens' fundamental rights and guarantees them, with the judiciary as their independent custodian. As a result, the judiciary not only has the authority to review and rule on the legality of laws in the context of the Constitution, but it also rules on the rights of individuals, organizations and 'public interest' qua the government. In the Indian context, the constitution is supreme and all three institutions of the state—the legislature, the executive and the judiciary—work within its framework. In fact, while amendments to the constitution are permissible, under the 'basic structure' doctrine, the Supreme Court of India has held that it is not within the Parliament's purview to bring changes to the fundamental tenets upon which the Constitution rests.

The Indian Supreme Court's recent expansion in its own
jurisdiction [...] has led to an unusually deep engagement of
the Court with administrative and regulatory processes. The
Indian Supreme Court acts to review regulatory decisions for
compliance with substantive fundamental rights; it determines
procedural compliance with statutes but also with stronger
due process requirements; it sits in appeal over decisions of
regulatory bodies when they act in 'quasi-judicial' capacities
but also over administrative decisions that are not judicial
in character; it occasionally takes control of, and directs,
regulatory measures itself; and, not least, it plays a significant
role in shaping the institutional design of regulators.[9]

The separation of powers and the supremacy of the written constitution
empower Indian citizens with rights and ensure their protection under
the adversarial Indian judicial system, acting as a check on executive
and legislative power. However, in the context of reforms, many of the
government's laws and policies have ended up in court, with many
facing delays or being struck down upon judicial review in High Courts
and the Supreme Court, creating an atmosphere of policy uncertainty.
Instances of judicial empowerment or overreach include suo-moto
cognizance and subsequent cancellation of the government's telecom
and coal mine allocation policies, the directive to auction all natural
resources (later reversed by a larger bench), issues related to telecom
adjusted gross revenue (AGR) dues, land acquisition matters, farm
laws, amendments to contractual obligations under force majeure,
and so on. It is notable that these instances of judicial intervention
coincided with a period when a politically weak executive was in power.

However, it isn't that China doesn't have a framework for law. Law
in China—till the extent it exists—follows civil law with European
(German) influence, in stark contrast to India, which has followed a
British common law tradition. Europe's civil law shares many values
with Chinese traditions. Furthermore, common law is individualistic
and does not fit the Chinese communitarian values enshrined in,
for example, the lineage associations of the *Tong* (family/kinship-

based merchant groups or 'Clan corporations,' particularly in South China).[10]

Under Mao, few private laws existed. The legal structure for economic growth was revised under Deng Xiaoping in 1982, with the drafting of civil and commercial law and civil contracts, including key property laws that distinguished between private property, state property and collective property. State property was sacred, while collective property was protected by law. However, within an ambiguous Confucian family structure (Tong) of extended kin or family in a village or rural area, collective land control was aligned with Marxist-Leninist collective state ownership, and the kin or extended family's local power remained dominant. This local—often kin or clan—rural land collective ownership was, however, later threatened by high urban property prices. This gradual conversion into urban land led to the dispossession and impoverishment of farmers. According to some estimates, the urban real estate boom resulted in the eviction of 40 to 50 million farmers by 2004.[11] However, as always, party policy took precedence, and those affected had little or no legal recourse.

It was China's admission to the World Trade Organization (WTO) that prompted a rapid modernization of its laws to meet the WTO requirements. The Property Law was revised to include elements of both civil and common law. The framework, however, retained features of a porous, sometimes situational, legal identity, justified by the pursuit of economic gain.

Communist principles continued to create friction between distinctions of public and private property. The CPC's firm belief in the community rights over law and state rule led to a neglect of the legal field during the period of economic reforms. However, the necessity to attract foreign capital shifted the focus to the legal reforms essential for a market economy. By 1986, there were 3,000 joint ventures and legal change was imperative. Another critical issue arising in relation to foreign investment in China was intellectual property law, which saw effective legislation only in the 1970s. Despite the passage of legislation, modest efforts were made to cooperate in international copyright and intellectual property protection systems.[12] As a result, law in China has largely been whatever the CPC has required it to be, modified to serve its policy goals while complying with international requirements, such as those of the WTO. Even within civil law codes that have been notified by the authorities, the Chinese legal system always places the party's interests first, followed by the people's interest, and only thirdly, the Constitution and the notified laws. Furthermore, unlike the English common law, civil law was not founded on principle or precedent, leaving little room for judicial constructive interpretation.

With propaganda being one of the CPC's founding tenets, media in all its forms has been strictly controlled and has toed the party line since the establishment of China's modern nation state. The single-party state with totalitarian control by the CPC also ensures no external dissent, with views or feedback being strictly communicated within the command structure of the party or bureaucracy, and the view taken by the *Zhuguan dangju* (the competent authority) being the final decision. As a result of the alignment between policy intent, communication and implementation, China's incremental reform process was undertaken in an integrated and holistic manner.

The reforms in India involved multiple institutions of Indian democracy, including the government, political parties and legislature, the judiciary, the media and private sector corporate groups, each with a distinct perspective and outcome objective. As a result, reforms were met with a barrage of regulatory, bureaucratic and judicial interpretation and dissonance, even as government policy was pulled in various directions to serve the interests of political and crony interest groups. All of this occurred in an environment of constant media speculations and allegations, which, in the competitive democratic electoral process, unravelled or stymied many of the reforms required to propel India's economy forward.

Despite economic evidence and numbers, the conclusion is not that the Chinese reform and opening up process is superior to the Indian path. China's reform and opening-up process has been characterized by a high-risk and all-in pursuit of economic growth.

Following the disastrous failure of the GLF, the Cultural Revolution and the lost decades under Mao, it worked spectacularly well under Deng's leadership. This momentum was sustained in subsequent years, aided by favourable global and geopolitical tailwinds. It now faces multifaceted and growing problems on multiple fronts, some of which are the result of its policy choices in pursuit of economic growth at any cost. These issues, if not addressed effectively by the party and Xi Jinping, have the potential to jeopardize not only China's economic prosperity but also the legitimacy of the CPC's 'Mandate of Heaven' among the Chinese people.

Since the beginning of the reform and opening-up process, delivering equitable economic prosperity has been a large part of the unwritten agreement between the party and the people. That compact is under increasing strain as China's growth slows, its engines falter and show signs of distress, and income and wealth inequality widens. Xi's crackdown on rampant corruption, widely viewed as one of the illegitimate sources of stark economic inequality, and his 'common prosperity' platform, are attempts to deliver on that social compact and return the party to its ideological moorings. In an increasingly adverse geopolitical environment and with limited room for manoeuvre, it all comes down to Xi Jinping's leadership abilities. It remains to be seen whether the outcomes will be similar to those of Mao or Deng.

In contrast, in an otherwise bleak global picture, India is well positioned and a source of economic growth. With an electoral majority government, political capital, strong institutional structures for necessary checks and balances, a vibrant democracy and a favourable geopolitical environment, India can expect sustained, balanced and risk-adjusted growth for the foreseeable future.

Part Three

The Drivers of Growth

7

The First Yang: Agricultural Land Reforms and Markets

I ndia and China both have long agrarian histories, which are reflected in their culture, civilization and empires. Interestingly, both countries are among the eight centres of origin, as identified by Nikolai Vavilov in his authoritative paper, 'The Phytogeographical Basis for Plant Breeding'. The cultivation of agricultural plants began in these regions before spreading to the rest of the world.[1]

In China, the emperor's 'Mandate of Heaven' has signified his legitimacy to rule, has always been closely and directly linked to the state of agriculture during his reign. The state owed supreme loyalty to the *she chi* (spirits of the land and grain)—'When a Prince endangers the altars of the spirits of the land and grain, he is changed, and another is appointed in his place.'[2] Chinese emperors made sacrifices and, alongside their ministers, took part in seasonal plowing ceremonies. Agriculture's dominant role in Chinese political and philosophical thought also reflected its economic importance. The Chinese state derived most of its revenue from land tax—a tax in kind that was levied directly from peasants on the produce of their land, throughout the imperial era.

The Chinese have been engaged in farming for several thousand years since neolithic villages in the Wei River valley and the Yangtze Delta began growing millet and rice around 5,000 BCE. China's large subcontinental size encompasses diverse regions that differ greatly in geography, climate, crops, agricultural techniques and tradition. China's modern nation state includes not only the vast and fertile floodplains of the Yellow River, the Huai River, the Yangtze River, the Pearl River and the inland mountains, but also the steppes of Mongolia, Central Asian deserts and oases, Tibet and the vast plains of Manchuria. However, even today, the main agricultural area corresponds to the traditional area of Chinese culture, or 'core' (Eastern) China:

> [...] from *Kansu* and *Szechwan* in the West to the China Sea, from *Peking (Beijing)* and *Liaoning* in the North to the tropical island of *Hainan*. The boundaries of this area have remained more or less unchanged (*for hundreds of centuries*)... This area corresponds very closely to the natural boundaries of arable farming-to the north and west it is bounded by arid steppes suitable for pastoralism, to the west and southwest by high, rugged mountain ranges.[3]

Although China has historically been a farming nation, only 14 per cent of its land is arable.[4] This land is mainly concentrated on the central eastern coast and along the Yangtze and Yellow River valleys, which has the highest sediment deposits among lands in China. With low arable land and historically high population density, agriculture has not only been central to China's economy, culture and civilization but also been a perennial battle between human endeavour and forces of nature throughout its history. While the arable lands of the valley have been highly productive, farms in China have been small because of increasing pressure from a growing population.

As China's population grew, supply of productive land was exhausted and new land had to be brought under cultivation. Many areas of high population density had exhausted their supply of productive land, leaving landless farmers with only two options: migrate to underpopulated regions where land was available or find a way to cultivate crops in a marginal land. This led to a continuous geographical dispersal until around 1800, by which time even remote provinces like Yunnan had received an influx of Chinese settlers. Some farmers, however, were unwilling to leave their ancestral villages, preferring to toil to reclaim land by draining marshy areas for rice fields, hacking narrow terraces from mountain slopes or patiently flooding and draining fields along the seashore to remove salt and enable rice cultivation. This reclamation process was not always wise and often short term, especially in the steep hills of the southern provinces, where the result was the denudation of the bedrock, leaving nothing but a barren waste. But farmers had little choice—the alternative often being starvation. Degraded land—both legacy and man-made—is one of the many severe environmental challenges that modern-day China faces.

China, today, has only about one fifth of an acre of arable land per person.[5] The scarcity of arable land has been at the root of China's distinctively labour-intensive agricultural practices over the centuries. Intensive cultivation in a small area to support a large human population has also been the cause of China's historical vulnerability to devastating droughts, floods, earthquakes, famines and other natural and man-made ecological disasters. In fact, the leitmotif of scarce arable land has been so pervasive throughout Chinese history that one of the reasons for China's lack of animal husbandry has been a lack of land to grow fodder to sustain a population of domesticated animals. The plowing and tilling of these small landholdings were done by the readily available human labour, which was less expensive than rearing and maintaining expensive draught animals. The intensity with which these lands were nurtured over millennia is also evident (as previously mentioned) in the use of night soil as fertilizers to increase land productivity. Arable land and agriculture, therefore, have shaped China's national psyche as few other factors have, and continue to dominate modern China's economic, political and social thought.

Agriculture has been equally important in India, with a long history dating back to the Neolithic age (7500–4000 BCE). The earliest historical references to agricultural activity can be found in the Rigveda (3700 BCE). During the Vedic period, farming was believed to have been practised across locations ranging from northwest India to the entire alluvial plains of the Ganga. The Vedic Aryans pursued pastoralism and agriculture as the mainstay of their livelihood. In fact, according to Max Müller, the noted Indologist and Sanskrit scholar, the term 'Arya', is derived from the root 'ar', meaning 'to stir' or the stirring of soil by means of sticks or plough. The mantras in the

Rigveda include prayers to various gods for rain and other favourable conditions required for raising *anna* (food crops) and domesticated animals. According to Sayanacharya, a fourteenth century Sanskrit scholar and influential commentator on the Vedas, agriculture was so important that the sun God, Surya—who was thought to have three bonds in the three *lokas* (worlds)—had tillage, rain and seed as his bond in the habitable world.

According to the Atharvaveda, the gods first cultivated *yava* (sweet corn) on the banks of the Sarasvati River for the benefit of mankind. The furrow master was the God Indra, and the plowmen were the Maruts. The *Krishi-Parashara*[6], estimated to have been composed around 400 BCE[7], is a Sanskrit treatise devoted to agricultural science. The *Krishi-Parashara* discusses all facets of agricultural practices including weather, irrigation, management of agriculture, management of cattle, agricultural tools and implements, seed collection and preservation, plowing, harvesting and storing crops. Kautilya (321–296 BCE), in his treatise on political economy, *Arthashastra*, emphasized on agriculture, cattle breeding and trade. He also proposed a separate post of head of agriculture, the Sitadhakashya.[8] According to researchers, agriculture was widespread in Peninsular India over the same time, with cultivation of pulses, millet, wheat, barley, and so on.[9]

The topography, soil conditions, crops and climatic conditions of the Indian subcontinent is varied. It is dominated by the fertile Indo-Gangetic plains, which curve in a large swath across the land from the north to the southeast. It was the site of ancient empires and now encompasses the large modern states of Uttar Pradesh, Bihar and Bengal. It is also the most populous region today, with marginal, fragmented agricultural holdings in densely populated areas. Other rivers that traverse the subcontinent include the Indus, which was the site of the ancient Harappan civilization, and its tributaries of the *Punj-Ab* (five rivers). This was also the site of the Green Revolution with the adoption of irrigation and high-yielding crop varieties in the 1960s. Furthermore, the Narmada, Tungabhadra, Godavari, Krishna and the Kaveri are principal rivers of Peninsular India. Beyond its river valleys and fertile alluvial plains, the monsoon has been the defining feature of Indian agriculture. For millennia, most of the subcontinent's crop cultivation has been dependent on the seasonal rains brought by the unusual geographical phenomenon of the monsoon. Rain-fed agriculture is as much a reality today as it has been throughout the subcontinent's long agrarian history.

Even when India and China became independent countries in the middle of the twentieth century, they were very aware of the looming food crises that had caused famines and deaths in the past. Both were large, populous and poor countries, with a significant proportion of their populations living below the poverty line, the majority of whom lived in rural areas and relied on subsistence agriculture. Food security was a national concern. Both countries recognized the urgent need to work on rapidly increasing agricultural output and reducing rural inequalities, achieving this even while shifting a large portion of the workforce away from agriculture in rural areas toward urbanized, industrial employment in their plans to become industry-led economies.

Both India and China embarked on strikingly similar agricultural and rural strategies to achieve this goal. The strategies had three key components: the first was to redistribute agricultural landholdings by giving them to cultivators; the second was to impose strict control on agricultural commodity hoarding and speculation to avoid profiteering, price shocks and runaway food inflation, which would be disastrous for their vulnerable population and economies; and the third was to eventually develop stable market mechanisms to guide farmers' crop selection through pricing incentives based on market demand and with minimal state intervention.

By keeping up with its long imperial legalist tradition of the absolute primacy of the state, China implemented land reforms by simply taking over all agricultural land from its owners and redistributing it. The trade of primary agricultural product was nationalized overnight, creating a state monopoly. However, the small size of the redistributed landholdings posed a problem in increasing agricultural output. Little agricultural surplus could be generated, which was required to feed its large, dependent population as well as fuel its industrial growth. Subsistence and self-sufficiency were the primary goals of most farmers at the time. Agricultural products were not heavily commercialized and were only available in rudimentary, local markets. Farmers also sought to increase their income by producing fewer products that were under state monopoly and more products under non-monopoly.

To address these issues and boost agricultural productivity, the state reclaimed all land and reorganized it in the 1950s. This time, however, instead of limiting itself to land, the Communist Party of China (CPC) reorganized the entire rural economy. The traditional rural village structure of household-owned land that was supported by ancillary village-level enterprises, was reorganized by establishing people's communes as the basic rural production unit throughout China. Zhou Li, currently the director general of the Chinese Academy of Social Sciences Rural Development Institute, writes:

> As the government could not make adjustments to state monopoly on agricultural products at the level of individual households, there was an objective need for an organisation system that would make managing peasants (*nongmin*, also referred to as rural citizens) more convenient. The people's commune was hailed as the best possible solution to this problem. Vice Premier Chen Yun, then in charge of economic work in China, used this vivid analogy 'Peasant households are like the hair on a woman's head. They are many and they're scattered and it's not easy to grab them. The role of the people's commune is to tie the many, scattered hairs into a single braid, which is easy to grab'.[10]

Under this people's commune system implemented in the 1950s, village communities were organized into collectives that cultivated the land; shared the labour and output; and met their target contribution to the state. This facilitated the transfer of surplus from the agricultural to the industrial sectors, as well as from rural to urban areas, by keeping rural wages and agricultural commodity prices low. During the Great Leap Forward (GLF) however, initial efforts were made to boost agricultural production based on unscientific practices such as 'close crop cultivation' (in which seeds were planted close together to increase yields). These resulted in widespread crop failures which were not reported to higher authorities. Output numbers were fudged and target quotas of supply continued to be met by the commune leaders. The resultant shortage of food grains in rural areas caused one of the worst man-made famines in human history, in which an estimated 30 million people perished.

While China recovered from the disaster and total agricultural output gradually increased over the 30 years of Mao's regime, there were constant food shortages. Agricultural commodities continued to constitute a significant portion of China's imports. Even in the late 1970s, when economic reforms were initiated, millions of Chinese farmers struggled to feed and clothe themselves. One notable reason for this was low agricultural productivity, with little incentive for commune members to increase production. The rural economic organization under the commune system was also inefficient.

Reforms in the agriculture sector began at the grassroots level in the late 1970s and garnered support at the policy level. In 1978, an experiment was initiated in Xiaogang, a small village in Anhui province under which 18 households took individual responsibility for the profit and loss of production on individual tracts from the collective agricultural land, in the first trial of what eventually came to be known as the household responsibility system (HRS). In the same year, the CPC Central Committee proposed a generic strategy objective of devolving production responsibility to production units. In 1979, a council was established where it was debated whether the HRS should be adopted. While the majority was supportive of the proposal, there was opposition too.

Hua Guofeng, Mao's successor, concluded that while collective production worked, some flexibility was required. It was, therefore, agreed that for impoverished households in remote regions, it was appropriate to delegate the production responsibility and rights to them. By 1980, the Anhui province had adopted the system. Even as the central government debated, more regions adopted the HRS. The growing trend caught the attention of the central leadership and gained Deng's support. In 1982, the CPC Central Committee issued an official document that established the HRS for China's agricultural production.

Initially, HRS was limited to contracting land to individual households that would be responsible for production and management. The village collective was still in charge of all accounting and profit distribution. The HRS quickly expanded to include households, being responsible for paying state taxes, meeting state agricultural product purchasing quotas and paying contracting fees to the collective. However, and most importantly, after meeting the agricultural product purchasing quota, the surplus was free to be sold in the market under the HRS, thereby, incentivizing production.

The 'opening-up' of the agricultural sector to sell surplus produce in markets occurred first in the areas undergoing rapid development on China's periphery—the first special economic zone (SEZ) of Shenzhen, adjacent to Hong Kong. Commune administrators in this area transformed rice paddies into fish ponds, vegetable fields, fruit orchards and medicinal herb gardens for sale in local and Hong Kong markets. These policies increased the value of agricultural products while also increasing rural incomes. Surpluses were reinvested to import more production equipment. Collaboration with foreign merchants enabled agriculture, animal husbandry and pisciculture to flourish. Some communes even collaborated with outsiders to develop quarries, tea fields and other ventures. As this new system met with success, it was expanded into other regions of China.

The growth of China's agricultural sector after the mid-1980s was primarily due to the successful implementation of a three-stage process of gradual reforms. These reforms enabled it to transition its agricultural and rural sectors from the planned economy to the market economy.

The first stage of the reforms was the nurturing of a rural market system. In the initial period of economic reform, the state significantly increased the prices of agricultural produce for both its own purchase and the surplus sold in excess of quotas. This increase in price greatly incentivized farmers to increase their farm investments and engage in multi-cropping. The state also reduced the number of agricultural products controlled by the state monopoly, as well as the quantities it purchased. This greatly facilitated the creation of rural markets, while also encouraging contract farming under terms of the HRS. From 1978, when 113 agricultural products were controlled by the state monopoly with price setting, the number was gradually reduced to just nine by 1991. By 1993, only cotton, tobacco, silkworm cocoons and a few other agricultural products were subject to price controls. By this time, agricultural product markets had matured to the point where only about one-third of farmer revenues for commercial grain came from state-planned grain purchases. The dramatic increase in the prices of agricultural produce purchased by the state, however, caused agricultural produce subsidies to increase 19.6 times over a six-year period from 1978 to 1984.

As this fiscal expenditure grew, the government pushed out the second stage of reforms (and stepped further away from the earlier state-controlled production and operation system) between 1991 and 1993 by opening grain sale prices to urban residents at market prices. This removed the fiscal burden of 'inversion'—buying high and selling low—between the prices at which the state obtained grain and the prices at which it sold it in urban areas.

In the third stage of reforms, China completely opened all the country's grain markets, creating an orderly, standardized and nationally integrated market. By 2004, it had abolished all institutions that required licences to move and sell grains across multiple jurisdictions. It also removed any regional barriers to the free trade of grains.

The agricultural reforms also sparked commercial and entrepreneurial ventures in many rural areas, particularly in the more commercial and rapidly developing regions. This resulted in an increase in ancillary financial and support activities and multiplier effects in the rural economy. China is now a full-fledged participant in globalized agricultural trade, post its World Trade Organization (WTO) accession in 2001.

The numbers in China's little-appreciated agricultural resurgence are astounding. According to the Food and Agricultural Organization (FAO) of the United Nations (UN):

> [China produces] one fourth of the world's grain and feeds one fifth of the world's population with less than 10 percent of world arable land [...] Currently, China ranks first in the world in terms of the production of cereals, cotton, fruit, vegetables, meat, poultry, eggs and fishery products. Thanks to the great importance attached to opening agriculture to the outside world, China has increasingly closer links with other countries in this field [...] built up agricultural exchange and cooperation relations with some major international agricultural and financing organizations as well as more than 140 countries.[11]

India had similar goals in initiating land reforms, intervening in agricultural produce markets and hoping for eventual development of market mechanisms to guide production according to demand while maintaining price stability. However, unlike totalitarian China, which had an imperial tradition of state ownership of land and resources, land ownership in India as recognized by the state dated back to a *zamindari* (permanent land settlement) system. It was a system introduced by the colonial government in 1793, with the primary goal of collecting revenues in a rural and feudal social order. As a result, contested land reforms were undertaken in India over a period from the 1950s to the early 1970s and remained incomplete in terms of acquisition and redistribution.

As P.S. Appu, a former land reforms commissioner and additional secretary in Ministry of Agriculture wrote, 'We have identified the lack of political will as the single most important cause for the failure of Indian Land Reforms.'[12] The claims made by the first generation of post-Independence leadership in India that they were ideologically committed to political democracy and socialism, were questioned as opportunistic political compromises with powerful propertied classes for the purpose of remaining in office by some analysts.[13]

The state's political inability to achieve its legislated redistribution goals persisted for two decades after Independence and beyond. As a result, large tracts of land remained in the hands of fewer landowning classes while most of the rural population remained marginal farmers and landless poor with few or no options for improving their economic circumstances.

This powerful political force of relatively prosperous landowning classes has since shaped the trajectory of India's agricultural and rural economy. It has also yielded dichotomous and often unfavourable outcomes in terms of its development objectives.

Starting in the late 1960s, the technology-led Green Revolution introduced new and hybrid varieties of seeds and improved agricultural productivity. The results were particularly noteworthy in larger farm holdings in India's semi-arid and irrigated northern region. This period also saw a substantial agricultural surplus, particularly in wheat and rice. However, the Green Revolution required large capital investments in irrigation schemes, electricity to power water pumps and increased fertilizer usage, all of which were heavily subsidized by the government. As additional support, grains were procured by the state at minimum support prices (MSP) or state-determined prices.

A significant portion of this procurement was used by the government's public distribution system (PDS) to supply subsidized food grains throughout the country. However, even as crop production grew and outpaced demand, powerful landed and politically active constituents in these states continued to demand and receive ever increasing subsidies from the state. This included subsidies on inputs like fertilizers, electricity, etc., increase in MSP, and higher—even compulsory—government procurement for these crops. These misguided and narrow subsidies cut into money that could have been used to improve infrastructure, health and education in rural areas. By taking 'the path of least resistance', successive governments seeking re-election continued to pander to these electorally important constituencies. This distortion prevented both a correction to the crop pattern and the development of a market mechanism for stable and remunerative agricultural produce pricing.

This entrenched system of vested interests led to four significantly adverse issues for the Indian agricultural and national economy. First, it created a system of large subsidies that distorted agricultural economics and were unrelated to the country's grain requirements. It also pre-empted the much-needed investments required for rural development. Second, the government continued to procure grain above its PDS requirement at ever-increasing prices. A significant portion of this procurement rots annually in the state-owned Food Corporation of India's godowns or open-air storage facilities, with no accountability. Third, scarce resources were diverted away from subsistence farming states with marginal landholdings, particularly in the poorer, poverty-stricken eastern parts of the country. Fourth, the continued overuse of water and fertilizers, particularly in India's irrigated northern region, has harmed soil health. The ecological damage of this overuse is significant, with the government unable to break this vicious cycle by incentivizing crop rotation changes or developing adequate market mechanisms to do so.

As a result, two distinct agricultural and rural economies have emerged, and both require government subsidies. The first economy necessitates government distribution-based safety-net interventions in inefficient PDS and implementation of minimum rural employment guarantee schemes (MNREGA) for landless rural poor and marginal farmers. The other economy requires high input subsidies from the government, procurement of food grains far beyond its economic demand and unsustainable prices, driven by politically influential farming communities. Both effectively shut out transition to the development of sustainable markets and pricing mechanisms that hold the promise of sustainable economic development and equitable social justice. Ironically, because of complexities of pricing controls, market incentives and deep inefficiencies in the labyrinthine and unwieldy system of procurement and distribution at both state and central levels, even the MSPs, are barely remunerative with respect to input costs and real incomes of farmers.

Indian reforms—particularly during its long political coalition era (1991–2014) when the state's will and capacity were at its weakest—have failed to address any of these issues. Direct benefit transfers (DBT) have made a start in transferring cash subsidies directly to farmers and the rural poor, thereby avoiding the significant inefficiencies and corruption that the distribution system entailed. However, efforts to develop agricultural produce markets based on demand and supply, as well as to change cropping patterns through price-incentivized contract farming, have been met with suspicion and resistance. This has forced even electoral majority governments to reverse these changes.

The growth trajectories of agricultural India and China make for an interesting comparison. As per the National Sample Survey Office (NSSO), the average size of agricultural holding in India was 1.2 hectares in 2010–11 (down from an average of 2.3 hectares in 1970–71 due to intergenerational fragmentation). The average Chinese (contract rights) holding according to the World Census of Agriculture was 0.6 hectares, though more evenly distributed than in India.[14] However, China's productivity per hectare is higher than India. China has also, unlike in the past, invested significant public sector resources in the agricultural sector, which has helped it boost both productivity and agricultural incomes.[15]

The rapid reduction in rural poverty has been a key outcome of China's substantial agricultural growth, largely attributed to the equitable distribution of land holdings among rural households and remunerative prices. Higher agricultural growth was the primary factor in reducing poverty from 33 per cent in 1978 to less than 3 per cent by 2001. The greatest decline occurred during the early years of reform (1978–84) and the implementation of the HRS, which provided Chinese rural households with both land and incentives to enhance productivity and improve economic condition. Over this six-year period, the agricultural gross domestic product (GDP) increased to 7.1 per cent per year, while rural poverty decreased from 33 per cent to 15 per cent.[16] In contrast, agriculture was not a major factor in poverty reduction during India's reform era. Between 1980 and 2003, the agricultural GDP growth averaged around 2.8 per cent per year.

According to Shenggen Fan and Ashok Gulati, China made agriculture—a sector which gave most people their livelihood—the starting point of its market-oriented reforms. By doing so, it could ensure a widespread distribution of the resultant gains and build consensus and political support for continued reforms. The use of incentives to encourage reforms resulted in greater returns to the farmers and more efficient resource allocation, which in turn strengthened domestic production and made it more competitive. It also facilitated the development of a dynamic rural non-farm sector as it provided additional sources of income outside farming. As Shenggen and Gulati noted:

A comfortable domestic food supply situation achieved through the various incentive reforms ensured a critical level of grain production before liberalization could begin and allowed Chinese policymakers to abandon the old agricultural policy framework geared towards self-sufficiency in food grains. The procurement system was dismantled everywhere except for the main grain-producing regions and the food rationing system was abolished in the early 1990s. As a result, private agricultural trade is now flourishing.[17]

They note that reforms in India, initiated in 1991, were prompted by imbalances in the economy and, therefore, started with macroeconomic and non-agricultural reforms. While these reforms led to economic growth, being limited to the non-agricultural sectors, they did not have as significant an impact on poverty as in the case of China. Policy changes related to agriculture were carried out much later, and even then, were only partial. As a result, India has continued with state food procurement and distribution, mainly as affirmative action for over two-thirds of the population, including the poorest, who are dependent on agriculture and the rural economy for livelihood.

The Vice Premier Chen Yun-led reforms relied significantly on traditional Chinese economic thought in shaping strategies and policies to make this transition. This caution and economic wisdom helped China avoid the implosion of other centrally planned economies like Russia (the former Soviet Union). As Shenggen and Gulati further noted:

> The Chinese policymakers first created the incentives and institutions required by the market economy and then, in the mid-1980s, they began to slowly open up markets, by withdrawing central planning and reducing the scope of procurement while expanding the role of private trade and markets. [...] This was because incentive reforms in China aided the gradual emergence of markets which kept at bay the negative effects of the sudden collapse of the old central planning system in the absence of market-based allocative mechanisms, as experienced in other transitional countries.[18]

The virtuous cycle of growth and multiplier effect spurred by these reforms in China were concentrated in the traditional core China region, with less impact on the sparsely populated Western, Northwestern and extreme northern regions such as Tibet and Xinjiang. The economic benefits of industrial and service sector growth during India's reform period were most visible in the already industrialized regions with better socio-economic indicators—the Southern and Western parts of the country. However, the marginal landholding and densely populated eastern part of the country has continued to be dependent on low income, low growth and subsistence agriculture.

A significant part of the difference in agricultural policy and outcomes can be attributed to the differing nature of institutions and structure of the political economy of the two nations. The institutional reasons for the non-effectiveness of India's agricultural reforms are many:

- The inability of the government to reorganize agricultural holdings through land reforms
- The continued fragmentation of marginal holdings under inheritance laws

- The cornering of state price support through MSP by a politically powerful and well-off constituency of regional farmers for select crops
- The trust deficit between farmers and administration and ineffective enforcement of law that in turn acts as a disincentive to aggregation of land for cultivation under a contract framework that hinders the development of land markets
- The cultural identification of farmers with their land ownership beyond its monetary benefits
- The lack of political will and political compulsions of parties seeking votes for re-election

There is, however, a stark contrast in agricultural policymaking between China and India. China's approach has been one of pragmatic and outcome-driven relativism of state intervention, evidently influenced by home-grown economic thought—its Guanzi, Qing zhong, Salt and Iron traditions, and so on. They have a delegation structure that has encouraged experiments of multiple policy choices at local and provincial levels, followed by a nationwide implementation from 'point to surface (*you dian dao mian*)' after successful experimentation and validation of a policy choice.

The Indian approach has been a Western neoliberal approach of predominantly unidimensional policy directives administered top-down by economic theorists rather than seasoned political economy administrators with the necessary political capital to mobilize change. As a result, the agricultural sector has largely been left unaddressed as a political 'hot potato', or has seen only limited success from the reforms that have been attempted. Urgent and substantial reforms are required to unlock India's and its agricultural sector's economic potential.

8

The Second Yang: Special Economic Zones

It is impossible to overstate the pivotal role that special economic zones (SEZs) have played in determining China's economic trajectory during the early years of reform and opening-up. Helped by favourable globalization tailwinds, it made China the 'factory of the world' and a manufacturing powerhouse. From the five SEZs in coastal areas (including Shenzhen in the 1980s) to the six SEZs, 14 open coastal cities, four pilot free trade zones and five financial reform pilot areas,[1] the success of China's SEZ story is remarkable in the annals of a nation's economic development. Special economic zoness have contributed to 22 per cent of China's GDP, 45 per cent of total national foreign direct investment (FDI) and 60 per cent of exports. These SEZs are estimated to have created over 30 million jobs, increased the income of participating farmers by 30 per cent and accelerated industrialization, agricultural modernization and urbanization.[2] A combination of unique factors of geography, history, diaspora, culture and the revival of latent regional ecosystems, contributed significantly in this remarkable rise.

Situated on China's southeastern coast, Shanghai, Guangzhou (Canton) and Hong Kong are exotic names that have fuelled popular Western imaginations of freewheeling and untold fortunes with a global and luxurious lifestyle to boot, for at least a few centuries now, and long before the current era of modern reforms. China was opened up to international trade by force in its century of humiliation beginning with the first Opium War in 1841. There were more than 80 treaty ports over this 100-year period in coastal China. While British, American and French commercial interests led the initial onslaught of forced unequal treaties, almost every major international power was involved by the end. These treaty ports operated on concessions of extraterritoriality, where an imperial China in decline not only gave up applicability of its laws on foreign citizens but also to land leased in the port areas, effectively taking them out of the control of local governments.

Those striking images in American films of gambling, night clubs and gangsters in China's coastal cities in the 1930s were actually of the 'bund', a narrow strip of prime land on the waterfront of these ports where all the foreign gentry's businesses, offices, warehouses and residences were located. The bund was self-governed, with its own shops, restaurants, parks, churches, courts, police and local government. Its facilities, like those in India and elsewhere in Asia, were off-limits to natives. The Shanghai International Settlement (SIS) created by 19 international powers that had treaty relations with China, rapidly developed into one of the world's most modern cities, comparable to London, Paris and Berlin, and set the urban standard for all of East Asia.

The impact of the port cities, led by Shanghai, in developing an economic ecosystem in East Asia, although neglected in most literature, cannot be emphasized enough. The Europeans brought in technological and economic innovation, as well as industries and banks. It was quickly adopted by Chinese entrepreneurs, and many industries were established, including shipbuilding, railway repairs and factories producing textiles, matches, porcelain, flour, tobacco, cigarettes, textiles and food products. The treaty ports were not only the entry point for all import and export trade but also for ideas and investments in China. They facilitated the spread of Chinese merchants across Southeast Asia—including British-controlled Singapore and Malaya, Dutch East Indies, French Indochina and American-controlled Philippines—as focal points for regional economic activity.

The roots of Chinese industrialization can be traced back to the years between 1912 (just after the fall of the Qing empire) to 1936 (just before the outbreak of World War II). According to Barry Naughton—a leading China expert and the So Kwan Lok Chair of

Chinese International Affairs at the University of California, San Diego—this was a period of rapid industrialization. In this period of industrial growth, two distinct patterns were identifiable: treaty ports industrialization and Manchurian industrialization.

The treaty ports were the site for factories established by foreigners around the turn of the twentieth century, which were quickly followed by the Chinese. This enclave industrialization primarily comprised light, consumer goods industries. According to an industry census, textiles accounted for 42 per cent of total industrial output in China (excluding Manchuria) in 1933, while food products (including tobacco) accounted for 26 per cent. There was a concentration of industry in a few treaty ports. For example, 70 per cent of textile production was concentrated in Shanghai, Tianjin and Qingdao. Shanghai alone accounted for 40 per cent of the industrial output in 1933. By the 1930s, Chinese-owned firms accounted for 78 per cent of the value of factory output.[3]

In contrast to the treaty ports, industrialization in Manchuria was undertaken by the Japanese government and its affiliates. Heavy industries and railroads were prioritized to exploit the region's rich deposits of coal and iron ore. These strategic industries produced raw materials for Japanese industries, while the machinery used to run these factories was imported from Japan. There were few linkages and spillovers from the industrialization in Manchuria to the rest of China. Japan, however, invaded Eastern China in 1937, sparking off warfare that lasted more than a decade until Japan's defeat in World War II and the Communist victory in 1949.

It was during this period that a Japan-centric East Asian economic system came into existence. This economic system had a distinct circle-within-circle structure, with Japan at its centre. It evolved during this relatively short period of a few decades, in part to Japanese imperialist initiatives and in part to the inherent economic dynamism of East Asia. Manufacturing and services, including government, were reserved for Japan. Next, came the core inner circle of food producers, Korea and Taiwan. The following circle consisted of raw material and semi processed goods suppliers like

Manchuria. It produced both agricultural and industrial materials for Japan. Finally, in the outermost circle was China, or Eastern China, that included regions with potential markets for investment and future expansion.

By the mid–1930s, Japan had surpassed Britain to become the largest foreign investor in Shanghai. This Japan-centric economic system functioned well until Japan's defeat in World War II, when it collapsed. Furthermore, in 1949, China effectively exited the East Asian economy. However, the dormant economic ties of its past remained.

In the context of China's high and consistent economic success, there has been a lot of debate over 'big bang' versus 'gradualist' approaches to transition of emerging economies. Much of this discussion, however, has largely ignored this aspect of its growth from the revival of its traditional economic relationships in East Asia. A dormant, highly commercialized and entrepreneurial Cantonese culture awoke in Southeast coastal China as Deng Xiaoping embarked on his gradual opening-up policy, in his words, by 'cross(ing) the river by feeling the stones'. Special economic zones were established in what were formerly treaty port areas, albeit this time under Chinese sovereignty. This 'dual track' approach of extraterritoriality of the SEZs under market-based rules while the rest of the economy and nation remained under strict, planned economic restrictions, was tried with success in the coastal SEZ experiment and then gradually applied elsewhere in China. It became a defining feature of China's institutional and economic transformation.

In August 1980, China declared four small cities in the southeastern coastal region—Shenzhen, Zhuhai, Shantou in Guangdong province and Xiamen in Fujian province—as SEZs. The goal was to promote exports, attract foreign investment, increase employment and achieve technology and management skill transfer. Businesses were allowed to make their own investment, production and marketing decisions. To attract investment, tax incentives were offered by the local governments to foreign investors. These initial SEZs were successful in attracting foreign investment. They

developed rapidly along with expanding light and consumer goods industries and a growing population. In 1984, 14 larger and older cities in the region—Tianjin, Dalian, Qinhuangdao, Qingdao, Yantai, Weihai, Lianyungang, Nantong, Ningbo, Wenzhou, Fuzhou, Guangzhou, Zhanjiang and Beihai—were granted the status of 'open coastal cities' for foreign trade and investment. In April 1990, the Pudong New Area in Shanghai became an 'open economic zone' with even more flexible policies.

Following Deng Xiaoping's visit to several SEZs during his historic and widely publicized Southern Tour in 1992, more restrictions were lifted, and other measures were implemented to further liberalize FDI. Similar policies were implemented in 23 major cities throughout inland China, including many provincial capitals.

A lot has been written about competitiveness, cluster development, network effects and, more recently, economic geography. However, the legacy of previous economic systems of East Asia that overlap those visible today is still a relatively unexplored subject. As Barry Naughton writes:

> Traditional economic centres suddenly revived with astonishing speed. […] There was even a revival of traditional market-based organizational forms, in which large numbers of very-small-scale specialized firms coordinated through markets with upstream and downstream producers. […] Indeed, that China has been able to grow so rapidly after 1978 is due in no small part precisely to the entrepreneurial and competitive behaviors that had been nourished by the traditional economy. Traditional links with parts of 'maritime China' outside the People's Republic of China also revived quickly.[4]

Traditional economic systems also reflected in the SEZs set up early in the reform era on China's coast to re-establish ties across boundaries. Indeed, the rapid economic growth of Hong Kong and Taiwan during the 1960s and 1970s could be considered a continuation and vindication of the traditional economy. After all, these were regions within the historical Chinese economy that had followed a path of evolutionary growth from traditional beginnings and had relied primarily on small firms to jump-start economic development. In the 1960s and 1970s, Hong Kong and Taiwan, which were regions of the traditional Chinese and East Asian economy, witnessed rapid economic growth by jump-starting economic development by relying primarily on small firms. Post 1978, the capabilities of these firms in Hong Kong and Taiwan were reintegrated with the labour and other resources within China, creating explosive growth of foreign trade. By 2007, free zones in China accounted for 18.5 per cent of China's GDP and more than 60 per cent of China's exports.

India, on the other hand, has no history of treaty ports, extraterritoriality or regional interlocking economic systems. Its colonial history of systematic exploitation for raw materials by the British saw the early development of railway networks into its hinterland. Trade and industry were concentrated primarily in its port cities—Calcutta, Bombay and Madras—all of which were established by the English East India Company. Other international powers had a minor presence on the subcontinent, like the French in Pondicherry (now Puducherry) and the Portuguese in Goa, among other small, scattered possessions. However, India's international trade and manufacturing were not as significant as China's. In fact, the opium trade from India—one of its largest exports at the time— was undertaken as currency to fund China's tea exports to Britain. The industrial clusters that grew up around these trading cities had their origins in colonial, foreign-owned companies and managing agencies. These covered a wide range of industries, such as cotton textiles, jute, tea and even engineering goods, especially in Calcutta and Madras.

The period also saw the rise of competing firms established by the subcontinent's mercantile communities, particularly the Marwaris, Gujaratis, Parsis and Chettiars. Post-Independence socialist India saw the licencing of manufacturing capacity, and restrictions on foreign ownership and overseas remittance. As a result, many foreign-owned firms were sold to these family-owned industrial groups by their expatriate owners. With the government raising significant import barriers to protect industry from foreign competition, most industries became insular, using obsolete technologies to manufacture outdated products under licence with limited production.

However, India recognized the importance of exports and the foreign exchange generated by them, and made early efforts to encourage industries to establish themselves in special zones with concessions. In 1965, Asia's first export processing zone (EPZ) was established at Kandla. The second EPZ was established in Bombay in 1974. In 1985, four new zones were established in Noida, Madras, Cochin and Falta. The Visakhapatnam EPZ was established in 1994. All of these were set up by the Indian government. However, unlike those in East Asian countries and China, attracting foreign investment was not a primary goal for these Indian EPZs. These were designed primarily to provide relief to domestic exporters from the regulatory regime.

In fact, while India has liberalized its trade since 1991, it wasn't until April 2000 that the Indian government announced the implementation of SEZs Policy modelled after the Chinese model to attract FDI. The Special Economic Zones Act of 2005, accompanied by SEZ rules, went into effect in February 2006. Existing EPZs were converted to SEZs, and new SEZs were proposed.[5]

Currently, India officially has one of the largest numbers of SEZs in the world. In 2015, the country had 348 notified and 202 operational SEZs. However, SEZs in India have had mixed results. While SEZs have accounted for roughly 80 per cent of total FDI inflows in early years in China, they have only played a minor role in attracting FDI in India. In recent years, several SEZs have been de-notified. The number of approved SEZs was reduced from 564 in 2014 to 437 in 2015.[6]

The story of India's manufacturing sector, till now, has been a mixed result. India's economic growth has been uneven in different sectors. Services have grown faster than agriculture and manufacturing. As a result, the manufacturing sector in India contributes less to GDP than as compared to other developing countries. Efforts to attract FDI in manufacturing through 'Make in India' and subsequently through schemes like 'production-linked incentive' have, so far, have achieved some success. Most of these efforts, however, have focussed on tax and production-related incentives. Greater emphasis is now being placed on becoming a part of the value chain cluster ecosystem and economic networks that have been critical to China's and other East Asian countries' SEZ success.

The other, and perhaps more serious, issue has been the negative public perception of SEZs because of previous large-scale land acquisitions, particularly for private SEZs amid allegations of land grabbing by corporate interests and real estate developers. These perceptions have gained traction because of the SEZs' poor performance in attracting FDI. Despite acquiring large tracts of land from individual farmers in the face of fierce opposition, many SEZs remain only on paper.

In this context, it is worth noting that, while Indian export growth has been among the highest in the world, trailing only China and Vietnam, it has been primarily driven by technology and business support services. These have also been spatially dispersed across regions like Bangalore (now Bengaluru), Hyderabad, Chennai, Pune, Noida, Gurgaon (now Gurugram) and others, as well as around urban agglomerations of existing pools of skilled talent, beginning with Tier I cities and progressing to Tier II. While the English-speaking educated middle classes have reaped the greatest benefits from this opportunity, the mass employment opportunities for labour—skilled and unskilled—that manufacturing facilities provide in the context of development have been missing in the Indian story.

Geography and medieval history have also played a part in the development of China's SEZs. China has a long, single eastern seacoast of nearly 14,500 km. The southern coast is rugged with hilly terrain hinterland, and its few good harbours are cut off from the inland regions. The coast in the North, particularly between the Yangtze River and the Shandong Peninsula, is low and swampy with few good harbours. These adverse geographic conditions contributed significantly to China's traditional imperial economy being inwardly oriented, with its global trade being more land-based along the Silk Road stretching across Central Asia.

There were some seafaring subcultures and maritime trade in coastal China, particularly during its medieval period. Maritime culture in China reached its apex with Zheng He's seven voyages, the first of which began in 1405. Zheng He's mission included exploration, trade and diplomacy in Southeast Asia, Sri Lanka, India, West Asia and the African east coast. His armada consisted of 317 ships, including 62 'treasure ships' loaded with gifts for wealthy heads of state, and commanded a force of 27,800 men. It was the largest armada ever assembled until the modern era. Following Zheng He's death, however, the new emperor moved to isolate China and prohibited any further expeditions. Zheng He's ships, as well as most of his voyage records, were destroyed. While maritime trade continued after the sixteenth century, it was mostly along the cut-off southeast coast, which was historically of little economic significance. This lack of a coastal and maritime orientation also contributed to China's delayed commencement in economic modernization. China's connections to the modern global economy began only when the extraterritorial treaty ports were forcibly opened up with the first Opium War. Even today, the vast interior west lags economically, whereas the rapidly urbanizing coastal east has surged ahead and become inextricably linked to the ocean transport web and the global economy.[7]

In comparison, the Indian subcontinent has approximately 7,500 km of coastline on both its western and eastern coasts, both of which have a long history of maritime trade. The western coast trade was historically dependent on monsoon winds, which allowed commodities to be exported from or imported into the Indian subcontinent across the Arabian Sea. Since Roman times, the Malabar (western) and Coromandel (eastern) coasts exported spices, teakwood, precious stones and a wide range of exotic luxuries, while imports were primarily limited to horses, spices and medicaments, rarities and exotic textiles for the consuming classes, along with base metals for the brass industry. In the seventeenth century, Bernier observed that gold had been 'dug out of the mines of all the corners of the earth, swallowed up, and lost when it came to India'.

Geopolitical developments that occurred in the early medieval period also gave impetus to Indian maritime trade. The Silk Road had been a major trade route for commerce between China and Rome for centuries. The old and mostly land-based Silk Road from China— which went through the Tarim Basin, and the passes of Afghanistan, were cut off. As a result, from the seventh century onwards, there was an increase in maritime activity on the eastern coast of India, with goods being transshipped between the China Sea, the Indian Ocean and the Persian Gulf. The seasonal monsoon winds played an important role in this division between the eastern and western parts of this transshipment trade. Due to the prevailing wind direction, the journey to the far East and China could not be completed safely by sail in a single season. As a result, trading communities of Arabs, Jews, Christians and Zoroastrians grew significantly in India's southern and western ports.

On the eastern coast of India, in the Indian Ocean and beyond, kingdoms of East and South India had a territorial, cultural and economic hegemonic status. They were at the centre of an ecosystem that gave rise to the great civilized states in Southeast Asia under Hindu and Buddhist influence. Tamil merchants not only carried culture and religion into the area but were also in direct trade with China. There is evidence that in the early twelfth century, the major portion of the export trade was in ships of Kling merchants from the Coromandel Coast and Ceylon (now Sri Lanka). At its peak in the early eleventh century, the Chola kingdom was mounting maritime expeditions to Srivijaya empire and embassies to China.[8] However, by the time of the advent of the East India Company in the seventeenth century, maritime trade had significantly declined. This was especially true on the eastern coast of India, where the earlier maritime ecosystem hegemony of the Tamil, Hindu and Buddhist empires in Southeast Asia faded as Buddhist and Hindu influence waned. In the face of invasions from the north and west of the subcontinent, South and East India, which were at the epicentre of East Asian maritime trade, also became insular and land-facing. Indeed, as the subcontinent's influence waned, some of the former Tamil, Hindu and Buddhist empires in the Indo-China region and Southeast Asia—Vietnam and Cambodia—came to be influenced by a China-centric system.

The migration of people, who carried their religion, culture, political influence and trade in their regions of influence, has been a feature of both China and India throughout their histories. The diasporas of both nations have played an important role in their respective economies, albeit in different ways. China has one of the largest populations of native origin living beyond its borders. The Chinese diaspora was estimated at nearly 11 million in 2023.[9] Over the course of its long history, Chinese people have emigrated from China and established themselves abroad.

According to some researchers, this emigration occurred in four distinct stages. In the first phase, from the twelfth to the sixteenth century, merchant trade missions were undertaken, and mercantile trade routes were expanded. These were backed by the rise in commodity production in China. In the second phase, beginning in the sixteenth century, the Ming dynasty (1368–1644) revoked an imperial edict prohibiting emigration. This resulted in the expansion of Chinese trading and industrial activities in the region. It lasted till Opium Wars (1839–42). The third phase began post the Opium Wars that marked the beginning of domination of China by the West and Japan. During this period, Chinese merchants travelled and settled outside China, mostly in Southeast Asia. Chinese workers also migrated to areas of Southeast Asia, even as these were colonized by Western industrial nations. Chinese migration also included indentured servitude in the Americas, Australia and Africa, and lasted till the founding of the People's Republic of China in 1949. The fourth and last phase from 1949 to present, represents a new era when China has not only regained its international status but overseas Chinese have become wealthy, educated and assimiliated in their adopted countries.

The attitude of China towards its diaspora, too, underwent

a significant change. For much of the country's medieval history, Chinese emigrants were considered outcasts, but they were expected to remain loyal subjects by maintaining a Chinese way of life and eventually returning to their roots. However, after 1900, emigration took on a new meaning as overseas Chinese were no longer viewed as disloyal subjects fleeing China, but as patriots by Chinese reformers and revolutionaries who looked up to them for financial and political support. Following World War II, the political landscape of the immigrants' countries of residence changed, with overseas Chinese gaining equal rights and becoming more upwardly mobile while retaining varying degrees of identity and ties to their homeland.

The idea of loyalty to a Chinese identity has been central to the description of Chinese overseas. The concept of overseas Chinese as sojourners, who eventually return to their homeland, is best captured in the term *huaqiao*. The term huaqiao became popular in the late nineteenth and early twentieth century in China as a positive connotation of Chinese people living overseas as zealous patriots and loyal supporters of China. It also implied a presumptuous jurisdiction of China over all ethnic Chinese outside of China based on a loose interpretation of descent (an assumption evidenced in 'Chinese police stations' in nations across the world[10]). It also creates a mentality among Chinese living abroad that connects them to China while distinguishing them from their adopted countries and local communities. The huaqiao are closely linked to the economic growth in the coastal regions of China prompted by market reform in the late 1970s, especially in the role they played in investing in China's rapid development.

The term 'new transnational Chinese economy' was coined by a professor at University of Virginia, Harry Harding, to refer to the links between the prosperity of China's coastal regions; the economic expansion of Hong Kong and Taiwan; and the financial influence of Chinese capitalists and firms within the international Chinese community. Other names for this broad economic system include the Asian Chinese common market, the Chinese economic community and the Greater China economic sphere. The role of overseas Chinese networks in facilitating the growth of this transnational Chinese economy has been particularly significant. As Professor Zhuang Guotu, chair professor at Institute of Overseas Chinese Studies, Huaqiao University of China, writes:

> Simply put, ethnic connections and personalized relationships among the international Chinese community are believed to be instrumental to Chinese capitalists and firms in facilitating their business ventures, and in promoting the economic growth in coastal regions of China since the market reform of the late 1970s. As well, the tendency of ethnic Chinese in different parts of the world to engage in business and commercial ventures is often attributed to their ability to preserve cultural values and cultivate ethnically based networks for business developments.[11]

Following Deng Xiaoping's policy of reform and opening-up to the outside world, the Chinese government's policy towards overseas Chinese underwent significant revisions beginning in 1978. The new policy towards overseas Chinese was also more practical and based on two significant changes in the Chinese diaspora. The first change was the great increase in overseas Chinese wealth. The two preceding decades had witnessed rapid economic growth of the overseas Chinese. The East Asian economic miracle was attributed, to a great extent, to local and interlinked overseas Chinese communities. Soon after, the economic development of Taiwan, Hong Kong and Singapore (all with a majority ethnic Chinese population) Chinese enterprises in Thailand, Malaysia, Indonesia and the Philippines also showed rapid growth. The combined output of overseas Chinese, according to World Bank estimates, rose from about $400 billion in 1991 to $600 billion by 1996.[12] The second change was the professional accomplishments and prospects of new Chinese emigrants (*xin yimin*, referring to those who emigrated from China since the 1970s). Since the 1980s, the vast majority of new Chinese emigrants have also been among the best educated Chinese from the mainland, Taiwan and Hong Kong, and regarded as potential resources for China.

With 'economic development' taking centre stage as the goal of the party and government, a focus on overseas Chinese as a source of both investment funds and human capital became a priority. China's State Council for Overseas Chinese Affairs (CSCOCA) was re-established in 1978, as was the All-China Federation of Returned Overseas Chinese.[13] As Zhuang Guotu writes:

> The heads of CSCOCA had come from a family with impeccable revolutionary credentials: first He Xiangning, the wife of Liao Zhongkai, one of Sun Yat-sen's comrades-in-arms; then her son Liao Chengzhi and then, after his death, his son Liao Hui. Soon afterwards, the sub-offices of CSCOCA were established in almost every province (with the exception of Tibet). In the National People's Congress and People's Political Consultative Conference (CPPCC), special committees to deal with overseas Chinese affairs were also organized in the 1980s.[14]

China's attention to overseas Chinese at all levels, and particularly local governments in South China's coastal areas, was unprecedented. The focus on the overseas Chinese's financial resources and strong commercial network, and how to utilize them for China's development, became a part of the national strategy.

The location of the four SEZs established in 1980 by the Chinese government were, as explained by Deng Xiaoping himself, geographical. They were placed to attract overseas Chinese investments—'Shenzhen is close to Hong Kong; Zhuhai is close to Macau; Shantou is the hometown of Chaozhou people, many of whom live in Southeast Asia; and Xiamen is chosen because there are many south Fujianese merchants in Southeast Asia'.[15] The SEZ experiment was a resounding success. Between 1979 and 1987, these four SEZs received 39.1 per cent of the total $5.22 billion in overseas Chinese capital invested in China, with the majority of investment coming from Hong Kong and Southeast Asia.[16] Deng Xiaoping acknowledged the unique contribution of overseas Chinese in China's development in 1993. As mentioned in *People's Daily* by Renmin Ribao, according to Deng, 'There have been rare opportunities for China to go into a great development. China is different from the other countries because China has several tens of millions overseas compatriots who can offer a unique opportunity to China's development and they have made great contributions to China.'[17]

Both the central government and local governments formulated new rules to offer preferential treatment to overseas Chinese capital investment in mainland China. Local governments at different levels of province, city and town, even offered more favourable conditions to the overseas Chinese in terms of investment, tax, land rent, import duties, special protection on some economic sectors, residence, etc. Goverment offices organized activities in China and sent delegations abroad to persuade overseas Chinese to invest in capital. This became so widespread that after the 1990s, the central government had to prohibit this practice. As a result, when other foreign capital was still hesitant to invest in China, overseas Chinese capital took the lead. Between 1979 and 1989, 55 per cent of mainland China's FDI came from Hong Kong and ethnic Chinese in Southeast Asia. In 2008, FDI investments in mainland China by overseas Chinese rose to 65 per cent.[18] Deng's successors, including Xi Jinping, have followed the same policy of leveraging overseas Chinese resources, networks and talent, particularly in the technology industry, as the Chinese government seeks to take its low-cost manufacturing economy to the next level of economic development.

The Indian diaspora story, although with a similar beginning as China, has a different trajectory. According to a UN report published in 2020, Indians today constitute the largest diaspora living outside their homeland (as compared to 10 million overseas Chinese), with a nearly 18 million population across over 100 countries.[19] Persons of Indian descent constitute more than 40 per cent of the population in Fiji, Mauritius, Trinidad, Guyana and Suriname. They are also a visible minority in Malaysia, South Africa, Sri Lanka, Uganda, the United Kingdom (UK), the United States (US) and Canada.

The story of Indian emigration can be broadly divided into three stages: pre-colonial, colonial and post-colonial. Prior to the sixteenth century, Indian emigration to the Asian region was primarily for trade or religious travel, and can be traced back to the first century, when merchants, princes, priests, poets and artisans travelled to East Africa and Southeast Asian countries. Pre-colonial India's maritime history reveals evidences of continuous contact between the Coromandel Coast and Southeast Asia. Southeast Asia was a thriving market for traders during the Chola period, from the ninth to the thirteenth century. Port towns such as Kaveripattinam and Nagapattinam flourished and enabled trade with this region, and through it, with China. It is also believed that merchants from Gujarat, Bengal and Tamil Nadu, settled down in the port cities of Southeast Asia and, along with trade and commerce, wielded a great deal of cultural and economic influence in these regions.

Inward looking and conservative practices gripped the subcontinent after the collapse of its maritime faring, eastern and southern Tamil transnational and Southeast Asian empires in the early medieval period. This resulted in less overseas migration for centuries. By the nineteenth century, the fear of crossing the *kalapani* (black waters of the deep seas), became entrenched in an insular, stagnant society. The transportation and incarceration of leaders of India's independence struggle to the Andaman Islands also imbued the term kalapani with new meanings associated with convict punishment. Post India's first War of Independence in 1857, nearly 90,000 emigrants left India in 1858 and 1859 to work on sugar plantations in Mauritius and became a key source of its prosperity.[20]

During the second phase, in the nineteenth and twentieth centuries, India was not only at the heart of a colonial interconnected network as a source of raw materials and a market for manufactured goods, but also as a source of labour for other parts of the British Empire. New plantations and other commercial ventures in distant British colonies as well as the abolition of slavery, created a demand for large quantities of labour, particularly unskilled and indentured or contracted workers. For most of the nineteenth century, Indian workers were transported to distant places to work in British Guyana, Trinidad, Jamaica, Suriname, Mauritius, Fiji and Natal (South

Africa). Indentured labour emigration to Southeast Asia, Africa and the Caribbean continued until the early twentieth century, with approximately 1.5 million Indians leaving India under indentured contracts. Following India's independence, migration from India changed geographically and demographically. A skilled and professional workforce was now emigrating, primarily to the developed countries of the West and Australia. The post-Independence diaspora narrative has also significantly changed in a new global economic and geopolitical context. In the 1970s, political upheavals, violence and the expulsion of Asians from Uganda resulted in an exodus of Indians to the West. There was also large-scale migration of skilled and unskilled labourers to the Gulf countries since the 1970s, giving rise to the 'money order' economy of some southern states and a significant source of foreign exchange remittances for India.

From 1990 to 2015, India's remittances grew from $2 billion to $72 billion (in comparison, China received $64 billion in 2015).[21] Since 2008, India has been the largest remittance-receiving country in the world. By the early 2000s, remittances contributed more to India's national revenue than software exports.[22] The Indian diaspora has also created multicultural spaces and social networks, and forged Indian communities overseas. However, rather than an overarching national identity of collaboration, the heterogeneity and division of class and caste identity persist.

India, too, has focussed on attracting investments from its diaspora through special policies. A committee appointed in 1979 suggested a range of incentives to increase non-resident Indian (NRI) investments. This led to the adoption of specific concessions in the early 1980s. Since the Indian economy opened up to foreign investment in 1991, various states in India have established specific regulatory frameworks, institutions and diaspora investment promotion policies for NRI FDIs.

The official effort to attract diaspora capital began in the 1960s, when India established the India Investment Centre (IIC) to increase both remittance inflows and investment. It, however, met with limited success. Other efforts followed. The Ministry of Finance established a special cell for NRI investment in 1983. In 2004, the government set up the Ministry of Overseas Indian Affairs (MOIA). The MOIA seeks to help overseas Indians with information, partnerships and other facilitation services. In 2007, the Overseas Indian Facilitation Centre (OIFC) was set up as a public–private partnership between the MOIA and the Confederation of Indian Industry (CII), one of the two largest industry associations, to encourage overseas Indian investments and business partnerships.

The government's recent flagship programmes, 'Invest in India' and 'Make in India' are aimed at both diasporic and non-diasporic populations. This is part of a broader trend of incorporating NRI investment issues into general policies. The Pravasi Bharatiya Divas, the government's annual diaspora convention, is an important part of the government's diaspora outreach programme. It has been held every January since 2003, around 9 January—the day Mahatma Gandhi returned to India from South Africa in 1915. This conference is held in various cities across India, and during the three-day gathering of 1,000–1,500 overseas and resident Indians, panel discussions take place. These discussions cover a wide range of topics including India's development, remittances and investment, diaspora philanthropy and diaspora grievances. Every year, the government organizes specific sessions on investment opportunities in states, during which chief ministers present their states as promising destinations for NRI investments. In 2003, India amended its citizenship act, introducing a new membership status (an extension of the Person of Indian Origin status)—the Overseas Citizenship of India (OCI)—which allows people of Indian origin who do not have Indian citizenship to live and work in India (without any political participation rights). Both initiatives were associated with the expectation that they would aid in increasing investment from the Indian diaspora.

The Indian diaspora's actual investments have, however, been limited and sector-specific. The NRI investment and involvement in India's IT and high-tech industries is widely acknowledged. According to one study, more than 22 per cent of Indian engineers in Silicon Valley invested in at least one start-up, with nearly 10 per cent doing so multiple times. In another study, it was found that three-quarters of the surveyed Indian professionals in Silicon Valley (77 per cent) had at least one friend who had returned to India to start a company, and half of the respondents (52 per cent) travel to India for business purposes at least once a year. A quarter of the respondents (23 per cent) self-reported investing their own money in Indian start-ups.[23] According to one study, nearly a quarter of Indians in Canada and more than half in the US have invested in India. However, according to another 2014 survey, nearly 23 per cent of Indians in the US planned to open a business in India, and nearly 30 per cent were interested in investing in a private commercial enterprise in India, but only 10 per cent had invested more than $50,000 in the previous three years.[24]

According to some scholars, the Indian diaspora differs significantly from the business diaspora of ethnic Chinese. Others argue that diaspora participation in FDI in China and India differs significantly because overseas Indians lack the skills necessary to manage export production with low-wage labour. They also claim that the relatively low level of diasporic investment was due to restrictions under which several products were reserved for small and medium enterprises (SMEs). This was a list that originally included over 800 items, of which the last 20 were finally de-reserved in 2018. Restrictions on foreign investments in SMEs made it difficult for many diasporic entrepreneurs, many of whom are retailers, to engage in those economic activities.

China's export-led manufacturing growth as a result of the opening of SEZs, and the role it played in China's explosive economic trajectory, is now a well-evidenced fact. Similar policies in India, while successful in the services sector, were unable to gain traction in encouraging the establishment of SEZs for the location of manufacturing industries.

Troubles with land acquisition, which led to political agitations, contributed to an environment of 'unease of doing business' for both domestic and overseas investors alike. This was directly attributable as much to the ever-changing uncertainty of India's political economy and lack of political capital as to the weaknesses of India's institutional framework and its uncertain outcomes. However, it must be acknowledged that historic ties to a pre-existing economic ecosystem via treaty ports, as well as a cultural diaspora of entrepreneurial overseas Chinese business organized around kinship, played an important—even determining—role in the early years of China's SEZs success story, an advantage India did not have.

9

The Third Yang:
Real Estate and Urbanization

Throughout China's imperial history, state authority over land has been a defining feature of its political economy. It has allowed China under the CPC to take over, redistribute, communize and lease land to its citizens. It has also enabled the relocation of local populations and seizing of land needed for its projects. Millions of Chinese citizens have been moved to make way for gargantuan infrastructure projects like the Three Gorges Dam (the world's largest hydroelectric power plant) and the South-to-North Water Diversion Project (three canals built to divert water from the Yangtze River to the water-scarce northern provinces).

Since the late 1970s' reform and opening-up, the authority to redistribute land has been the linchpin of local governments' development model. Local governments have used land to compete and attract investments to their jurisdictions from large concessional tracts to set up SEZs to industrial parks with attractive subsidies. However, land could not be sold. It was, and continues to be, owned by the state. About a decade after the reform process began, as a result of fiscal reorganization, China permitted local governments to raise funds by selling rights to the long-term use of land, and to borrow from banks that are willing to accept land as collateral. This monetization of urban land lease rights—residential and commercial—set off a fundraising spree that generated funds at an unprecedented scale and sparked a property and infrastructure boom in China that is now in its third decade.

'During the early days of reform, the problem in attracting foreigners to open factories and businesses was that our infrastructure was not good enough,' Zhao Ziyang, China's former premier and Deng's chief lieutenant, wrote in his memoirs. 'We had no funds to build roads for cities or to bring in water and electricity.' According to Zhao, a Hong Kong property developer introduced him to the idea of land finance when Zhao had mentioned that he just couldn't find the funds for urban development. 'He asked me, "If you have land, how can you not have money?"' Zhao wrote, 'I thought this was a strange comment. Having land was one issue; a lack of funds was another. What did one have to do with the other?' The funds from state-owned land monetization would finance both, the building of property and infrastructure, in the most rapid urbanization the world has ever seen.

To accommodate growing cities, local governments seized large tracts of agricultural land. They rezoned these areas for housing or retail and connected them to utilities. These rezoned lands were then routinely sold for 10 times more than what they paid the farmers as compensation. Estimates of displaced or affected Chinese range as high as 65 million over a decade, roughly equivalent to the entire population of the UK. However, land expropriations were a lifeline and manna from heaven for fiscally strapped local governments seeking to meet expenses, fund deficit budgets, expand, build world-class infrastructure and offer competitive incentives to attract investment to their jurisdiction. It was a trend that rapidly accelerated after the global financial crisis (GFC) of 2008.

The extent to which China's economic growth in the post GFC era was funded by land sales was unprecedented. As Dinny McMahon, former Wall Street Journal journalist and author writes:

> From 2009 to 2015, the seven years following the (GFC), China's governments collected 22.01 trillion yuan ($3.3 trillion) just from selling land. That's comparable to selling all the land in Manhattan two and a half times over. Nationally, land sales in China account for roughly a third of all fiscal revenue. [...] This... has made it possible for China to transform its infrastructure. [...] Foreigners often look upon this transformation as a sign of the superiority of China's economic system, when in fact

it was made possible solely by the one-time privatization of a state asset.[1]

A significant part of the funds raised by local governments from land sales were applied to build infrastructure. However, as McMahon also notes:

> [...] it's a privilege that has been abused by local governments that treat land finance as though it's free money. They've built whatever they wanted—subways, airports, new cities and districts—without reference to any underlying need, and without financial consequence. And even worse, they've become addicted to it. In 2014 alone, local governments raised thirty-one times more money from land sales than they did in 2001.

Land sales helped stimulate the economy by funding an increase in real estate and infrastructure in the wake of the GFC. However, stimulus is supposed to be a temporary measure but China's stimulus never stopped. Massive land sales and correspondingly large real estate and infrastructure works became business as usual. Experts repeatedly warned of the risks of a real estate bubble and the unsustainability of this policy. Ba Shusong, one of China's most influential economists, wrote presciently in the *People's Daily* as early as 2013, 'If the land markets cool, land prices drop and the volume of land sales fall, not only will the funding of some projects experience difficulties, but it will likely produce financial crises...'

News about China's urbanization and real estate is now making headlines around the world for the wrong reasons. Its largest real estate group, Evergrande (which has a staggering $300 billion in debt) as well as other real estate firms, are facing bankruptcy, which could jeopardize global financial stability. It has been dubbed China's 'Lehman moment', and if the real estate sector and its companies are allowed to fail by the Chinese government, it would undoubtedly have disastrous consequences for both the Chinese and global economy.

In many ways, Evergrande is symptomatic of the China real estate story. Founded in 1996 by Hui Ka Yan in Guangzhou, the real estate arm of the group (it also has business interests in electric vehicles, food and drink manufacturing, wealth management and owns a football club) owns more than 1,300 projects in 280 cities across China. Undertaking construction at a frenetic pace for decades with easy availability of land, funds and patronage, Evergrande's dizzying expansion saw Hui as the richest person in Asia at some point. However, China's real estate markets are softening (by some accounts, there are at least 65 million empty homes in China, enough to house the entire population of France[2]) after prolonged exuberance.

With enormous housing projects going unoccupied and its loans falling due, Evergrande and the real estate sector teeters on the edge of default. Even as the central government works to avoid defaults that could cause a confidence crisis—which would threaten not only China's huge real estate and urban infrastructure sectors which are important for local government revenues, household savings and construction, and on which much of the country's famed success is built—but would also cause a global crisis. However, to understand how China's real estate and urbanization story began and reached this place, it is important to start at the very beginning, with land and its exceptionally unique context in China.

Land has dominated Chinese economic and social consciousness throughout its history and has been a matter of life and death— particularly in East and South China. Over centuries, limited cultivable land, combined with historically high population density, has resulted in great human ingenuity in harnessing natural resources as well as highly sophisticated cultivation techniques. It has also witnessed massive natural and ecological disasters when these techniques have failed. The importance of land to China and its political processes was recognized by both the Kuomintang and the CPC as they fought for control of China's future. As Sun Yat-sen said in 1924, 'If the land problem can be solved, one half of the problem of livelihood will be solved'. Mao went a step further in 1936, unambiguously prophesying, 'Whoever wins the peasants will win China. Whoever solves the land problem will win the peasants.'

After decades of a war effort that was predominantly based

and fought in the rural areas of China, Mao and the CPC won the Chinese Civil War in 1949 and formed the government. It came to power by occupying parts of the countryside and then implementing land reforms in these areas by redistributing land to farmers. This earned the CPC political support along with a primary ideological tenet to foment class struggle. Implementing land reforms, first as redistribution, then as cooperatives and finally as collectives or communities as individual ownership was revoked, was thus one of the first tasks undertaken by the CPC once it came to power.

It was not till the 1980s that reforms to this arrangement, by way of the HRS began under Deng Xiaoping's leadership. The HRS reforms led to the recognition of private land use rights, and the eventual creation of markets for land use rights in respect of urban land. According to the Constitution of the People's Republic of China, all urban land is owned by the *guoyou* (state) and all rural land is owned by the *jiti* (collective). Prior to 1986, land use rights were granted without charge, by municipal or village governments, to individual state units or farmers. However, in 1988, the land management law underwent a landmark revision that separated land ownership rights from rights to use. This allowed the landowners (the guoyou and jiti) to lease land use rights for fixed periods in exchange for fees. For the first time in communist China's history, land markets (of some kind) became legal in both rural and urban China. Ever since, property rights have been central to China's reforms and economic development strategy at both the national and local levels. Land lease has been used to raise capital by monetizing it, to plan city and regional urbanization, to develop infrastructure, to control population migration from one region to another and to accelerate the rise of real estate as an economic activity multiplier and macro control lever for the economy.

For the sake of clarity, it must be borne in mind that Chinese property rights bear no resemblance to what is commonly understood as the Western concept of 'individual ownership'. Land in urban China is still owned by the state, and land in rural China is owned by the collectives. The government has de facto control over all land. While rural land use is privatized in household farming, the members of rural collectives—collective landowners by their rural household registration (hukou) status—cannot legally sell either their share of collective farmland or their own homestead land (although there have been some recent changes with regard to homesteads). On the other hand, urban land is owned by the state, represented by the local government. Until recently, only urban land could be leased for construction (this was amended under the new Land Administration Law of 2020, which now allows 'collective land for for-profit construction' in a rural area to be transferred or leased out, subject to collective committee approval).[3] Furthermore, only the local government has the authority to convert land from rural to urban status.

It is impossible to overstate the enormous economic and financial power that this urban land ownership and conversion rights bestowed on local governments in a communist state that had no private property and was just opening up and growing as a market economy. To give a reference point, according to a McKinsey report, nearly 68 per cent of global wealth is on account of real estate.[4]

Applying the same metrics to a then-emerging market economy in China—a nation with a long history of and proclivity for saving—the channelling of higher household savings resulting from the initial impetus of the manufacturing-led export boom into a nascent real estate sector can only be described as mind-boggling in scope and scale for monetization. Furthermore, in Asia's emerging economies, real estate accounts for nearly 7 to 8 per cent of the annual GDP, has the greatest multiplier effect and contributes the greatest percentage to GDP growth.[5] Local governments in China were at the epicentre of this exceptional, greenfield opportunity for economic wealth creation through the sale of state-owned real estate rights to private companies and households.

The nearly three-decade-long land and real estate boom began in 1994, when local governments gained monopoly of urban public land. This was due to a reorganization of the fiscal distribution system between the central government and local governments at the provincial, municipal and county level, which saw local governments' share of tax revenue decline to less than 50 per cent, despite no change in their expenditure burden. Between 2002 and 2006, their tax revenues were further reduced as local fees and then the millennium-old agricultural tax was abolished.

In fact, it was this deprivation of tax revenues at the local level, throughout the first decade of the 2000s, that sparked the rush among local governments to monetize property rights. Local governments increasingly relied on revenues received from leasing out land to fund basic budgetary expenditures. As this was the only source of revenue under their control, they used it to bridge budget deficits. Since then, sales of land use rights have been a primary source of revenue for local governments. The urban land use rights were and are leased through a variety of mechanisms, some of which are public (such as auctions) and others that are private (such as negotiations). Lease terms vary depending on the type of land (from 40 years for commercial land to 70 years for residential land). Notably, from the local government's point of view, user fees for the whole length of the lease accrue up front at the time of lease.

Despite recurring crises and long-held fears (that are fast becoming true) of a real estate bubble that might burst one day, land has now become central to the Chinese development model. Chinese cities have grown rapidly in the last 25 years. Between 1996 and 2010, the area of urban construction doubled (from 20,000 to 40,000 sq. km), and real estate investment as a percentage of GDP increased from near zero in the early 1990s to a remarkable 15 per cent in the last decade.[6] A research paper by Harvard professor of public policy and economics Kenneth Rogoff and International Monetary Fund (IMF) economist Yuanchen Yang, estimates that real estate sector activity accounts for around 29 per cent of China's GDP.[7] In fact, China's real estate market has been called the most important sector in the world economy. Valued at about $55 trillion, it is now twice the size of its US equivalent, and four times larger than China's GDP.[8]

Land is also the most debated economic and political issue in China. Every year, large-scale protests in rural and adjacent urban areas in China erupt, along with petitions to higher governmental authorities, as the struggle for rural land has become a flashpoint between peasants and local governments. In urban China, the demolition and relocation of residents has been a source of disaffection. According to Chinese academics, as many as 60 million peasants have lost their land since the early 1990s.[9] Scholars argue that if current trends continue, China will have 110 million landless peasants by 2030 as a result of land conversion from agriculture to construction. 60 per cent of peasants who file complaints (*shangfang*) with higher-level governments do so over lost land, most of which is lost as a result of state acquisition (*zhengyong*). The process of land conversion is contentious and often violent. Chinese journals frequently report beatings, assaults, incinerations and mass brawls among peasants and local leaders over land disputes.[10]

As a result of this insatiable appetite of local governments to convert rural land into urban land, the central government strengthened control over the land supply since the late 1990s. The Ministry of Land and Resources (MLR), established in 1998, adopted increasingly rigorous methods of controlling conversions of farmland and investment in urban development. In 2004, the ministry began setting quotas of land for urban construction, allocating each province an amount of land for urban built-up areas and restricting how much agricultural land they could convert. The provincial governments then negotiate with municipal governments, who in turn negotiate with county and township governments about the allocation of development land.

The need of land for urban development and the historically limited arable land available in China for its food security has also brought this inherent conflict of fast urbanizing China into sharp focus. The central government designated non-negotiable land—land that cannot be developed in any way—as a 'Red Line' of 120 million hectares of arable land, which according to them is the baseline required for China's food security. Local governments throughout China also acknowledge the Red Line as a sacred number. Local governments, however, have an incentive to lease as much land as possible, resulting in an urban sprawl and misuse of resources. These local governments stand to benefit the most when expropriating rural land from peasants at low prices and selling use rights to urban users at high prices (though this has been mitigated in part by the new Land Administration Law of 2020, which allows rural collectives to sell property rights for for-profit development). This has generated widespread discontent and land disputes, as rural residents seek increased compensation and urban governments seek to prevent collective action. The over-reliance of Chinese cities on land-based and real estate investment has also become a matter of growing international concern.

However, this is the result of a deliberate policy process in the Chinese style. The original goal of creating markets for land use in China was to generate capital for cities, which it has done through a process of experimentation, crisis and learning. Between 1986 and 1988, policymakers ran two experimental land leasing programmes in Shenzhen and Shanghai. The Shanghai lease marked the first time a foreign company had independent control over a plot of Chinese land since the Chinese Revolution. Both were a success, and real estate in China took off in a big way, especially after 1992. Nationally, there were 117 development zones at the end of 1991, and 1,993 by the end of 1992.[11]

Cities grew at a breakneck speed, as urban officials converted rural land on a grand scale for the first time. The craze for cashing in on real estate, however, was not limited to local governments. Universities, hospitals, businesses and government agencies of all kinds established real estate arms, claiming state land and attempting to develop commercial real estate. The majority of land use was determined by administrative allocation at the time, in which 'the state' (typically the local government) would assign land use rights to institutions free of charge. After land was assigned to an institutional user, the user could allow the land to enter the real estate market and profit from it.

As Meg E. Rithmire, associate professor at Harvard Business School writes:

A 1992 investigative report from *Xinhua* revealed changes in land prices that alarmed central authorities. In addition to uncovering the sale of central urban land at incredibly low prices in cities like Xiamen and Shenzhen, the report also concluded that commercial housing prices had risen on average 5.5 times in the larger cities, a rate far faster than that of wages. Central authorities, concerned about a bubble and fearful of social instability and a housing crisis, concluded that the real estate sector needed discipline. As [they began (contract) lending as] part of a 'macro adjustment' in response to fears about property oversupply and overinvestment [...] all kinds of firms and institutions struggled to repay debt they had taken on toward real estate investments.[12]

One of the primary causes of the 1992–93 chaos was identified as low barriers to entry in the real estate sector, which created conditions for overinvestment. Policymakers concluded that the state would have to limit who could enter the real estate business at what stages of development, and also regulate the supply of land for development. Furthermore, because real estate has significant cascading effects on the overall economy, leaving land development entirely to markets would create dangerous distortions and jeopardize urban plans for infrastructure, land use, transportation, etc.

The solution devised was to combine the ability to lease land with the ability to create urban plans, thereby designating urban governments as the sole legal owners of land. According to the new policy, the Chinese government would monopolize land supply to strengthen economic and land planning, and control the macro supply of land. A National Bureau of Statistics (NBS) report stated: 'After several years, when virgin land becomes mature land, through real estate markets we can preserve value, add value, and in this way add to the wealth of the country. China has 25,000 square kilometers of state-owned urban land. This is an indispensable condition for economic and social development and the first great source of national wealth.'

As an economic tool in the hands of the state, changes in the land supply worked directly and indirectly to expand or contract the country's economic output in three ways. First, land development increased China's GDP directly through investment and economic activity related to real estate investment. Increasing land for urban construction meant more construction jobs, more purchases of durable goods, and so on, thereby boosting demand. China's NBS even estimated a fiscal multiplier: for every yuan invested in real estate development, GDP would grow by 1.34 yuan.

Second, increasing the supply of land for development served as an indirect fiscal stimulus to local governments. As local governments cannot issue debt or levy taxes, they have little control over their resources other than the revenues generated by the sale of property rights. The central government used the supply of land and the allocation of quotas to the local governments as a proxy for fiscal expansion and contraction, in addition to the direct fiscal transfers undertaken. The central government also used this mechanism to boost regional development, promoting growth and investment in regions left behind by the economic boom along the east coast. This it did through campaigns like 'Open Up the West', 'Rise of Central China Plan' and 'Revitalize Northeast China'. A critical source of resources for these regions was an increased land quota for development, thereby allowing more direct investment and greater revenues for local governments to invest in infrastructure and public services.

Third, changes in land quotas act as an indirect form of monetary stimulus through the financial system. Local governments cannot directly borrow from banks but do so indirectly through local government financing vehicles (LGFV). These semi-public investment vehicles borrow with the implicit support of local governments and use real estate as collateral. Increasing the supply of land increases the collateral available to local governments (as well as developers and businesses), and thus, the volume of loans disbursed by banks. Between 1994 and 2009, these investment platforms essentially converted land into monetized capital for local governments via the financial system. Beginning in 2010, soon after the central government realized the potential of a debt problem in the local government, a futile attempt was made to restrain the growth of these vehicles and their balance sheets.

Since the late 1990s, local governments throughout China have been successful in innovating ways to maximize land for development while maintaining their assigned quotas. Some of these innovations have been institutional in nature, such as the transfer of development rights between jurisdictions in order to preserve quotas at higher (e.g., municipal or provincial) levels; the establishment of systems in which rural residents can trade their land certificates and land rights for urban citizenship; and the sale of those land certificates in government-sponsored markets. Other less transparent and potentially abusive innovations include village redevelopment projects that consolidated villagers into high-rise housing developments, frequently displacing them from their farms to maximize the amount of transferable land.

The state's use of land as a macroeconomic policy tool, on the other hand, was most visible in China's response to the 2008 financial crisis. The GFC necessitated an increase in construction in China to generate domestic demand and sustain economic growth. It resulted in unprecedented land development and construction activity, with cities of all sizes across regions engaging in infrastructure development projects and creation of new urban areas. Investment as a percentage of GDP increased to nearly 50 per cent as banks and local governments responded overwhelmingly to the stimulus.[13] According to one OECD report's 'conservative' estimate, the stimulus had grown to nearly 27 per cent of GDP by the end of 2010.[14] Between 2000 and 2015 alone, more than 270 million people—equivalent to the combined population of Germany, France, the UK and Spain— moved from the rural areas to China's cities.[15]

However, the stimulus ballooned far beyond the central government's intentions, and likely control, as did the balance sheets of LGFVs and local governments. Just as state monopolization and control of land was used as a macro policy tool in the aftermath of the 1993 real estate bubble, the CPC managers of the economy have been searching for new management mechanisms in the aftermath of yet another crisis since 2012—and again more recently—with little success.

Farmers have paid the highest price as a result of China's political economy and institutional structure, with little power to negotiate compensation or redress abuse by local governments. While this land acquisition process has impacted over 300 million rural residents, their inability and limitations in organizing themselves for political protests have allowed local and provincial governments to exercise totalitarian power. The central government and the party, on the other hand, have benefitted in a variety of ways from this arbitrary land governance. By retaining its ownership over land and exercising absolute control over how much land gets converted, the state has control over the pace and geographical distribution of urbanization.

Along with population migration control from rural to urban areas (under the hukou permit system), this has allowed China to benefit economically from urbanization and urban construction. This has led to a rapid growth in real estate markets without being vulnerable to the political fallout of massive urban agglomeration that other comparable developing economies have experienced. Local government and party officials have benefitted greatly from decentralized land ownership too, as control over the land is not only a powerful tool for managing the local economy but also a lucrative source of distribution, patronage and personal enrichment. Corruption and financial connections between officials and developers abound in China's guanxi or relationship-centric social structure. In fact, firms with political connections to the central government are more able to flout land regulations.[16]

However, because local governments own land, they can use land pricing as a competitive incentive to attract investors to their jurisdiction. Urban Chinese households benefit as savers and homeowners as well, because the government—at all levels—has a monopolistic interest in ensuring that land prices, and thus housing prices, do not fall. Because of this, even when local governments' greed for land development has resulted in overinvestment and an ever-inflating property price bubble, there has been an official central government intervention to keep asset prices from falling and to keep local debt (guaranteed by land as collateral) from becoming a problem and sparking a collapse.

This monopolistic feature of the real estate markets, as well as government intervention are unique to communist China and have allowed it to continue its unbridled expansion for nearly three decades. For years, external observers have warned of an impending 'burst' of China's now $5 trillion housing bubble, but no such collapse has occurred. The reason has been the overarching institutional framework within which this bubble has been managed. The problem of real estate oversupply has been addressed by recruiting rural migrants to generate demand, for example, by liberalizing household registration (hukou) and relocating these rural residents to cities with excess housing. High savings rates, limited alternative investment and fiscal incentives, and ever-increasing real estate prices (till now) has resulted in increased housing investment by most urban households. Further, urban households have resisted levy of property taxes, which is the other—more obvious and balanced—alternative to land leasing as a source of revenue for local governments.[17]

When they took power in 2012, China's fifth-generation leaders, Xi Jinping and Li Keqiang, had emphasized a 'new-style urbanization' as a strategy for continued economic growth. According to this strategy, real estate would drive growth by increasing domestic demand. It was envisaged that small- and medium-sized cities would be the focus of growth, creating new urban residents by liberalizing migration for new rural migrants. Cities would focus more on service sector economic activity and shift away from reliance on industry and production for export. This stage of urbanization would create a secure, permanent and consuming urban middle class to support growth at the 'new normal' target of 7 per cent per year. While target economic growth rates have been revised in light of current global and domestic economic scenarios, the plan's long-term trajectory remains uncertain.

Real estate and urbanization is, however, a different story in India. Other than land owned by the government and public sector units, all land in India is privately owned. In rural and densely populated India, with many farmers engaging in subsistence farming with fragmented landholdings, land is a deeply emotive issue. With a large part of its population continuing to be dependent on agriculture, acquisition of land has been emblematic of the struggles of India's economic policy in its post-liberalization phase. It still continues to be a highly sensitive and political subject in democratic India.

Landholdings in India have also been plagued by poor records, disputes and conflicting legislation. By some estimates, nearly 66 per cent of all pending civil litigation that is clogging India's courts is land related.[18] A complex web of rules, regulations and land ceilings have limited the availability of large parcels for planned development in urban India, breeding widespread corruption through a deeply entrenched builder-bureaucrat-politician nexus in municipal and state governments. There has also been widespread illegal occupation of public and government land in urban areas as the rural poor migrated to cities in search of a better life. This has resulted in sprawling slums devoid of even basic amenities and unplanned urban growth. The real estate industry—like other asset classes— has followed traditional economic boom–bust cycles in India, unlike in China where the once-in-a-lifetime monetization of government ownership and policy has fuelled an intense impetus to its GDP growth for nearly three decades.

The history of land and its ownership in India has deep cultural and sociological roots. According to the ancient Hindu text *Manusmriti*, cultivated land is the property of those who clear and till it. Land was generally abundant in pre-colonial India, and rulers were more concerned with land cultivation than land ownership. The ruler had the right to levy and collect taxes. The state, on the other hand, made no claims to absolute ownership of all land in their territory, and individual property rights were recognized. In fact, in some areas, if a farmer's crops were destroyed due to movement or encampment of the army, the ruler would compensate to the extent of destruction (*paimalli*).

Land ownership and acquisition by the state began during the colonial period as a result of public infrastructure projects such as roads, railways and dams, which necessitated the acquisition of large tracts of land. The Land Acquisition Act of 1894 provided legislative teeth to government land acquisition, allowing it to take over private property for public use while compensating the owner. Following India's independence, the planned, state-led economic development path saw a further and even more significant increase in demand for land for infrastructure and industry. With an increasing population, the pressure and demand for land in the country also grew exponentially.

Acquisition of private land by the state has, however, always been contentious and faced public protests. When the Hirakud Dam was being built, Nehru exhorted in 1948, 'If you are to suffer, you should suffer in the interest of the country.' Many such dams were built—Pong, Chandil and Tehri to name a few—in the 1970s and 1980s which faced local agitations. None were able to stop the land acquisition or get good resettlement terms. The landscape for public purpose land acquisitions, however, changed with the Narmada Bachao Andolan, against the Sardar Sarovar project on the Narmada River in the late 1980s. This landmark movement and activism, which coincided with the liberalization of the Indian economy (as well as the electoral vulnerability and low political capital of coalition governments at the Centre), saw greater attention paid to the social aspects of these public projects, with displacement and resettlement becoming part of the project's plan and costs.

Dhanmanjiri Sathe, professor of Economics at Savitribai Phule Pune University, calls this 'the civil society phase', which saw greater mobilization by farmers even while the legal framework remained largely unchanged. According to her, this was due to two factors. First, as landholdings became smaller and more fragmented, there was increased pressure on scarce agricultural land.[19] Second, the farmers were better organized, more aware of their rights and more vocal, with the support of non-governmental and civil society organizations, the media and opposition political parties. An active judiciary was also sympathetic to their rights. This period also saw a significant increase in the compensation paid to farmers for land acquired, with many settlements satisfying both parties. However, in the case of some, such as Singur, the state's attempts to acquire land failed. Private property rights have been recognized in India even before Independence. In its legislative and judicial context and intent, the right to property in India has, however, undergone significant evolution. Originally a fundamental right under the Constitution, this individual right clashed with the state's socialist reforms as it sought to acquire and redistribute land starting from the 1950s. In 1979, the right to property ceased being a fundamental right and was reclassified as a constitutional right. Adding to the complexity, land is a state subject under the Constitution, whereas land acquisition is a concurrent (Centre and state) subject. As a result, while the central law remained the antiquated colonial Land Acquisition Act of 1894 (with amendments) for most of India's post-Independence period, individual states passed their own laws and were not entirely reliant on this central law. Some states acquired land using various models, methods and laws in their respective jurisdictions. As a result, during India's liberalization period, there was no integrated land acquisition law that addressed the private sector's massive land requirements for infrastructure and industry. There were also no institutional mechanisms for fair market-based compensation; rehabilitation and resettlement in the changed economic scenario of private participation in public infrastructure and manufacturing projects; and political environment of rights-based agitations and weak coalition governments. It was only after widespread protests against land acquisition, particularly large tracts of agricultural land for SEZs, that the then central government led by the United Progressive Alliance (UPA) enacted a new Land Acquisition Act in 2013, more than 22 years after reforms began, to replace the more than 100-year-old colonial law. The UPA was voted out of power in 2014, which was exacerbated in part by the mess in land acquisition.

To make the land acquisition process easier, the then newly elected National Democratic Alliance (NDA) government amended the Act through an ordinance in 2014, which was extended twice in

2015, but it was not legislated in Parliament due to a lack of support in the Rajya Sabha and political opposition in the upcoming Assembly elections. It did, however, exhort individual states not to wait for a consensus and enact their own legislation to facilitate industrial and infrastructure development. The 'triumvirate' economic growth model of SEZs, infrastructure and urbanization—which is heavily reliant on land acquisition—was played out in this political-legal theatre over the three critical decades of reforms, with mixed results.

The story of the Singur–Nandigram fiasco in West Bengal best exemplifies the post-liberalization land acquisition narrative. In August 2005, the West Bengal Industrial Development Corporation (WBIDC) signed a memorandum of understanding (MOU) with the Salim Group of Indonesia to promote an industrial SEZ with accompanying urbanization in West Bengal. After much deliberation, the communist-led state government had decided to embark on what was to be the new model of industry-led development in post-liberalization India. With centrally funded projects drying up, major states were now competing with one another to attract private investments in India's competitive federal economy. The challenge was especially acute for West Bengal's Left Communist Party of India (Marxist)—CPI(M)—government, and it was not just ideological. West Bengal's land was fertile agricultural land, yielding multiple crops per year due to its location in the Ganges Delta. It was also land that had been fragmented into small, individual holdings, with a high density of rural population relying on it for subsistence.

The CPI(M) government had just won its seventh election in a row in May 2006 with a landslide victory, and had enthusiastically embarked on an industrialization programme as promised in its election manifesto. The re-elected government began by acquiring 997 acres of land on the newly built six-lane Durgapur Expressway for a small car project by the Tata Group in Singur, about 45 km from Kolkata—the state capital. The state government was eager to secure this prestigious project and had shown the Tata Group various sites for locating its plant, including a large tract of land already owned by the state government near the industrial town of Durgapur. However, it was reported that the Tata Group insisted on this specific location (Singur)—a fertile stretch of farmland spread across six zones: Gopalnagar, Beraberi, Bajemelia, Khaser Bheri and Singherbheri—with road and rail connectivity advantages.

In July 2006, a state gazette notification was issued declaring that the land was to be acquired under the Land Acquisition Act of 1894 by the government or its undertaking 'at public expense for a public purpose' such as 'employment generation and socio-economic development of the area by setting up a Tata Small Car Project'. The disconnect between the announcement and the ground reality was immediate and obvious. When the Tata Group officials visited Singur, they were met with angry protesters shouting anti-factory slogans. Meanwhile, in June 2006, the chairman of the Salim Group, Indonesia, visited Nandigram and Haldia, where the company planned to acquire land for the development of a chemical hub, an SEZ and an urban township with schools, colleges and hospitals.

Even as the state government prioritized the Tata-Singur land acquisition, local protesters blocked the expressway along the busy route. They demanded that the project be relocated and that the land acquisition process be halted immediately. In July 2006, the state government signed a contract with the WBIDC and the Salim Group for the setting up of a chemicals complex at Nandigram. The project entailed the acquisition of 38,650 acres of farmland and a proposed investment of ₹40,000 crore. West Bengal had never received such a large investment, and both Tata-Singur and Salim-Nandigram were widely publicized as 'historic' projects. However, by July–August 2006, several protests had been organized, with the support of various Opposition parties, criticizing the state government's initiatives on the grounds that they had been made without any consultation with those who would be affected—those who would lose their land to accommodate these megaprojects. The farmers' fear of losing their land to corporate interests and getting a raw deal was exacerbated by a lack of communication between the state government and the ruling communist party.

The private-sector-led development model, which envisaged the acquisition of large tracts of land from farmers—undertaken or facilitated by the state on which capital-intensive industries and export-oriented SEZs would be established—came under increased public scrutiny and debate. A significant difference in public perception was that, unlike previous land acquisitions justified by governments as public projects, the 'sacrifices' demanded for the 'public good' this time were not for state projects like the Hirakud Dam, but for a private corporate enterprise for profit. This private-sector-led model was being tested not only in Nandigram and Singur but also in Dadri, Uttar Pradesh; Kalinganagar, Orissa; and Raigad, Maharashtra. Acquisition of agricultural or tribal lands took place in these areas to varying degrees. As political commentators wrote at the time, there was no reason to believe that in a parliamentary democracy, this corporate-led and urban-centric growth strategy would not be rejected by the overwhelmingly rural and poor electorate in West Bengal and elsewhere. Given the importance of land acquisition to the triumvirate model of economic growth, it is critical to understand this story from the perspectives and motivations of both the government and the protesters.

In February 2007, the West Bengal government presented its position on the issue of land acquisition and industrial policy at a party meeting. West Bengal, under Left-wing rule, had maintained a consistent agricultural growth rate of 4 per cent per year, compared to the country's 2 per cent after decades of extensive land redistribution. This was accomplished despite concerns raised about the viability of smallholdings following land reforms. The state was also first in the country in the production of fish and vegetables, and it is now self-sufficient in paddy production. This had resulted in a large amount of disposable cash for rural West Bengal, transforming it into a huge market for consumer goods.

'Our kisans', Chief Minister (CM) Buddhadeb Bhattacharjee had asserted, 'possess the highest purchasing power of industrial goods in the whole of the country today in the retail sector, be it cement, radio, cycle, motorcycle, or apparel'. For West Bengal to develop, however, he argued that it was imperative that it accepted that 'the transition from agriculture to industry is an inevitable phenomenon both in capitalism and in socialism'. He highlighted the crisis that West Bengal would face if the government did not fulfil its responsibility to modernize agriculture and create jobs. Agricultural land was becoming fragmented as a result of rising demographic pressure. Agriculture accounted for 65 per cent of the state's population while accounting for only 26 per cent of the state's economy. Rising input costs had made agriculture less profitable. Furthermore, the younger generation was disinclined to stay in agriculture. With meagre investment in infrastructure—such as refrigerated chains, transportation and food processing—massive amounts of perishable produce were routinely wasted.

Industrialization, from the standpoint of the West Bengal government, was not a matter of choice. To accomplish this, two major challenges had to be overcome—a lack of capital and land. While the state's demand for capital was not unusual, West Bengal, with its high population density, faced a serious problem with land availability. Since the early 2000s, the government had been getting investment proposals, particularly in iron and steel, chemicals, petrochemicals, information technology and other industries, and had found it difficult to provide suitable locations for the majority of these proposals. Only 1 per cent of the state's land was fallow (compared to 17 per cent nationally), 13 per cent was under forest cover, 23 per cent was under urban and industrial settlement and 63 per cent was under intensive cultivation. To set up industries, it was pointed out that acquisition of agricultural land was unavoidable. Land acquisition had already become a contentious issue across the country.

'Under capitalism, in India, the expropriation of the land of the farmers is taking place in a brutal manner,' the then CM of Bengal observed. 'In our drive for industrialisation in West Bengal', he assured, 'we will not proceed this way'. He compared West Bengal to other states where 'the zamindars own the land and the *lathi*-wielding *pehelwans* run the panchayat,' citing Left-led farmer struggles in the

1960s and 1970s that resulted in 83 per cent of the state's agricultural land being in the hands of poor and marginal farmers. He promised: 'We are committed to protect the interest of the farmers. If land needs to be taken, it will be done by providing those owning and dependent on land a fair deal, without coercion.' Barely five weeks later, the police open fired on protesting farmers in Nandigram.

Critics claimed that the Left Front government made undue concessions to the Tata Group in Singur for the establishment of a car factory, and that it tried to force its way into Nandigram for the construction of an SEZ by keeping farmers in the dark. The government admitted that concessions were made because without the incentives, the state had no chance of obtaining the project. Following the mass agitation that followed the firing, the government admitted that land 'is a very sensitive issue'. The CM said: '...The Left always looks after the interests of the poor. The effort should also be on to develop industries. We feel we are at a crucial phase of development. With agriculture as our basis, we shall build industry'.[20] The outcome of the mass agitation over the state's acquisition of land for Singur and Nandigram saw the relocation of the Tata Nano project to Gujarat, the abandonment of SEZ and industrial zone plans in the state, and eventually, as predicted by political pundits, the end of communist party rule in West Bengal.

Some analysts argue that the outcome could have been different if the acquisitions had occurred under the subsequent, and more modern and contemporary framework of market-based compensation and rehabilitation of the Land Acqusition Act of 2013. They also argue that the outcome could have been different if the Tata Group had accepted the state government's offer of a project site at Guptamoni near Kharagpur, where large tracts of vested lands were already with the district administration; or if the state government had communicated with the affected farmers better rather than trying strong-arm tactics to force the acquisition. These arguments, however, ignores India's multi-institutional framework and political processes, as well as its electoral democratic outcomes.

Previously, public sector companies had acquired land for setting up large industrial projects and ancillary townships with strong state support. The compulsory acquisition was justified as necessary for public purposes, and a unilaterally determined compensation was paid to those whose lands were acquired, overriding any protests. The land that was acquired did not create any right for the landowner to get a job or any assurance of employment for displaced families. Cash compensation was also strictly by the book, determined by the price of land based on historical value. There was often excess acquisition of land undertaken, far in excess of their requirements, by government agencies and public sector companies in these projects. Land, which continues to be in their possession even now.

The land acquisitions by the state were not limited to establishing industrial projects alone. During the 1950s, the state also established large towns such as Chandigarh in Punjab/Haryana, Durgapur in West Bengal and Bhubaneswar in Orissa, which required significant relocation. The comparison of land acquired for/by the state for the public sector in the earlier phase and for/by the private sector in the name of SEZs in the post-liberalization phase is revealing.

Table 1
Comparative Chart of the New Towns Developed after Independence and the Largest/Proposed SEZs[21]

Town	Size (hectares)	SEZ	Size (hectares)
Chandigarh	11,400	DLF Universal, Gurgaon	8,097
Durgapur	15,400	DS Constructions, Palwal	5,000
Bhubaneswar	13,500	Navi Mumbai	4,377
Kalyani	2,914	Maha Mumbai	10,000
Rourkela	20,000	New Kolkata	5,000

While the scale of land acquisitions envisaged under the SEZs was smaller than those previously undertaken for urban townships and industrial projects, the key difference was in the beneficiaries. It was private developers who were developing the SEZs instead of the government or its agencies. It was not acceptable in India's democracy for the government to use its unilateral power to force poor and marginal farmers to sell their land at low, notified prices in order to benefit private developers.

Furthermore, land markets across the country were difficult to understand. In many cases, they were nonexistent with no market prices that could be benchmarked. Two limitations imposed on landowners under the earlier 1894 legislation further complicated land markets and contributed to the farmers' misery. The first did not allow for judicial review of acquisition orders. The second was a ban in many states on converting agricultural land to non-agricultural use, which required a non-agricultural use clearance (NAC) from the state government. This depressed the price of agricultural lands, resulting in large windfall gains for the purchaser at the expense of the farmers, who were unable to seek an NAC for their land because it required clear terms of use to be submitted. Landowners' claims for higher compensation were also hampered by the fact that many—by some estimates, more than 90 per cent—of land parcels in India are subject to ownership disputes that take decades to resolve in courts.

The method used to determine the cost of buying the land was based primarily on the average registered price of previous transactions, and it disregarded the benefit that would come from the development of the land. With most previous transactions having been registered at less than market price to save on high stamp duty (the balance being mostly paid in unreported cash), there was further loss to those whose lands were being acquired at the average of these under-reported registered prices.

Significant land was acquired for SEZs and urbanization by the state as well as by private developers despite the numerous protests and opposition to the land acquisitions. However, neither the SEZs nor the real estate market took off as anticipated.

In 2017, a non-governmental organization (NGO) petitioned the Supreme Court, requesting that farmers be given back 90 per cent of the 4,842 hectares of land that had been acquired for SEZs but had remained idle in the states of Andhra Pradesh, Maharashtra, Karnataka, Tamil Nadu, West Bengal and Punjab. It stated that, while the government had acquired 2,048 hectares for SEZs in Andhra Pradesh alone, only 4.13 hectares had been used. Quoting a Comptroller and Auditor General of India (CAG) report, the NGO said, 'Of the 50 SEZs approved for the states, only 15 are operational, 6 have been denotified and 29 are still to start commercial activity. Of the 12.47 lac job opportunities these SEZs were intended to create, only 42,000 have come true'. It went on to say that since the SEZ Act of 2005 came into effect, 77 per cent of the notified SEZ land had been concentrated in four states—Andhra Pradesh, Gujarat, Maharashtra and Tamil Nadu—and that these states have acquired 35,415 hectares of the total 45,782 hectares acquired by 20 states. Citing a government committee that stated that more than 2.1 million hectares of agricultural land had been transferred for non-agricultural purposes between 1990 and 2003, it claimed that the land acquired for SEZs was a fraction of the land acquired by governments under the Land Acquisition Act of 1894. It was alleged that industries that were allotted land in SEZs at concessional prices waited for years for the price of the land to rise, and then mortgaged these lands with banks to obtain loans that were diverted for purposes other than setting up industries in the SEZ.[22]

These allegations have some validity. While the acquisition of SEZ land was undertaken with great enthusiasm and fanfare in its early stages, industrial SEZs failed to take off for a variety of reasons. Some reasons included—a change in taxation with the introduction of the minimum alternate tax (MAT), large capital requirements for setting up SEZs of scale, uncompetitiveness, lack of ease-of-business environment, agitations, etc. Many jumped on the bandwagon to aggregate contiguous land at cheap prices, particularly in proximity to existing urban centres, to be used as a land bank for subsequent real estate ventures.

The urbanization and real estate story too has played out differently in India, despite similar imperatives as China. Both faced stagnant agricultural productivity combined with high population dependency in rural areas. Furthermore, both sought to drive economic growth through industrialization and services. Agriculture's contribution to India's GDP fell from 37 per cent in 1981 to 17.5 per cent in 2011. But the proportion of the population that was dependent on agriculture did not decline proportionately, falling only from 66 per cent to 53 per cent during that time.[23]

India's urban population increased from 286 million in 2001 to 377 million in 2011, according to the census of 2011. However, this represented only 31 per cent of the Indian population, compared to 45 per cent in China, 54 per cent in Indonesia and 87 per cent in Brazil. Rural–urban migration contributed about 20 per cent to the growth of urban population. According to experts, India's urban population is expected to reach 600 million (40 per cent) by 2031, and the urban sector's share of the country's GDP is expected to increase from its current 66 per cent to 75 per cent by 2031.[24]

Despite its growth and increasing pace, urbanization in India has taken place in a largely haphazard manner. One major flaw of India's master planning approach has been that it has not allowed market forces to determine the scale and location of economic activity. Urban and government master plans have not included financial planning as a critical component while drafting their plans. They have also not seen land value as a significant source of revenue or a driver of real estate and urban infrastructure financing and growth.

The lack of a properly functioning land market based on clear property rights; ease in transacting the purchase or sale of land; effective enforcement of contracts to buy and sell developed properties; and transparent rules and regulations for redeveloping land or property has hampered the growth and orderly development of Indian cities. As a result, property transactions in India have historically been opaque. Land values are increased by non-transparent changes in land use, higher permitted FSI (total permissible built-up area divided by plot area) or proposed transportation infrastructure in an area. This, in turn, becomes a breeding ground for speculation and corruption through insider trading.

As a response to some of these issues, major projects in a number of cities are now incorporating integrated land use and transportation planning, similar to the China model. As roads and metro corridors are built for connectivity, they are supported by land use changes along their routes, with targeted levies funding a portion of these large infrastructure projects. In Hyderabad, a 1-km stretch on each side of the Outer Ring Road has been designated as a Growth Corridor, with a proposed development fees. Similar transportation-led land use planning is taking place along the corridors of Ahmedabad's Outer Ring Road and Indore's Super Corridor.

Opportunities for urban planning with integrated transport and land use on a much larger scale are also planned in the Golden Quadrilateral, freight corridors and other networks, with enormous scope for planning new cities at nodes of these major intercity transport systems. Similar to the China model, the Delhi–Mumbai Industrial Corridor (DMIC) and the Eastern Dedicated Freight Corridor (EDFC) plan to build a number of hubs for manufacturing and commerce, as well as self-contained, state-of-the-art townships with world-class infrastructure for planned urban and regional development. However, these plans for large-scale urban planning with integrated transport and land use have been hampered by delays in the transportation corridors, the existence of other urban nodes competing with proposed new cities, the large capital outlays involved in these integrated schemes, the lack of institutional financing mechanisms and the limitations of Indian real estate markets and real estate companies.

Urban planning in India has historically relied heavily on compulsory public acquisition of land under the erstwhile 1894 law. Different state governments experimented with various land aggregation models. The state-owned development authority in the national capital of Delhi has long held an inefficient and apathetic monopoly in land acquisition and housing development. Other state governments have adopted the route of private sector initiatives and public–private partnerships (PPP) for land aggregation and development, e.g., in planned developments in Gurugram, Noida, Hyderabad and Bengaluru.[25] These models have, however, also posed their own problems, resulting in large-scale speculation in land and corruption of local town planning and urban authorities.

Ironically, delegation of authority, revenues and empowerment of municipal local government in matters of urban development in democratic India, despite contributing nearly 70 per cent of GDP[26], has been significantly less as compared to authoritarian China. It is only now that tentative efforts in this direction are being made in India, along with a programme to monetize government land in order to raise revenues. However, even if these cut through the red tape of legislation and bureaucracy that has historically entangled them, the monetization opportunity is modest in comparison to the size of the Indian economy.

Real estate, construction and infrastructure will continue to be key drivers of the India economic trajectory, with the highest GDP multiplier (incremental GDP per rupee spent). But, simply put, there is no trillion-dollar privatization opportunity based on government ownership or acquisition of land to monetize, and underwrite a real estate, construction and infrastructure boom for decades as happened in China due to its unique circumstances.

10

The Fourth Yang:
Policy and Infrastructure

China's economic success is most visibly associated with the remarkable story of its infrastructure. Chinese infrastructure is now routinely associated with superlatives such as fastest, longest, largest, most, greatest, best, and so on, thanks to high-speed bullet train networks, fast multi-lane expressways and bridges, gigawatt power projects and cutting-edge telecommunications. The Chinese predilection for centrally directed grand public works, stretching from Shi Huangdi's 'Great Wall' to Chairman Mao's 'Great Leap' has continued in the age of reforms. Its modern achievements in infrastructure, however, dwarf all that has been done before.

China's economic growth story that began with manufacturing and exports-led engine of the coastal SEZs, continued through its domestic demand-led twin engines of real estate and infrastructure. All three engines have powered China to become not only the manufacturing workshop of the world but also its real estate and infrastructure Zhongguo.

The current state of infrastructure in China and India is vastly different, despite the fact that both were comparable till as late as the 1970s. China produced 7.3 billion kWh of electricity in 1952, while India produced 6.3 billion kWh. In the 1950s, India's road network was nearly three times that of China, at 400,000 km. India's railway network in the 1950s was 53,000 km, more than double that of China at 23,000 km.[1] Both had approximately the same low number of telephone subscribers. The story has obviously changed since then. The breathtaking scale of China's and India's growth post its reform and opening-up, is captured in the metrics of just four key infrastructure sectors: power, roads, railways and telecommunications.

Table 2
China's and India's Growth Post Economic Reforms[2]

Key infrastructure sectors	China		India	
	1980	2022	1980	2022
Power				
Installed Capacity (GW)	65.9	2,564	33.3	416
Power Generation (billion Kwh)	285.5	8,389	119.3	1,492
Roads				
Length ('000 km)	883	5,350	644	6,332
Railways				
Length (km)	49,940	155,000	61,240	128,305
High speed network Length (km)	n.a	38,000	n.a	nil
Telecommunications				
Telephone (per '000 persons)	4.3	–	2.3	–
Mobile (per '000 persons)	–	1,206	–	827

The story of China's infrastructure creation is as much an outcome of its economic growth and rapid urbanization as it is of policy. The unlocking and monetization of real estate by local governments have funded this frenzied and symbiotic construction activity-led virtuous economic cycle in housing and infrastructure that has sustained the continued high growth rate of the Chinese economy. Since the introduction of the reform and opening-up policies, the number of China's mainland cities grew from 193 in 1978 to more than 650 in 2018, and towns grew from more than 2,000 to about 20,000.[3] China's policies demonstrated a strategic vision for not only the construction of cutting-edge infrastructure but also for the development of a national competitive advantage over other nations, and building of national champion companies, across manufacturing and technology sectors.

The telecom sector best exemplifies the differences in approaches to infrastructure policy between China and India. The story of the mobile telecom revolution in both countries begin around 1994. In China, it was designated as a national priority. A newly formed Ministry of Information Industry established three competitive state-owned telecom giants—China Telecom, China Unicom and China Mobile—from its previous monolithic telecom department in 1999. It then allowed progressive and calibrated participation by foreign telecom companies under a new regulatory regime, in accordance with its WTO obligations. Its primary focus for private participation in the telecom sector, however, was on telecom equipment and building domestic capabilities in cutting-edge telecom technologies. It accordingly stipulated that foreign equipment vendors, who were eager to enter the massive Chinese market, were required to undertake in technology transfer along with their investments. As a consequence, today Huawei and ZTE—despite multiple allegations and accusations—are global giants that dominate world markets for telecom equipment, having acquired or decimated erstwhile suppliers and collaborators like Nortel and Lucent Technologies. At the end of 2020, around 1.22 billion people—83 per cent of China's population had mobile subscriptions. China is now at the cutting edge of adoption of 5G technology, accounting for nearly 87 per cent of all global 5G connections.[4] China, by all accounts—even as it pivots in its policy and regulatory choices—is now well positioned to ride the crest of the next wave of global value creation on a strong digital foundation.

India's telecom story began in late 1994, with a quasi-markets policy that allowed both state-owned and private players into the telecom market through an auction of licences to private carriers on a competitive bid basis. India also established a separate regulatory authority and tribunal for tariff regulation, dispute resolution and protection of stakeholders' interests while ensuring the telecom sector's orderly growth. However, the high licence fees paid by private companies to obtain licences became a barrier in lowering tariffs, thereby stifling the country's telecommunications growth. Furthermore, the telecom companies were unable to pay their licence fees.

In 2000, the Department of Telecommunications (DoT) reduced licence fees and switched to a gross revenue-sharing model, in which telecom carriers bid on what percentage of revenue they were willing to share with the government. It also increased the permissible stake for foreign investors. The floodgates opened, and many players rushed into the high-potential Indian mobile telecommunications markets, all of which aggressively bid for telecom licences with high revenue sharing, even as they invested massive amounts of capital in equipment rollout and marketing to gain market share. As a result, mobile telephony grew exponentially, and India became one of the world's largest and cheapest telecom markets. However, concerns began to be raised about the policy's costs, effectiveness and long term viability. The massive amounts of capital expenditure being undertaken even as telecom services were priced at unviable levels due to competition was fast turning into a fight to the death among a swarm of telecom companies. This was being done even as they continued to pour in huge sums raised from private and public investors, as well as banks, into this winner-takes-all market bloodbath.

Tasked with balancing stakeholder interests and ensuring market order, India's telecom regulator took a hands-off approach, largely delegating its public policy and public interest role to unbridled and irrationally exuberant markets. The government, too, limited itself to opportunistic financial extraction from the sector through highest revenue sharing and even retrospective taxation. As a result, many companies were taken over, merged or went bankrupt, even as allegations of manipulation and policy adhocism were made.

Allegations of rent-seeking in government processes prompted the judiciary to intervene in policy, directing an auction and revenue maximization approach to all natural resources, including the telecommunications spectrum. This added to the confusion among telecom companies, the government and the judiciary, with each playing multiple roles as players, regulators or adjudicators. As a result, the Indian telecom sector now has only four carriers, two of which are terminally ill and require government assistance. To prevent their collapse and to forestall the Indian telecom market from turning into an unhealthy duopoly, the government is now hard pressed to find solutions to the mess created by a short-sighted policy.

A similar story of technology transfer and absorption, as well as rapid rollout, can be found in China's most visible infrastructure growth—high-speed railways. China, like India, had no high-speed railways at the beginning of the twenty-first century. Since the inception of its rapid rail transit programme in 2008, it has built approximately 38,000 km of high-speed rail that connects all of its major mega-city clusters. Even more remarkably, more than half of that has been completed in the last five years alone. The network's length is expected to double by 2035. Additionally, 75 per cent of China's cities with populations of 500,000 or more have high-speed rail connections. In comparison, Spain has approximately 3,000 km, the UK has 107 km and the US barely qualifies on a single rail route.

China's high-speed rail, like Japan's Shinkansen (bullet trains) in the 1960s, are a symbol of its economic power, rapid modernization and most importantly, growing technological capabilities. It also forms a part of Xi Jinping's plan of integrating its vast national market through 'coordinated development'.

China's policy playbook for establishing itself in the high-speed rail industry was similar to that of telecommunications. It initially relied on technology imported from Europe and Japan to build its network, with global behemoths like Bombardier, Alstom and Mitsubishi eager to collaborate given China's massive market size and ambitious plans. However, as its rail networks have rapidly expanded over the last decade, its domestic companies have emerged as world leaders in high-speed rail technology and engineering.

China's high-speed rail networks are being built at an unprecedented scale and speed. The 815-km, $13.5-billion Zhengzhou East-Guangzhou line was completed in less than five years.[5] With the completion of the new 180 km Xuzhou–Lianyungang line in February 2021, there is now a continuous 3,490 km high-speed rail connection between Jiangsu province and Urumqi, in the Xinjiang autonomous region.[6] Trains on its high-speed network can now travel

1,700 km from Beijing to Harbin in just five hours, at an average speed of 340 km/hr. China's high-speed train network runs more than 9,600 trains per day. On some routes, more than 80 per cent of the track is elevated.[7] Its track, built on concrete viaducts, soars above densely packed cities and valuable agricultural land.

More than 100 tunnels—each 10 km in length, have been built to complete this network, including massive long-span bridges over rivers like the Yangtze. With the technology transfer and experience gained, Chinese companies are now at the cutting edge of new autonomous (driverless) train operation and advanced signalling and control technology. Driverless trains equipped with the latest technologies between Beijing and Zhangjiakou are capable of achieving speeds up to 350 km per hour, making them the world's fastest autonomous trains. China has also tested a prototype of a very high-speed electric train for international routes which can operate at speeds as high as 400 km per hour. Not only can it operate in extreme temperatures, but it also has gauge changing wheelsets that will allow it to operate on other national standard rail networks.

High-speed rail, like telecom, power, ports and roads, is a critical component of China's Belt and Road Initiative (BRI) which was launched in 2013. It has already completed the $5.3 billion Laos–China Railway, a 257-mile line that, although not high-speed, improves connectivity between South China and Vientiane, Laos' capital city. China is also constructing a railway link to Bangkok, Thailand and further south to Singapore. It is already the world's largest supplier of rail transit equipment and technology, and now well-positioned for global exports under its BRI.[8]

It is also important to note that, like other infrastructure sectors like telecom and power, its high-speed network has been built at competitive costs. According to a World Bank report[9], China's high speed rail has cost between $17 million to $21 million per km, even though it has a high ratio of expensive viaducts and tunnels. In Europe, the costs are between $25 million to $39 million per km, while in California, the only US state currently planning a high-speed rail line, it is about $56 million per km.

In comparison, India's first 508-km high-speed bullet train rail link between Mumbai and Ahmedabad is expected to cost between $28 to $30 million per km. Originally scheduled to be commissioned by 2023, its construction schedule has been delayed due to issues in land acquisition for the project.[10] India also plans seven other new high-speed rail link corridors covering a total distance of 4,869 km, including Delhi–Varanasi (865 km), Mumbai–Nagpur (753 km), Delhi–Ahmedabad (886 km), Chennai–Mysore (435 km), Delhi–Amritsar (459 km), Mumbai–Hyderabad (711 km) and Varanasi–Howrah (760 km).[11] The newly introduced high-speed Vande Bharat trains aim to reduce travel time between major cities, but it remains to be seen whether they are also part of a larger and integrated transportation-urbanization high speed corridor-led development nodes network strategy.

The cost competitiveness of China's infrastructure industry is worth investigating. Part of this can be attributed to its authoritarian state, where the cost of removing people from land and acquiring it is low, and labour is cheap. According to a World Bank report on China's high-speed rail, site work and right-of-way costs in litigious California are approximately $10 million per km, or approximately 17.6 per cent of the total cost. In comparison, land acquisition and resettlement costs in China account for less than 8 per cent of total project costs.[12] However, a significant portion of its cost competitiveness and advantage can be attributed to its policy and strategy, which has significant implications for its BRI exports.

To start with, the sheer magnitude of China's high-speed rail programme, as well as a credible plan and commitment to build 10,000 km of network, energized the construction and equipment supply ecosystem. Companies and state institutions increased capacity and invested in innovative techniques as they were assured of high volumes. According to Gerald Ollivier, a World Bank senior transportation specialist, this resulted in lower unit costs as a result of the development of competitive multiple local sources for construction (earthworks, bridges, tunnels, trains, and so on) that used mechanization in construction and manufacturing.

Furthermore, high-cost construction equipment was amortized over a number of projects, which contributed to lower unit costs.

The second factor was standardization. China standardized designs for embankments, track, viaducts, electrification, signalling and communication systems, reducing costs even further. It also standardized construction techniques. For example, by standardizing the design and manufacturing the viaduct bridge beams, the costs of expensive viaducts were reduced. Their span was standardized at 24 or 32 m and was cast in temporary factories set up along the railway alignment. Each beam was transported no more than 8 km by a specially designed vehicle with up to 18 axles. Similar standardization in tunnel construction enabled China to reduce unit costs between $10 million and $15 million per kilometre, compared to New Zealand ($43 million), the US ($50 million) and Australia ($60 million). It also enabled it to tunnel at a faster rate of nearly 5 to 10 m per day.[13]

A similar story has played out in the case of solar energy as the world finally responds to climate change by shifting to renewable energy sources. Eight of the world's top 10 solar companies are Chinese. Its solar supply chains' economies of scale now dominate global manufacturing. Chinese firms control 64 per cent of global polysilicon and wafer production and 80 per cent of global solar cell production.[14] China also leads the world in electric vehicle batteries and ecosystems, with a similar hold on global supply chains. All have followed a similar policy, strategy, scale and finance pattern as in telecommunications and thermal power, except this time it is in technology-led sunrise industries that will shape the global future.

In contrast, India has struggled to capitalize on early opportunities to build globally competitive infrastructure and industries. Since 1991, its policy across sectors has been defined by an abdication of responsibilities to private participation, opening the sector and its markets to global competition and limiting itself to a regulatory and fiscal role. Market forces and finance, it was hoped, would enable the emergence of globally competitive industries and national champions. However, the result has not materialized as planned.

A part of this can be attributed to the political processes and the nature of institutional power in the Indian democratic state, coupled with challenges related to land acquisition, procedural delays of PPPs, a lack of political capital and will in coalition governments, allegations of corruption, judicial intervention into executive policy domains, the need to win elections and the intertwined funding relationship among politicians, industry and the bureaucracy. However, a significant part of this can also be attributed to the manner in which policymaking in India during the reform period lacked political capital and direction. It thereby became a limited domain of senior economists and bureaucrats, rather than an integrated political and administrative machinery with feedback loops at all levels of government from the grassroots upwards.

The euphoria of private investments-led growth in telecommunications, power, roads and airports between 2004 to 2014, built amid allegations of crony capitalism for obtaining contracts and loans from state-owned banks, ended in denouement, recrimination and electoral loss of the political formation that adopted this policy. The resulting wreckage in terms of overleveraging, bankruptcies, non-performing assets of banks, reluctance to lend and setback to the sentiment and momentum of the economy took nearly eight years to normalize.

Even in sunrise industries like solar, having earlier missed the bus in terms of building national competitive advantage or national champions in telecommunications equipment by leveraging its huge domestic market, the India story so far has been as an importer of Chinese equipment than having any domestic manufacturing capability.

Only recently, in cutting-edge technology sectors such as electric vehicles and hydrogen, efforts are underway to capture global leadership in innovation and manufacturing. Simultaneously, 5G and 6G telecom technologies, solar and semiconductor manufacturing facilities are being developed indigenously to secure key geostrategic concerns in a polarizing and increasingly protectionist world. Its outcomes, in light of the multiple centrifugal forces that act upon it, are however, uncertain.

11

The Fifth Yang: Entrepreneurship

Beyond the aerial, 30,000-ft view of policy and strategy, totalitarian administration and enabling environment, lies the story of entrepreneurship—the invisible ingredient or the secret sauce of economic success. It is inarguable that despite its authoritarian political system, dominance of state-owned enterprises and poorly designed and enforced institutional infrastructure, communist China has offered scope for large scale and widespread entrepreneurial action at an unprecedented scale. It has enabled an environment in which new factories, new age businesses, cities and infrastructure have been built for both global and domestic markets, as a result of which, its economy has grown so rapidly as to be among the largest in the world.

It is important to note that, as against the Anglo/European model of privatization followed in England and Russia, China's success in transitioning its economy has been in creating new enterprises rather than selling off old ones. As Douglass North notes, 'the Chinese developed an incentive structure which managed to produce rapid economic development without any of the standard recipes of the West.'[1] What is even more remarkable is how an entrepreneurial culture has not only emerged but prospered despite the heavy weight of China's totalitarian institutions. All entrepreneurship has an inherent risk-taking and rule-breaking nature, which is mostly at odds with a state's inherent role of reducing uncertainty and enforcing rules, more so in a communist totalitarian command economy. How then did China's political and economic institutions promote entrepreneurship? Or is it that entrepreneurs manage to thrive despite the institutions?

It is evident that the factors that have contributed to China's economic growth and achievements would not have come together without the organization and leadership of entrepreneurs, known as *neng ren* (capable men) in many parts of China. There is also evidence that entrepreneurial ventures grew resiliently and quickly despite a changing, unstable and even hostile institutional environment. This story of private entrepreneurial resilience is best narrated by Zhang Chunlai, an entrepreneur in the city of Tangshan, and his 'theory of wild chickens':

> Who are the *minban* (non-state) enterprises? They are those who do not rely on the State, do not occupy any critical industries of the national economy, but have to grow at the periphery. By way of an analogy, they are like a flock of wild chickens searching for any eatables in deserted mountains. […] Excellent *minban* entrepreneurs are the strongest of surviving the 'wild environment'; therefore, they are more efficient in producing eggs. The smartest investment by the State is to adopt an easy-going policy, nursing a favorable, supporting and protecting environment. In return, we will let the State and the government pick up more eggs.[2]

The analogy clearly suggests that state-owned enterprises (SOE) were the domestic chickens that were raised in much better conditions but produced far fewer 'eggs'. Therefore, it was in the interest of the state to provide more support to the private sector. But how has the state's easygoing tolerance or forbearance policy translated into entrepreneurial success on the ground?

This has been a subject of academic interest as well, given the complexities of the process of creating a legally valid entrepreneurship in a communist economy transitioning to a market-oriented one. Entrepreneurs operating at the periphery in this rapidly dynamic environment have to acquire political and administrative protection from within the fast-changing institutional boundaries. In a totalitarian state with no 'rule of law' as understood in its Western context, successful entrepreneurs connect business opportunities in the market to institutional gaps so that opportunities can be seized without provoking political, administrative or public relations problems. In this environment, legitimizing business innovations becomes a constant and necessary part of the entrepreneurial process. This is especially true when entrepreneurial ventures are deemed as potentially threatening to the dominant political ideology and system, administrative authorities or the widely accepted moral codes. Two features of the Chinese institutional structure have created a unique entrepreneurial culture. Firstly, during the initial years of reform and opening-up, the CPC ruled China more through policy rather than formalized law. In practice, this means that the CPC leaders proposed ideas that were then debated in a larger group, likely the Political Bureau of the Central Committee, and a final decision was reached collectively. These ideas were then technically and administratively specified as regulations by the State Council and the People's Congress. The roots of prioritizing policy over law can be traced back to the CPC's struggle for political power during the Civil War and the fight against the Japanese. It discovered that, when compared to laws, policies were more adaptable in dealing with complex problems across a large country. Since then, the practice has largely continued. Laws demand a high logical consistency, leave little room for errors and manipulation, but most importantly, acquire a defined principle and interpretation of their own. In comparison, party policies, while comprehensive, are logically coherent and consistent, and can be formulated as general principles in a short period and applied in all relevant situations without sacrificing flexibility. As a result, policymakers can tailor policies to their own interests based on the existing situation.

Secondly, unlike in other economies where government agencies are officially far less involved—if not outright prohibited—from profit-making activities, the political careers and personal well-being of Chinese government officials are directly related to improving local economic conditions. Party policy at the local level is, therefore, likely to be interpreted and implemented in this context, with bureaucrats having the authority to determine the legitimacy of new enterprises. The manner in which this has played out in China's new entrepreneurial culture is best represented by two stories: one of toasted sunflower seeds that allowed entrepreneurship; and the other, more well known, of new-age technology companies that reminded entrepreneurs their subservience to the CPC and state objectives.

In 1972, a local entrepreneur named Nian Guangjiu (nicknamed 'the Fool') started a business of toasted sunflower seeds, a popular snack in China. Local officials initially encouraged him to grow sunflower seeds in order to demonstrate that they were following the general policy of promoting individual businesses. The business, however, became a roaring success, and local officials quickly realized that it was a risky political gamble. By 1981, the Fool had already employed more than 100 people and paid a tax of more than 300,000 yuan, an amount likely equivalent to a local area's total revenue in those years. According to them, the company was no longer an 'individual' now, but had evolved into a 'capitalist' enterprise. Some local officials proposed putting him in jail on the charge of exploitation. Evidently, the rule-makers at that time were not united behind a clear principle. In fact, they were torn between developing their local economies and remaining politically correct. Clarity was achieved through the following policy document, published in 1983:

> We are a socialist nation, and thus will not allow the existence of exploiting institutions. But we are also a developing nation with still a relatively low level of production and underdevelopment of commodities, particularly in rural areas. It is therefore beneficial for the development of socialist economy to allow a certain level of mobility and various combinations of finance, technology, and labor ... For those who have employed more than what the regulation has permitted, we should not recommend or disseminate publicly, but nor shall we be in a hurry to eliminate them. What we should do is to provide proper guidance so that they will develop into various types of cooperative economy.[3]

In the matter of the Fool's toasted sunflower seeds, the pragmatic Deng Xiaoping suggested a 'wait and see' policy and dismissed the hostile approach to solving the case:

With regard to some other problems, we don't have to be impatient for quick solutions. For instance, the emergence of privately hired labor was quite shocking a while back [...] In my opinion, that problem can be set aside for a couple of years [...] If we act on the question now, people will say the policies have changed, and they will be upset. If you put the man who makes 'Fool's Sunflower Seeds' out of business, it will make many people anxious, and that won't do anybody any good. What is there to be afraid of if we let him go on selling his seeds for a while? Will that hurt socialism?

There were two outcomes to this 'wait and see' policy, which lasted for about four years from 1983 to 1986 and gave tacit consent to private businesses while only a few ambiguous rules were published by the CPC. To the entrepreneurs, the absence of rules was an encouraging sign but with great uncertainty. They could go ahead, but they had to proceed with caution. Also, China's top leaders actually put the fate of private businesses in the hands of local authorities. Businesses in areas with a liberal local leader, mostly in the coastal provinces, benefitted from friendlier policies and better administration while those in areas with conservative leadership faced harsher treatment.

So, how did this new 'wait and see' policy play out within the party and the state institutional structure during the reform era? The emergence of private enterprise posed a dilemma for many local officials. These enterprises could significantly contribute to the much-needed economic growth in their area. However, they were not the type of businesses that the CPC was supposed to support based on the ideological principles that it had held for so long. Debate within the CPC over how to solve the dilemma prevented the formation of a clear policy. As a result, the CPC adopted a 'wait and see' strategy, allowing but not openly encouraging private enterprises.

Between 1978 to 1986, the CPC largely relinquished its responsibility for guiding this sector of the national economy. There was no talk, no discussion, no document, no research and no indication of its position. In short, there were no institutional rules in place during this time period. After identifying potential market opportunities to address, entrepreneurs started their businesses with the goal of escaping poverty.

By 1987, economic pragmatism had gained an upper hand over communist ideology and the CPC granted private enterprises a legitimate status in its thirteenth Congress in October 1987. The big lesson that the CPC learnt during this period and from managing economic reforms was the importance of keeping their policies as stable as possible. Recalling the case of the Fool's sunflower seeds in 1992, Deng Xiaoping made this point very clear in his famous South China tour:

> In the initial stage of the rural reform, there emerged in Anhui Province the issue of the 'Fool's Sunflower Seeds'. Many people felt uncomfortable with this man who had made a profit of 1 million yuan. They called for action to be taken against him. I said that no action should be taken, because that would make people think we had changed our policies, and the loss would outweigh the gain. There are many problems like this one, and if we don't handle them properly, our policies could easily be undermined and overall reform affected. The basic policies for urban and rural reform must be kept stable for a long time to come.

As a result, entrepreneurship thrived in a regime of no or few rules and flexible policy, particularly in sectors where there were few SOEs operating in nationally strategic sectors. Even in sectors with rules and the presence of institutions that discriminated against private ownership, entrepreneurs would try to circumvent these constraints. The 'red cap' phenomenon best exemplifies the flexible nature of policy and even the business form in China not being a barrier to entrepreneurship. Keming Yang, associate professor of sociology at Durham University writes in his book, *Entrepreneurship in China*:

> A firm has two ownerships, one nominal and the other actual. The nominal ownership is registered with the Bureau of the

Administration of Industries and Commerce. The actual ownership is the firm's true nature. A private firm can obtain a legitimate ownership once it is registered as, or becomes a part of, a public enterprise, either state-owned or collectively owned. This strategy is dubbed as 'red cap' or 'fake public' phenomenon in China.[4]

There are a variety of ways of putting on a red cap. One method is to pay an extra fee to a local government for obtaining a public identity. The fee amount is negotiable between the firm and the local bureaucracy. Another method is to set up a private firm within a state or collective enterprise, with the private firm negotiating financial terms with the protecting firm. As Yang writes:

> Obviously this behavior is cheating, but to many people in China, it is absolutely understandable and acceptable. Although no one has stood out to defend such cheating publicly, the fact that so many entrepreneurs and officials are involved [...] it is claimed that about 80 percent of collective firms in Guangdong province were private in 1999 [...] In March 1998, the State Council issued a directive requiring private firms to take off their 'red cap' and show their true private ownership.[5]

In China, entrepreneurship has long required a partnership between entrepreneurs and officials or any agent with access to valuable information, power or tangible resources. The Western concept of entrepreneurship focusses on an individual's ability to identify and capitalize on profitable opportunities. In contrast, the ability to form an alliance with those economic agents who possess or control the financial, physical or human assets required to succeed in the marketplace is the key determinant of successful entrepreneurship in China.

Guanxi, a social construct unique to China, played an important role in forging alliances as entrepreneurs capitalized on opportunities in the early years of the reform and opening-up process. The 'dual track' price system introduced in 1984, for example, allowed state enterprises to sell a portion of their resources to other firms at market price. As a result, many commodities had two prices: one set by the government and one set by the market, with the market price typically being much higher. While private enterprises would mostly have to pay the market price, some with connections could pay less by 'yielding some of the difference between the two prices to the person in control of these resources. In such situations, competition was more about connections to powerful persons than better products and services.'[6]

In many ways, it is crony capitalism with Chinese characteristics. It has also resulted in a scale of corruption that is so rampant, widespread and deep that it threatens the very foundations of the communist Chinese state. Cracking down on corruption is now one of Xi Jinping's topmost priorities. But the role of flexible policies, entrepreneurship and alliances in China's remarkable entrepreneur-fuelled economic growth is undeniable.

However, the recent crackdown on technology companies, particularly Jack Ma's Ant Group, exemplifies the uncertainty of entrepreneurship and the subservience of all activity, including private business, to the CPC's objectives. Ant Group, arguably China's most famous private conglomerate, was set to go public in November 2020 with an initial public offering of $37 billion and listing on international stock exchanges. Jack Ma, the billionaire Alibaba e-commerce tycoon, was China's biggest corporate star and had wielded statesman-like powers with proximity to the CPC leadership.

In 2017, he travelled to New York to meet then President-elect Donald Trump just days before his inauguration, promising to create a million American jobs in an informal and televised press conference. It was an outing that attracted the displeasure of the Chinese government, who reportedly had no prior knowledge. This came at a time when there were tensions between the two countries on account of Trump's repeated criticism of China during his electoral campaign, holding it responsible for the loss of American jobs. A concern that was apparently communicated to Ma. However, Ma continued with his global outreach between 2018 and 2020, meeting high-profile figures including the UN Secretary General, the Queen of Jordan and the Belgian premier. The relationship between Ma and Beijing, however, reached its nadir when authorities cracked down on Ma's business empire after a speech he gave in Shanghai in October 2020, accusing financial watchdogs of stifling innovation.

China's regulators swiftly suspended the proposed listing of his Ant Group just two days before its launch on 5 November 2020, ordered restructuring of the Ant Group and launched antitrust investigations into Ma's businesses. It further imposed a record $2.75 billion fine on Alibaba in April 2021. In larger concerns regarding concentration and dominance of economic and monopoly power, it also clamped down across the private sector space, tightening oversight and regulations of companies in technology, real estate, gaming, education, cryptocurrencies and finance. It is likely that Ma was provocative and out of step with the new approach to governance as enunciated by Xi Jinping and was, therefore, a natural first target for sending out the message.

However, his fall from favour with the CPC authorities was abrupt and immediate. According to reports, Ma requested an audience with at least two people in Xi's inner circle immediately following the suspension of his initial public offering (IPO) but his requests were turned down. He subsequently disappeared from public view, only emerging after nearly a year on a visit to Europe, ostensibly on an 'agriculture and technology study tour related to environmental issues'. During this year, he apparently wrote to Xi Jinping directly, offering to devote the rest of his life to China's rural education. Tsai, his co-founder at Alibaba is quoted downplaying Ma's influence, saying: 'He's lying low right now. I talk to him every day. The idea that Jack has this enormous amount of power, I think that's not quite right… He is just like you and me, he's a normal individual.'[7] Jack Ma was (then) reported to be presently residing in Japan on a teaching sabbatical.

However, as with all other policies in China, policy on technology and entrepreneurship has been recalibrated after the necessary message has been delivered and the impact assessed. Rules on certain sectors

and platforms have been eased, promising stability and transparency while concerns on data security and online content remain.[8] However, again, as with everything in China, what ultimately matters is the CPC, its leadership and the paramount leader's point of view. In India, by contrast, private entrepreneurship has co-existed with state-owned enterprises since Independence. Private enterprise during this period was, however, hobbled by manufacturing capacity licencing, limited credit and shareholder ownership restrictions. It was also viewed by the state administration and a large section of public as a grubby version of exploitative crony capitalism through corrupt politicians and bureaucrats. By the time liberalization began in the 1990s, India had a large number of established industrial houses of significant size and presence. These industrial houses have grown since, as have other new homegrown entrepreneurs.

The growth of services, particularly in technology and software, has been a remarkable success story in India, with India's exports increasing exponentially. However, in comparison to China's explosive industrialization and entrepreneurial growth since reform and opening-up process in 1978, the scale of activity in India was modest. There are several possible explanations for China's explosive industrialization and entrepreneurial growth. First, the unleashing of an inherent but dormant spirit of risk-taking, particularly in coastal South China's Cantonese-speaking communities. Second, the risk capital flowing in from a strong and commercially vibrant diaspora community from Hong Kong and Taiwan—contentious parts of China but with strong family ties. Third, the greater incentive to escape from the bone-grinding poverty and scarcity that characterized Maoist pre-reform China.

However, the nature of the relationship between India's institutional framework and entrepreneurship also played a significant role. India's institutional framework, patterned on the British model, is dominated by two features. The first, an administrative bureaucracy. The second, the bifurcation of powers between the legislature, executive and the judiciary. During its colonial period, which required the British to rule the vast subcontinental landmass and its large population with only a handful of expatriates, a pyramidal administrative structure was created throughout British-ruled India. A small and elite cadre of expatriate officers, the Indian Civil Service (ICS) was created. Ruled territories were divided into districts, with an ICS officer at its apex. The officer represented the colonial state in all its primary civil functions—collecting tax as the district collector; ensuring law and order; and administering justice as the district magistrate. The district collectors and magistrates in turn reported to provincial governments and a central government, all staffed by senior expatriate ICS officers. It was an administrative design for ensuring a colonial power's control over its territories. The institutional administrative structure, however, remained largely unchanged after Independence. The only change undertaken was that the earlier judicial function was bifurcated into a separate judicial service from the district level upwards, with the Supreme Court as the apex judicial institution. The administration continued to remain small and elite with the erstwhile ICS being replaced, in all its other positions and functions, by the Indian Administrative Service (IAS).

The hegemony of the executive and bureaucracy in unquestioned decision-making was, however, impacted in the constitutional separation of powers of the state between the legislature, executive and the judiciary. Envisaging as a system of 'checks and balances', the history of independent India is also a story of contestation for power between the executive and judiciary. Indira Gandhi's Emergency of 1975 was the nadir of an independent judiciary. However, the long period of coalition governments over the three decades of reforms saw an assertion of judicial 'activism' and 'public interest litigation' that expanded its remit into matters that, till then, were exlusively the domain of executive policy. This contestation of power between these two powerful arms of the state and the continuation of a colonial administrative framework, had two adverse outcomes from an economic point of view. The impact of the first is best illustrated in what became widely known as the 'coal scam'.

During the liberalization period in early 1990s, the central government decided to relinquish its coal monopoly and, in order to increase coal production and availability, allocated identified coal blocks that were not part of its public sector units to private companies. However, there were no concrete guidelines for block allocation because coal mining had previously been restricted to public sector units and many locations were deemed unprofitable for mining. Allocation guidelines were developed, and they were revised in 1993, 1998 and 2003. Based on these, between 1993 and 2005, 70 coal mines were allocated. Between 2006 and 2010, an additional 146 blocks were allocated.[9]

A report issued in 2012 by the CAG, a statutory and independent auditor under India's constitutional framework, revealed irregularities in coal block allocation. It estimated the loss to the government exchequer at ₹18 lakh crore. According to the CAG, the government had the authority to auction the coal blocks but chose not to do so. As a result, those who got the coal block allocation received a 'windfall gain'. As the Opposition targeted the UPA-led coalition government, the Central Bureau of Investigation (CBI), India's premier law enforcement agency, opened investigations. A Parliamentary Committee also looked into the matter and found that the coal block allocations from 1993 to 2008 were done illegally. In light of the ongoing mess, the Supreme Court took matters into its own hands, ordering the CBI to report directly to it rather than the government. Many prominent industrialists, politicians and bureaucrats became embroiled in the controversy, with the CBI even conducting an investigation into then Prime Minister (PM) Manmohan Singh.

Prime Minister Manmohan Singh refuted allegations of fraud, calling the CAG's computations of 'loss' misleading. He argued that the primary coal-producing states of West Bengal, Chhattisgarh, Jharkhand and Orissa, which were then ruled by Opposition parties, were strongly opposed to switching to competitive bidding. These states believed competitive bidding would raise the cost of coal, thereby negatively impacting value addition and industrial development in their states, while also diluting their prerogative in selecting coal mine lessees.

In response to allegations of windfall gains to those allotted mines without competitive bidding, he argued that calculating extractable reserves based on averages was incorrect because the cost of coal production varied from mine to mine, even for public sector units, and the units allocated to private companies for captive mining were those outside the public sector units' production plans and generally in areas with more difficult geological conditions. In terms of 'loss to the exchequer', he argued that a portion of the profits would be appropriated by the government through taxation, with an additional 26 per cent of profits required to be allocated to local area development.

Since 2012, the CBI has filed numerous chargesheets. In 2017 and 2018, it secured the convictions of senior bureaucrats, including the Secretary—the highest official in the coal ministry—who were sentenced to jail on charges of withholding information from the PM (who was also the coal minister at the time) and distorting facts in granting approvals. In the 2G telecommunications spectrum allocation case, widely known as the '2G scam', the CAG made a similar allegation, estimating the loss to the exchequer at ₹1.75 lakh crore.

The coal block allocation and the 2G spectrum allocation cases were among the reasons that the UPA government came to be perceived as corrupt, contributing to its subsequent electoral loss in 2014. More importantly, it prompted the Supreme Court to intervene in executive policy, cancelling allocations retroactively and ordering that all 'sovereign natural resources' be auctioned off to maximize revenue to the exchequer. It later clarified that not all resources would require to be auctioned, and acknowledged the right of the government to set policy. But the uncertainty in the business environment had already set in.

The consequence of this contestation between policy and 'public interest' law in its economic impact was immense. Private participation across sectors, particularly infrastructure, collapsed. Those who had already undertaken significant capital expenditure on their projects under implementation based on these allocations, mostly with loans from public sector banks, were now stranded.

Projects stalled, cost overruns mounted, defaults and non-performing assets at public sector banks ensued. Many private entrepreneurs and companies were bankrupt. Coal reserves remained unmined and production was lower than what it could have been with private participation. There was also a missing positive impact that lower coal costs could have had on industrial growth in general.

In telecommunication and other infrastructure sectors, which followed the auction model, exuberant bidding and rigid 'letter of the law' rules versus policy guidelines saw visibly unviable bids being awarded public projects by a now cautious administration, even while all stakeholders acknowledged their impossibility. With subsequent efforts failing at changing bid terms of these projects to make them viable through crony lobbying in the new environment, these projects stalled, leading to defaults on huge loans taken from public sector banks.

In economic terms, the clash between a crony capitalism *jugaad* (makeshift) of entrepreneurship and rule-based governance structure of administrative institutions (particularly law), the resultant business paralysis and environment uncertainty resulted in a significant setback to India's economic growth as projects stalled, were abandoned or bankrupted in the crisis that followed. Interestingly, China's flexibility of policy guidelines, as interpreted at multiple levels of government, has enabled it to pursue a growth that is consistent with its objectives. China too has faced rampant corruption, and crony capitalism in its reform process. The CCP has attempted to tackle these separately through periodic anti-corruption campaigns such as 'tigers and flies'.[10] Corruption has, however, been prosecuted at the individual level in both party and state organizations, while ensuring no adverse fallout on either policy or implementation.

The complexities of the Indian state and the democratic process have shaped and hobbled entrepreneurship and its outcomes at every turn. The incentives for performance are few in an unaccountable bureaucracy dominated by a small and elite service cadre, where officers are generalists with short tenures. As a result, rent seeking often becomes rampant, with every rule providing yet another opportunity for obstructive corruption in the system. The story of Sajan Parayil—a 48-year-old NRI businessman from Kerala who committed suicide in 2019 due to alleged institutional harassment and no redressal mechanism or accountability—made national headlines.

According to media reports, he had spent about ₹18 crore of his life savings to construct a convention hall in Anthoor municipality in Kannur district, only to be denied permission by municipal officials. The entrepreneur reportedly made about 19 visits to the municipality office but was sent back every time by the officials citing minor issues, like pillars of the building were 1.5 inches off the construction plan, and so on. The family of the businessman blamed local ruling party members for pushing Parayil over the brink. The case brought other similar stories to public attention. These included a 'contract' between a granite quarry owner and local ruling party leadership seeking 'rent', a business in Kozhikode that waited for three years for permission from the city corporation to run a manufactured sand unit, the suicide of an NRI entrepreneur who was asked by local politicians to pay them a large sum of money to construct a workshop on leased land, and so on.

The stories have largely been the same across states, scale and types of businesses, ranging from large enterprises to small- and medium-sized businesses, to retail mom-and-pop convenience stores and street vendors. There have been significant reductions in permissions required and improvements in 'ease of doing business' rankings—a measure of the difficulty of undertaking entrepreneurial ventures. However, concerns about the entrepreneur's and business's vulnerability to predatory and unaccountable bureaucrats and politicians adept at raising red tape objections or creating operational difficulties on the ground persist.

Part Four

The Costs of Growth

12

The First Yin: Debt

High economic growth stories always have an underbelly of vulnerability—usually consisting of large amounts of financial debt that have fuelled unprecedented expansion and, when the peak is reached, widespread defaults that cause the economy to slow and contract. This boom-bust cycle consumes much of the attention of financial markets and central banks alike. Companies and markets attempt to time the cycle in order to profit from it, while central banks attempt to manage the cycle's path through monetary policy in order to extend it as long as possible while also ensuring a soft landing on the inevitable downward curve. This has been the pattern in all modern market economies, with banking systems and institutions that have evolved over time as a largely efficient and sustainable financial ecosystem. The case of China, however, is different.

The financial sector in China was underdeveloped when the reform and opening-up of the economy began to gather pace in the early 1980s. Being a command economy, its focus under Mao was on agricultural and industrial productivity, growth in output, and so on. The communist state allocated capital for new projects or plant operations based on a national priorities assessment, with no concept of returns, profits, repayments, interest rates or commercial principles that underpin the modern monetary capitalist economy. The initial export-led manufacturing special economic zone (SEZ) boom in coastal China was financed by foreign funds, primarily from Hong Kong and Taiwan, with little involvement from state-owned Chinese banks. Even as the Chinese economy liberalized and expanded, and the real estate market began to emerge in 1994, state-owned banks continued to lend primarily to state-owned enterprises (SOE), with much of the financing for the rest of the economy coming from the country's shadow banking sector. It wasn't until the 2008 global financial crisis (GFC), which resulted in a dramatic drop in Chinese exports and national employment along with a manufacturing crisis, that real estate and infrastructure were fired up in a big way as domestic engines of economic growth. That stimulus has never stopped since then.

Many people believe that China's economy is primarily driven by exports which renders it the status of the 'factory of the world'. While this was especially true in its early years, its economic growth over the last decade-and-a-half has been driven by the state's massive expansion programme in urbanization and infrastructure, which has seen its financial system lend huge funds for the construction of new housing and infrastructure. A government-led economic stimulus, however, is not unusual. It is a standard tool of post-Keynesian economics used by countries all over the world.

What makes China different is that, unlike most others, it was not a full-fledged market economy, or an economy with a developed financial sector. As a result, debt has become the core of the Chinese growth engine. China's total debt to gross domestic product (GDP) ratio, as of 2021, stands at 290 per cent, up from below 150 per cent in 2006. In itself, it is comparable to the United States (US) (296 per cent), the eurozone (292 per cent) and far below Japan (405 per cent).[1]

The issue with China's debt is, however, not its size but the rate at which it has grown, along with the composition of the debt. Since 2008, China has added roughly the size of the entire US banking system. Over the last decade, the size of China's banking system has quadrupled. Not all of that debt has been productive. Unoccupied apartment towers and districts, underutilized infrastructure, huge manufacturing capacities that sit idle and land reclamations that have gone unused are evidence of debt that has been squandered on such projects and will never be repaid. Further, unlike other economies where the largest component is government debt, the largest portion of borrowings in China is by the corporate sector, or non-financial sector borrowings (160 per cent of the GDP).[2] However, unlike in functioning markets where bank and company ownership is separate and transactions are based on commercial creditworthiness, the majority of this debt is lending by state-owned banks to state-owned firms on the directions of the state. Many of these state-owned firms are 'zombie' firms with no commercial or financial viability, and the lending is based only on an implicit state-backed guarantee. State-owned firms account for between 23 per cent to 28 per cent of China's economy[3], but have borrowed, by some accounts, over 80 per cent of all corporate debt.[4] Further, the bottom 90 per cent of state-owned firms account for 45 per cent of corporate debt.[5] According to McKinsey, between 2007 and 2014, China's corporate debt went from $3.4 trillion to $12.5 trillion, the fastest ever by any economy in modern times. At the end of 2015, corporate debt in China had grown to 163 per cent of GDP, up from 120 per cent in 2011. This was significantly higher than the US (71 per cent) and Germany (52 per cent).[6] The productivity of these loans in the tsunami of borrowings undertaken in this short time span, particularly by the state-owned corporate sector in the last decade, is anyone's guess. It is also a growing cause of global concern.

The borrowings of China's state-owned firms from its state-owned banks are, however, only one part of its growing debt problem. The other—and perhaps, even greater risk—is the threat posed by its shadow banking sector that is now facing a deepening crisis. Shadow banking refers to financial services and loans that are outside the highly regulated formal banking system. China's shadow banking sector has provided funds to non state-owned businesses that have found it hard to tap the traditional state-owned banks for financing. The size of China's shadow banking sector, according to a report by China's top banking regulator, was estimated at $12 trillion accounting for 86 per cent of China's GDP in 2019.[7]

The biggest of the businesses that shadow banking has financed is the real estate sector, which comprises an estimated one-fourth of China's economy. China's real estate sector—critical to local government finances, financing of real estate companies for construction and inventory, and a significant investment asset for many Chinese households—is heavily dependent on funds from shadow banking. In turn, the shadow banking sector is critically dependent on the real estate sector.

Over the last two decades, and particularly post the GFC in 2008, local government financing vehicles (LGFVs) have pledged land to raise funds for their budgets and regional development plans, while real estate companies like Evergrande have raised construction funds from the shadow banking sector. Chinese households too rushed to buy their homes—or speculate on property—as prices rose. With funds being available with few restrictions, real estate companies embarked on ambitious expansion, thereby setting in motion a cycle of ever-increasing land and real estate prices. The shadow banking sector, in turn, promised high returns on their 'investment management' products to investors to raise funds to finance these loans.

This frenzied cycle in the real estate sector continued for long despite evident and increasing signs of stress of unsold inventory and softening real estate prices. At the root of the problem was the unsustainable debt that real estate companies had borrowed from the shadow banking sector. The government finally cracked down on real estate companies in August 2020 by setting limits on their debt levels. Unable to meet their repayments, Chinese property giants such as Evergrande and Country Garden defaulted. The defaults of real estate companies caused a crisis in the shadow banking sector. In a domino effect, shadow banks like Zhongrong, which had given large loans to real estate companies, were unable to repay their investors. This snowballed into a crisis that has spread from the real estate sector to the shadow banking sector, and now threatens the financial savings and real estate investments of Chinese investors and households. According to Logan Wright, Chair in Chinese Business and Economics, Centre for Strategic and International Studies:

> The deleveraging campaign that China's leadership launched in 2016 to reduce systemic financial risks is the only logical starting point to explain how China's structural economic slowdown

began. [...] China's economic growth over the next 5 to 10 years will depend upon how successfully and efficiently the financial system can shift its resources away from property-related lending and local government investment projects and towards more productive private sector firms.[8]

Resolving its growing debt crisis will, however, be only the first step. Difficult reforms shall have to be undertaken in an uncertain global economic environment. As global companies adopt a China Plus One strategy by shifting of supply chains, increasingly fractious geopolitics and a slowing growth rate, there is nervousness about the scale of the problem and its potential impact on China's growth and future. China's underdeveloped financial sector also faces structural issues that pose significant challenges to reforms. Unlike market economies that have well developed and independently regulated banking and financial sectors, which offer a wide range of options for both household savings and borrowings, household participation in China's financial sector is comparatively less.

The Chinese have traditionally been debt averse, and household borrowings comprise a relatively small segment of debt in China. High savings rates have been among the traditional habits of the Chinese with a significant part of their growing financial prosperity being deployed in owning a home. In fact, with historically low interest rates being offered by the state-owned banks in the controlled economy, a significant component of their household savings has been parked as real estate investments. China today, has nearly 65 million vacant houses, enough to accommodate the entire population of France. As real estate prices soften, these household savings in real estate investments are at risk of losing value.

Further, under communist China's command economy, all government, non-government, corporate, bank and investment or wealth management products are perceived to come with an implicit state guarantee. In other market economies, forces of creation and destruction keep people running only commercially viable businesses in both the corporate and financial sectors. However, the moral hazard of China's implicit state guarantee, and therefore state intervention, has kept the bubble growing, as even more money has been lent to state-owned zombie firms and the property boom has continued to grow over the years. This sweeping under the rug of non-performing assets (NPAs) in pursuit of record economic growth has now reached unsustainable levels and these sectors are now in crisis.

Lack of transparency and credible data in the Chinese economic and financial system, particularly the real estate and shadow banking sectors, make an assessment of the size of this problem difficult, if not impossible. Yet, the dominoes may not fall. In the banking and financial sector in which the state controls all levers of power, including interest rates, it is likely that the cost of most NPAs may be inflated away on bank balance sheets, as was done earlier.

At the end of the 1990s, China's banking system was reported to have been technically insolvent, with nearly 40 per cent of its loans turning non-performing as state-owned firms were unable to repay loans. With funds being scarce, the Chinese authorities recapitalized the faltering banks by setting an upper limit on the maximum deposit rate that banks could offer on savings and a floor limit on the minimum rate at which the banks could lend. This fixed minimum margin by banks on their loans ensured both their profitability and their recapitalization. What, however, was neglected in the process was the 'moral hazard' of this method of recapitalization. With every loan the banks lent to borrowers, their profits increased. And when the banks massively expanded lending during the GFC, their profits expanded accordingly.

In late 2013, Yao Jingyuan, the former chief economist and spokesman of National Bureau of Statistics of China compared banking in China to a highway toll system, remarking, 'With this kind of operational model, banks will continue making money even if all the bank presidents go home to sleep and you replace them by putting a small dog in their seats'.[9] The problem was further exacerbated by the reluctance of banks to lend to the now over-the-decades well-grown private sector. As a result, banks sought to exponentially expand its loans to SOEs with their implicit state guarantee.

While solutions to deal with a growing debt problem may be found at the financial level, what would, however, be more difficult to deal with is the impact on the non-financial economy. Property prices continue to be soft, after decades of strong growth, threatening both the story and the sentiment upon which much of China's prosperity has been achieved. Efforts to reduce the dependence of local governments on real estate monetization have been met with limited success, with alternate sources of raising revenue for them through the introduction of property tax, meeting with stiff resistance. Attempts to turn off the loan financing and widespread shutdown of state-owned zombie firms could also lead to job losses and social strife in a slowing economy.

Another significant cause of worry is the impact on the construction and its allied industries, which employ more than 50 million people in China. While bad loan estimates in China's strictly controlled financial data economy vary and are difficult to rely on, evidence of underutilization and wastage of the assets created from this financing indicates that the problem is of a humongous scale. The massive construction capacity that has been created during the boom is the greatest economic multiplier in its economy, fuelling its growth over decades.

The need to keep this enormous engine running, irrespective of financial constraints and domestic overcapacity, has also been among the key reasons for the concerted overseas push of China under its Belt and Road Initiative (BRI). The BRI ports, power plants, airports, and so on, with limited project feasibility and on unviable terms, have been hard sold to developing countries across Asia and Africa. A key part of the incentives offered were loan financing from China. These unviable projects are now in default and Chinese companies are taking over these assets as compensation for their debt. This is further adding to a mounting debt problem and an increasingly fractious geopolitics of mistrust in China.

A key challenge posing questions of urgent reforms is the structure of China's financial system which, while superficially familiar, is quite different from those elsewhere around the world. China's money market funds, for example, are not managed by traditional market fund managers like Fidelity and Vanguard but by Chinese technology firms, China's equivalent of Amazon and Google. Insurance companies generate most of their premiums not from selling insurance policies but from selling term maturity financial products that offer a fixed return slightly higher than bank deposits.

Financial trusts, as a class of institutional asset managers, are the second-largest class of financial institutions after banks and lend to a wide range of borrowers from property developers to local governments. While households in most developed and developing economies own equity shares in publicly traded companies as part of their savings portfolios, households in China have significant resources invested in short term, fixed-income investments called wealth management products (WMPs) which are sold by banks as a no-risk, higher-return alternative to deposits. These WMPs were introduced in 2004, but they really exploded as an investment class after 2010. By the end of 2016, the amount under WMPs aggregated to nearly 20 per cent of bank deposits.

Another systemic feature and challenge of China's financial system has been the preponderance of weightage to collateral in lending, than credit assessment of potential cash flows and the ability to service the loans. The Chinese financial system lends not on the basis of a company's needs but according to the value of its assets. Nearly 60 per cent of all loans made by the banking system are made against collateral, mostly property. Shadow banking institutions also lend in a similar manner, requiring anywhere between two to three times the value of a loan as collateral. In cases where the company doesn't have adequate collateral, banks have been willing to accept third-party guarantees. The premise of this collateral-based lending is that if the company that has borrowed is unable to repay the loan, the collateral can be sold and funds recovered. Similarly, third-party guarantees can also be encashed to recover any losses on the loan to the bank.

This entire collateral-based model of lending by the financial system is, however, based on two critical assumptions: first, that China will continue to grow at its scorching fast pace. The second assumption is that property prices, the primary collateral, will continue to remain buoyant. Both, however, are flawed not only in the assumption of endless economic growth and price buoyancy but also in ignoring the interconnectedness and risk between themselves. If economic growth slows, as it has, prices are likely to soften. This may lead to defaults by borrowers—a situation property developers like Evergrande and Country Garden find themselves in. This may further lead to sale of property held as collateral, further weakening the already weak prices in the property market. The third-party guarantees to these loans would further widen the scope of distress to other sectors and areas, turning these into local crises as complex networks of interlocking mutual guarantees fall like dominoes. It is also one of the primary reasons that the government has intervened to prevent any significant weakening of property prices in China, in view of the household savings and financial system investments locked up in the sector.

This unique Chinese financial system is not one that has been designed by the Chinese authorities on any global principles of prudence, supervision or risk mitigation in an interconnected financial system. It has grown from an unprecedented tolerance to financial experimentation and innovation by markets. It is, however, widely speculated that this tolerance has also unleashed a perpetual machine of debt creation, which the state is increasingly finding difficult to rein in for concern of the consequences. At the heart of this problem is the moral hazard of 'implicit state guarantee' that underlies all excesses of its financial system on both sides—asset and liabilities—of its balance sheet.

The state has always played an overarching role in China's political economy since its imperial times. Its reform and opening-up and 'economics with Chinese characteristics' have been guided as much by its ancient texts of political economy like the Guanzi, as by Keynes and Western neoclassical economics. Its Qing Zhong (Salt-Iron) principles of economic relativity continue to guide state interventions in market dynamics based on circumstances and importance. This principle has served well so far on the 'unitary totalitarian balance sheet' that China runs, despite an ostensible 'privatization of ownership'.

On the basis of 'implicit state guarantee' and unitary balance sheet, China has been able to prolong its unprecedented real estate, infrastructure and construction-led yang boom cycle. This has enabled it, in the short term, to avoid consequences similar to that of India's privately-led infrastructure and real estate investments that took place between 2004 to 2014. However, in the process, all the yin of project economics—poor selection of projects, implementation and operational inefficiencies, project cost overruns, lower than projected revenues, corruption, etc.—have also been swept under the carpet in China in its single-minded pursuit of economic growth.

In India, government spending on capital investment, on the back of record tax collections and fiscal conservatism, is already at an all-time high. The NPA mess in the banking system has now been cleaned up under a new administration, and the stage is set for fresh ideas and a renewed private sector capital investment cycle to start. In China, however, the bubble grows even bigger as further expenditure is proposed to keep its construction sector busy and the economy running. This is happening even as its economy teeters on the brink of collapse, with softening property markets, rising NPAs and growing defaults of major real estate companies and shadow banking institutions. It is possible that China, with complete control over its economy, banks and domestic interest rates, will be able to inflate away the financial problems and avoid the type of market meltdown that observers have been fearing and predicting for a long time. Its problems in the non-financial sector economy, on the other hand, may prove to be a more difficult boat to sail. Its recent attempts to impose a property tax have met with stubborn resistance.

Financial reforms are one of the keystones of Xi's vision and agenda. China has announced plans to deepen financial reforms and attract global investment, even as it recognizes the growing risks in its economy.[10] Given the turmoil in financial markets, its own deep systemic and institutional issues, and the overriding imperative of propping up growth in a slowing economy are challenges that will shape China's economic trajectory over the next few decades.

India by comparison, has always had a mixed economy. Its relatively robust financial system has also mostly functioned on market incentives of risk and return. While its banking system has been dominated by state-owned banks, following a wave of bank nationalization between 1969 to 1980, it has had other financial intermediaries from the non-state sector too operating in its banking and financial markets. This includes robust stock markets that have been in existence since 1875. The banking and financial sector received early priority in the reforms process, with the Narsimham Committee report setting out the path for banking reforms in November 1991.

Besides setting out prudent banking norms, these reforms also liberalized foreign exchange rules to prepare a planned transition to a market-determined exchange rate system. Subsequent initiatives included the setting up of the Securities and Exchange Board of India (SEBI) as capital markets regulator in 1992, licences for new private banks in 1993, current account rupee convertibility, deregulation of interest rates and insurance sector reforms in 1994, and universal banking in 1998.

While the state continued to encourage lending in keeping with its objectives through policy directives, like priority sector lending to agriculture and rural activities, mostly through its state-owned banks, the share of such directed lending reduced in the years following liberalization. Further, while public sector enterprises continued to receive loans from banks, this was increasingly based on the perception of their state ownership and therefore, sovereign guarantee for their loans. Progressively, banks also began favouring better performing state-owned units over the zombie units. Development of professional banking culture, particularly at state-owned banks was, however, a significant challenge. While decision-making was progressively decentralized to bank management and boards, control of banks and accountability was not. It was a policy flaw that saw indiscriminate lending, mostly by state-owned banks, with scant regard for viability, security or prudent banking norms during 2004–14, particularly after 2008.

The year 2004 saw the onset of a fresh wave of liberalization, with a large number of infrastructure projects in roads, power and telecom, along with an improvement in availability of large credit funds from banks for private sector-led projects. This decade-long investment-led growth cycle, with many poor credit decisions by banks, allegedly based on crony considerations, came to a crashing conclusion as these projects stalled. Amid accusations and investigations, the banks and the state-owned banks in particular, faced mounting NPA losses. With infusion of funds from the central government and improved margins and performance, most of these losses have been written off over the past decade.

The Indian banking system now is the healthiest it has been in decades. The equity markets have also overcome their challenges for raising fresh capital and as providers of liquidity. Both the primary and secondary markets are at record highs in market capitalization and fund raising. The financial sector as a whole is, therefore, in a relatively robust condition to meet the investment requirements of renewed growth. Further, learning from previous experience and challenges faced, the central government has modified its infrastructure development model.

Instead of being led by greenfield private sector investment, which failed in setting up or operating projects on issues of land acquisition, project approval, payment delays, litigation and bureaucratic red tape in the last cycle, it is proposed that the government and its agencies shall undertake the project development and implementation phase of most infrastructure projects. After de-risking the project development and implementation phase, and a few years of seasoning of the project cash flows, the government will bid out these projects for private sector ownership. As a result, the private sector would be able to secure viable cash flow streams for their investments at market-determined prices, while the government would recycle its investments. This process would also enable the government to absorb any viability gaps or subsidization requirement issues of projects before sale.

India has now begun identifying resources, projects, institutions and models for its new investment cycle, including the National Infrastructure Pipeline (NIP), with projected capital expenditure on infrastructure projects aggregating $1.4 trillion between 2020 and 2025. It has also created the National Land Monetization Corporation to identify and monetize surplus land under the control of its public sector units. It further seeks to now focus on local and state governments as the primary unit of administration for competitive policy implementation and resource allocation. It has revived megaprojects like the Ken-Betwa link, the first interlinking of rivers project. It has also created a new co-operative ministry to strengthen the co-operative movement in the country to lead and bring reforms, including in farmer co-operatives leasing of land and agricultural markets. With a reformed financial and banking sector and revised format of public-private partnership (PPP) in place, the next cycle of investments in India is poised to catapult India into a higher trajectory of economic growth.

13

The Second Yin: Corruption

On 14 November 2011, a British businessman Neil Heywood was found dead in Nanshan Lijing Holiday Hotel in Chongqing city, under mysterious circumstances. It was a murder that would end in high drama, rock China to its foundation and also give an insight into corruption, power and politics within the all-powerful, totalitarian Communist Party of China (CPC) and the Chinese state.

Initially, the death did not attract much attention. However, on 2 February 2012, the Chongqing city government announced that its Police Chief Wang Lijun had been transferred to another job. It was a public confirmation of his fall out with Chongqing's powerful communist party boss, the high-profile and one of the top 'next generation' leadership contenders, Bo Xilai. This announcement attracted much speculation, as Chief Lijun was widely considered Bo Xilai's right-hand man in all his dealings and activities. The speculation, however, quickly turned to astonishment and high drama when just four days later, Chief Lijun fled to the US consulate in Chengdu city, near Chongqing. He spent the night in the US consulate, which was quickly surrounded by Chinese police. The next day, the Police Chief was persuaded by Chongqing's mayor to leave the consulate and was quickly whisked away. On 8 February, the Chongqing government released a statement that Wang Lijun was under a 'holiday-style medical treatment', when in fact, he was under investigation and detention.

Between 5–14 March 2012, Bo Xilai attended China's annual parliamentary session in Beijing where he kept an unusually low profile. Rumours swirled that Chief Lijun's actions had tarnished his chances of promotion to the party's Politburo Standing Committee (PSC) scheduled for later in the year. On 14 March, Premier Wen

Jiabao indirectly criticized Bo Xilai for the Lijun incident. It was the first statement made by a senior leader, emphasizing Bo Xilai's precarious position within the party leadership. Matters moved quickly after this. On 15 March, China announced that Bo Xilai had been removed from his post as party chief in Chongqing because of the Wang Lijun incident. Bo Xilai disappeared from public view.

On 20 March, a leaked audio recording suggested that Bo Xilai and his Police Chief Wang Lijun fell out when Wang Lijun told his boss Bo Xilai of an investigation into the latter's family. Rumours spread that Bo Xilai could be linked to the death of Neil Haywood, the British businessman who died in Chongqing five months earlier. On 26 March, the United Kingdom (UK) government confirmed that it had asked China to re-examine Neil Heywood's death. On 10 April, China announced that Bo Xilai had been removed from all his CPC posts and that his wife Gu Kailai and an associate were being investigated in connection to Heywood's death. In a subsequent trial, both Bo Xilai and Gu Kailai were found guilty of various crimes, including corruption, after which they were convicted and sentenced to prison.

Bo Xilai was as blue-blooded China's communist party royalty as anyone could get in red China. He was born in 1949 to prominent CPC leader Bo Yibo, one of the party's Eight Immortals, who served as minister of finance in the early years of communist rule but fell out of favour with Mao for advocating for more open trade relations with the West. During the Cultural Revolution, which began in 1966, he was labelled a 'rightist' and a 'counter-revolutionist', stripped of his posts and imprisoned, where he was reportedly tortured. His wife, Hu Ming, was abducted by Red Guards in Guangzhou and was either beaten to death or died by suicide.

At the time, Bo Xilai was 17 years old and attending one of Beijing's most prestigious and best schools, from which he was removed and imprisoned for five years before being released to work at a hardware repair factory. Following Mao's death in 1976, Bo Yibo was politically rehabilitated and appointed vice premier in 1979. His son, Bo Xilai, got a degree from Peking University and joined the CPC in 1980 while the Bo family regained its political influence during the period that followed. Bo Xilai's subsequent rise within the CPC was rapid, as he served in successive positions of increasing responsibility even while being visible and often controversial. As a princeling—the offspring of a leading CPC revolutionary leader—he inherited his family's political influence which assisted in this rise. It is also interesting to note that at the time of his downfall, he was widely seen as a serious contender for the top post of the CPC, locked in competition with another equally blue-blooded princeling, Xi Jinping. With Bo Xilai's fall and subsequent conviction, Xi Jinping emerged as the uncontested leader of the CPC and the state.

Corruption has been identified by Xi Jinping as one of the biggest challenges to the future of the CPC and China. Along with 'common prosperity' to address China's growing income and growth inequalities, it is one of the cornerstones of his 'China Dream' vision and policies. Both are intertwined in many ways. Corruption during the reform and opening-up process and beyond has been a defining characteristic of China's rise to economic growth. Students protesting in Tiananmen Square in 1989 had denounced 'official profiteering'. By 2001, economist Hu Angang estimated that corruption accounted for 13 to 16 per cent of China's GDP.[1] While the estimate is undoubtedly high, it reflected the public sense that corruption was deepening and beginning to get entrenched in the communist party and state as the 'opening-up' gathered pace and market-based processes generated opportunities for rent-seeking by party and government functionaries.

The GFC of 2008 saw a stimulus of nearly $750 billion to the Chinese economy, even as the twin engines of its future growth—real estate and infrastructure—were fired up. According to reports, corruption has only accelerated and grown since then. Infact, corruption was so significant that a crackdown on it was among the first tasks Xi undertook on assuming the position of the CPC's general secretary in November 2012. While its immediate trigger may have been the Bo Xilai incident, it was also a crackdown on the party indiscipline that preceded it, which challenged the CPC's decisions and threatened party unity. As Xi said:

> Among the Party's discipline and rules, none is greater than political discipline and political rules. In recent years, we have investigated high-level cadres' serious violation of discipline and law, especially the case(s) of Zhou Yongkang, Bo Xilai, Xu Caihou, Ling Jihua, and Su Rong. Their violation of the Party's political discipline and political rules was very serious; it has to be viewed seriously. These people, the greater their power and the more important their position, the more they ignored the Party's political discipline and political rules, even to the extent of being completely unscrupulous and reckless![2]

There is little doubt that Xi also likely used the opportunity to crack down 'tigers and flies' to purge his political enemies. 'Tigers' denote senior party or government officials of vice-ministerial rank and above, while 'flies' are middle or low-ranking functionaries. Over 184 tigers and tens of thousands of flies have been targeted so far. But the anti-corruption campaign cannot be seen as limited to a political struggle. To Xi and his allies, the party faces serious challenges that could destroy it, similar to the challenges that brought down the Communist Party of the former Soviet Union. The collapse of the Communist Party and its control over the Soviet Union has been an obsessive theme for the CPC leaders who keep returning to it to glean lessons and avoid a similar fate. As Xi put it, shortly after being elevated as party chief, 'Why did the Soviet Union disintegrate? Why did the Soviet Communist Party collapse? An important reason was that their ideals and convictions wavered...' According to Xi, it was the loss of their ideals and convictions that caused the collapse of the Soviet Communist party, which was also the root of a growing crisis of legitimacy in China.

The problem and contradictions, however, run much deeper, with corruption being just one of the many manifestations. Since 1982, the CPC had promulgated a new constitution and emphasized 'rule of law' in its rhetoric, contrasting with the earlier focus on party, policy, hierarchy and individual-centric approaches. This emphasis on rule of law and institutionalization, potentially implied an end of the party's revolutionary mission in favour of institutionalized government. As Xi said in 2012:

> To manage state affairs according to law, first we must run the country in accordance with the Constitution. The key to holding power in accordance with the law is to first rule in accordance with the Constitution. The party leadership formulates the Constitution and the law, and the party itself must act within the scope of the Constitution and the law to truly achieve the Party leadership's establishment of the law, ensuring the enforcement of the law, and taking the lead in abiding by the law.

This was misinterpreted by many as 'China's Dream is the dream of constitutional government', suggesting a liberal agenda, supporting rule of law, individual rights protection and, more broadly, the emergence of civil society. The contradiction that this represented was immediately apparent. While this vision offered a path to a 'peaceful evolution' to institutionalized and constitutional government, it also undermined the party's legitimacy. Corrective action soon followed and in April 2013, the party's General Office issued the famous Document No. 9, which outlined seven areas that should not be publicly discussed, including constitutional government, universal values, civil society, freedom of the press and historical nihilism.

The concept of 'historical nihilism' is particularly important to maintain the legitimacy of the CPC, according to its leaders. The CPC's rule over China before Xi came to power in 2012, can be broadly divided into two 30-year periods—the harsh Mao period of the Great Leap Forward (GLF) and the Cultural Revolution; and the post Mao period of 'reform and opening-up'. There are inherent ideological contradictions between the two periods. For Xi and the party, an overemphasis on the Mao period would undermine the later reforms, just as an overemphasis on reforms risks repudiating Mao, and thereby the legitimacy of the revolution itself.

It is a troubling question that is increasingly being asked—how does a revolution from nearly 75 years ago, in its individual context and circumstances at that time, justify the party's continuation in power today? In an authoritative article, the CPC Central Party History Research Office stated that the negation of Mao Thought by the party would lead to 'serious political consequences'. According to the CPC, 'One important reason for the disintegration of the Soviet Union and the collapse of the CPSU (Communist Party of the Soviet Union) is the complete negation of the history of the Soviet Union and the CPSU, the negation of Lenin and other leading figures (by Khruschev and subsequent leaders), and the practice of historical nihilism, which confused people's minds.'[3]

In many ways, the party's challenge is one of squaring the circle. How to reconcile the two ideologically distinct periods while retaining and reinforcing the party's public legitimacy? Xi's anti-corruption campaign is directly related to interpretations of the CPC's history and legitimacy issues. The emergence of corruption is directly related to the loss of 'ideals and convictions' among the CPC members. If CPC members have lost their ideological bearings, civil society and the rule of law may be able to restrain them. However, this does not address the issue of the party's continued legitimacy. Instead, if party discipline and idealism can be restored by attacking corruption, then perhaps, the idea that only the CPC represents the true interests and ideals of the Chinese people is more sustainable. But beyond the politics and legitimacy of the party, why does corruption matter so much in China? How is it different from corruption as it exists in other countries?

In scarcity-plagued and state-controlled Mao's China, there were few opportunities for corruption. The reform and opening-up, however, presented many opportunities for corruption as market processes were introduced in policy-driven, top-down, decentralized approach to decision-making and implementation. The setting up of industries in the SEZs in the first phase saw significant patronage and corruption in state-owned land allocation, permissions and incentives. Corruption only increased exponentially in the subsequent phase of real estate and infrastructure boom. This phase saw increasing social conflict as well, with local governments colluding with private builders to acquire rural, agricultural land from farmers for low compensation, and in turn selling it at high prices as urbanization grew at a rapid pace. With a weak and non-institutionalized party and government framework to keep corruption in check, it quickly became a rampant and most visibly contentious feature of China's economic growth. Corruption in China is also a significant contributor to the public perception of being the source of increasing wealth and income disparities between China's urban rich and rural poor. It is also the reason why Xi's 'tigers and flies' anti-corruption campaign and his 'common prosperity' vision are two key policy planks on which the future legitimacy of his and the party's rule and legitimacy rest.

Corruption captures the public mind like few other issues do. It is among the most visible, hotly contested, but least understood aspects of public policy, growth and governance. A survey of almost 70,000 people in 69 countries conducted by WIN/Gallup International in 2013, identified corruption as the world's number one problem.[4] Across countries, regardless of their level of development, corruption is resonating in the public imagination and causing much outrage. It has even led to political regime changes in places as unconnected as Ukraine, Thailand and India in 2014 alone. Yet, there is little consensus on what constitutes corruption. In its broader sense, the study of corruption draws extensively on the work of anthropologists, criminologists, economists, historians, lawyers, political scientists and sociologists. It also has ethical, moral, religious and social connotations. However, its most common usage is in the context of economic or financial corruption.

Even the United Nations Convention Against Corruption (UNCAC), the only legally binding universal anti-corruption instrument, could not agree on a definition. A broad consensus, though, now agrees that corruption is 'the abuse of public office (or entrusted power in the case of private corporations) for private gain'. What constitutes 'private gain' is, however, again a subject of debate, particularly in the context of beliefs, attitudes and behaviours in different societies. For example, is nepotism, patronage and clientelism (providing support in exchange of goods or services) perceived differently in Asian societies as compared to the West? So why is corruption, beyond its moral and ethical aspects, a problem from an economic point of view? As a paper on 'Corruption and Economic Growth' by the Organisation for Economic Co-operation and Development[5] points out, there is strong prima facie evidence that points to a negative correlation between perceived corruption and the reduced level of output. If corruption is curtailed, the resultant gains in output can be invested in human and civic capital necessary to make further progress. The true social cost of corruption, however, cannot be measured by the amount of bribes paid or even the amount of state property stolen.

Rather, the real cost of corruption to society and economy, is the loss of output due to resource misallocation, incentive distortions and other inefficiencies caused by corruption. In addition to these losses, corruption can also impose additional welfare costs in the form of adverse effects on income distribution and disregard for environmental protection. Most importantly, corruption undermines public trust in the government, reducing its ability to carry out its primary mission of providing adequate public services and fostering a favourable environment for private sector development. In extreme cases, and particularly where there is little public scrutiny or accountability mechanisms, it could even lead to the delegitimization of the state, causing political and economic instability. Furthermore, since this kind of delegitimization creates a general sense of uncertainty, private businesses are less likely and less able, to commit to a long-term strategy for development. This makes it hard for such countries and economies to achieve sustainable development.

However, is all corruption the same? And how has China prospered over the last three decades despite evidence of vast and rampant corruption? Professor Yuen Yuen Ang has deconstructed corruption in her authoritative work, *China's Gilded Age: The Paradox of Economic Boom and Vast Corruption*. She suggests a framework that provides insight on how, despite rampant corruption, China has managed remarkably and sustained economic growth over a long time. According to professor Ang, economic corruption can be analysed and plotted along two dimensions. The first, whether it involves exchanges or whether it is outright theft. The second, whether it involves elites (of the governing or ruling class) or whether it is mostly non-elites. The resultant matrix from this juxtaposition is described by her as follows:

Table 3
Analysis of Economic Corruption[6]

	Non-Elites	Elites
Involves Theft	Petty Theft	Grand Theft
Involves Exchange	Speed Money	Access Money

Research suggests that, from an economic perspective, corruption that involves theft and non-elite exchange (speed money) is more obstructive for growth than corruption involving exchange between elites (access money). Accordingly, she offers a four-part explanation for China's growth-with-corruption conundrum. First, she argues that the dominant type of corruption in China is access money—elite exchanges of power and wealth between decision makers—rather than petty bribery or outright theft. This is in contrast to economies such as India, where the common citizen is typically plagued by petty theft and speed money. She, therefore, posits the standard argument that 'corruption...lowers private investment, thereby reducing economic growth' does not hold true across various types of corruption. In fact, access money may often raise private investment—and even spur over-investment, as seen in China's real estate sector—thereby increasing growth, at least until the onset of a crisis. In the case of China, in the face of its growing real estate and economic crisis combined with its slowing growth, it appears to be a prediction that is increasingly coming true.

India and China are political polar opposites, with China being the world's largest autocracy and India being the world's largest democracy. Both have vast territories with multiple levels of government, both governing the world's largest populations. According to standard indices, they also have nearly identical aggregate levels of corruption. In 2017, according to a global list released by anti-graft agency Transparency International, China had a corruption perception index (CPI) score of 41, while India had a score of 40.[7] Bundled scores of corruption, however, do not tell the entire story, and mask important structural variances.

Between 2015 and 2017, the Global Corruption Barometer (GCB) conducted a survey across countries that focusses on the personal experiences of citizens with petty corruption. In the survey, the respondents were asked whether they had to pay a bribe in order to access public services in the previous 12 months. According to the survey, petty bribery is most prevalent in India, where 69 per cent of respondents reported paying a bribe, compared to only 26 per cent in China. According to the GCB, petty bribery is also less common in China than in Vietnam (65 per cent), Thailand (41 per cent) and Indonesia (32 per cent).[8] That is not to say that China does not have a corruption problem, just that its nature of corruption is different. Yuen Yuen Ang writes:

> Although China may have less of a problem with petty bribery than India, access money flows abundantly... The scandal of Zhou Yongkang [...] a former member of the Standing Committee of the Politburo [...] revealed that top Chinese politicians cultivate an extensive network of clientele through which massive bribes flow, even if the patron doesn't personally take bribes. [...] this style of elite, network-based bribery is more prevalent in China than in India. [...] To sum up, in India, people pay bribes to override obstacles; in China, graft buys lucrative business deals. If the former is analogous to grease, then the latter is more like sludge.[9]

Power is concentrated in the hands of individual leaders in China's autocracy, who can easily waive restrictions and open doors. In contrast, India's democratic system of checks and balances empowers numerous and diverse authorities to block decisions. These authorities, however, cannot unilaterally approve requests or extend deals. In India, a high-level official in New Delhi has been quoted saying: 'If you want me to move a file faster, I am not sure if I can help you. But if you want me to stop a file, I can do it immediately.'

While access money corruption also exists in India, its limitations in the Indian system of checks and balances were best illustrated during India's gilded age—the period between 2004 to 2014. In the aftermath of allegations regarding allocation of telecom spectrum and coal mine allocation, and widespread public and media outrage, India's independent judiciary struck down government process and allotment. It further decreed that natural resources would thenceforth be allotted by a public auction process.

It is also notable that the economic and social effects of access money and speed money are starkly different. In India, where petty bribery is seen as 'routine', such corruption directly stifles growth by imposing delays, inefficiencies and costs on businesses. Worst of all, the poor bear the brunt of the burden of petty bribery. By contrast, access money feeds China's capitalist machine, enriching entrepreneurs who pay for deals. It also rewards communist officials for promoting rapid economic growth. Its serious negative consequences are felt only in the long run by increasing inequality and distorting policies and capital allocation.

Why has corruption in China primarily taken the form of access money as opposed to other forms of corruption, such as in India? The answer lies in both China's autocratic system of government and the rapid opening-up of its economy since the 1980s. China's political system has followed a profit-sharing logic since the early days of market opening, with both elites and non-elites benefitting from wealth creation in their respective geographical jurisdictions. The entire Chinese bureaucracy is incentivized to promote development of their provinces, cities and autonomous regions, even as officials engage in rampant deal-making. To understand how this works, it is important to distinguish between the mechanisms of profit-sharing among political elites, about 500,000 high-ranking officials and the rank and file employees in the bureaucracy, numbering about 50 million in total.

Economic growth is a key determinant in the promotion of local leaders in China. Political elites have both career and financial incentives to promote development aggressively. However, because of the limited number of seats for advancement as the administrative pyramid narrows, not all leaders aspire to or achieve higher office. As a result, the financial incentive for these leaders is greater. The more prosperous their local economy, the more local leaders will profit. Successful Chinese politicians, therefore, typically aspire to kill two birds with one stone: by spurring development and awarding projects to favoured businesses, they achieve their political targets and also garner bribes. Further, unlike democratically elected politicians, authoritarian local leaders can bulldoze old properties, order new projects and mobilize vast amounts of resources at command.

This incentive structure is also aligned and formalized for rank and file bureaucrats, who share profits through remuneration. Although their salaries are set at low levels, they are supplemented by a range of fringe benefits, such as allowances, bonuses, gifts and free meals, which can comprise up to three-quarters of their official compensation. These fringe benefit components are linked to financial performance: the more tax revenue a local government generates—as well as the amount of non-tax revenue (such as fees and service charges) that individual offices collect—the more fringe benefits they can provide to their employees. This supplemental compensation not only encourages revenue-generating efforts but also discourages bureaucrats from engaging in petty bribery. This also gives officials a personal stake in ensuring economic growth.

In addition, the Chinese government has reduced forms of corruption that directly impede entrepreneurial growth. While corruption may induce communist officials to enthusiastically embrace market reforms, the central government has to steer them away from corruption (theft and extortion) that damages growth and undermines state performance. These forms of corruption—petty theft, grand theft and speed money—were brought under control through an ambitious but understated capacity-building programme that began in 1998 under Premier Zhu Rongji and is still being expanded. The programme includes establishing a new law for civil servants[10], standardizing tax rates, strengthening oversight through budgeting and accounting reforms, replacing cash payments of fees and fines with direct electronic deposit, consolidating public bank accounts and other initiatives.

According to research, while bribery has increased significantly since 2000, embezzlement and misappropriation of public funds has decreased. Arbitrary extortion of fees and fines, which was common in the 1980s and 1990s, have become less common. Regional competition in China has also helped curb predatory corruption. Local leaders are motivated to reduce petty corruption among rank and file bureaucrats in the face of intense competition for projects and investors. Such efforts to foster an investment-friendly environment in their region are perhaps best exemplified by the leadership's slogan in Hubei: 'Investors are Gods, prospectors of investors are heroes, bureaucrats are humble servants, and those who harm corporate interests are sinners.'

Deal-making too, by local leadership, is part of this growth promotion. Leaders compete to offer 'preferential policies' to selected businesses while also projecting competence and upgrading their development strategies by positioning their regional competitive advantages. Taken together, all these characteristics not only explain the Chinese paradox of growth with corruption but also help in reconciling contradictions in China's uniquely authoritarian yet economically decentralized and highly competitive political economy. It is an economy in which growth is impressive yet imbalanced and risky, and where local officials are corrupt but in pursuit of development.

Elite corruption in India has also been of grand (at times, petty) theft. A former Chief Minister (CM) of Bihar was convicted in a 'fodder' scam involving fraudulent withdrawals from the state treasury, and a former CM of Haryana was convicted in a 'teacher' scam involving fraudulent appointment of school teachers in return

for bribes. Successful access money corruption in India, involving co-opting of elites and their families as partners in the enterprise in comparison to China—as vividly described by China insider Desmond Shum in his autobiography *Red Roulette: An Insider's Story of Wealth, Power, Corruption, and Vengeance in Today's China*[11]—has been relatively less, and more so in the years of India's liberalization. The fragmentation of power in the political economy has been a key factor, with electoral results from 1991 to 2014 failing to give any political party a majority, necessitating coalition rule. With weak ruling political coalitions, other arms of the state, particularly the judiciary and the media, have effectively acted as a check (or expanded their writ, depending on perspective) as seen in the telecommunication and coal scams.

Elite corruption in democratic India, however, besides institutional checks and balances, also faces the check of political elections every five years at various levels of government. The potential loss of power that this could involve if faced with a public electoral backlash, prevents the elite, particularly the political elite, from entrenching itself in grand corruption without fear of consequences. Ironically, it is also the need for electoral funds to fight these recurrent elections at all levels of government that drives a significant part of elite corruption—whether access money or grand theft.

The rising tide of frictionless access money corruption that lifted China's economic growth over the last three decades has resulted in overinvestment and distortions that threaten not only its economic stability but also pose dangers to the legitimacy of the CPC rule. It is a key existential challenge that Xi Jinping faces, as he is China's elected leader for an unprecedented third term—and possibly for life—the only leader after Mao to be so. India by contrast, with its institutionalized system of checks and balances on corruption and a vibrant democracy, has already course corrected to a large extent with learnings from its past, and is poised for significant growth over the foreseeable future.

14

The Third Yin: Geopolitics

In 1792, an embassy led by George Macartney arrived in Beijing with a letter from the British King George III to the Chinese emperor Qianlong requesting British diplomatic representation at the imperial court, an easing of trade regulations and the opening of more Chinese ports to trade. The Qianlong Emperor rejected all the requests in his reply to the British king, a letter that is more notable for its tone than its content, giving an insight into Chinese imperial worldview:

> You, O King, from afar have yearned after the blessings of our civilization, and in your eagerness to come into touch with our converting influence have sent an Embassy across the sea bearing a memorial [memorandum]. I have already taken note of your respectful spirit of submission, have treated your mission with extreme favour and loaded it with gifts, besides issuing a mandate to you, O King, and honouring you at the bestowal of valuable presents. Thus has my indulgence been manifested.
>
> Yesterday your Ambassador petitioned my Ministers to memorialise me regarding your trade with China, but his proposal is not consistent with our dynastic usage and cannot be entertained. Hitherto, all European nations, including your own country's barbarian merchants, have carried on their trade with our Celestial Empire at Canton. Such has been the procedure for many years, although our Celestial Empire possesses all things in prolific abundance and lacks no product within its own borders. There was therefore no need to import the manufactures of outside barbarians in exchange for our own produce. But as the tea, silk and porcelain which the Celestial Empire produces, are absolute necessities to European

nations and to yourselves, we have permitted, as a signal mark of favour, that foreign hongs [groups of merchants] should be established at Canton, so that your wants might be supplied and your country thus participate in our beneficence. But your Ambassador has now put forward new requests which completely fail to recognize the Throne's principle to 'treat strangers from afar with indulgence,' and to exercise a pacifying control over barbarian tribes, the world over. Moreover, our dynasty, swaying the myriad races of the globe, extends the same benevolence towards all. Your England is not the only nation trading at Canton. If other nations, following your bad example, wrongfully importune my ear with further impossible requests, how will it be possible for me to treat them with easy indulgence? Nevertheless, I do not forget the lonely remoteness of your island, cut off from the world by intervening wastes of sea, nor do I overlook your excusable ignorance of the usages of our Celestial Empire. I have consequently commanded my Ministers to enlighten your Ambassador on the subject, and have ordered the departure of the mission. But I have doubts that, after your Envoy's return he may fail to acquaint you with my view in detail or that he may be lacking in lucidity, so that I shall now proceed ... to issue my mandate on each question separately. In this way you will, I trust, comprehend my meaning.[1]

The Confucian view of a hierarchical, Sinocentric *tianxia* (all under heaven) world saw imperial China regard itself as the centre of civilization, receiving tributes from other, lesser nations whom it indulged by permitting them trade and other favours, but in turn had no requirement for their goods, commerce or goodwill. This self-image of Chinese exceptionalism and isolation from the world received a severe blow in the century of humiliation that followed, sparking widespread turmoil and soul searching among the Chinese elite as they sought to understand the reasons behind China's economic and cultural downfall.

The rapid spread of Western thought in China, including Christianity under the protection of Western powers, saw the Taiping Rebellion (1850–1864) establish 'The Heavenly Kingdom of Great Peace' with its capital at Nanjing, before being put down by the Qing army with aid from British and French forces. It also sparked the Boxer Rebellion (1899–1901), an anti-foreign, anti-colonial and anti-Christian uprising in China by the Society of Righteous and Harmonious Fists (*Yìhéquán*), towards the end of the Qing dynasty. The fiercely contested arena of political thought and organization also saw China turn to Western models. The Republic of China was established in January 1912, following the Xinhai Revolution, which overthrew the Qing dynasty and ended over 2,000 years of imperial rule in China. Initially led by Sun Yat-Sen, its authority waxed and waned as China was plagued by warlordism, Japanese invasion and the Chinese Civil War in the decades that followed. Its central authority was at its strongest during the Nanjing decade (1927–37), when most of China came under the control of the authoritarian, one-party military dictatorship of the Chiang Kai-shek led Kuomintang (KMT). The KMT was defeated by the People's Liberation Army (PLA) of the CPC, after which it retreated to the island of Taiwan where a multi-party democracy now exists. The CPC's own authoritarian Marxist-Leninist origins lie in the philosophy of a German economist and a Russian revolutionary. Furthermore, Mao's fledgling People's Republic of China relied upon the Soviet Union for assistance in its initial years.

After Joseph Stalin's death in 1953 and the rise to power of a 'revisionist' Nikita Khrushchev, who denounced Stalin's personality-led cult, the gap between Mao's China and the Soviet Union widened. By 1961, the split was irreconcilable, with China denouncing the Soviet Union model as 'social imperialism'. In addition to its historical animosity towards the US, whom it denounced as 'imperialists' and who in turn supported Taiwan and blocked it from the world institutions that it dominated, China's relative global isolation in the Cold War period from both geopolitical superpowers was largely complete.

Its initial regional efforts at diplomacy include the signing of the Panchsheel, the Five Principles of Peaceful Coexistence with India in 1954. The five principles, while rooted in a shared pan-Asian cultural heritage, were also an expression of modern Western Westphalian geopolitical thought that recognized equality and sovereignty of individual nations (as against traditional Chinese tianxia geopolitical thinking). The five principles were:

1) mutual respect for each other's territorial integrity and sovereignty;
2) mutual non-aggression;
3) mutual non-interference in each other's internal affairs;
4) equality and cooperation for mutual benefit; and
5) peaceful coexistence.

The then foreign minister of China, Zhou Enlai, is credited with the first public formulation of the principles of Panchsheel, where he enunciated them as 'five principles governing China's relations with foreign countries'.[2] According to then Indian Prime Minister (PM) Jawaharlal Nehru, 'if these principles were recognized in the mutual relations of all countries, then indeed there would hardly be any conflict and certainly no war'.[3] In fact, it was Sukarno, the Indonesian nationalist leader, who first declared five general principles, or *pancasila* in 1945, on which future institutions were to be founded. Indonesia became independent in 1949.

It was an underlying assumption of the five principles that newly independent states after decolonization would be able to develop a new and more principled approach to international relations. It was also no coincidence that the five principles had their origins in Buddhist thought, which was a shared heritage of these three nations. The principles were part of a statement issued in April 1955 at the historic Bandung Conference in Indonesia of newly formed, post-colonial states. The principles eventually formed the basis of the Non-Aligned Movement (NAM) of countries formed in 1961 as an independent alternative to the bipolar Cold War world order.

Interestingly, China did not join the NAM, instead it limited itself to being an observer. In October–November 1962, a war broke out as China crossed the Line of Control on the disputed border with India. For much of the 1960s, China also attempted to export its brand of Maoist communism to parts of Asia and Africa, actively providing ideological and alleged material support to communist movements and insurgencies. Growing tensions between an increasingly powerful and militant Communist Party of Indonesia (Partai Komunis Indonesia or PKI), a Left sympathetic President Sukarno and Right-wing military and religious forces in Indonesia came to a head on 30 September 1965, when a group of militants captured and executed six of Indonesia's top military generals. The militant movement declared itself President Sukarno's protectors, justifying its actions as a preventive strike against a potential coup by the 'anti-Sukarno', pro-Western council of generals.

The militant movement was quickly crushed by Major General Suharto, but the assassination was seen as linked to the PKI, though subsequent information revealed no direct linkage between the CPC, PKI and the militant group. A widespread purge and massacre followed, targeting the PKI members and communist sympathizers, in which nearly 500,000 to 1.2 million were killed. It also led to the overthrow of Sukarno, suspension of diplomatic ties with China in 1967 and Suharto's three-decade-long authoritarian rule.

The fear of China's long and hegemonic shadow continues to haunt Southeast Asian countries even today. China's support (along with the Soviet Union, then under Stalin) and participation in the Korean War (1950–53), when North Korea under Kim Il Sung invaded South Korea; and its deep involvement in Vietnam, with aid and active participation to the communist Viet Minh in its wars between 1955 and 1975, speak as much of a Confucian tianxia worldview as they do of the export of Maoist revolutionary communism in its cultural and territorial backyard and beyond. It was a schizophrenic geopolitical perspective that alternated between articulating Westphalian Panchsheel democratic principles; Confucian tianxia hegemonic and hierarchical authoritarianism action; and the export of Maoist revolutionary communist ideology. The irony of

China's Cultural Revolution (1966–76), which rejected all forms of Confucian thought and practice in favour of Maoist communism, is unmistakable.

The journey of communist China's diplomacy and geopolitics has been a troubled one. Only 12 countries—all members of the Soviet Bloc—recognized the formation of the People's Republic of China (PRC) in 1949. Even a decade after its founding, the PRC had established diplomatic ties with only 35 countries.[4] Its break with the post-Stalinist Soviet Union only increased its global isolation, with increasing tensions in the Sino-Soviet relationship putting added pressure on China's national security.

The Soviet Union's invasion of Czechoslovakia in 1968 and the articulation of the Brezhnev Doctrine, under which Moscow claimed to reserve the right to intervene in any socialist state to prevent 'counter-revolution', put communist China under existential threat. Military conflict along the disputed Ussuri River border only exacerbated fears. The Soviet Ambassador in Washington also alerted the newly formed Nixon administration that the Soviet Union was considering a 'surgical strike' against China's nuclear facilities. It became clear to Mao that it was not feasible to battle on two geopolitical fronts. Furthermore, the 'social imperialist' Soviet Union represented a greater and more immediate danger to the PRC than the 'imperialist' US.

While inherent contradictions persisted between China and the US, the pragmatic Cold War realpolitik (epitomized by the notion of 'the enemy of my enemy is my friend'), facilitated a rapprochement between the two nations in 1971–72. This diplomatic effort was led by Henry Kissinger as secretary of state and President Richard Nixon of the US. Nixon's February 1972 visit to China was dubbed 'the week that changed the world'. In the light of the events that followed, it was not an overstatement. China in the 1970s began the process of 'joining the world' after two decades of totalitarian isolation.

By the time full normalization of diplomatic ties between the two nations was established in January 1979, the Mao era and the xenophobic Cultural Revolution had ended. Additionally, Deng

Xiaoping's 'reform and opening-up' was beginning to get underway. The establishment of relations with the US had a significant impact on China's geopolitical presence, both economically and diplomatically. At the end of the 1960s, only 45 nations had diplomatic ties with the PRC. By the end of the 1970s, this increased to 115 nations. The US facilitated the PRC taking Taiwan's seat in the United Nations (UN) in 1971, following the expulsion of Taiwan. China's establishment of ties with other Western and Asian countries that were American allies, and its coordination with them in alignment against the Soviet Union, also facilitated the opening up of commercial and cultural exchanges with them.

The 1980s saw a single-minded exclusive focus on economic growth by China, excluding all other geopolitical concerns. Massive foreign investment in manufacturing facilities in newly opened SEZs, largely from Taiwan and Hong Kong, resulted in rapid economic growth. China also expanded its foreign trade; sent students abroad to study; began interacting with Western militaries and purchasing weapons; and opened up to foreign visitors. The visible success of the economic 'reform and opening-up' process fuelled enthusiasm inside and outside China, leading many to believe that the PRC was throwing off the shackles of communist dogmatism, political totalitarianism, command economy and social strictures of the Mao era.

It was an enthusiasm that directly led to the Tiananmen Square protests in June 1989, where demonstrators demanded greater civil freedom and change. Grievances included inflation, corruption, restrictions on political participation, the call for greater accountability, constitutional due process, democracy, freedom of the press and freedom of speech. At the height of the protests, nearly 1 million people assembled in Tiananmen Square, and it soon spread to other cities.

The growing movement was viewed with concern by the party leadership and seen as disturbing the social order and stability— an inviolable canon of the CPC rule and anathema in the party lexicon. Party moderates such as Zhao Ziyang advocated negotiating with demonstrators and offering concessions. They were, however, overruled by hardliners led by Chinese premier Li Peng and supported by paramount elder statesman Deng Xiaoping who, fearing anarchy, insisted on forcibly suppressing the protests. Lethal force was used to disperse the demonstrators, while Zhao Ziyang was removed from his position and placed under house arrest till his death in 2005. The Tiananmen incident, televised and widely reported, set back China's diplomatic efforts and badly tarnished its international reputation. It also set back its ties with Western countries for many years, which invoked multiple sanctions.

Interestingly, the condemnation and outrage of Western societies, governments and media was, however, not shared globally, with the rest of the world remaining relatively silent. Japan joined G7 sanctions, but wiggled out of them within a year. South Korea only noted it as a 'regrettable incident'. Singapore's Lee Kuan Yew stated his shock, horror and sadness at the disastrous turn of events, but did not condemn them. Other nations, too, remained silent and did not suspend or sever ties. Within five years, the G7 countries had lifted most of their sanctions and by 1995, China emerged from the isolation imposed on it due to the Tiananmen incident.

The world that China re-emerged into had, however, changed dramatically. In the interim, the communist states of Eastern Europe had collapsed one after another, culminating in the disintegration of the Soviet Union and the end of the Soviet Communist Party rule in 1991. Paranoia and trepidation gripped the CPC leadership, which feared a repeat in China. The security lockdown following the Tiananmen incident and a recalibration of strategy prevented such occurrence.

Deng Xiaoping, who had formally retired from all positions and was in poor health, first enunciated the new 'grand strategy' of *taoguang yanghui*. The Chinese phrase has been differently interpreted by various scholars as 'keep a low profile and remain calm in the face of such pressures and uncertainties', and 'bide your time and hide your strengths'. In early 1992, he also embarked on his famous Southern Tour, which re-energized economic reforms and re-engaged the country with the rest of the world.

China quickly pivoted its focus to establishing relations with the new Russian Federation, as well as the 14 other newly independent members of the former Soviet Union. Throughout the 1990s, China's renewed engagement with the European Union (EU), the return of Hong Kong to Chinese sovereignty in 1997, participation in various Asian multilateral institutions, enhanced engagement with its Asian neighbours, assistance provided to Southeast Asian states in the aftermath of the Asian financial crisis and the exchange of state visits between Presidents Jiang Zemin and Bill Clinton in 1997–98, all contributed to China deepening its integration into regional and international systems by the decade's end. Over the decade, the PRC added 32 nations with which it established formal diplomatic relations. Following the establishment of formal and relatively stable relations with the majority of nations, as well as the expansion of its international footprint through foreign trade and diplomacy, China moved on to the next phase of its economics-driven geopolitical strategy: deepening its global presence.

The goal—articulated as 'going out' or 'going global'—was to make Chinese companies competitive in global markets. In the 2000s, Chinese companies, institutions, students, media and individuals established a global presence. Chinese presence across Africa, Europe and Latin America increased significantly, with China's rapidly growing and seemingly endless appetite for raw material and energy supplies driving much of this expansion.

While some of this activity was undertaken by the Chinese private sector, the predominant activity was by SOEs, national oil companies and state media. China joined the World Trade Organization (WTO) in 2001, a watershed moment for its manufacturing, exports and economy. It also strengthened ties with Russia while expanding ties with Central Asian members of the Shanghai Cooperation Organization. Its relations with India also stabilized, and it experienced its best period of relations within East Asia.

Sino-American relations also saw stable development through the presidency of George W. Bush. If the 1990s under Jiang Zemin were defined by a focus on China's relations with the major powers (the US, Russia and the EU), the 2000s under Hu Jintao saw a more varied and omnidirectional diplomacy with a new emphasis on the Global South. China established a wide range of regional multilateral institutions and dialogue groupings with every continent. China also recognized and embraced 'soft power', leading to a concerted effort to improve China's global image and influence its international narrative.

In 2009–10, following the GFC in 2008 and China's surpassing of Japan as the world's second largest economy, a notable and unsettling change unfolded in China's external relations for which it came to be known as the 'year of assertiveness'.[5] During this period, China confronted its neighbours over seemingly insignificant events in rapid succession, using a more caustic and confrontational approach. It threatened Japan with diplomatic and economic retaliation over the arrest of a drunken Chinese fisherman who had strayed into Japanese waters near the disputed Senkaku Islands. It repeated the same against the Philippines on conflicting claims in the South China Sea. It upset South Korea by blocking a UN Security Council resolution condemning the North Korean sinking of a navy submarine ROK *Cheonan*, taking the lives of 46 sailors. It escalated its claims to disputed territory with India and increased the size of its military units in these areas. It arrested and jailed Australian businessmen, allegedly in response to Australia blocking a mega-merger of Chinese and Australian metal and mining giants Chinalco and Rio Tinto. It downgraded diplomatic relations with Denmark for hosting the Dalai Lama and with Norway for their decision to award the imprisoned Chinese intellectual and dissenter Liu Xiaobo the Nobel Prize. At multilateral fora, China's diplomats blocked a final agreement and communique at the Copenhagen Climate Change Conference, engaged in disputes with the EU over multiple issues and gave a cold reception to US President Barack Obama when he undertook a state visit to Beijing in November 2009.

China's assertion and proactiveness has increased since Xi Jinping's rise to becoming the leader of the CPC and China. David Shambaugh writes:

Xi has replaced Deng's prescription for passive diplomacy-'bide time, hide brightness' […] with his more activist dictum of 'striving for achievement'. Xi has also emphasised China's 'great rejuvenation', the 'Chinese Dream', and a 'community of a shared future for mankind'. Xi has prioritised foreign policy, he has asserted that China should practise 'major country diplomacy' and he has advocated a 'new type of major power relations' […] Xi has notably emphasised that China should play a more prominent role in global governance and multilateral diplomacy. Xi has also advocated improving China's 'external propaganda' and by 'telling China's story well'.[6]

The roots of this change lie in China becoming the world's second largest economy (and the world's largest trading economy since 2013) and the GFC. The crisis of confidence that the GFC sparked in the global financial system convinced the Chinese leadership of the need for China to exert global economic influence. During the 'miracle growth' period from 1978 to 2010, China grew at an annual rate of around 10 per cent on average.[7] Rapid growth was fuelled by the seemingly limitless availability of cheap labour, giving it a global competitive advantage in labour-intensive manufactured exports. It also became the world's largest buyer of iron ore, copper and oil.

To further encourage exports, China's foreign exchange policy emphasized a low and stable yuan value. By the mid-1990s, current account controls—transactions involving payments for real goods and services—had been liberalized, boosting trade even further. China joined the WTO in December 2001, sparking an unprecedented export boom. Between 2000 and 2007, China's exports more than quadrupled, accounting for an unprecedented 35 per cent of its GDP.[8] China itself, however, remained largely a less-than-open economy, particularly on the capital account. Firms could not freely move funds in and out of China, or convert yuan into foreign currencies (except as needed for their trade transactions). Only a few firms—mostly SOEs, and particularly the three state-owned oil companies—were permitted to invest and operate internationally.

The unprecedented export boom had two immediate outcomes. First, the seemingly inexhaustible supply of cheap labour came to an end and wages began to rise, threatening China's export competitiveness. Second, as a result of the boom and rising wages, Chinese households, businesses and governments began to accumulate wealth. Domestic savings reached an extraordinary high of 50 per cent of total national income, putting pressure on productive investment both at home and abroad.[9] Initially, Chinese policymakers invested China's current account (trade) surplus funds in official foreign exchange reserves—buying and holding foreign currency and selling yuan to keep the Chinese currency's value low in order to facilitate labour-intensive exports. However, it became increasingly clear that this policy was costly, ineffective and unsustainable. If China was becoming less competitive in labour-intensive exports, it made little sense for it to continue buying low-yielding US treasury bills in order to keep the yuan's value low. Its old policies based on cheap labour export-led growth, and large but limited engagement with the world financial system and economy were no longer appropriate to China's requirements in the changing circumstances.

The three years preceding the GFC (2006–08) saw trade surpluses equalling a potentially destabilizing 7 per cent of China's GDP[10], with the accumulation of official foreign exchange reserves emphasizing the unsustainable nature of this policy. By the end of 2007, it was clear that this was a serious problem. China's official reserves had risen to a more-than-comfortable $1.5 trillion and policymakers faced rising inflation and increased trade frictions as a result of the artificial suppression of the yuan price caused by Chinese policy.

China was at a crossroads, and it needed to rethink its strategy. It was widely expected that China would respond to the new circumstances by pursuing its previously announced policies of market-oriented reform and deeper integration into the global economy. China had committed to capital account convertibility as early as 1996, and while it had been repeatedly postponed, it was seen as the logical next step. Furthermore, following the end of their own miracle growth phases, the economies of Japan, Korea and

Taiwan had followed the same path. It was, therefore, anticipated that China too would make gradual progress towards a more open economy. The GFC, however, disrupted this anticipation by forcing an unexpected and skewed rebalancing in China. As China's trade exports plummeted and its trade surplus shrank dramatically in 2008, the country embarked on a massive domestic stimulus programme to offset the massive impact of the sharp drop in exports on its economy. This government-led increase in investment in infrastructure and real estate aimed to boost domestic demand and offset a drop in exports.

From 2009 to 2014, gross fixed capital formation (GFCF) was an incredible 45 per cent of GDP.[11] However, as a consequence, China's economy became even more unbalanced and reliant on domestic investment, rather than increased domestic consumption to drive growth. In 2017, the GFCF to GDP ratio fell, only marginally, to 42 per cent.[12] With economic growth slowing once more, Chinese policymakers have launched another round of infrastructure-led growth stimulus. It is now a persistent imbalance that continues to grow and haunt policymakers in China and around the world for its future consequences.

The GFC not only forced China to deviate from its widely anticipated path of gradual open market reforms but also altered China's perception of its own place in the global economy. Barry Noughton writes:

> The GFC had been created by regulatory and policy failures in the United States - thus greatly impairing the appeal of the US model of the financialised, market economy. Moreover, China's decisive stimulus program was seen to have contributed to managing the fallout from the crisis. Did this not signify that the Chinese government could and should be bolder in using its newfound economic strength to achieve both political and economic objectives at home and abroad? Further market-oriented reforms seemed less urgent, and a leadership consensus emerged that the government could 'concentrate forces to accomplish big things'.[13]

This leadership consensus, in turn, focussed on increasing the Chinese government's intervention to grow the country's technology sector (a cause of subsequent friction with the US and other trade partners). It also sought new policies, initiatives and instruments to match its growing economic strength and status as a high-saving, middle-income economy—a strategy that would allow it to convert its external savings from low-yielding US treasury bills to higher-yielding investments while also allowing it to use its economic clout to exercise more international influence.

As a consequence, China increased its lending to developing countries and stepped up its overseas investments—particularly in natural resources (which it mistakenly saw as a natural hedge to its import requirements). It also undertook two significant initiatives: the internationalization of the yuan as a global reserve currency as an alternative to the US dollar and other currencies, and the BRI. With China being the world's largest trading economy, using the yuan as a global reserve currency made logical sense, and it worked well for several years. By 2015, the yuan was being used to settle nearly one-third of all Chinese trade transactions.

Furthermore, the People's Bank of China (PBC) had signed 'swap agreements' with 34 central banks, providing access to emergency liquidity and encouraging foreign banks to hold the Chinese currency in their official reserves. However, its internationalization was hampered by China's reluctance to provide a freely convertible capital account. China's policymakers rejected this idea, arguing that the Asian and global financial crises demonstrated the need for countries to maintain some emergency controls over capital flows. Instead, they proposed establishing a framework for investment capital to flow in and out of China in response to differences in opportunities and interest rates.

This 'macroeconomic policy with Chinese characteristics' assumed that policymakers would have more control to make investments more straightforward and efficient, increase returns on Chinese overseas investments and improve domestic economy efficiency. This 'managed' convertibility, however, was abruptly interrupted in August 2015 by a confidence crisis. Following a modest move by the PBC, exchange markets turned sharply negative on the yuan. The capital account which had been partly liberalized to allow some outflows of capital, saw a sudden and dramatic acceleration in outflows. Official foreign exchange reserves fell by almost $1 trillion, from a peak of $4 trillion to $3 trillion by the end of 2016. In response, the PBC retreated, reinforcing strict controls on capital outflows to stabilize the yuan.

Chinese overseas foreign direct investment (FDI), which had surged and exceeded incoming FDI in 2016 and 2017, fell as a result of stricter controls. The failure of yuan internationalization has since pushed Chinese policymakers back to a slower and more orthodox path. China has made new commitments to market reforms and capital account liberalization. However, its future trajectory in the volatile post-Covid global scenario remains uncertain.

The BRI—launched in 2013—is a comprehensive and high-profile Xi Jinping-led programme that follows on the earlier 'influencer efforts' made after the GFC, of setting up 'development funds' in developing countries including Venezuela and Africa. It has also been seen by many as an alternative 'Chinese model of development.' In essence, the BRI is a programme of infrastructure construction that links China to its neighbours and beyond by signing bilateral agreements between China and individual countries for the construction and financing of a wide range of infrastructure projects, including ports, power projects, railway lines, electricity transmission grids and IT networks.

The BRI envisages six land corridors radiating out from China spanning Asia, Europe and Africa. The BRI aims to improve China's global connectivity; transportation infrastructure such as ports, highways and railroads (including high-speed rail) will reduce transaction costs and knit a transnational economic network with China at its centre, while communications infrastructure will connect this network to common information standards. The building of this infrastructure will also provide opportunities for Chinese construction companies and IT hardware and service providers. It will also allow Chinese foreign currency reserves to be deployed in a more profitable manner through loans and equity investments. The BRI platform is, however, not a multilateral platform. Agreements and policy coordination exist only bilaterally between China and individual countries, and range from comprehensive joint planning and projects like the China–Pakistan Economic Corridor (CPEC) to a few pilot projects.

Given the poor infrastructure and connectivity in its surrounding regions, as well as the fact that most states on China's periphery are generally small, with weak development capabilities and limited financial and planning resources, the BRI is, conceptually, well-articulated. China has also put in place financing institutions for supporting its initiative, setting up the Asian Infrastructure Investment Bank (AIIB) which, while having 93 members (end-2018), is often seen as 'China's multilateral development bank'.

The BRI has, however, run into difficulties in recent years. Expensive but unviable projects built by Chinese companies and funded by Chinese debt have become white elephants for many of these countries, unable to generate sufficient revenues to repay these often high-cost loans. China's tough approach to the recovery of its investments include taking over projects, like Sri Lanka's Hambantota port for 99 years[14], on terms that resemble its own past with treaty ports and extraterritoriality, instead of modern terms of bilateral debt restructuring between two sovereign nations of Westphalian order. The aggressive approach has inflamed public opinion in many of these nations, which view these as an attack on their national sovereignty, even amid allegations of crony collusion by China with their political leaders. China has, however, continued with its deliberate and uncompromising approach to assert these acquired rights and aggressively push its maritime and other interests, rather than adopting diplomacy and conciliation, even in stressed post-Covid economic and geopolitical times. This approach was evident in the controversy of a Chinese surveillance ship provocatively docking at the China-controlled Hambantota port even as Sri Lanka faced a humanitarian crisis, much to the concern of India that was engaged in providing relief and assistance to the beleaguered island nation.[15]

It is in the background of the above that China's proactive diplomacy has rapidly grown in the decade since Xi's rise to power, much to the consternation and suspicion of large sections of the international community. China's revised and aggressive approach to modern geopolitics is best described in what is called its 'wolf warrior' diplomacy. *Wolf Warrior* and *Wolf Warrior 2* are Chinese action blockbuster movies that highlight agents of Chinese special operation forces against external (Western) forces. The movies have tapped into a rich vein of national pride among Chinese viewers. Perhaps, taking a cue, the Chinese foreign ministry, too, has taken an increasingly strident, even offensive, tone against the US, Australia, Japan and other countries in a new approach that seems popular in China and reinforces a presumed transition of Chinese diplomacy from conservative, passive and low key (as advocated by Deng) to assertive, proactive, confrontational and high profile (as practiced by Xi Jinping). More worryingly, wolf warrior diplomacy is not limited only in combative words but aggressive actions.

In April 2020, a Chinese coast guard ship allegedly sank a Vietnamese fishing trawler near the Paracel Islands. When Vietnam protested, the Chinese foreign ministry responded by saying that Vietnam's claims to the area are 'illegal'. In the same month, the Chinese Ministry of Natural Resources and Ministry of Civil Affairs jointly announced the naming of 80 islands, reefs, seamounts, shoals and ridges in the South China Sea, triggering angry protests from other claimants. The last time China named islands and other geographical features in the South China Sea was in 1983.

The Galwan Valley clash on the disputed Indo-China border on 15 June 2020, led to loss of lives of soldiers on both sides, making it the first such incident in 45 years. While border skirmishes were frequent earlier, the loss of lives and the aggressive forward stance taken by China resulted in hardening of public opinion on both sides and escalation of tensions and military buildup along the long Himalayan border that have yet not ebbed.[16] The impact of the border clash continues to cast a long shadow on Indo-China ties across the spectrum of their engagement. It is a pattern that is repeated across most of China's borders at land and at sea, where it is in aggressive confrontation with its neighbours—Japan, Philippines, South Korea, Indonesia, Vietnam, Malaysia, Australia, and so on—escalating to what earlier would be minor disputes.

China, as the world's second largest economy, also has the second largest military force in the world today, accompanied by a strong maritime presence that is on its way to becoming a blue water navy. It also has a maritime militia that it has used to capture and assert control over islands, rocks, reefs and the South China Sea, including construction of artificial island outposts in the disputed Spratly Islands in 2016.

While the maritime militia has been used by China in the past (it was used in 1974 to seize the Paracel Islands from Vietnam), its involvement in aggressive operations increased in the 2000s, when militia vessels physically interfered with the navigation of multiple US Navy ships. This continued into the early 2010s, where the militia played a key role in China's seizure of Scarborough Shoal in 2012, as well as the deployment of a Chinese oil rig into Vietnamese waters in 2014. According to a report of the CSIS, 'Militia have accompanied Chinese law enforcement at several oil and gas standoffs with Malaysia and Vietnam and have participated in mass deployments at targeted features; nearly 100 militia boats were deployed near Philippine-occupied Thitu Island in 2018, and approximately 200 gathered at unoccupied Whitsun Reef in the spring of 2021.'[17] According to the Chinese perspective, as China becomes more powerful, some countries increasingly view its development as a threat to their national interests and are unprepared or unwilling to accept China's rise. Many Chinese believe the Western media portrayal of China is highly biased with ideological and racist undertones, and wolf warrior diplomacy is part of the Chinese government's effort to 'tell the China story'.

China's uniquely authoritarian worldview, particularly regarding people of Chinese descent who are non-Chinese citizens or residing overseas in other countries, has an aggressive element of extraterritorial actions that have alarmed and fuelled public and government reactions around the world, particularly in the US, the UK, Australia and Canada. This includes alleged overseas 'police stations'[18] that reportedly coerce or put undue influence on overseas Chinese to comply or return to China for accountability to Chinese law.

Allegations of aggressive wolf warrior behaviour have included accusations of consular staff pulling in a pro-democracy Hong Kong protestor into its consulate compound in Manchester, England and beating him up, an incident that caused widespread public outrage and withdrawal of six Chinese diplomats by China.[19] It has also fuelled demands to review Confucius Institutes, China's soft power evangelization of its culture and language at a global level and a potential ban in Britain.[20]

China's global image has further suffered during the Covid-19 crisis due to its bungled handling of the outbreak at the early stage, with many blaming China for initially covering up the human-to-human transmission of the virus and not sharing complete information with the international community. In early 2020, the US and China were engaged in tit-for-tat expulsion of journalists that started after the publication of an op-ed in *The Journal* (The Wall Street Journal podcasts) titled 'China is the Real Sick Man of Asia'. When *The Wall Street Journal* refused to apologize, China expelled three of its journalists. Shortly afterwards, the US declared five Chinese media outlets as 'foreign missions' and cut the number of Chinese nationals working there. In retaliation, China expelled more American journalists. The Chinese foreign ministry spokesperson claimed that the coronavirus might have been brought to Wuhan by the US military. This was widely seen as a response to the US politicians, notably the then Secretary of State Mike Pompeo in the Trump administration, continuing to call it the 'Chinese virus' or the 'Wuhan virus'.[21]

While there is no consensus within the Chinese foreign policy establishment on whether this confrontational diplomacy is desirable, and some traditionally minded diplomats continue to suggest that Chinese diplomacy should uphold 'the spirit of humility and tolerance, and adhere to communication, learning, and openness', these are voices in the wilderness.[22] Wolf warrior diplomacy and geopolitical aggression is already hurting China's interests, since it has generated mistrust and pushback across nations. With China's soft power being weak globally, a belligerent approach further damages China's global image with many seeing it as a return to its truant and unpredictable ways. More importantly, as American and Western public opinion of China and Xi turns more negative, so does Chinese public opinion on America and the West, along with views on its neighbours with most of whom it has a fractious relationship.

Hardening attitudes have resulted in actions with real life consequences, including Xi's 'zero-Covid' strategy that has caused great hardship to urban Chinese, slowed economic activity across China and disrupted global supply chains. It has accelerated the increasingly frantic search of companies and nations for a 'China Plus One' strategy, relocating manufacturing bases away from the 'factory of the world'. This has also led to growing Chinese global isolation as military, security and economic realignments took place in a fast-changing world that is grappling with its own crises. However, perhaps most importantly for its future prospects, it has also progressively restricted China's access to high technology in cutting-edge research domains like semiconductors and artificial intelligence, where the West maintains a competitive edge.

While China continues to be deeply, and perhaps irreversibly, integrated with global manufacturing and supply chains, it presently faces its most significant geopolitical challenges since 1972—the year it established ties with the US and embarked on a path of re-engagement with the world, a journey that has been a significant source of its subsequent economic prosperity as the factory to the world and its ascent to the position of the world's second largest economy. The question that is increasingly being asked is, what has led China to abandon Deng's *taoguang yanghui*—low profile strategy—that yielded it significant economic prosperity and global clout for over two decades, for an aggressive geopolitical posturing that seems to be attracting more enemies than friends, and yielding negative returns? Is a course-correction possible?

Some scholars suggest that China's increasingly aggressive nationalist posture to the world, and more importantly to the Chinese people, has its roots in legitimacy issues that the CPC rule presently face. Over 70 years of the CPC rule, and over 30 years of reform and opening-up, have made China the world's second-largest economy, propelled it to the status of a middle-income country and lifted millions of its people out of poverty. In the process, however, it has adopted a market-based 'socialism with Chinese characteristics' model that has sharpened wealth and income inequalities—particularly among the urban rich and rural poor, with land conflicts and social unrest. Accompanied by widespread and rampant corruption among the CPC elite and rank and file, and deviation from the ideals and objectives of the party, it has brought its 'Mandate of Heaven'—an important determinant in Chinese psyche—under growing public scrutiny. If the CPC is no longer communist or adhering to its ideals and objectives, what is its legitimacy to rule China?

The roots of many of Xi's initiatives lie in addressing these issues—for example, the anti-corruption campaign, 'common prosperity' and a return to 'more pure' idealism. However, none of these fully address the question of legitimacy, or square the circle of the inherent contradiction of Mao's revolution phase and the post-Mao market reforms phase. Xi has sought to answer this question by travelling back in time to imperial China and its Confucian values. His 'China Dream' of making China great again seeks to evoke a nationalism, led by the CPC, which legitimizes continued rule by the party towards this national purpose. It is ironic that Confucian and traditional Chinese values that were reviled and persecuted during Mao's Cultural Revolution—including the desecration of Confucius's family cemetery by Red Guards seeking to establish the absolute authority of Mao Zedong Thought—have been revived with state patronage.

Confucianism and China's glorious past are increasingly referred to in speeches, publications and state media as the CPC seeks to aggressively claim an unbroken lineage with the nation's imperial past. In fact, Xi's signature BRI, of building infrastructure in developing countries, too, is based on the Silk Road—land-based and maritime—route, with hints of the Qianlong Emperor's letter to the British monarch. All these speak to and resonate with the deep cultural pride of the Chinese, of China regaining centrality in its tianxia and also its sense of national exceptionalism. To many observers, it is remarkable how today's PRC has inherited and resembles the much reviled—and 'foreign' non-Han Manchu—Qing empire's notions and practices.

As Odd Arne Westad, the Elihu Professor of History and Global Affairs at Yale University writes:

> Many of the concepts of extreme centralisation are from the Qing era, as are institutions such as the *hukou*, the household registration system by which Chinese are permitted or denied the right to settle outside the region of their birth. In overall terms, the PRC's current authoritarianism, its state reverence, its methods for controlling and fashioning private enterprise, organisations and religious communities all come from the Qing (although many of them, of course, have deeper roots). China today has done away with less of its imperial legacies overall than most other post-imperial states. For the purposes of understanding the PRC's international affairs, grasping this relative continuity and its effects is central. It has a strong effect both on what China is and how it constructs its outer worlds.[23]

With a third term, and as likely authoritarian leader for life in an increasingly centralized state, unchallenged CPC General Secretary (including his other, equally important military position as chairman of the Central Military Commission [CMC] of the People's Liberation Army) Xi Jingping resembles a Chinese Emperor with a Mandate of Heaven, as no other has since Chairman Mao. If this foundational construct were to be true, it will be increasingly difficult for Xi's China to adopt any alternate path to nationalist exceptionalism at home or abroad—and attempt to reclaim its historic role as regional hegemon, if not global 'major' power—while retaining the legitimacy of the CPC rule. This challenge unfolds against a backdrop of slowing economic growth, increasing social unrest, unfulfilled promises and a rapidly changing adverse geopolitical situation in which it finds itself increasingly isolated and under suspicion.

In one of those quirks of history, the roots of the geopolitical strands that continue to entangle India and China in the modern world stretch back to the same Qianlong Emperor whose reception of the British ambassador George Macartney in 1792, set in motion events that led to the Opium Wars and China's century of humiliation—a turbulent phase that continues to haunt Chinese policymakers and scar its geopolitics even today. It was under the Qianlong Emperor that the Qing dynasty finally achieved its long-held ambition of expanding its empire westward into Inner Asia by defeating and extinguishing their tenacious foe, the Junghar Mongols.

It was in July 1757 that Amursana, the last pretender to the rule of an independent Jungharia, fled from pursuing Qing forces into Russia. When the Qing absorbed Amursana's domain two years later, the Qing empire reached its greatest extent ever, and its western border in Tibet and Xinjiang abutted the Indian subcontinent. Ironically, it was in June 1757, barely a month earlier, that the Battle of Plassey was fought in which the East India Company defeated the Nawab of Bengal, setting the stage for British colonial rule in India. The British colonial territories bordering the Qing empire stretched in an arc across the Himalayan borders to its maritime presence and colonies in the South China Sea. It was opium grown in India that was used by the British to pay for its Chinese imports of tea and other valued goods, forcing the Opium Wars (1839–42 and 1856–60) on China, a war in which it extensively used Indian troops. It was also a war which inflicted a devastating defeat and blow to Qing's prestige and ignited questions among the Chinese elite that eventually led to path-dependent events leading up to the present.

One of the questions that has intrigued historians is 'how did Qing rulers, officials and scholars interpret the rising British power in India between 1750 and 1860, and how did this understanding influence the policies proposed or implemented to maintain the empire's security?' In his book, *From Frontier Policy to Foreign Policy: The Question of India and the Transformation of Geopolitics in Qing China*, Matthew Mosca writes:

> In the eighteenth century, the (Qing) empire was conceived by its rulers to be surrounded by a collection of discrete frontier areas, each to be analysed and managed according to its own political circumstances. The formulation by the emperor and his ministers of segmented, regionally specific strategies to guide Qing relations with the outside world... (was a) 'frontier policy'. This approach, well suited to flexibly governing the far-flung diversity of the empire's borderlands, became less effective when the Qing confronted European empires that operated simultaneously in multiple, non-contiguous areas and could not be managed, or even fully comprehended on any single frontier.[24]

Simply put, Qing statesmen and scholars never conceived a comprehensive 'grand strategy' to deal with ascendant European empires because they perceived the world differently.

British interests drove Indian geopolitics during British rule, with the primary goal of retaining British dominance in India. Throughout the nineteenth and early twentieth centuries, British rule in the subcontinent was shaped by 'The Great Game'—a strategic rivalry with an expansionist Russia as it extended its influence into Central Asia, threatening the northwest of India. British India, from the 1880s onwards, followed a policy of 'buffer states' on its borders. A buffer state was a protected state between the territory actually administered by the British Raj and the territories of its adversarial neighbours—Russia and China. By definition, this was not a neutral state but one that excluded all outside influences in its foreign relations.

A Ring Fence policy was enacted in which 'ring fence' included Nepal, Bhutan and territories that the British nominally regarded as independent or autonomous, like Tibet and Thailand, which the British Raj tried to keep free of outside influences and hostile powers.

To British strategists, India commanded the strategic centre and its Asian presence hinged on the subcontinent's power and stability. It was a role that India would continue to play, even as Russian and Chinese power consolidated in Central Asia, remaining pivotal to the maintenance of balance of power in the continent.

Indian foreign policy after Independence was largely guided by PM Jawaharlal Nehru's vision of a socialist republic, while being deeply conscious of its civilizational heritage and its role in an Asian and global context. A mix of realist and idealist, he continued to follow many of British India's policies and role, concluding similar treaties with Bhutan and Afghanistan, and intervening in Nepal in an attempt to manage India's civilizational sphere of influence. His anti-imperialist and socialist inclinations, however, convinced him that India's future did not lie in aligning with either the Cold War bloc of Soviet Union or the US. Instead, he advocated for a non-aligned approach—maintaining equal distant from both superpowers.

The Non-Aligned Movement (NAM) of recently independent, developing countries under his leadership—along with Sukarno of Indonesia and Josip Broz Tito of Yugoslavia—gathered pace as an alternative in a deeply polarized world order. Yet, India retained its membership of the British Commonwealth after Independence, retaining the Westminster model of government and seeking guidance from Britain regarding legal and governance precedents. In large part, the foreign policy and military institutions that the newly independent Republic of India inherited were creations of the British Raj, thereby perpetuating ongoing colonial habits, traditions and attitudes.

In his thoughts of geopolitical continuity, anti-imperialism, subcontinental leadership and idealism lay Nehru's conviction:

India is not a poor country. She is abundantly supplied with everything that makes a country rich, and yet her people are very poor. She has a noble heritage of culture-forms and her culture-potential is very great; but many new developments and the accessories of culture are lacking only two factors may come in the way: international developments and external pressure on India, and lack of a common objective within the country. Unfortunately, it is the latter alone that will count. If India is split up into two or more parts and can no longer function as a political and economic unit, her progress will be seriously affected. There will be direct weakening effect, but much worse will be the inner psychological conflict between those who wish to reunite her and those who oppose this.[25]

The Indian subcontinent was, however, split into two parts on religious lines, with the creation of Pakistan with territories to the west in the Punjab plains and beyond, and in the east, encompassing parts of the Ganges Delta.

The legacy of British colonial 'divide and rule' saw India engage in multiple wars and conflicts, including those over Kashmir and the 1971 war for the liberation of Bangladesh in the eastern part of the subcontinent. The divided subcontinent became a sub-theatre of the changed Great Game during the Cold War, with Pakistan as a forward allied state of the US and Western nations against Russian influence in Afghanistan, while counterbalancing India's regional power. The unresolved border with the buffer state of Tibet along the long Himalayan range also had long term geopolitical implications, as China's 1949 invasion of Tibet saw the two Asian regional powers sharing a direct border which they could not reach an agreement upon. The disputed border has seen multiple skirmishes, military build ups and even war in 1962 in which China captured Aksai Chin, bordering its troubled Xinjiang province.

The border dispute has cast a long shadow on Indo-China relations, even as China and Pakistan have formed an axis to keep India off-balance, to the extent of Pakistan ceding India-claimed territory to China. Pakistan ceded the Yarkand River and Shaksgam Valley to Beijing in 1963, followed by the Sino-Pakistani construction of the Karakoram Highway, an 810-mile road cutting through the Khunjerab Pass in India-claimed Gilgit–Baltistan towards Xinjiang in 1973. The Sino-Pakistani strategic partnership has been greatly expanded in recent times, with the CPEC building significant infrastructure including roads, ports and power plants since 2013, and enabling Chinese access to the Arabian Sea and the Persian Gulf. China now seeks to expand the CPEC to Afghanistan and Iran. China's primary interest in Afghanistan lies in the Wakhan Corridor, a 217-mile-long and nine-mile-wide strip of land in Afghanistan that connects to the Wakhjir Pass in Xinjiang. The Wakhan—the only land border between China and Afghanistan—provides access to Turkmenistan and Uzbekistan, the only two Central Asian states that do not share a contiguous border with China.

Beijing began the construction of a highway through the Wakhjir Pass into Wakhan, which connects with the Karakoram Highway to interact with vital CPEC-related components. China has also signed the 25-Year Cooperation Programme in March 2021 by leveraging Tehran's desperate need to counter Western sanctions. Both states are looking to build a north-south corridor between the Chabahar Port—Iran's only oceanic port—and Central Asia, and a south-west corridor connecting Chabahar and Bandar Abbas with Turkey and Azerbaijan. Chabahar Port is also perceived as India's gateway to Afghanistan and Central Asia, to secure a trade transit route into Uzbekistan and Turkmenistan, and to counter Chinese influence over Gwadar. In 2016, India secured a $500 million deal to develop and operate Chabahar port and signed an MoU to construct a 628-km railway from Chabahar to Zahedan to facilitate greater trade with Afghanistan.[26] More recently, India and Iran have been reported as being close to finalizing a long-term agreement on Chabahar port.[27]

The Great Game on the Asian landmass lives on well into the present, except the players have changed. Instead of Russia and Britain, it is now China and India—as rising powers—that since 2013, are increasingly jockey for power, influence and containment in the Persian Gulf and Central Asian regions vital to global geopolitical interests. It is a contestation that extends further to Indo-China, and increasingly in the Indian Ocean, where China aggressively pursues Belt and Road alternate land and sea routes to the potential chokepoint (Malacca Straits) for its trade, while India looks to secure its regional security influence in the region through its 'Neighbours First' and 'Look East' policy.

The US and Western countries' alignment in this lies naturally with India, as they seek to counter the growing influence of China at land and sea, with a series of economic and security agreements with nations at the periphery of China's borders with whom it is often engaged with in fractious conflict. Equally, the reconvergence of a Russia and China axis—with Pakistan as China's all-weather friend—in a multipolar world geopolitical order is not only a distinct possibility, but an emerging reality. China's deep economic integration with Western supply chains, and the consequences of this rapidly changing realignment of global geopolitical forces on it, is a multi-trillion dollar question that remains unanswered.

India, since 1991 and even earlier, has adopted market-led change and improved its relations with the US and Western countries in the unipolar world that emerged following the collapse of the Soviet Union. Its liberalization reforms, opening up of markets and joining the world trade order have been largely as per policy prescriptions prescribed by West-dominated Bretton Woods institutions. Its liberal democracy with familiar institutional mechanisms that have survived the test of time, while other postcolonial regimes in Asia and Africa have fallen to dictatorships or failed nations, has been a source of geopolitical stability in the region. Since 1991, it has focussed its geopolitics almost entirely on its economic growth and the practice of strategic autonomy. With 30 years of more than 6 per cent economic growth, India has improved its position relative to all powers except China. In a multipolar world, its importance as a regional stabilizing counter-weight to an aggressive China will only grow.

Since 2014, the Narendra Modi government has renewed focus on India's economic growth and embarked on a policy of pragmatic geopolitical strategic autonomy. In the process, policy objectives have been revisited, as also changes in how India strategically perceives its role on the global stage and proactively engages with an increasingly multipolar world. The old 'grand strategy' of foreign policy, as described by Shivshankar Menon, former National Security Advisor

(NSA) to the Government of India (also former foreign secretary, and Indian ambassador to China), 'was a Nehruvian legacy of working within the existing order to create an enabling environment for India's development and to encourage an open, plural, and democratic international order, while improving the order, and India's say in it, where possible.'[28]

The world today is, however, facing a rapidly changing global scenario with multiple challenges of emerging realignments, evolving alliances and regional hegemons of economic and military power. And, unlike Xi Jinping's 'China Dream' of Chinese civilization and national exceptionalism resulting in wolf warrior behaviour and belligerent diplomacy that has caused alarm and concern among the global political community as well as public opinion across countries, India's inclusive soft power projection has not been aggressive or fractious in its geopolitics.

India has, in addition to its pragmatic diplomacy, sought to develop and project its soft-power—the Yoga day at the UN for example, to engage with decision makers and public opinion across nations and at international forums at a cultural level, to increase their familiarity of shared democratic and universal values, while maintaining the primacy of the strategic autonomy of India's foreign policy as guided by India's proactive economic and security interests. As Shivshankar Menon also points out, 'India is fortunate in having a tradition of strategic thought that, unlike China's, prepares it for the polycentric or multipolar world of contention among today's powers of differing capabilities'.

As global geopolitics rapidly changes, China's quest to aggressively rise as a 'major power' by an emphasis on its civilizational exceptionalism and its status as the world's second largest economy and military achieved over the last 30 years, is likely to face many challenges. India on the other hand, while mindful of its civilizational heritage, remains proactively focussed on its economic and security interests in its practice of inclusive geopolitics, pursuing a course of strategic and pragmatic autonomy in a fast-emerging multipolar world.

15

The Fourth Yin: Demographics

In January 2023, according to estimates by the World Population Review, India's population increased to 1.423 billion, overtaking China's 1.412 billion and became the world's largest country by population.[1] What also grabbed headlines the world over, was the release of data from China's National Bureau of Statistics (NBS) which estimated that China's population fell in 2022, its first decline in population since the famine-hit 1960s. China's population is projected to continue to rapidly decline, while India's population grows and is projected to peak at 1.7 billion by 2064.[2]

Estimates also show a younger population structure of India as compared to China, where half of India's current population is under the age of 30 years, as compared to about 35 per cent of Chinese in the same age group. Further, the ageing population (60 years and above) of China is almost double that of India.[3] China's demographic dividend—of a higher working age population—has disappeared, while India's is likely to rise over the next few decades. It presents both an opportunity and a potential threat if not addressed appropriately, to both economies and nations.

Most nations face an ageing and declining population as their economies grow, accompanied by higher levels of education, improved socio-economic indicators, urbanization and gender participation in the workforce. For China, the problem is, however, more acute as its demographics undergo a rapid ageing transformation, the roots of which can be directly traced to a state policy intervention undertaken decades ago, the consequences of which are becoming evident now. This rapid change will require a significant transformation in the present composition, productivity and trajectory of China's economy, addressing the increasingly prevalent question, 'Will China grow old before it grows rich?'

How did China reach this severe demographic dilemma?

In the late 1970s and early 1980s, China first announced—and then enforced—its one-child policy. China's population had reached nearly 1 billion by then, and was growing at a rate of nearly 1.5 per cent annually. Earlier the CPC's views on population, expressed by Mao as 'Ren Duo, Liliang Da (With Many People, Strength is Great)', saw China follow the post-World War II depopulated Soviet Union celebrating 'mother heroines' for giving birth to large families. The rejection of Malthusian dogma under socialist doctrine, eventually gave way to growing concern, followed by alarm, as gains of growth and mortality over the following decades were increasingly diluted by a burgeoning population. Mao's view of a growing population as a national strength was, however, not only an expression of orthodox communist thought (which posited that labour was the only factor of production that could be productive without limits) but also a traditional Confucian view that had been long held in China.

Fertility was encouraged in China by both the imperial state and social traditions. State promotion of fertility over civilizational millennia in an agricultural era included various imperial edicts to make widows and widowers marry each other, making it a punishable crime for parents if a woman remained unmarried at 17, or a man at 20 years of age. It was also illegal for young men to marry old women, or for old men to marry young women. Incentives offered included exemption from two years of labour service for women who gave birth to a baby. Imperial governments also provided nutritious food for pregnant women, and their husbands were exempted from one year of labour service. For Confucians, xiao (filial piety), meant continuing the family heritage and propagating the family line by giving birth.

According to Mencius (372–289 BCE), the most famous Confucian thinker after Confucius himself, 'There are three ways to be unfilial; having no posterity is the worst'. Family and children were thus central to Chinese state policy and tradition. Even Sun Yat-Sen, the founder of the KMT which battled the CPC in a long war, was of the view that China's problems were not caused by overpopulation. Comparing China to the population growth in other countries, he was, in fact, worried about China's 'racial destruction' if this population race was lost.

It was Deng Xiaoping, as vice premier in the early 1950s, who advocated and championed birth control amid much opposition from other leaders. Even Mao initially supported a voluntary birth control policy by 1957, before backing off in the chaos of the GLF and its horrific consequences in the Great Chinese Famine. The tragedy of the Great Chinese Famine saw a sudden rise in fertility in China, particularly between 1965 and 1970. The rise in fertility temporarily reversed a downward trend in the 1950s, perhaps as a cultural response to the loss of so many people. It had, however, already reverted to a long-term downward trend between 1970 to 1979, when the total fertility rate (children per woman of child bearing age) fell from six children per woman to three.[4]

Deng's reform and opening-up brought a laser focus on economics as the driving force of China's development. If Mao's era saw 'politics in command', under Deng it was economic development that became the touchstone on which policy was determined. According to Deng, 'Economic work is the biggest political work now. The economic issue is the overwhelming political issue… We must control population growth. If we allow people to give birth to children desperately, our development would fall.'

The direct result of this line of thought was the one-child policy in 1980, a policy that, with a few exceptions, was so strictly enforced that it had disastrous social, economic and demographic consequences until it was modified 35 years later. The one-child policy was deeply controversial from its inception. China officially credits the policy with preventing 400 million births, helping the nation improve its economic situation and limiting further strain on natural resources, while lifting millions out of poverty, thereby improving human and developmental quality of life for its people. But the policy has also had severe consequences. The most evident, and the reason for the relaxation of policy in 2015, is an ageing population.

China has one of the fastest-aging populations in the world.

According to Chinese officials themselves, 20 per cent of China's population will be 60 years and older by 2025. This figure will rise to 30 per cent of the population by 2035, when 400 million people will be 60 years and older.[5] Rural areas face a larger and more severe ageing problem than urban areas. Many provinces in Northeast and Southwest China already had more than 20 per cent of their population aged 60 and above in 2020.

There are several economic and social consequences of this ageing problem. As the number and percentage in population of elderly people rises, its proportion to the working population falls. This means there are fewer working persons to support each elderly person. This dependency ratio is rising and is expected to peak around 2050. Furthermore, it will pose great challenges to China's future economy, growth, public services and the sustainability of its social security system. Additionally, Chinese preference for boy children over girl children has also resulted in illegal abortions, infanticide and led to a skewed gender ratio that jeopardizes the social fabric.

The costs of this policy are, however, not limited to economics and society alone. As the Chinese demographic pyramid has rapidly inverted to a 4-2-1 (four grandparents, two parents, one child) structure, nearly two generations of Chinese have grown up as single children. Ageing parents have traditionally lived with their children in Chinese culture, who have felt a responsibility to take care of them. This social convention is, however, rapidly breaking down under urbanization and the one-child policy.

The 'only child' has become a much-discussed and written about socio-psychological phenomenon in Chinese society since the early 1980s. The only child are precious, and therefore, pampered and spoilt as 'little emperors' and 'suns' around whom the entire family revolves. The generations that have grown up as a single child is best illustrated in a story from the book *Buy Me the Sky: The Remarkable Truth of China's One-Child Generation* by Chinese expatriate journalist Xinran.

Xinran writes of coming across a family of six people, spanning three generations. The toddler was throwing a tantrum, wanting her mother to buy her the river that was flowing through the city centre. Her mother was trying to explain to the child that it was not possible to 'buy this big river'. In the background, the grandparents were debating the matter, with some advising them not to tell her that they couldn't afford it. Instead, they suggested she tell the child that they would buy it when she grew up. Or to ask her father how to buy a river. Some were concerned about teaching her from an early age to believe in lies, while others just wanted to keep her happy. The entire focus was on not to upset the child.

> [The child spoke again and] the quietly arguing family suddenly fell silent, as though they were listening to an imperial edict. 'Then I want to buy a star in the sky,' the little girl demanded in her babyish voice. I did not stop to listen anymore, so I never knew if the little girl had further requests, but I found it impossible to understand these old people's words, and the way they took their little granddaughter's naive demands so seriously.[6]

Shenshen Cai writes in her book:

> After more than three decades since the implementation of the one-child policy […] the first generations of single children […] have become the 'backbone' of the society. Because of the inappropriate education and spoiling from their parents, together with the 'lonely' environment in which they grew up, it is believed that a considerable percentage […] show many ostensible flaws concerning their character, living aptitude, emotional adaptability and values. Commonly, (they) […] lack a sense of family duty and traditional values, […] become selfish and deficient in social skills, and perform comparatively poorly in domestic and career situations.[7]

The Yao Jiaxin incident in 2011 sent shock waves in China and made headlines around the world. Yao Jiaxin was a 22-year-old student at the Xi'an Conservatory of Music. On the night of 20 October 2010, the car he was driving ran over a 26-year-old female rural migrant worker. Not only did he make no attempt to help her, he was so afraid that this migrant worker would create trouble for him when he saw her memorizing his number plate, that he stabbed her eight times with a fruit peeling knife, killing the mother of a three-year-old child on the spot. He then fled in his car to another junction where he injured another pedestrian and was finally apprehended by a passer-by. The local public security bureau, however, released him after only questioning him about the incident at the second junction. He turned himself in to police only three days later, accompanied by his parents. He was subsequently charged with premeditated murder, and after being found guilty, was sentenced to death and executed in June 2011.

The case deeply divided Chinese public opinion along theoretical and moral lines. According to some, the circumstances of the crime were so heinous that death was the only option if Chinese law was to maintain public trust. Others saw Yao as a victim of being an only child who was not adequately socialized and had a poor moral framework, thus advocating against imposing death penalty. Many university students held a surprising third point of view, claiming that the life of an only child who had received higher education in the arts was of greater intrinsic value than that of an uneducated peasant. Since then, the challenge of defining rights and wrongs, glory and shame, from the perspectives of multiple and very different generations has only grown. The first generation had no siblings, and their children had no uncles, aunts or cousins, and the third generation will have no family at all. The impact on Chinese society, where family ties and affection have been a core value and a goal pursued by both individuals and society, is undeniably enormous.

Aside from the gender imbalance, the growing elder care problem, the erosion of traditional values and the socio-psychological issues in one child generations, the one-child policy's implementation also resulted in gross human rights violations. Compulsory sterilizations, abortions, the prohibition of births to mothers under the age of 23, imprisonment of those who fled elsewhere, no official documents for an unauthorized second child and steep fines were among the draconian measures undertaken. The policy also brought the party and the state into conflict with the masses.

As state personnel directly interacted with women, family planning staff and local officials not only needed to persuade some 10 million women with unplanned pregnancies to undergo abortions, they also had to visit hundreds of millions of families to collect fines for unplanned births. According to Chen Jian, a senior official who used to work for the National Family Planning Commission, 'In the history of our Party, there has never been anything like birth control which has been based on confrontation with the masses. The one child policy seriously trampled on the rights of citizens, especially their reproductive rights. This severely endangered the legitimacy of the ruling party and government at lower levels in rural areas.'[8]

The radical impact of the one-child policy on China's social and economic fabric was exacerbated by the stringent hukou household registration system, a feature that Chinese imperial authorities had once used for taxation and migration control. The hukou that was introduced in CPC-ruled China in 1958 was designed for three purposes—government welfare and resource distribution, controlling internal migration and criminal surveillance. Each town and city issued its own hukou, a kind of domestic passport, which gave residents access to social welfare services in that town, city or county. People were broadly classified as 'rural' or 'urban' based on their place of residence. The hukou was hereditary, with strictly controlled migration. The apparent logic of the hukou system was to ensure that China's rural population continued to stay in rural areas to cultivate and provide food and other resources for urban area residents as China sought rapid industrialization in its pursuit of economic development in a planned manner.

However, the 1980s reform and opening-up fuelled an unprecedented demand for cheap labour. Hundreds of millions of young men and women from rural areas relocated to coastal China in one of the world's largest migrations to work in factories and on construction sites. As unregistered migrants, they were cut off from access to any state welfare services, including education, health, rations and even law. In the singular focus on economic growth, their conditions were largely ignored till 2003 when, in response to the death of a migrant in police custody, as he did not have a valid hukou, barriers to migration began to be addressed. Rural migrant workers, whose cheap labour has powered China's spectacular economic growth over the last three decades, however, remain marginalized and subject to institutional discrimination. Their children have limited access to education and healthcare if accompanying their migrant parent(s), and, if left behind in the rural area of their hukou registration, they are separated from their parents for years.[9]

The magnitude of this hukou migration issue is highlighted by the fact that there were an estimated 292 million rural migrant workers in China in 2021, comprising more than one-third of China's entire working population.[10] Over the last decade, the average age of migrant workers in China has steadily increased as fewer young people enter the workforce and older workers with no pension protection are forced to continue working. In 2021, the average age was 41.7 years, up from 34 years in 2008.[11] The vast majority of rural migrant workers are still employed in low-wage industries such as manufacturing, construction and service (transportation and logistics).

According to a NBS sample survey conducted in 2020, the total number of children of migrant workers that year was around 138 million, or about 46.4 per cent of all children in China. Out of this total, there were an estimated 71 million children who migrated with their parents and 67 million children who remained in their hometown, in both rural and urban areas.[12] Three decades of reform and opening-up and spectacular economic growth later, however, the hukou system remains in place, particularly in major cities. According to some experts, there is a pressing need for a genuine commitment to enhancing social justice, reducing the gap between rich and poor and increasing social mobility.

China's Gini coefficient—the measure of income inequality (the lower the coefficient, the less the inequality)—saw a rise from 0.31 in 1980 to a peak of 0.49 in 2008, before falling to 0.47 in 2021.

That is more unequal than the US (0.39).[13] One per cent of China's top earners hold a greater share of wealth than the bottom 50 per cent. Less than one fifth of Tsinghua University, one of China's top-ranking educational institutions, were from rural or less developed areas. An apartment in Shenzhen costs 43.5 times the average annual salary in the city.[14] 'Common prosperity', unsurprisingly, is one of the keystones of Xi Jinping's proposed policies in his third five-year term. Cai Fang, a well-known economist and adviser to the central bank, has argued that in order to achieve common prosperity, China should aim to reduce its Gini coefficient to 0.4 by 2025, which will require various forms of distribution and redistribution as well as the construction of a 'basic public service system covering the entire life cycle of all people, which can also be called a social welfare system'.[15]

China's economic growth, at least initially, was due to its nearly limitless supply of cheap labour from rural areas, which fuelled its SEZs and earned it the title of 'factory of the world' manufacturing base. Its subsequent rapid urbanization and infrastructure construction also benefitted from a demographic dividend of a large population, with rising incomes and a high savings rate, as it transitioned low-productivity labour from rural agriculture to industrial or services-oriented urban areas. Its gender participation rate, or the proportion of women in the labour force, has also been consistently high and stable.

China has also performed well on other socio-economic indicators, such as nutrition, education and healthcare, when compared to other developing countries. However, with a shrinking workforce, rising labour costs and an ageing population, many of the conditions that propelled its rise no longer apply. These challenges arise as it seeks to transition to the next phase of its growth trajectory through technological innovation and productivity. China today faces real risks of being caught in the 'growing old before it grows rich' middle-income trap.[16] This predicament is exacerbated because of its skewed demographics arising from the reform and opening-up period, along with the poor policy choices.

India, on the other hand, is facing a different set of opportunities and challenges with its young and growing population. With the youngest working age population of any major economy in the world, it is poised to reap a demographic dividend of higher levels of economic activity and GDP growth over the next three decades. The forecast, however, is accompanied by an ominous caveat. Productive employment opportunities for the increasingly large number of young people entering the job market every year need to be exponentially scaled up to encash this demographic dividend and avoid possible social issues that may arise if there is large scale unemployment. India needs to maintain high GDP growth, even as it is transitioning a large part of poorly skilled/educated, low productivity, agriculture-based, feudal and socially stratified surplus rural labour to higher skilled/ educated, better productivity or value added manufacturing services centred in meritocratic social structures and growing urbanization. The barriers to creating conditions for large-scale labour mobility and productivity improvement are well known. Most of these barriers are being addressed at the policy and implementation levels.

Settlement and digitization of land records, creation of land and agricultural produce markets, promotion of contract farming, formation of agricultural land co-operatives to aggregate fragmented landholdings and enhance productivity yields and incomes, facilitation of farmer producer and marketing organizations, introduction of large scale manufacturing production-linked incentive (PLI) scheme, skilling initatives, decentralization of power with local or municipal government as the focal point of empowerment and financial support to drive competitiveness are some of the steps being undertaken. Above all other factors, how well India tackles this pressing issue will determine not only its growth trajectory but also its economic future.

'*san da fa* (three great cuttings [of trees and forests])': the [...] the Cultural Revolution and the third in the early 1980s—after [...]s death—when the state owned farmland, including forests, were [...]racted out to families under the household responsibility system. [...] war against Nature wasn't limited to claiming tillable land:

[In 1958] one of the most extreme measures was an effort to [...]top birds eating grain. As part of the Four Pests campaign [...] people were called upon to shoot sparrows, destroy their [...]ests and bang pots and pans until the birds died of exhaustion. [...]Millions of sparrows, perhaps even hundreds of millions, were [...]illed. The measure though left crops vulnerable. Pests such [...]s locusts became the real winners, as they had lost a major [...]redator. Mao called off the sparrow campaign, but it was too [...]ate [...] A toxic combination of widespread deforestation, misuse [...]f poisons and pesticides and misinformed agricultural policy [...]ombined with poor weather to create a devastating famine. Up [...]o 45 million people died.[7]

[...]'s changing attitude towards nature over time in the pre-Mao, [...]and post-Mao periods was summarized by some as: traditional [...]'s *Tian Ren Heyi* (harmony between the heavens and [...]nkind), yielding to Mao's *Ren Ding Sheng Tian* (man must [...]er nature), replaced in reform era China by *Yiqie Xiang Qian* [...]look toward money in everything), as commercialization and [...]et forces became predominant. Mao's war on nature was an [...]cedented disaster. As Professor Judith Shapiro at the School [...]ernational Service, American University, writes:

[...] revolutionary China's environmental problems resulted [...]rimarily from over extraction of resources, impoverishment [...]f the land's productivity through attentive farming schemes, [...]nd drastic reshaping of the physical landscape [...] An [...]xploding population and massive human transfers into wildlife [...]abitat altered fragile ecosystems ... Intense efforts to increase [...]able land failed to compensate for declines in agricultural

16

The Fifth Yin: Environment

Growing pollution and increasing human population in the modern era, brought about by technological changes and advances in science, has been a global feature since the Industrial Revolution in England in 1760. Industrial-scale coal combustion for power and heat; widespread deforestation for wood and agriculture; ground and surface water pollution from chemicals, plastic, mining, sewage and untreated waste; and land degradation from overuse of chemical fertilizers and poor agricultural practices have all been lethal outcomes of the modern Anthropocene epoch. Global population has increased from approximately 770 million in 1760 to nearly 8 billion today[1], with nearly 56 per cent living in urbanized and industrialized towns and cities.[2] The degradation of the environment—air, water and land—in this energy intensive, natural resources exploitative cycle has only accelerated in the recent decades.

According to the Living Planet Report of 2022, published by the World Wildlife Fund for Nature (WWF), there has been a 69 per cent decline in the wildlife populations of mammals, birds, amphibians, reptiles and fishes across the globe in the last 50 years.[3] The scale of degradation has been such that environmental issues are not limited anymore to regions and nations but threaten the entire planet and life on it. Climate change is now a reality for billions of people across the world. Global and national efforts are on to combat it by accelerating the transition to greener technologies, building a new framework of sustainable existence and growth.

As late entrants to industrialization, with large and poor populations comprising nearly 36 per cent of humanity and the increasing need for energy and natural resource for development, the challenges for China and India have been, and continue to be, particularly enormous.

In China, however, the challenges are more acute, having lived on the environmental edge for a long period of its civilizational history. China's geographical conditions have seen it grapple with severe natural disasters—particularly floods and droughts—for millennia. The collision of the Indian subcontinent with Eurasia, besides forming the still growing Himalayas, has also created the Tibetan Plateau, also known as 'the roof of the world'. China, therefore, has a steep west-east gradient between its mountains and sea coast, with its prime cultivable lands in the plateaus, river basins and mostly southeast lowlands.

Around 58 per cent of China's land area is covered by either mountains or high plains[4], largely unsuitable for cultivation and more prone to soil erosion after deforestation. Further, located on the eastern fringe of Eurasia, China is open to cold, dry outflows of the Siberian anticyclone in the winter and to the monsoonal flows including typhoons, in the summer. There is also a significant irregularity in the rains, and most of China's annual precipitation falls during the monsoon between May and September. As a consequence, China does not go a single year without some serious drought or flood. Land for agriculture and controlling the waters have been central to Chinese civilization for millennia.

Yu, a legendary king who founded the Xia dynasty and whose records are lost beyond recorded time, was given the rare honorific title—'the Great'. He was known for his legendary work on flood control more than 4,000 years ago. His story is immortalized in *Da Yu Zhi Shui—(The Great Yu Who Controlled the Waters)*. In this constant struggle against nature, water conservation projects and granaries against famine were the primary responsibilities of imperial administrators. Early examples of these works that still exist include the Dujiangyan irrigation works built during the Qin dynasty (221–206 BCE), and the Grand Canal, built in the seventh century to connect North and South China.

As nature has always played an important role in Chinese civilization, China's efforts to reshape lands and waters, open up forested areas for agriculture and feed a growing population, date

back beyond recorded history.[5] In traditional three schools have existed about how humankind nature. The first was a Daoist tradition that advo nature's ways; the second was a Buddhist tradition reverence for all living beings; and the third tradition that actively sought to manage, utilize a The anthropocentric and hierarchical Confucian the dominant thought over time, and while it ha prescribing sustainability and against overexploita is on regulation and ordering of the natural en good of society. It was on these same Confucia implicit, that Mao launched his devastating 'War coming to power in China in the middle of the

By the Mao era, China's fertile and tillable land transformed by millennia of use, while large land degraded from deforestation and overexploitation being the Loess Plateau near X'ian, the site of capital and the famed Terracotta Army. What wa about the Mao era was that it rejected both Ch modern Western science. Mao's effort to conque concentrated and oppositional—a socialist utop upon, conquering and changing nature through at a scale never before seen in human history growing population as a national asset. Ignoring on agriculture and the environment, Mao declare *Da* (With Many People, Strength is Great).

The GLF respected neither nature nor scien was the only metric that counted. The failure seeds and other unscientific practices saw a stee agriculture production, resulting in the Great 1959–61. In response, Mao said '*kaihuang zhor* wilderness to plant grain). Large tracts of fore restraint to plant grains in the mountains. Only and other crops were destroyed. Even fruit tr chopped down. In the recent environmental hi productivity due to other unsustainable activities such as deforestation, excessive well-digging and reclamation schemes that led eventually to desertification. A 1982 Beijing Review article acknowledged, for example, that between 1957 and 1977, China had a net loss of 29 million hectares of farmland despite reclamation of 17 million hectares from 'wasteland'.[8]

Focus on heavy industry and industrial development in rural areas for a variety of economic, social and security reasons saw significant industrial contamination of land, air and water. In the reform and opening-up era, economic growth replaced Maoist authoritarianism in China's environmental difficulties. Exclusive focus on economic development, uncaring of environmental impact of decades of unchecked industrial growth and rampant environment abuse permeated policymaking until 1993, when a pea soup smog over Beijing and other parts of China brought home the message of environmental pollution.

The crisis in the Eastern regions was particularly severe in the pollution of air, water, soil and food. The manufacturing industries set up for making products for export and domestic consumption had turned vast rural coastal areas into urbanized and polluted ghettos, while mining and heavy industrial agglomerations emitted heavy air and chemical pollutants, poisoning the countryside. The outsize and widespread impact of this pollution on the general populace, even as its economic benefits accrued to only a few, sparked widespread concerns of potential instability caused not only by economic inequality but environmental depredation.

Failure on the part of the state to address this issue could mean an increase in protests, of what the government called 'huanjing quntixing shijian (environmental mass incidents)'. The fear of luan (chaos) in society has been intrinsic to Chinese cultural thought dating back for millenia, and there was a real fear that environmental issues could become a rallying point for mass public mobilization. As a direct consequence of the severity of this crisis, the environment has become increasingly central to the CPC, and its leadership's thinking and policy.

China's approach to its environment issues has been much the same as it tackled economic matters. It was in 2007, under Hu Jintao, that the term '*shengtai wenming* (ecological civilization)' became an explicit goal of the CPC. It was soon incorporated within the party and national constitutions, elevating it to the level of official political philosophy. In keeping with the CPC's views on historical nihilism, it projects the continuity of China's development path under the party's leadership—transforming from an agricultural to an industrial civilization under Mao, then to a material civilization under Deng and now, to an ecological civilization under Xi.

Xi Jinping's ubiquitous quote, '*lushui qingshan jiushi jinshan yinshan* (clear waters, green mountains are in fact gold mountains, silver mountains)' underlines the party's commitment to its rejuvenation as an ecological civilization, a path on which the CPC under Xi will lead China's, and the world's, efforts. In its efforts at realizing its vision of ecological civilization, Chinese think tanks and research institutions have focussed on the negative influence of interest groups and capital, on the unhealthy 'deification' of economic growth and development, along with the growing risks of an overly anthropocentric worldview. They have sought to weave and integrate the concept of ecological civilization into policymaking, governance reforms and promoting technological innovations for environment protection—a perspective that the state has then converted to goals to be achieved through decisive interventions. Its achievements and appeal in a global environment facing a climate catastrophe with weak leaders and an inability to tackle a growing crisis, are evident.

China, today, leads the world in wind and solar energy. It is the world's largest manufactuer of clean energy equipment and components. It is also the world's largest generator and consumer of clean energy. It is the largest manufacturer and buyer of electric vehicles and buses. It has, a tad ironically, shut down the import of low-grade recyclables and hazardous e-wastes. It has switched systems from coal to natural gas and banned ivory sales. It has built entire ecosystems of green power including rechargeable batteries for storage and energy-efficient high-speed rail, while

16

The Fifth Yin: Environment

Growing pollution and increasing human population in the modern era, brought about by technological changes and advances in science, has been a global feature since the Industrial Revolution in England in 1760. Industrial-scale coal combustion for power and heat; widespread deforestation for wood and agriculture; ground and surface water pollution from chemicals, plastic, mining, sewage and untreated waste; and land degradation from overuse of chemical fertilizers and poor agricultural practices have all been lethal outcomes of the modern Anthropocene epoch. Global population has increased from approximately 770 million in 1760 to nearly 8 billion today[1], with nearly 56 per cent living in urbanized and industrialized towns and cities.[2] The degradation of the environment—air, water and land—in this energy intensive, natural resources exploitative cycle has only accelerated in the recent decades.

According to the Living Planet Report of 2022, published by the World Wildlife Fund for Nature (WWF), there has been a 69 per cent decline in the wildlife populations of mammals, birds, amphibians, reptiles and fishes across the globe in the last 50 years.[3] The scale of degradation has been such that environmental issues are not limited anymore to regions and nations but threaten the entire planet and life on it. Climate change is now a reality for billions of people across the world. Global and national efforts are on to combat it by accelerating the transition to greener technologies, building a new framework of sustainable existence and growth.

As late entrants to industrialization, with large and poor populations comprising nearly 36 per cent of humanity and the increasing need for energy and natural resource for development, the challenges for China and India have been, and continue to be, particularly enormous.

In China, however, the challenges are more acute, having lived on the environmental edge for a long period of its civilizational history. China's geographical conditions have seen it grapple with severe natural disasters—particularly floods and droughts—for millennia. The collision of the Indian subcontinent with Eurasia, besides forming the still growing Himalayas, has also created the Tibetan Plateau, also known as 'the roof of the world'. China, therefore, has a steep west-east gradient between its mountains and sea coast, with its prime cultivable lands in the plateaus, river basins and mostly southeast lowlands.

Around 58 per cent of China's land area is covered by either mountains or high plains[4], largely unsuitable for cultivation and more prone to soil erosion after deforestation. Further, located on the eastern fringe of Eurasia, China is open to cold, dry outflows of the Siberian anticyclone in the winter and to the monsoonal flows including typhoons, in the summer. There is also a significant irregularity in the rains, and most of China's annual precipitation falls during the monsoon between May and September. As a consequence, China does not go a single year without some serious drought or flood. Land for agriculture and controlling the waters have been central to Chinese civilization for millennia.

Yu, a legendary king who founded the Xia dynasty and whose records are lost beyond recorded time, was given the rare honorific title—'the Great'. He was known for his legendary work on flood control more than 4,000 years ago. His story is immortalized in *Da Yu Zhi Shui—(The Great Yu Who Controlled the Waters)*. In this constant struggle against nature, water conservation projects and granaries against famine were the primary responsibilities of imperial administrators. Early examples of these works that still exist include the Dujiangyan irrigation works built during the Qin dynasty (221–206 BCE), and the Grand Canal, built in the seventh century to connect North and South China.

As nature has always played an important role in Chinese civilization, China's efforts to reshape lands and waters, open up forested areas for agriculture and feed a growing population, date back beyond recorded history.[5] In traditional Chinese thought, three schools have existed about how humankind should behave in nature. The first was a Daoist tradition that advocated adapting to nature's ways; the second was a Buddhist tradition that emphasized reverence for all living beings; and the third was a Confucian tradition that actively sought to manage, utilize and control nature. The anthropocentric and hierarchical Confucian tradition became the dominant thought over time, and while it has many principles prescribing sustainability and against overexploitation, its emphasis is on regulation and ordering of the natural environment for the good of society. It was on these same Confucian traditions, albeit implicit, that Mao launched his devastating 'War against Nature' on coming to power in China in the middle of the twentieth century.[6]

By the Mao era, China's fertile and tillable lands had already been transformed by millennia of use, while large land areas of China were degraded from deforestation and overexploitation—a stark example being the Loess Plateau near X'ian, the site of the First Emperor's capital and the famed Terracotta Army. What was, however, distinct about the Mao era was that it rejected both Chinese tradition and modern Western science. Mao's effort to conquer nature was highly concentrated and oppositional—a socialist utopia of declaring war upon, conquering and changing nature through mass mobilization at a scale never before seen in human history. Mao saw China's growing population as a national asset. Ignoring growing pressures on agriculture and the environment, Mao declared '*Ren Duo, Liliang Da* (With Many People, Strength is Great)'.

The GLF respected neither nature nor science. 'Record output' was the only metric that counted. The failure of close planting of seeds and other unscientific practices saw a steep fall in nationwide agriculture production, resulting in the Great Chinese Famine in 1959–61. In response, Mao said '*kaihuang zhong liangshi* (open the wilderness to plant grain)'. Large tracts of forest were cut without restraint to plant grains in the mountains. Only grains were planted and other crops were destroyed. Even fruit trees were relentlessly chopped down. In the recent environmental history of China, there

were '*san da fa* (three great cuttings [of trees and forests])': the
GLF, the Cultural Revolution and the third in the early 1980s—after
Mao's death—when the state owned farmland, including forests, were
contracted out to families under the household responsibility system.
The war against Nature wasn't limited to claiming tillable land:

> [In 1958] one of the most extreme measures was an effort to
> stop birds eating grain. As part of the Four Pests campaign
> [...] people were called upon to shoot sparrows, destroy their
> nests and bang pots and pans until the birds died of exhaustion.
> Millions of sparrows, perhaps even hundreds of millions, were
> killed. The measure though left crops vulnerable. Pests such
> as locusts became the real winners, as they had lost a major
> predator. Mao called off the sparrow campaign, but it was too
> late [...] A toxic combination of widespread deforestation, misuse
> of poisons and pesticides and misinformed agricultural policy
> combined with poor weather to create a devastating famine. Up
> to 45 million people died.[7]

China's changing attitude towards nature over time in the pre-Mao,
Mao and post-Mao periods was summarized by some as: traditional
China's *Tian Ren Heyi* (harmony between the heavens and
humankind), yielding to Mao's *Ren Ding Sheng Tian* (man must
conquer nature), replaced in reform era China by *Yiqie Xiang Qian
Kan* (look toward money in everything), as commercialization and
market forces became predominant. Mao's war on nature was an
unprecedented disaster. As Professor Judith Shapiro at the School
of International Service, American University, writes:

> [...] revolutionary China's environmental problems resulted
> primarily from over extraction of resources, impoverishment
> of the land's productivity through attentive farming schemes,
> and drastic reshaping of the physical landscape [...] An
> exploding population and massive human transfers into wildlife
> habitat altered fragile ecosystems ... Intense efforts to increase
> arable land failed to compensate for declines in agricultural

productivity due to other unsustainable activities such as deforestation, excessive well-digging and reclamation schemes that led eventually to desertification. A 1982 Beijing Review article acknowledged, for example, that between 1957 and 1977, China had a net loss of 29 million hectares of farmland despite reclamation of 17 million hectares from 'wasteland'.[8]

Focus on heavy industry and industrial development in rural areas for a variety of economic, social and security reasons saw significant industrial contamination of land, air and water. In the reform and opening-up era, economic growth replaced Maoist authoritarianism in China's environmental difficulties. Exclusive focus on economic development, uncaring of environmental impact of decades of unchecked industrial growth and rampant environment abuse permeated policymaking until 1993, when a pea soup smog over Beijing and other parts of China brought home the message of environmental pollution.

The crisis in the Eastern regions was particularly severe in the pollution of air, water, soil and food. The manufacturing industries set up for making products for export and domestic consumption had turned vast rural coastal areas into urbanized and polluted ghettos, while mining and heavy industrial agglomerations emitted heavy air and chemical pollutants, poisoning the countryside. The outsize and widespread impact of this pollution on the general populace, even as its economic benefits accrued to only a few, sparked widespread concerns of potential instability caused not only by economic inequality but environmental depredation.

Failure on the part of the state to address this issue could mean an increase in protests, of what the government called 'huanjing quntixing shijian (environmental mass incidents)'. The fear of luan (chaos) in society has been intrinsic to Chinese cultural thought dating back for millenia, and there was a real fear that environmental issues could become a rallying point for mass public mobilization. As a direct consequence of the severity of this crisis, the environment has become increasingly central to the CPC, and its leadership's thinking and policy.

China's approach to its environment issues has been much the same as it tackled economic matters. It was in 2007, under Hu Jintao, that the term 'shengtai wenming (ecological civilization)' became an explicit goal of the CPC. It was soon incorporated within the party and national constitutions, elevating it to the level of official political philosophy. In keeping with the CPC's views on historical nihilism, it projects the continuity of China's development path under the party's leadership—transforming from an agricultural to an industrial civilization under Mao, then to a material civilization under Deng and now, to an ecological civilization under Xi.

Xi Jinping's ubiquitous quote, 'lushui qingshan jiushi jinshan yinshan (clear waters, green mountains are in fact gold mountains, silver mountains)' underlines the party's commitment to its rejuvenation as an ecological civilization, a path on which the CPC under Xi will lead China's, and the world's, efforts. In its efforts at realizing its vision of ecological civilization, Chinese think tanks and research institutions have focussed on the negative influence of interest groups and capital, on the unhealthy 'deification' of economic growth and development, along with the growing risks of an overly anthropocentric worldview. They have sought to weave and integrate the concept of ecological civilization into policymaking, governance reforms and promoting technological innovations for environment protection—a perspective that the state has then converted to goals to be achieved through decisive interventions. Its achievements and appeal in a global environment facing a climate catastrophe with weak leaders and an inability to tackle a growing crisis, are evident.

China, today, leads the world in wind and solar energy. It is the world's largest manufactuer of clean energy equipment and components. It is also the world's largest generator and consumer of clean energy. It is the largest manufacturer and buyer of electric vehicles and buses. It has, a tad ironically, shut down the import of low-grade recyclables and hazardous e-wastes. It has switched systems from coal to natural gas and banned ivory sales. It has built entire ecosystems of green power including rechargeable batteries for storage and energy-efficient high-speed rail, while commercializing hydrogen and other new electricity generation and storage technologies. While its reliance on fossil fuels for its legacy industries continues, it has developed the most visible path to energy transition among major economies in the world.

This 'sustainable development with Chinese characteristics', or authoritarian environmentalism—the use of authoritarian methods to accomplish environmental goals—has, however, faced a set of challenges and outcomes, quite different from its economic predecessor. A primary concern and hurdle, of drafting environment policy is a feature known as the 'tragedy of the commons'. Articulated by Garrett Hardin in 1968, it posits that rational individuals will necessarily and inevitably over-extract resources from shared spaces because their self-interests, collectively, outweigh the good of the group. Its most visible forms in practice are overfished seas, overgrazed common pastures, overexploited forests and discharge of private effluents and pollutants into common air, water and land. According to Hardin, the only way to avoid this overexploitation of shared resources is by 'mutually agreed-upon coercion'.

In China's top-down, authoritarian model, this has posed a problem of reconciling systemic design and incentives with the objective of achieving such an equilibrium. As Yifei Li and Judith Shapiro write, 'The effectiveness of state leadership in environmental affairs is thus premised on its incorporation of civil society inputs into the policy process. Some environmental initiatives...went awry because the state went too far, too fast.'[9] For a party bureaucracy incentivized over decades to achieve economic development targets for either promotion or financial incentives, the broader and consensus-based 'mutually agreed-upon coercion' to avoid the tragedy of the commons in implementing environment goals has yielded mixed results. However, since 2011, promotions and bonuses are officially supposed to be tied not only to economic growth and social stability but also environment protection.

The perverse incentives that allowed officials to benefit from allowing polluters to operate and are being eliminated, and local environment officers are less likely to require a steady levy of fines to meet their own salaries. By contrast, according to Yifei Li and Shapiro, the state has done better when people have participated in environmental governance or undertaken 'qunzhong jiandu (supervision by the masses)'. The results of authoritarian environmentalism have therefore, been mixed, yielding marked improvement in some conditions such as urban air quality, but others such as desertification and deforestation—barring a few successes—appear to have worsened. The target-setting approach in an environmental authoritarianism set up can yield perverse outcomes.

In June 2019, during the wheat harvest, farmers in Henan province were ordered to undertake manual harvesting. Machine harvesting, which was the norm, had been prohibited for that season. Faced with labour shortage and multiple issues, the farmers could not undertake the harvesting operation within the window available and as a result, entire wheat fields were left to rot, with some colonized by sooty mould because of rains. Farmers were devastated and upset with this directive. Post facto investigation revealed that the order originated in the county's automated air monitoring station. Like other newly installed stations in China, this station too sent real-time readings of air pollutants to the powerful Ministry of Ecology and Environment.

The county had been given specific clean-air targets and local officials were reluctant to allow machine harvesting due to the large quantities of air blown chaff that it generated, which could potentially result in a spike in pollution readings. Local officials initially attempted to defend the move, suggesting that 'in this tough battle of environmental protection, the interests of a very small group of people shall be compromised for the benefit of the vast majority of the people'. Faced with widespread public protests, provincial authorities subsequently denounced local officials for their 'failure to fully comprehend the Xi Jinping thought on ecological civilisation'. Harvest machinery was once again allowed to be used, but it was too late for the season and the damage had been done.

In another instance of target and directive driven outcome

gone wrong, a detailed transition plan for switching from coal to liquified natural gas (LNG) was drawn up for the heavily polluted Beijing–Tianjin–Hebei metropolitan area in 2014, which required an effective ban on coal in three years, by 2017. By February 2017, under pressure, the Beijing–Tianjin–Hebei authority—responsible for more than 110 million people across two municipalities and 26 cities across four provinces—outlined detailed localized targets. Four months later, 13 of China's most powerful ministerial level agencies reiterated these targets and demanded that cadres at all levels be evaluated on their performance in this regard. As a consequence, local cadres took drastic measures to meet the targets. The state-owned Beijing Gas Group Company Limited invested an amount of $1.3 billion, five times its annual expenditure, to retrofit residential energy infrastructure. In Shanxi and Heibei provinces, about 3.5 million households were retrofitted, nearly three times their targets. The coal reduction target was met sooner than planned, and the percentage of coal in the national energy mix dropped to 60.4 per cent because of over-enforcement at subnational levels.[10]

Across homes and factories, coal burning equipment was destroyed to make the quickest transition to LNG. In November 2017, gas companies across the region warned of tight supply. Hebei province had to suspend gas supplies to commercial users, barely able to meet residential demand, and LNG gas prices skyrocketed. By December, it was clear that the supply gap was too wide to be covered by emergency measures. Thousands of ordinary people were left out while the gas shortage crisis spread nationally. The Ministry issued a short communication, directing local governments to lift the ban on coal and switch back to the earlier infrastructure. Most of the equipment had, however, already been scrapped. The ministry rushed teams to distribute electric heaters—bought from funds earlier earmarked for air pollution mitigation. However, many people went without heaters even as the temperature plummeted. In this instance, the problem was not that target setting did not work, but that it worked too well. An overachievement as it was, not met or balanced in another critical input, led to an adverse outcome.

China has also used techniques of mass mobilization for behavioural modification, launching slogans and campaigns to encourage and inculcate environmentally conscious behaviour in the public. This included banning of fireworks—a centuries old tradition at the Chinese New Year, banning stubble burning by farmers, giving free licence plates to buyers of electric cars, preventing food wastage, segregating dry and wet waste in urban waste management, and so on. In the village of Yangde, about 250 km from Shanghai, a social behavioural modification experiment is being undertaken.

A social credit system, known as a 'morality bank', awards credit points to villagers for recycling waste and hosting other 'virtuous deeds'. It deducts points for 'extravagant' funerals and birthday parties and other 'acts of immorality'. The morality bank is a part of China's ambitious and controversial social credit system, which is designed to monitor the citizen's behaviour and rate it across a range of activities, including public behaviour, compliance with rules and law and creditworthiness. The pervasiveness of monitoring and behaviour modification techniques was last seen during the outbreak and the zero-Covid lockdown.

The limitations of this 'one-size-fits-all' approach to conserve environment is best illustrated in its afforestation programme. Tree planting is one of China's most ambitious environmental initiatives. From programmes ranging from conversion of croplands to forests, to anti-desertification campaigns, to urban and infrastructure afforestation initiatives, planting of trees is as ubiquitous as it is mandatory. Afforestation is also deeply integrated into the policy and planning of the multi-level framework of the state. 'Green plots' are demarcated on planning maps, which may be farmlands, rural settlements or deserts, but which are deemed necessary to be reforested or afforested within the specified time to meet the set targets.

An unintended consequence of this type of simplified perspective in an authoritarian state-led system is a cookie-cutter approach to complex and differentiated local issues. This quest for uniformity and efficiency under a sweeping state authority, a 'yidaoquie (cutting everything with the same knife)' approach that has been a feature of environmental governance since the Mao era, has been most evident in China's monoculture afforestation programmes. Monoculture (cultivation of a single crop) afforestation is infamous among environmentalists for its increased vulnerability to diseases, poor wildlife habitat and lack of shelter and forage for local flora and fauna. Monoculture afforestation, however, has obvious advantages from the viewpoint of the state. It can be implemented by local officials quickly and effectively, easily monitored, evaluated and rewarded at higher levels with tangible outcomes during the limited tenure of officials appointed by the CPC from Beijing. It is also a low-cost option due to economies of scale in growing and transporting seedlings, training workers and manufacturing and using chemicals in newly planted forests. The monoculture afforestation, as a result, has now become an endemic, setting in motion a self-perpetuating cycle of state-owned business interests that continue to expand in line with China's afforestation targets, making this coercive monocultural approach the new normal.

The limitations and vulnerabilities of this monocultural approach are in stark contrast to the success of the rehabilitation of the Loess Plateau. In the mid-1990s, a group of Chinese and international experts worked with local villages to restore one of the world's most highly eroded environments. In this initiative, while planting trees was central to the rehabilitation, it was not the only activity. An integrated local area development approach was undertaken through a long process of consultation with the village communities. This included an understanding of the processes that led to soil erosion and some of the local practices that could help restore the functions of the ecosystem.

In turn, this led to changing methods of unsustainable farming and herding, along with a deeper understanding of the plateau's complex topographical characteristics. As a result, an integrative rehabilitation programme of tree planting, terrace farming and small sediment-holding dams was undertaken and a revamped land ownership structure—which contracted parcels of lands to individual households and required them to set aside plots for planting and nurturing trees—was implemented. The terraced fields and orchards provided local livelihoods while the ecosystem was gradually restored. The rehabilitation was successful because the trees were selected based on the local soil structure and climate conditions across the plateau, nourished by an intricate system of dams checks and layered canopies of shrubs and trees to provide cover and stabilize the land against erosion. The Loess Plateau rehabilitation continues to be one of the success stories of local communities-involved distributive afforestation and ecosystem restoration under an integrated approach, over a monocultural, state-driven approach.

Besides forests, water has been and still is the most important environmental issue in China. From hydropower to flood control, to addressing increasing water scarcity in the densely populated core China through grand water transfer projects like the South–North Water Transfer Project to a Sky River project that envisions seeding clouds on the Tibetan Plateau to attract monsoon moisture from the Indian subcontinent, it has been among the most contentious initiatives, with significant cross-border and geopolitical implications.

China's national energy goal is to generate 35 per cent of its electricity from renewable sources[11], with hydropower playing a significant role. China, with 352 GW, already has nearly one quarter of the world's installed hydroelectric capacity. Dams have, however, become among the most contentious of all power projects around the world, with even multilateral financing institutions like the World Bank turning away from mega dams. It has, however, not discouraged China from pushing ahead with its ambitious mega dam projects. Many of China's new and proposed dams are in the Western Himalayan region where the river currents are strong. It is also an area of frequent seismic activity.

According to some experts, the weight of the water in some catchment areas is thought to trigger earthquakes. It is posited that the massive weight of the stored water causes deformity in the Earth's crust and can lead tectonic plates to shift. In fact, some scientists have hypothesized that a new dam at Zipingpu in the

Sichuan region led to increased seismic activity before the devastating earthquake in 2008 in Wenchuan which killed an estimated 70,000 people. Many hydroprojects are on international rivers descending from the Tibetan Plateau with cross-border implications, including the Mekong (Lancang), Nu (Salween), Jinsha and the Brahmaputra. Further doubts on the nature of China's sustainable ecological civilization makeover from Mao's 'war on Nature' mindset are raised by the controversial Sky River cloud-seeding project on the Tibetan Plateau. China's cloud-seeding experiments date back to its target-set requirements for 'blue sky days' for the 2008 Beijing Olympics, and even before. Between 2012 and 2017, China spent about $1.3 billion on weather modification 'for the sake of ecological civilisation'.[12] It has sparked regional tensions, with some areas accusing others of 'stealing' their rain and others complaining of the potentially toxic effects of the chemicals used to precipitate the rain.

The Tibetan Plateau is also known as the 'water tower of Asia' or Earth's 'Third Pole' because of the enormous amount of water it stores in glaciers at its stratospheric heights. All major rivers of China, South East Asia and the Indian subcontinent have their origins in the Himalayas, including the Yangtze, Yellow, Indus, Brahmaputra, Ganges and Mekong. Glaciers on the Tibetan Plateau are, however, rapidly melting due to global warming. The extra water that this rapid melt is generating will soon disappear, threatening the existence of large urban populations on its banks or in its riparian zones. China's technocratic and authoritarian environmentalism response to this has included an effort to change the weather on the 'roof of the world'. The highly controversial Sky River Project envisages:

> [...] building a cloud-seeding system [...] to induce cloud-formation with the goal of increasing rains with such volume and regularity that it would be equal to 7 percent of China's water consumption. [...] 500 experimental chambers have already been deployed in Tibet, Qinghai, and Xinjiang, with a plan for tens of thousands more. These relatively inexpensive chambers [...] burn solid fuel that produces ice-like iodide. This is then

carried upward by monsoon breezes from South Asia to interact with water vapor and form snow—and rain—releasing clouds. Thirty planned weather satellites will monitor winds over the Indian Ocean so as to guide the chambers with real-time data. The project is to be jointly implemented by the China Aerospace Science and Technology Corporation, Tsinghua University and the government of Qinghai province. In an echo of the 'rain stealing' complaints in Eastern China, sceptics have noted that intercepting moisture in Tibet would likely reduce it in South Asia, with potentially devastating effects.[13]

China's attempt to change the weather for water is fraught with geopolitical conflict, particularly with India—its largest Asian and Himalayan neighbour.[14] It is, however, not the only contentious and potential flashpoint between the two countries, besides their long and undefined border issues. China's plans for massive capacities of large hydro projects in the Western Himalayas and Tibet involve water diversion to the East. It also involves power generation and includes the world's largest dam on the Brahmaputra bend at Medog, of 60 GW located just a few kilometers from the Indian border.[15] This move has sparked fears of military intent, escalating tensions for potential water wars.[16]

India, too, faces similar challenges of air and water pollution along with land degradation owing to rapid industrialization, urbanization and population growth over the last 30 years. Like China, it also has a problem that has been exacerbated by climate change and renders its large population more vulnerable to environmental and economic impacts. Air pollution in cities due to vehicular and industrial emissions, groundwater and river pollution due to chemical and untreated sewage and wastewater discharge, stubble burning on farms, waterlogging, salinization, land degradation of agricultural land due to excess usage and use of chemical fertilizers, extensive deforestation and illegal mining are just few of the challenges posed to India's environment. Climate change further poses growing challenges in the form of more frequent heat waves, erratic weather patterns and rising sea levels, leaving India vulnerable to floods, droughts and extreme weather conditions. India today, is among the top 10 countries affected by climate change.

Several measures have been taken at the central and state levels to tackle these challenges, including the National Action Plan on Climate Change (NAPCC), Swachh Bharat Abhiyan, National River Conservation Plan (NRCP), National Clean Air Programme (NCAP) and the National Mission for Clean Ganga. An important difference has been how India has responded and continues to respond to its increasing environmental challenges within its social and institutional framework. Following liberalization and the growing environmental challenges that accompanied economic growth, environmental checks and balances were established, along with an environmental adjudicatory infrastructure.

A framework of mandatory project clearances from the Centre and respective state environment ministries based on project size, preceded by detailed environmental impact assessment reports and public hearings, and followed by stringent rules and monitoring of these projects, was put in place. India has also had a vibrant civil society questioning governments and projects, particularly as the pace of industrial and infrastructure development accelerated following the 1991 reforms. Protests by non-government organizations against the Sardar Sarovar Dam through the Narmada Bachao Andolan which began in 1985[17], protests against mining of bauxite in 1997[18], among many others, were as much environmental protests as they were about project displacement, private land rights, compulsory land acquisition, compensation and resettlement. The resulting situation and logjam, which in many cases resulted in project delays, cancellation or unviability, prompted the establishment of an independent adjudicatory body to arbitrate these environmental concerns and disputes, as well as serve as a specialized environmental court.

The National Green Tribunal Act was established in 2010. It has played an active, even activist, role in the recognition and resolution of environmental issues based on well-defined and articulated rules and laws. As a result, India has a thriving environmental democracy, which, while resulting in more measured industrial development, has avoided the excesses and severe consequences of both a single-minded pursuit of economic growth and the resulting environmental authoritarianism.

Part Five

The Authoritarian Dragon and The Democratic Elephant

17

Understanding the Differential

As evident from earlier chapters, any comparison of China and India is fraught with complexities at multiple levels of analysis. As Prasenjit Duara and Elizabeth J. Perry write:

China and India not only have vastly different political systems; their social systems are also markedly divergent. As is well known, India is a parliamentary democracy, whereas China is ruled by a communist party-state. Social divisions in India are deep and myriad, including caste, language, and religion, among others, whereas in China the principal social cleavages are economic (along class lines), political (in relation to state power), and regional (especially urban versus rural but also coastal versus interior). These various disparities obviously have major implications for... development, labor relations, social welfare, higher education, internal and external migration, entrepreneurship, foreign investment, legal reform, and popular protest...[1]

In their view, the extent to which the Chinese and Indian states are able to address these issues is a function not only of the familiar 'democracy vs autocracy' arguments but also of their distinctive social contexts. As they point out, '...viewed from a historical perspective, the divergent foundational events of the two states—a massive social and political revolution in China and a more gradual transition from colonialism in India, along with the very different political institutions to which these events gave rise—have generated strikingly different trajectories over the last (75) years.'[2]

At the heart of this debate, lies the nature of the relationship between the nation state and its citizens. The Indian state is a creation of its people, with fundamental rights and welfare of its citizens as its core enshrining principle of the Constitution and an inalienable and basic structure of its parliamentary democracy. The Chinese state is a creation of the Communist Party of China (CPC), which won the contest for power in 1949, with the primacy of the CPC and its right to rule. In India, governments of majority and coalition, with different ideologies—socialist and communist, industry and business-friendly—have ruled at different levels of its democratic structure at various points of time.

At times, it has also overlapped, with each offering different manifestoes of electoral promises to voting citizens to win elections and attain power. China, in contrast, has been ruled by a single party— the CPC (there are other political parties that exist, but nominally), with the party being the state. In keeping with Mao's famous maxim 'political power grows out of the barrel of a gun'[3], the CPC is the only ruling party with an army, among major nations of the world. The control of the party's People's Liberation Army (PLA), through the chairmanship of the Central Military Commission (CMC), is as important institutional mechanism of retaining and exercising political power in China as the general secretaryship of the CPC.

Unlike constitutional and democratic India with political parties and governments of different ideological persuasions being voted to and out of power throughout its history since its independence, the CPC's continued legitimacy for power (Mandate of Heaven) in the post-Mao 'reform and opening-up' period (and after the disaster of the Cultural Revolution) has been based on two promises: the promise of continued economic growth and the promise of restoration of China to its Zhongguo status in the world order. These promises have been best articulated by Xi Jinping who, in late 2012, just after becoming the general secretary of the CPC, announced the 'China Dream' as the great rejuvenation of the Chinese nation.[4] Formulated by Wang Huning, one of China's leading political theorists and ideologists, the China Dream was described as achieving the two centenaries: the material goal of China becoming a 'moderately well-off society' by 2021, the hundredth anniversary of the CPC; and China becoming a fully developed nation by 2049, the hundredth anniversary of the founding of the People's Republic of China (PRC).[5] It is these two objectives that have driven the CPC and Chinese policies, almost to the exclusion of all else. These objectives also provide context to both its economic policies and geopolitical strategies now.

The trajectory of the authoritarian Chinese state has seen many achievements: land and agricultural reforms; improved health, education and socio-economic indicators; urbanization and infrastructure; economic growth and prosperity; and rising geopolitical clout as a potential superpower. These have been achieved amid the backdrop of remarkable social mobilization, perhaps unparalleled elsewhere in the world, or even in history. These, however, have not been without significant costs—the disasters of the Great Leap Forward (GLF) and the Cultural Revolution serve as reminders of the dangers of totalitarian decision-making concentrated in one or a few leaders.

Rights of citizens continue to be a concern across a wide spectrum, ranging from rural land acquisition protests against predatory local governments to the horrors of zero-Covid lockdown. The continued fragility of private rights to property, corporate and individual agency, and their subservience to objectives of the state policy are best illustrated in the recent cases of Huawei, Jack Ma's Ant Group, crackdown on the tech sector, increasing golden share for the state in the corporate sector and increasing incidents of individuals and families fleeing from China along with their wealth. It is notable that despite its position as the second largest economy in the world, China does not allow unfettered convertibility of its yuan, which is a major hurdle in its rise as a global reserve currency. The continued high propensity of most Chinese to continue to save at high rates, despite significantly higher prosperity, may also perhaps suggest historical memories and fear of uncertain times, as much as cultural value of thrift. As a result, low domestic consumption to the ratio of its GDP is a challenge that China's economy continues to grapple with, forcing it to ramp up investments and keep its economy going by building even more infrastructure and increasing urbanization that is now reaching saturation levels.

While India's achievements in comparison may appear modest over the same period, these have been more stable and robust with greater sensitivity to rights and aspirations of its citizens. Its resounding rejection of authoritarianism in the Emergency of 1975 has since seen deepening and widening of its democratic processes. Its institutional structure of checks and balances have helped prevent catastrophic mistakes and concentration of political power, thereby safeguarding citizen's rights and properties. Its moderation and democratic coalition of diversity, and its civil liberties have also enabled greater acceptability of its geopolitical policies and have helped in crafting sustainable alliances based on shared values. India is particularly well positioned to reap the benefit of its strong democratic foundation—based on constitutional values of citizen rights, secularism and the rule of law—in its economic trajectory over the next 30 years.

18

Influence of Culture

The subject of culture as an influence on economic development has been one of the most contentious topics among social scientists and economists. The difference in the economic trajectories of, say, South Korea and Ghana—both with similar economies and gross domestic product (GDP) in the early 1960s— and the factors that led to different outcomes have been a subject of intense debate. The contention of culture being an important factor in the political, institutional and economic development of nations has now largely been accepted in theories of economic behaviour by economists. According to Daniel Patrick Moynihan, a leading American sociologist and politician, 'The central conservative truth is that it is culture, not politics, that determines the success of a society. The central liberal truth is that politics can change a culture and save it from itself.'[1] Both truths have found resonance in the economic history of China and India.

China's (in fact, most of East Asia's) historical identity as a Confucian society based on widespread social values of thrift, investment, hard work, education, hierarchical organization and discipline has had as much of a role to play in its modern development as Mao's frontal attack on feudalism, class identity and the disastrous Cultural Revolution with its attack on the 'Four Olds'—Old Ideas, Old Culture, Old Customs and Old Habits.[2] It may be controversially argued that the disastrous social and cultural upheaval and suffering caused in conservative and stratified Chinese society during Mao's regime, also created social mobilization that churned the fertile sociocultural ground for Deng's eventual 'reform and opening-up' that set China on the path of economic development. The role of an obedient and objective-driven, hierarchical party, bureaucracy and society that is highly responsive to central policy directive is visible in both the GLF, as also subsequent—and more successful—initiatives. Equally, all social structures of potential protest or resistance were ruthlessly crushed in the process.

There is growing recognition of the multipolar and multi-civilizational history of the world, which is a relatively recent development. Monolithic Western civilization-centric colonial narratives have begun to undergo changes. Samuel P. Huntington, an eminent American political scientist and director at Harvard University's Center for International Affairs, was a leading proponent of this new, post-Cold War understanding of civilization-based economic development and global relations. His book, *The Clash of Civilizations and the Remaking of World Order*, first released in 1996, posited:

> [...] modernisation is distinct from Westernisation and is producing neither a universal civilisation in any meaningful sense nor the Westernisation of non-Western societies...a civilisation-based world order is emerging; societies sharing cultural affinities cooperate with each other; efforts to shift societies from one civilisation to another are unsuccessful; and countries group themselves around the lead or core states of their civilisations.[3]

The economic success of each civilization nation states has come from their core shared values. If the economic growth of the West has been attributed in large part to what German sociologist and economist Max Weber called 'the Protestant Ethic'[4] for the rise of capitalism, the more recent rise of East Asia has been attributed to 'Confucian values'. Interestingly, the attributes that facilitated the rise had little to do with religion per se, but with cultural values of hard work, thrift and, in most cases, an intense sense of group responsibility. Group responsibility, a particularly dominant feature of Confucian traditions, was often translated into 'nationalism' in East Asian societies. The most prominent example being the Meiji Restoration (1868), sparked by isolationist Japan's first contact with Western Civilization, when the feudal Tokugawa shogunate was overthrown and control of the state was restored to Japan's Emperor.

The Meiji Restoration set the tone for Japan's rapid modernization and economic rise. Its biggest challenge, however, lay in the creation of a mobilizing identity for its citizens—a question that was answered in identification with the Emperor and the imperial nation. As David Landes, professor of economics and history at Harvard University writes in his essay, 'Culture Makes Almost All the Difference':

> Most Japanese peasants and workers did not feel this way to begin with—under *Tokugawa*, they scarcely had a notion of nation. That was a primary task of the new imperial state: to imbue its subjects with a sense of higher duty to the emperor and country and to link patriotism to work. A large share of school time was devoted to the study of ethics; in a country without regular religious instruction and ceremony, school was the temple of virtue and morality. As a 1930 textbook put it: 'The easiest way to practice one's patriotism (is to) discipline oneself in daily life, to help keep good order in one's family, and fully discharge one's responsibility to the job.' Also to save and not waste.[5]

It is worth that all were core Confucian values. Even in the Chinese experience, Mao's Marxist-Leninist communism was modified with Deng's socialism with Chinese characteristics in the reform and opening-up era. A policy that tapped into deeper cultural values and which has followed by all his successors, including Xi Jinping who now seeks to leverage those same attributes for a cultural national identity, the 'China Dream', at home and abroad.

These civilizations have, however, also been shaped by Moynihan's 'central liberal truth', of politics shaping culture and, (at times) saving it from itself. Japan's mass mobilizational politics were of nationalism (which also led it to World War II). China's mass mobilization under Mao was first on communist, 'classless' principles and breaking down feudal values and systems, then followed by Deng's 'to get rich is glorious' (paraphrased).

The shared citizen and rights-based mass mobilization of Western civilization nation states, that created its institutions, political and cultural philosophy, lie even further back in time. From the Magna Carta in 1215, to the American (1775) and French revolutions (1789), the interplay of shared cultural values, and globe colonizing history, of Western civilization has been among the most influential tour de force of modern political thought and institutions (and in some cases, neo-colonialism) over the past century, particularly among newly independent nations.

Diversity and tolerance are central to the idea of India, in both its civilizational and nation state form. Answers to Moynihan's conservative and liberal truths about culture are, however, more complex and entangled. The conservative truth is that, unlike the commonality of identity, shared values or even religion and philosophy found in civilizations that have channelized these to realize their economic potential, India's cultural history is multi-layered rather than homogenized or unitary.

At its broadest level, in modern times, three identities—a pre-Delhi Sultanate (Hindu) pluralist liberal identity (1206); a Sultanate or Mughal (Islamic) monoist, mostly conservative identity (1206–1719); and a colonial (Western) institutional identity (1757–1947)—have shared cultural space in the Indian subcontinent. At the narrower level, identities of region, language, caste, tribe, food and worship continue to shape and define micro-identities of individuals on its modern cultural landscape. The liberal truth is that politics has been unable to reconcile these cultural differences which, at its broadest level, even resulted in the two-nation theory and partition of the subcontinent.

Two competing political mobilization narratives have sought to shape India's modern cultural and civilizational history. First, by Mohandas Karamchand (Mahatma) Gandhi, as the unquestioned leader of India's mass independence movement, for a secular, pluralist, liberal nation accommodative of diversity that has defined the modern Indian state's creation as a constitutional and secular democracy. The second, by a narrower, religio-cultural Hindutva movement, first articulated by Vinayak Damodar (Veer) Savarkar and—in parallel—carried forward by the Rashtriya Swayamsevak Sangh. Both have, however, failed to find a thread of social identity broad enough to bind a common culture. Mahatma Gandhi, besides the political struggle for Indian independence, had also identified and worked on two key aspects of modifying culture as a part of his mass movement. The first was the eradication of caste discrimination by breaking down distinctions and creating a unifying identity. The second was the village as local government or Panchayati Raj being the primary constituent of the state and its primary level of social organization and administrative governance. We can only speculate the change he may have brought about in the social sphere, outside of state power (unlike Mao's use of the state), if he had lived long enough in the newly independent India. In subsequent years, there were few mass mobilizations on a pan India scale. Jayprakash Narayan's 'Sampoorna Kranti[6] (total revolution)' on socialist ideals in 1975 sought to bring about a total social transformation, and directly led to the imposition of the infamous Emergency by Prime Minister (PM) Indira Gandhi. The mass mobilization around the 'Ram Janmabhoomi' in Ayodhya from the mid-1980s saw the rise to nascent political power of the Hindutva movement which, after a prolonged period of coalition politics, was voted to electoral majority in 2014.[7]

It is pertinent to note that the significant period of India's reforms that began in 1991 was undertaken during a span when political capital was scarce, and cynical electoral considerations were paramount. It was also a time when minority–majority caste-based arithmetic politics particularly flourished, in the art of politically possible coalition governments. An electoral majority at the Centre has, however, been returned by India's voters since 2014, enabling political stability and a long term view on India's development requirements to be undertaken. Tentative, if symbolic, steps for the evolution of a new and overarching cultural national identity have been undertaken through the construction of a new Parliament House—a newly built national memorial to independent India's war martyrs—and renaming of the Raj Path as Kartavya Path.

However, whether socialist-secularism or religious-nationalism, the liberal truth is that modern politics has not been able to reconcile these differences between short-term compulsions of political parties winning votes by pandering to multiple identities, and the long-term requirement of development of a unifying national and cultural narrative. The challenges of transformative mass mobilization to address India's deep-rooted sociocultural issues that impede its economic development remain. There are many who have been, and continue to be, pessimistic of the relative failure of the Indian state or its political leaders to bring about this cultural transformation.

However, as David Landes writes, in his conclusion on sociocultural attributes that make a difference to the economic development of nations and reasons for their high productivity:

> You want high productivity? Then you should live to work and get happiness as a by-product. Not easy. The people who live to work are a small and fortunate elite. But it is an elite open to new-comers, self-selected, the kind of people who accentuate the positive. In this world, the optimists have it, not because they are always right but because they are positive. Even when wrong, they are positive, and that is the way of achievement, correction, improvement, and success. Educated, eyes-open optimism pays; pessimism can only offer the empty consolation of being right.

Or more simply, as Lord Krishna advised Arjuna in the Bhagavad Gita (Chapter 2, Verse 47), 'Karmanye Vadhikaraste Ma Phaleshu Kadachana, Ma Karmaphalaheturbhurma Te Sangostavakaramani. (You have the right to work only, but never to its fruits. Let not the fruits of action be your motive, nor let your attachment be to inaction).'

Whether Harvard or the Bhagavad Gita, even in the economic development of nations, building positive cultural attitudes matters.

19

Democracy with Indian Characteristics

If Mao Zedong were to revisit China today, he may likely find it difficult to identify the party-state that he was instrumental in creating in 1949. From the imported European ideology of Marxist-Leninist communism, to Deng Xiaoping's 'socialism with Chinese characteristics', and then further to the 'factory-of-the-world' market economy under state control today, China's trajectory has been as evolutionary as it has been revolutionary. Reconciling these supposed contradictions into a seamless official narrative is a major focus point for the CPC, going as it does to the very core of the legitimacy of the party's continued rule. In fact, 'historical nihilism', challenging the party's official narrative of evolutionary history in thought and practice from Mao to Xi, and highlighting any possible contradictions, is a political crime of the highest order with severe consequences. One of the reasons for this is the CPC's obsession with understanding the collapse of the former Soviet Union in 1991.

According to the CPC, and as also repeatedly expressed by Xi Jinping, the practice of the Soviet Communist Party to criticize its past leaders and to repudiate their legacies and party histories, weakened the party's ideological base and led to their eventual collapse. Starting with Nikita Khrushchev's repudiation of Stalin and his policies and ideologies (a key cause of Mao's break with the Soviet Union in 1960), the CPC believes that criticism of the Soviet Communist Party and its history by its own leaders weakened the communist movement in the Soviet Union. It is a mistake that the CPC is determined not to repeat. Furthermore, historical nihilism is officially banned in China.[1]

Despite the disasters of the GLF and the Cultural Revolution of the Mao era, the primacy of the paramount leader, along with the consultation and consensus of key party elders during the Deng era and after, enabled this evolution of the CPC strategy and policies to meet objectives in the context of an evolving situation. Statements like 'it doesn't matter if the cat is black or white, as long as it catches mice' and 'cross[ing] the river by feeling the stone', reflected this cautious, realpolitik pragmatism. China has had four constitutions since 1954, with multiple revisions in its situational context that are modified almost every five years. However, it has always been the CPC leadership—and CPC leadership alone—that has set policy objectives and targets for its hierarchical machinery at all levels of party and government.

Since 1947, India's journey as a constitutional democracy has been remarkable, more so when fledgling nations of similar vintage, geography and culture have collapsed into authoritarianism, dictatorship, or even worse, failed states. India is also the only large democracy to have survived and succeeded outside of Western liberal democracies. Strongly influenced by the Westminster style of government, and combined with India's own rich traditions of plurality, diversity and secularism, the Indian democratic republic is a creation of a written constitution, the longest in the world, of a sovereign nation. Its institutional structure of 'separation of powers' between the legislature, executive and the judiciary has inbuilt checks and balances that prevent concentration of state power in any one branch. This system has successfully safeguarded the fundamental rights of citizens since Independence, most notably during the Emergency (1975–77)—the darkest hour of challenge for Indian democracy. The drafting of the Constitution and institutions in anglicized form was, however, criticized even in the Constituent Assembly.

K. Hanumanthaiah, a Constituent Assembly member remarked— 'We wanted the music of a veena or sitar, but here we have the music of an English band.' This purported lack of indigeneity to Indian conditions has been a subject of political debate ever since. However, as historian and author Tripurdaman Singh argues, while indigenous, and particularly Gandhian, alternatives were rejected, the creation of the Constitution was far more than just a transplantation of the Westminster system. He writes:

> Desperately poor, largely uneducated, with little real knowledge or experience of parliamentary democracy, deep-seated social divisions and an absence of enabling background conditions, the India of 1947—its political and judicial institutions - lacked the traditions, precedents, and conventions on which their Westminster counterparts rested. It was the need to address this [...] [that] India's Constitution [...] [went into] extensive detail. This was [...] [driven by] the need to explicate rules and provide firm and detailed guidance for institutions. It was an indigenous answer to India's circumstances: the absence of experience, tradition and precedent emblematic of Westminster.[2]

Or as political theorist and legal scholar Madhav Khosla, associate professor of law at Columbia University, puts it, 'The Constitution was, in other words, conceptualized as a pedagogical tool. It would be an instrument of political education—aspiring to nothing short of building a new civic culture.'[3]

Electoral democracy has been successful and resilient in the face of multiple challenges, and has taken deep root in Indian soil. Outcomes on achieving the revolutionary social objectives (as enshrined in the Constitution), and individual rights, however, have been a mixed bag of results. An interesting insight into the rooting and functioning of democracies and institutions in different cultural environments has been suggested by David Stasavage (dean for the Social Sciences of New York University) in his book, *The Decline and Rise of Democracy*. Professor Stasavage posits the argument that while modern democracy coexists with a state bureaucracy that manages day-to-day affairs, the pre-existence of institutions and bureaucracy before the introduction of democracy has a direct bearing on the subsequent level of trust and active participation in governance by its citizens.

According to him, rights-based Western liberal democracies (England, France, the US and Germany) arose from initially weak states with rudimentary institutions and bureaucracies, thereby empowering greater and negotiated rights to landed gentry and citizenry from the ruler. State democratic institutions and bureaucracy evolved on this already preset stage of negotiated relationships and wider democratic participation of its citizens. As these states grew in size and faced external threats, democratic practices were already deeply anchored and scaled up to operate in larger polities. As a consequence, bureaucracy did not substitute democracy as an autocratic alternative in these Western liberal democracies, but instead, functioned in a complementary manner.

It is also why African countries with weaker state structures are more likely to be democracies today, as compared to countries in, say, the Middle East where state coercive structures have pre-existed for centuries. Stasavage also suggests that large democracies tend to have lower levels of trust in government as compared to small democracies. According to him, larger democracies tend to be more distant and episodic, rather than direct representation, and citizens tend to trust local and state governments more than they trust central governments. He further suggests that in a democracy, people will feel that their property is more secure.[4]

This construct contributes significantly in explaining India's authoritarian bureaucracy that predates Independence, its continued feudal style of functioning vis-a-vis the citizens and also to an extent, weak state capacity (this aspect is dealt with in the next two chapters on institutional reforms and local governments respectively). It provides insight into the long-prevailing weakness of democratic citizen rights at the individual and grassroots level in India, the 'mai-baap' or non-assertive supplicancy, of individuals trapped in their interactions with formal (institutions, bureaucracy) and informal (caste, religion, language, cultural) power structures. It explains the control and trade of identity conglomerations or coalitions by a few leaders for electoral gains, and a share of power, in a hijacking of representative democracy with little accountability in India's electoral processes.

It also explains the proclivity of the state to legislate, thereby adding to a library of laws, which it finds difficult to implement on the ground, but which a bureaucracy (that derives its authoritarian power from this every growing law-rules-regulations maze going back even to the colonial period) thrives on in either rent-seeking or in tying up citizen rights and government policies in red tape. The farcical depth of legislation of citizen rights, at times as a response to the state's inability to deliver on-ground solutions, is best illustrated in an example from Professor Kaushik Basu's 2018 book, *The Republic of Beliefs: A New Approach to Law and Economics*, that demonstrates the gap between law, state capacity and political will to resolve difficult challenges.

The National Food Security Act (2013), popularly known as the Right to Food Act, was part of an effort to protect the poor from some of the extreme vagaries of the market which had been a longstanding part of India's foodgrain policy. It was also recognized as a fundamental right under Right to Life of Article 21 of the Constitution. Yet, beyond legislation, it did little to tackle the well-known distortions and ills of the food procurement policy, process, unsustainable minimum support prices, regional inequalities, leakages, profiteering, and so on. As a consequence, this law, like many others in a growing library of legislation, was widely violated.[5]

The logjam in India achieving its constitutional objectives, amid the realpolitik of its electoral politics, that seek to pander to the lowest common denominator of entrenched and competing denominational interest groups seeking their share of power, has been evident for decades. The problem has only worsened during the coalition era between 1984 to 2014. A recent case in point is the New Pension Scheme (NPS) for government employees that was introduced in 2003 as part of the reforms initiated by the then government. It was a much needed reform in the light of the worsening fiscal burden of the state and it capped government contribution to the pension scheme of new government employees. It was a policy continued by subsequent governments. Yet, in 2023, the same political coalition that undertook the reform of the NPS is now promising restoration of the unlimited Old Pension Scheme if voted back to power, to woo the sizeable and influential section of government employee voters.

Competitive politics is forcing other political parties to match or improve this offer, at the obvious cost of fiscal prudence and meeting constitutional objectives, as all parties attempt to build as wide a coalition of interests and promises to return to power.

Corresponding to this are coalitions of interests and promises to fund increasingly expensive elections that, in India's multiple levels of government, are a 365-day, non-stop cycle in the largest democracy in the world. It is worth noting that India's electorate at nearly 900 million (2019), is larger than the combined electorates of 36 other democracies.[6] It is estimated that a significant part of the unaccounted (black) money generation in the country is for funding elections. It has also brought in unsavoury elements of muscle and money power (*bahubalis*) into the election process and legislatures.

While representative politics in a large democracy may be expected to face such problems till the electorate matures, a proposal to slow down this race to the bottom in both vote and funds seeking, by synchronizing the cycle for the multiple state and general elections is worth consideration. Held at the constitutional interval of five years, it may give a fair chance to whichever political party is elected, to implement a mandate aligned to constitutional objectives rather than for all political parties to constantly function in election mode, and be hostage to populism and political imperatives of winning the immediate next elections or by-elections.

The proposal has, however, not found traction among political parties, who have very legitimate fears of being shut out of the power cycle for a prolonged period which may make their political return more difficult, and lead to an entrenchment of political power based on prevailing electorate trends, which would be detrimental to the health of India's democracy. It is a difficult problem with no easy solution. There is, however, no denying that India needs a 'democracy with Indian characteristics', to be able to formulate and implement policies that deliver on its constitutional objectives of economic development and social justice. Furthermore, common political ground will have to be found to address this growing issue.

20

Institutional Reforms

Public institutions are important pillars of the state, as they are the mechanisms through which specific outcomes are produced. The only public—and state—institution, which wields absolute and unquestioned power in China is the CPC. The party has regulated all aspects of national, public, business and individual life since coming to power in 1949. As the recent zero-Covid lockdown and crackdown on private sector technology entrepreneurs and companies reminded, all institutions, rights and laws are subservient to the CPC policy.

Since 1978—the beginning of the 'reform and opening-up' with the single-minded policy purpose of economic growth—the CPC has created and strengthened other institutions under itself by creating a new constitution, strengthening a civil law legal framework, creating proto-property rights to attract foreign investment and facilitating transition to a market-led economy. A key institutional change has been political decentralization and enhancement of powers of local governments, who now enjoy a wide range of authority under the market-oriented reforms.[1]

The role of local governments in raising finances through local government financing vehicles (LGFVs), rapid urbanization, building infrastructure and competing to attract investments to their jurisdictions has already been discussed. Actions of local governments, however, continue to be strictly in pursuit of, and circumscribed by, objectives and policy direction as instructed by the party Politburo, its standing committee, and the paramount leader.

In contrast to China, public institutions are central to India's governance structure. Empowered with powers from the Constitution, the legislature, executive and judiciary work in a system of checks and balances that have been instrumental in holding up India's constitutional democracy since Independence. While there are multiple public institutions at the state, local and sectoral levels—for the sake of simplicity and brevity—only the primary, 'load bearing' public institutions at the central level are discussed. The role and impact on the trajectory of India's democracy and economy—in the context of Professor Stasavage's argument that the pre-existence of institutions and bureaucracy before the introduction of democracy has a direct bearing on the subsequent level of trust and active participation in governance by its citizens—bears examination.

All three public institutions and their respective bureaucracies have pre-existed India's independence and constitution as an electoral democracy. Many aspects of a centralized and paternalistically authoritarian style of governance, culture and attitudes of these institutional bureaucracies have continued well after India's independence. This approach, while initially advanced as a plausible argument of preventing India's democracy from collapsing into anarchy in its fledgling years of independence, has not significantly evolved or kept pace with change over the years. It can also be held responsible in part for stifling individual rights-based democracy (as against simply an electoral representative democracy) from reaching grassroots, thereby stifling initiative and encouraging a continued supplicant attitude towards colonial power and authority aggregated within these institutions. Many have argued that India's improved economic performance since its reform processes began, has been despite, and not because of, the state. As Gurcharan Das, author and former CEO of Procter & Gamble, put it, 'India grows at night while the government sleeps.'[2]

The fact that India's public institutions have not kept pace with India's growth and change in other aspects of its national polity is now a deep cause of concern. As Devesh Kapur, Pratap Bhanu Mehta and Milan Vaishnav write, '[...] continued welfare gains, better distributional outcomes, and the resilience and sustainability of rapid economic growth are in considerable doubt in the absence of better-performing public institutions.'[3] The numbers they offer in support of this argument are startling. While India's population increased from 846 million to 1.2 billion (now 1.4 billion) between 1991 (the year India's reforms began) and 2011, the absolute size of the elite, centrally recruited and controlled Indian Administrative Service (IAS, successor to the colonial Indian Civil Service) that dominates policymaking and administration in the country across most public institutions, except the judiciary, dropped by 10 per cent. By 2010, the total strength of the IAS and Indian Police Service (IPS) was less than 11,000, while the vacancy rate stood at 28 per cent.

India has one of the lowest per capita police rates among major countries at 1.3 constables per 1,000 citizens. Official estimates of police vacancies stand around 23 per cent. India's judicial system presently has a backlog of more than 31 million cases. Government estimates suggest that as many as 10 per cent of all cases are pending for a decade or more. However, understaffed has not meant under-bureaucratized, with each public bureaucracy weaving its own tangled web of power accretion, patronage and denial of citizens and private enterprise.

India's poor performance on global ease of business rankings has been in large part due to this public institutional atrophy, and while there has been significant improvement since, there is still a long way to go. Even rights-based reform legislations such as the Right to Information (2005) and the Right to Education (2009) have not been able to achieve desired outcomes in the face of poor public institutional capacity and entrenched interests. Some of the reasons for this have been weak and compromised policymaking, fragmentation of decision-making, poor incentives and competencies of key decision makers, lack of internal accountability in these public institutional structures and inherent tendencies of self-perpetuating institutional bureaucracies to accrue power and turf.

The lack of a strong political centre to envision and drive a reforms agenda in the legislature and government, during the coalition years from 1991 to 2014, saw both the judiciary and the bureaucracy expand jurisdictions. The Supreme Court, over the course of three cases during this period, evolved the principle of judicial independence to mean that no other branch of the state—

including the legislature and the executive—would have any say in the appointment of judges. It instead created the collegium system—a panel of seniormost judges—to undertake selection, bringing the practice into use first in 1993, following what is known as the Second Judges Case. On a question of law regarding the collegium system, raised by the then President in July 1998, through a reference to the Supreme Court under his constitutional powers, the Supreme Court gave an opinion upholding the collegium system (known as the Third Judges Case). It is pertinent to note that there is no mention of the collegium either in the original Constitution of India or in successive amendments. The Supreme Court has since dismissed all challenges to the collegium system of appointment.

In 2013, in a rare display of political unanimity, the Constitution (120th Amendment) Bill was passed which established the National Judicial Appointments Commission, on whose recommendation the President would appoint judges to the higher judiciary.[4] The amendment was, however, struck down by the Supreme Court for being unconstitutional in 2015, reading it as a basic and unalterable structure of the Constitution, and the collegium system has continued amid public debate and contestation. While there is need to insulate India's public institutions—particularly the judiciary—from a deteriorating political climate and abuse by politics of self-interest with roots going as far back as events leading up to and during former PM Indira Gandhi's Emergency, there is no denying the dangers and conflict of interest inherent in judges sitting in their own cause and selection, particularly in an environment of poor internal and external institutional accountability of its functionaries. The fact that this unaccountability has often led to whimsical and arbitrary expansion and intervention into the executive domain of policy by judges in the past, has only heightened uncertainty in the economic and business environment.

The reforms and liberalization process that began in 1991 saw a rethinking on the issue of regulation for India's growing market economy (the other rethinking was on decentralization and devolution of power to local governments, which has been dealt with separately).

Recognizing the shortcomings of existing public institutions (of a ministerial executive and judicial adjudication) in meeting requirements of specialized sectors of the economy—as also pressures from international financial institutions to adopt institutional innovation, particularly in the financial and infrastructure sectors— the government set up quasi judicial–legislative regulatory bodies to frame rules, oversight orderly development and undertake regulation and adjudication of individual sectors of the economy. There was also the hope that these regulators would 'depoliticize' areas of economic activity—particularly infrastructure—that had become heavily driven by political considerations rather than the economy's requirements. The outcome of this institutional initiative has, however, been underwhelming.

As Devesh Kapur and Madhav Khosla write, '[...] if liberalization was meant to roll back the state, the rise of the regulatory state is a testament to the fact that, far from rolling back, the state has simply rolled over. It has, however, led to a more fragmented state apparatus. The emergence of the "independent regulatory agency" has been a defining element in this institutional fragmentation.'[5] Performance has varied across regulators, and some failures can be attributed partly to faulty design. However, the larger and more consistent feature has been the 'lack of attention to the reform of the market structure and an inadequate understanding of interaction between the market structure and the effectiveness of the regulatory process'.[6]

A familiar pattern of the dynamics of India's dominant institutional bureaucracies has seen the civil services of the state and the judiciary, manning most of these decision-making regulatory positions as post retirement sinecures. This has impeded development of these regulators as their members have continued to be an extension of the institutional weaknesses of their parent public institutions, rather than building the regulators as specialized market-knowledgeable, interactive, effective and independent institutions. Beyond the capture of new regulatory institutions by older institutional bureaucracies, the fragmentation of state power also brought to the fore heightened concerns of regulatory capture by dominant market players that the regulators were tasked to regulate. The continued failure of India's public institutions, now fragmented and compounded by the multiplicity of poor market interaction and poorly functioning new regulators, is a significant retardant to economic growth across sectors. It is an urgent and deep reform that needs to be undertaken if India is to achieve its economic potential in the next 20 years.

21

Local Government

Much of China's economic growth has been driven by local governments. While policy objectives were decided and communicated from Beijing, local leadership had significant autonomy in how they planned to achieve those objectives. It was a delegation and decentralization of power that was encouraged under Deng's leadership. 'Cross[ing] the river by feeling the stone' and a delegation structure that encouraged experiments of multiple policy choices at local and provincial levels, followed by a nationwide implementation as *you dian dao mian* (point to surface) after successful experimentation and validation of a policy choice, worked across diverse sectors. These sectors include the setting up of special economic zones (SEZs), the shift to the household responsibility system, agricultural market reforms, the township and village enterprises (TVE) intermediate experiment, urbanization and infrastructure. The intense competition for development among local and provincial governments, in order to attract investments to their jurisdiction, was aided by an incentive structure for their bureaucracies. This structure was tied to their success in attracting and retaining industries.

This alignment largely ensured that all local bureaucracies were aligned to the primary party objective of economic growth. This is also why corruption in China took the form of the arguably less retardant elite 'access money' than petty corruption 'speed money'. The initial decentralization and delegation of powers to local governments that took place during Deng's era got a fillip that was forced more by circumstance when, following a reorganization of the fiscal distribution system in 1994, the lion's share of taxes was appropriated by the central government.

Local and provincial governments and its leaders nominated by the central government, were left to their own devices to meet their expenditure budgets and funds for undertaking capital works. Local governments were, however, given monopoly ownership over urban public land in that reorganization. It sparked a rush by local governments to monetize property rights, a boom which has continued unchecked for the last 30 years and has funded the urbanization and infrastructure engines that have driven China's economy, particularly since 2008. It is a structural weakness that is a major cause of worry in China's growing economic troubles.

From the late 1980s and early 1990s, decentralization (along with regulatory bodies for specialized supervision, dealt with earlier) was a growing trend across developing economies. It was an institutional reform design that was supported by multilateral financial institutions like the World Bank, which encouraged governments to devolve authority to local governments, delegate services to quasi-independent organizations or the private sector and de-concentrate central delivery of services to improve governance. As against an earlier centralized model of governance, national governments now insisted that local and provincial (state) authorities took on the fiscal responsibility of managing budgets, generating revenues and rendering accounts. Legislation to elect officials at these levels of subnational government was also passed, while also making them administratively responsible for delivery of significant public services and local infrastructure. Local institutions that had decayed from decades of centralization, like panchayats in India, were sought to be revived to take on these complex challenges.

Decentralization not only brought about new responsibilities for local officials and agencies, but it also brought about additional relationships that required to be managed, in addition to the traditional, centralized reporting structure. The arguments in support of this decentralization and the benefits it brought were many. Economists argued that decentralization prioritized public spending based on local demand, with services being made more readily available to citizens by local governments based on their feedback, and greater accountability in elections of local politicians. Local taxes would also lead to citizens demanding better services, and holding officials and service providers more accountable, thereby deepening democracy. With local tax and expenditure by the local government, transparency and reduction of corruption could also be expected under improved citizen participation.[1]

India's effort at decentralization began with the landmark amendments to the Constitution that created a framework for rural and urban local governments, giving them constitutional status and mandating regular elections to locally elected bodies. It further mandated reservations of positions in these local bodies for women and individuals from traditionally disadvantaged (and constitutionally recognized) groups. Beyond these mandates, it called upon (but did not explicitly require) individual states in India's federal system to enact legislation to devolve power and resources to these local bodies to fulfil their role as institutions of self-governance. The Panchayati Raj constitutional amendments marked as much a recognition of Mahatma Gandhi's idea of village proto-democracy as it recognized the failure of the existing centralized and bureaucratic public institution framework in delivering constitutional aims and objectives.

Efforts at decentralization, however, met with mixed success across states. The primary reason was that the Constitution assigned exclusive legislative domain over local governments to the states, upon whom the final responsibility for the design and local government reforms rested. Each state in the federal structure of India had their own historical trajectories and existing sociopolitical and economic conditions, resulting in significant variations in the design, scope and extent of devolution to local governments. Further, in light of earlier attempts to revitalize local governments, the Constitutional amendments were not entirely a 'greenfield' initiative.

Earlier efforts by states, with varying rates of success, put them at different points on the local government devolution trajectory. As Shubham Chaudhari writes, 'The provision mandating regular elections to rural local bodies clearly had different implications in the state of Bihar (where elections to rural local bodies were last held in 1978) than it does in the state of West Bengal (where elections have been regularly held every five years since 1978).[2]

The vision of a truly participative and empowered grassroots democracy was, however, stunted by realities of India's identity-based and feudal politics, dominant interest groups' capture of power and existing powerful bureaucracies that neglected the nurturing of fledgling local governments. The vitality of a rights-based and empowered citizenry—driving economic development and growth through locally empowered governments and accountable institutions—that was expected to emerge from these reforms never occurred.

Another key aspect for these reforms not taking off as expected was also regarding finances of these local governments. Historically, both governance and finance have had a centralized nature in India. The central government has been reluctant to devolve finances to states, which in turn have resisted giving financial autonomy to local governments. Without adequate resources, and few other sources of funds or monetization, the effectiveness of local bodies to undertake the public services and capital expenditure expected of them in their jurisdictions has been limited. This has, however, improved following the acceptance of the fourteenth Finance Commission, which—along with the goods and services tax—shall increasingly see greater resources being made available to the states. Further reforms for devolution of finances are also being undertaken, with urban reforms being a key component of future economic growth strategy.

Of the ₹1.3 lakh crore earmarked as capital expenditure support to states in the Union Budget 2023–24, ₹20,000 crore is specifically tied to urban planning and financing reforms.[3] There is also an effort to push urban local bodies to prepare themselves to raise funds by way of municipal bonds from capital markets, to be repaid from user fees and local cess. However, much more will be required to be done, and institutions and finances reimagined, if the vitality and initiative of an empowered citizenry to undertake local government-driven economic activity and growth, as promised by the local government template, is to be realized.

22

Land and Agricultural Market Reforms

The reform of land and agricultural produce markets have been an integral component of China's economic story. It was the reorganization of land and agricultural produce markets, under the household responsibility system and the dual-track system that enabled generation of agricultural produce surplus and its transfer to finance China's industrialization. It was the availability of large tracts of land to be allotted by local or provincial governments that enabled the setting up of SEZs. In later years, it was the monetization of land by local governments that financed rapid urbanization and infrastructure build out, generating decades of uninterrupted economic growth. It was also resources from land, along with high mobilization capacity of the party-state, that enabled widespread improvement by local governments in education, healthcare and other socio-economic parameters over this period.

In contrast, India's gains in agricultural productivity have primarily come from the Green Revolution which improved agricultural yields in the early 1970s in parts of the country. However, it also required greater capital outlays for irrigation works, electricity for water pumps and fertilizers, along with minimum price support and provision of credit. The government provided extensive subsidies to improve productivity and make India self-sufficient in foodgrains. Over time, however, these subsidies became entangled in electoral politics, and eventually became institutionalized, with successive governments becoming committed to providing heavy subsidies for these inputs.

The subsidies which were not well-targeted and over time benefitted large, albeit entrepreneurial, land owners and fertilizer companies at the expense of investments in rural infrastructure, health and education, have continued in the decades since, despite the evident distortions and inequity they create. As a consequence, instead of generating an economic surplus to support growth, political clientelism has created an entrenched system of continuing subsidies and wastage that benefits only a small section of the agricultural and rural community with wide geographical and economic discrimination.

The failure of land reforms, disputed and outdated ownership and revenue land records dating back to colonial times, along with poorly regulated and adjudicated tenancy laws, have prevented the development of an active market in both purchase and sale of land. It has also hindered the development of land aggregation on lease for undertaking contract farming. Litigation over land, pending for decades, is one of the largest contributors to the backlog of cases choking the judicial system.

According to a news report in 2019, an estimated 7.7 million people were affected by conflict over 2.5 million hectares of land, threatening investments worth more than ₹14 lakh crore. Land disputes account for the largest number of cases in Indian courts—25 per cent of cases decided by the Supreme Court involve land disputes, of which 30 per cent of all civil cases in India are related to land or property disputes. The average pendency of a land acquisition dispute case from its creation to its resolution by the Supreme Court is 20 years.[1] The progressive fragmentation of land holdings to unviable levels under inheritance laws, besides emotional, social and cultural prestige with owning land have also contributed to the lack of development of an active land market.

Acquisition of large and undisputed land has been among the single largest hurdles for economic development across sectors— whether for SEZs, infrastructure projects or urbanization. Outdated policies of compulsory land acquisition by the government for SEZs and infrastructure projects at 'revenue' land rate and significantly below market prices, led to widespread mass agitations that wrecked many development initiatives in their infancy. Legislative changes have since been made, providing for land compensation in multiples of its market value. Land records have also been updated and digitized. Legislation to ease tenancy provisions and to encourage contract farming has also been enacted. Farmer cooperatives and producer organizations are also being encouraged to enable land pooling, contract farming and build sustainable organizations and frameworks for marketing agricultural produce at remunerative prices to farmers. Cold storage chains and shift to value added horticulture is being encouraged. Urban land reforms are also being undertaken. Yet, significant challenges remain, both with developing active land markets and freeing and creating viable and sustainable agricultural produce markets, especially because of electorally powerful entrenched interest groups that weaken the larger, constitutional resolve of any government when faced with opposition from critical vote banks.

The issue of land and agricultural produce markets, however, continue to be the core differential of the development conundrum, including improving agricultural productivity; offering remunerative prices to farmers; improving rural economy and socio-economic indicators of health, education and rural consumption; development of infrastructure; setting up of large industries and reaping the economic benefits of urbanization. How well the solutions are found for these complex and pressing issues will play a key role in determining the future trajectory of the Indian economy.

In Conclusion:
Parrots and Tea Leaves

China's economy has grown over the last 45 years almost uninterruptedly, on the backdrop of state-directed growth that first saw success in the SEZs and then in the rapid development and growth of urbanization and infrastructure. While facilitated by its history, geography and culture of treaty ports, shared kinship and economic ties with Chinese business diaspora and East Asian networks—along with Confucian hierarchical social order traits of popular mobilization to larger objectives—the unprecedented and miraculous growth was primarily based on two once-in-a-lifetime vectors.

The first vector was China's accession to the World Trade Organization in 2001 that gave it unrestricted access to international markets at a time when globalization was at its peak. It helped it in establishing itself deeply in global supply chains and across markets, making it the factory of the world. The second vector was the multi-trillion dollar monetization of state-owned land that began in 1994 but gathered pace post the 2008 global financial crisis. The opportunity and resources these put in the hands of the Chinese state has been unprecedented in human history and has enabled a rapid growth in industrialization, urbanization and infrastructure that is now into its fifth decade.

China's trajectory, guided by state directives and entirely focussed on economic growth driven by manufacturing, urbanization and infrastructure development has been skewed, and led to severe imbalances. These imbalances include disparity in income and wealth, concentration of unproductive and unsustainable debt and assets in LGFVs and real estate; underdeveloped markets and institutions; continued state-directed lending to state-owned 'zombie' enterprises; brittle foreign exchange mechanisms; low domestic consumption as a percentage of its GDP; and concerns about social, political and economic risks lurking beneath a monolithic and opaque surface.

The imbalances of yin-yang that have crept in were not addressed during the rapid growth phase, as they were hidden amid the rising tide of prosperity. All three engines are, however, now under stress. The strain of Covid-19 disruption, increasing forces of globalization and protectionism, fractious geopolitics, rising wages and manufacturing costs in China and global economies battling the threat of recession are leading to weaker global demand and shifting of manufacturing and supply chains away from China to lower cost countries in a growing China Plus One strategy by companies seeking a resilient and de-risked approach.

Overcapacity in domestic urban construction and infrastructure, and declining—even negative—marginal returns on capital deployed threaten its land monetization and investment-led growth model. This in turn has begun to seriously affect local government finances, which have depended on this monetization to fund not only its investments but also meet its social security obligations of pensions, medical care, etc. Worrying signs suggest looming real estate and municipal debt crises of an unprecedented scale and size.[1] Its export-oriented geopolitical Belt and Road Initiative—which envisages deployment of its financial resources through investments and loans in infrastructure projects in developing countries that would keep its huge construction industry running—also faces headwinds in the form of growing defaults, resistance and geopolitical suspicion, as those economies battle challenges of their own.

China's growth till now has been led by its manpower-intensive manufacturing, real estate and construction sectors. Its next stage of economic growth from a higher middle-income country to a high-income country, however, shall be dependent on its migration to an invention or innovation-led model, where its economy develops capabilities to lead sunrise sectors. China, today, leads the world in the rapid commercialization and building of economies of scale in many nascent technologies like electric vehicles, battery storage, digital technology and commerce, and solar and wind capacity. Its geopolitics, however, suggests, that it may have to contend with increasing trade barriers and growing distrust in a fast-changing world. The US has already enacted the CHIPS Act, that prevents at a global level not only the supply of latest generation semiconductor chips, but actively hampers the development of core cutting-edge chip manufacturing technology in China. In the current geopolitical scenario, these restrictions may affect the very technological foundation from which China hopes to make the leap to a services and innovation driven economy.

In 2019, China's urban-based services industry accounted for nearly 54 per cent of its GDP, which is projected to grow to 63 per cent by 2035 even as contributions by other sectors decline. As the share of urbanization and services increases in China's economy, the pressure of making a successful transition to the next stage of innovation-led economic growth increases even more. The challenge is further compounded by China facing a rapidly ageing demographic trend, which will increasingly require a decreasing base of young population to support a larger population, and its increasing healthcare and social costs in retirement. High value added and higher wage employment for these urbanized youth in innovation-led services and industries will have to be generated to meet these challenges. It is a strain already visible as local governments cut back on social security benefits and protests grow around these cutbacks. A question that is now being increasingly asked is, can China grow rich before it grows old?

That, however, is not the only question facing China. Its growth as a rising superpower, increasing belligerence in its global relations over the last few years and its implications has seen the formation of numerous military and economic alliances, with the US as the existing global hegemon at its centre as they perceive an attempt to overthrow the existing rules-based, post World War II global order. The Thucydides Trap, which posits an inevitability to a conflict between an existing and an emerging superpower, as it did between the ancient Greek cities of Sparta and Athens, is very much a subject of growing concern in diplomatic and military circles.[2]

While China continues to flog its infrastructure-led investment strategy with more capital expenditure to prop up a flagging economic growth rate and keep its key engines of the economy running, there is growing recognition that long-neglected structural problems can no longer be ignored. As global demand falls, China's domestic consumption must rise to compensate while also driving future growth. China is one of the world's largest markets, and it represents a significant opportunity to become the next engine of both domestic and global growth.

Raising household consumption is, however, easier said than done in a country with prolific and exceptionally high saving habits that have been ingrained for decades by deep uncertainties and fears of the future, as well as limited robust investment opportunities. Disparities in income and wealth have exacerbated the problem, contributing to rising social and regional tensions. Consequently, addressing these disparities lie at the heart of Xi Jinping's 'common prosperity' theme. Promoting even more conspicuous consumption by the wealthy to generate domestic demand is, however, a policy line fraught with multiple social and political implications in communist China.

At a macro level, however, China's model of authoritarian development has resembled the fabled hare, which has raced ahead on four sectoral legs of policy steroids that gave it tremendous speed but are now showing signs of strain, while the rest of the body has struggled to keep pace. China will most likely need to spend the next decade, if not two, in correcting systemic imbalances in its economy, restoring yin-yang harmony, as well as strengthening and deepening institutional and market reforms.

Xi Jinping's recentralization of power, which reverses China's collective leadership vector since Deng's era, suggests a political will and authority to make difficult policy decisions. The risks of such an approach, of a policy misstep or unknown or unfactored risks emerging unexpectedly and causing great damage, like in the GLF or the Cultural Revolution, are also at their highest since the opening-up process began in 1978. However, the rapid reversal of the widely unpopular and prolonged zero-Covid lockdown, which caused social unrest and protests, particularly in cities, also suggests a pragmatism rarely seen in previous totalitarian CPC leaders like Mao, to whom his growing power is frequently compared.

There has also been a visible scaling down of China's vaunted 'wolf warrior' belligerent style of diplomacy, much of it undertaken for domestic audiences, in the post-Covid, de-globalization and rapidly realigning geopolitical scenario. Even as China finds itself increasingly at loggerheads with the West and its Asian neighbours, it seeks to grow new alliances in West Asia, East Europe and Russia.

The legitimacy of the CPC to rule China has widely been seen as a compact with the Chinese public to first, deliver economic prosperity; and second, and more recently, to restore and claim China's respect and primacy status in the world order. Well set to achieve the first, its approach to the second has brought it into fractious conflict with its neighbours as also with other global powers and trade partners. Over the course of the next decade or more, Xi Jinping and the CPC will have to address and resolve significant questions and challenges that may arise, as its public compact of continued growth and prosperity in the reforms and opening-up for the Mandate of Heaven comes under increasing strain.

India, in contrast, stands out as a rare and successful pluralistic and secular modern democracy, a form of government that speaks to its very civilizational core of culture and political ethos. It is an ethos that has deeply influenced its economic trajectory, with much discussion, debate and contestation of citizen rights and powers of the state, the individual and collective or common good within its robust framework of institutional checks and balances. While, like the proverbial tortoise, its pace has been slow—at times taking two steps forward, one step back—it has made steady progress. India's liberalization reforms that began in 1991 were triggered by a crisis too. Effective policy formulation and implementation were, however, hampered for nearly 23 years, from 1991 to 2014, with no political party achieving an electoral majority and thus, lacking the political capital required to provide firm leadership and direction.

Despite this, it has experienced rapid growth, ranking alongside China as one of the fastest growing large economies over the last two decades. Its investment-led growth, particularly between 2008 and 2014, exposed fragilities in its institutional and regulatory systems, resulting in a crisis of confidence that led to a non-performing asset debt crisis in its banking sector. It also saw an electoral majority government being voted into power in 2014, for the first time in nearly 25 years. This has led, within its institutional and democratic framework, to a firmer direction for the economy. The mobilizational success of the JAM trinity—Jan Dhan, Aadhaar and Mobility in poverty alleviation, Direct Benefit Transfers, the Swachh Bharat campaign of nationwide toilet construction, the Pradhan Mantri Awas Yojana and the Har Ghar Jal scheme have seen improved implementation on the ground, with fewer leakages than in the past.

With targets and increased accountability, India's bureaucracy and institutional framework are responding to a government with a political mandate for democratic governance. Challenges, however, remain. While India has performed better than most other economies and remains a bright spot in a darkening post-Covid global scenario over the long term, critics point to a K-shaped recovery (when different sectors of the economy recover at different rates) and increasing stress in the rural economy and households. There is, however, a broad consensus of opinion that India is well poised to rapidly transition from a low middle-income country to a higher middle-income country status in the upcoming years.

India's young population represent a significant opportunity to drive this economic growth over the next two decades. As a large number of young people enter the workforce, it could lead to increased productivity and consumption. While a growing trend of de-globalization is a long term threat, in the short and medium term, the shifting of manufacturing and supply chains in China Plus One strategies, offer significant opportunities to position India as a reliable, low-cost manufacturing hub. It is also made more attractive by shared democratic values and rapidly changing geopolitical realignments that make India a globally trusted and reliable partner in a multipolar world. This opportunity is sought to be capitalized on in policies like the production-linked incentive scheme, Atmanirbhar Bharat, etc., which seek to become part of global supply chains even while undertaking value-added manufacturing and supplying to domestic markets.

This demographic dividend, however, has a double edge. Even as an increasingly large number of young people enter the workforce, it is of critical importance that adequate quality jobs are generated. Failure to do so could potentially lead to significant social and economic issues. Improving education outcomes and skill development in a fast-changing environment are critical to encashing this once-in-a-lifetime demographic opportunity. Addressing the deep-rooted structural inequalities and reform barriers in India's agricultural and rural economies, which continue to support nearly 65 per cent of its large population[3], is central to India's future economic trajectory. Legislative initiatives that were undertaken on developing agricultural produce and land markets but were retracted in view of agitational opposition, will have to be reworked for popular acceptance and undertaken to improve rural incomes and livelihoods. Steps to address the growing income and wealth inequalities, exacerbated in the post-Covid recovery, will also need to be taken on priority.

Industrialization, urbanization and infrastructure development represent the single biggest opportunity after agricultural and land reforms, to shift people from their present low productivity and disguised unemployment in the rural agricultural sector, to higher productivity urban jobs. It is a shift that is central to putting India on a sustainable high growth path.

Ongoing infrastructure development, including the development of highways, Vande Bharat high-speed rail networks, smart cities, ports and airports, backed by significant state investment, can drive this economic growth and attract foreign investment. It would not, however, be feasible for the state alone to undertake the multi-trillion dollar investments required. Furthermore, private participation in partnership with the state will have to be reimagined to address the shortcomings in the previous public–private partnership infrastructure-led investment cycle.

Urban reforms, including legislative, financial and empowerment of local bodies that are being undertaken, will bring more autonomy and accountability to the urbanization process. Efforts are also being made to focus on innovation and technology, to develop new industries and products, including clean energy, semiconductors, artificial intelligence, biotechnology, and so on.

Besides its efforts to attract large-scale manufacturing investments, India also needs to focus on its strong services sector, including IT, finance and healthcare, by leveraging technological changes, which have the potential for it to become the 'back office' or 'the healthcare centre of the world'. In this development process, India also needs to address existing and future environmental challenges at both the national level and climate change concerns at the global level. This will require a reimagination of the economic development trajectory to be environmentally sustainable over the medium term, while reconciling the short-term compulsions of economic activity and growth.

India also needs to focus on technologies and industries of the future, to leapfrog its technological and industrial development to develop cutting-edge manufacturing expertise in emerging sectors such as green hydrogen, semiconductor manufacturing, space technology, financial technology and digitization. The rapid and exponential expansion of invention to innovation in the ongoing Fifth Industrial Revolution and beyond, also presents first principle *de novo* greenfield opportunities for India to reimagine and chart its future development trajectory in a sustainable, low ecological impact and balanced manner for its citizens—an option not available to other large middle-income and rich economies that are already locked into high energy, high impact and high investment ecosystems and path-dependent trajectories.

India is also well poised to offer an alternative vision of inclusive growth and sustainable development to the Global South and to developing countries in Africa and Asia—a growth that balances improved economic outcomes for their peoples with individual rights and aspirations, and a collaborative approach of partnership and mutual benefit rather than of dominance or hegemony, that suggests a world order different from either neocolonialism or economic exploitation.

Amid the growing differences between China and the West-led world order, India is increasingly being called upon to participate and lead in reshaping existing global institutions to meet the changed geopolitical scenario. Its participation in discussions to reshape institutions like the World Bank and the International Monetary Fund, to prepare them to fund new development requirements like climate change and renewable energy, while also being a cofounder of the Asian Infrastructure Investment Bank—an active contributor to the Shanghai Cooperation Organization—and a key constituent of the New Development Bank (popularly known as the BRICS bank)—all point to its increased role and importance in the rapidly emerging multipolar world. It is a role that it is exercising with pragmatic self-interest, while adhering to its civilizational principles of equity, mutual respect, mutual sensitivity and mutual interest. It is also a framework upon which India seeks to build a pragmatic relationship with China.

The political stability and transparency of India's democratic institutions, alongside the continuity provided by an electoral majority government, offer the direction and impetus needed for driving reform. India's political capital and will to deliver required reforms with grassroots mobilization and its benefits to citizens along with a comparatively robust economy, a cleaned up and ready-to-lend financial and banking sector, a growing domestic market for products and services, and favourable tailwinds of geopolitical collaboration and trust indicate that India is well poised to lay strong foundations and reap the benefits of sustained higher economic growth over the next few decades than in the past.

It is, however, important to remember that, unlike the proverbial hare and the tortoise, China and India are not in a race. Both are individual nations with many overlapping and shared civilizational and cultural values, although with different forms of political government, seeking to deliver benefits to their people. In an evidently identifiable Asian Century, the world shall be increasingly reliant on these two largest nations for both leadership and growth on issues that confront the planet and humanity. Sustainable models of development and tackling climate change are the most immediate and pressing global concerns that leave no nation or individual untouched. Beyond fractious differences and catering to domestic audiences, China and India need to demonstrate statesmanship and cooperate in finding solutions to the many pressing issues that might darken the global horizon over the next two decades. The universal principles of Panchsheel, as espoused by Zhou Enlai and Jawaharlal Nehru could be a good starting point, if subscribed to in letter and spirit.

Both countries have a cultural history of fortune telling and attempting to predict the future, with the Indian subcontinent using card reading parrots and China using tea leaves. However, neither is a science with any level of predictability or certainty. The future remains uncertain, with many complexities, risks, pitfalls and opportunities that will require skilful navigation and leadership. What is certain, though, is that the choices made by the two giant Asian neighbours over the next few decades in their respective complex trajectories will, quite literally, decide the world's future.

Endnotes

Introduction

1   Allison, Graham, *Destined for War: Can America and China Escape Thucydides's Trap?*, Houghton Mifflin Harcourt, 2017.

2   'AUKUS: UK, US and Australia Launch Pact to Counter China', *BBC News*, 16 September 2021, http://tinyurl.com/2p9b3tce. Accessed on 6 September 2023.

3   U.S.–China Economic and Security Review Commission, *2020 Report to Congress of the U.S.–China Economic and Security Review Commission*, December 2020, http://tinyurl.com/52u9wu6y. Accessed on 6 September 2023.

4   Smil, Vaclav, 'China's Great Famine: 40 Years Later', *BMJ*, Vol. 319, No. 7225, 1999.

5   Inoue Kosuke, and Iori Kawate, 'China Overtakes U.S. In National Net Worth to Grab Top Spot', *NIKKEI Asia*, 19 December 2021, http://tinyurl.com/yscmdf3c. Accessed on 6 September 2023.

6   'From Burj Khalifa to Changsha IFS Tower: Check Full List of World's Top 15 Tallest Buildings', *News9*, 3 September 2022, http://tinyurl.com/bddc2x9x. Accessed on 11 September 2023.

7   'Three Gorges Dam Hydropower Station', *NS Energy*, http://tinyurl.com/43a4xt77. Accessed on 6 September 2023.

8   Marcus, Lilit, 'China Debuts World's Fastest Train', *CNN Travel*, 21 July 2021, http://tinyurl.com/33yhtjzp. Accessed on 6 September 2023.

9   'How China Built the World's Largest Highway Network', *InSITE*, 22 March 2021, http://tinyurl.com/2jmyccf5. Accessed on 6 September 2023.

10 'The World's 10 Longest Railway Networks', *Railway Technology*, 19 February 2014, http://tinyurl.com/4vyvfvs7. Accessed on 6 September 2023.

11 'China Has Built the World's Largest Water-Diversion Project', *The Economist*, 5 April 2018, http://tinyurl.com/mwa3dauv. Accessed on 6 September 2023.

12 'China Opens World's Longest Sea Bridge near Qingdao', *BBC News*, 30 June 2011, http://tinyurl.com/3yrzrnkm. Accessed on 6 September 2023.

13 Swanson, Ana, 'How China Used More Cement in 3 Years than the U.S. Did in the Entire 20th Century', *The Washington Post*, 24 March 2015, http://tinyurl.com/yh64r82k. Accessed on 7 February 2024.

14 Baer, Drake, 'A Simple Design Innovation Let a Chinese Entrepreneur Build a 57-Story Skyscraper in 19 Days', *Business Insider India*, 19 June 2015, http://tinyurl.com/52uxrmx6. Accessed on 6 September 2023.

15 Pang, Kelly, 'The Great Wall of the Qin Dynasty', *China Highlights*, 22 December 2022, http://tinyurl.com/2r3255zd. Accessed on 6 September 2023.

16 'Deng Xiaoping: Socialism with Chinese Characteristics', *Works & Days*, http://tinyurl.com/4dywvtts. Accessed on 6 September 2023.

17 'India vs China by Population', *Statistics Times*, 24 January 2024, http://tinyurl. com/kjyenfvr. Accessed on 6 September 2023.

18 'Comparing China and India by Economy', *Statistics Times*, 8 December 2023, http://tinyurl.com/eehxwedt. Accessed on 26 February 2024.

19 'Projected GDP Ranking', *Statistics Times*, 2 November 2023, http://tinyurl. com/374yspkd. Accessed on 6 September 2023.

20 'Comparing China and India by Economy', *Statistics Times*, 8 December 2023, http://tinyurl.com/eehxwedt. Accessed on 26 February 2024.

21 Krishnan, Ananth, 'India's Imports from China Reach Record High in 2022, Trade Deficit Surges beyond $100 Billion', *The Hindu*, 13 January 2023, http:// tinyurl.com/y9yaze8e. Accessed on 6 September 2023.

22 Dhar, Biswajit, 'The Ultimate Captive Market', *DNA*, 22 January 2019, http:// tinyurl.com/5cs6rmh3. Accessed on 6 September 2023.

23 'International Land Border', *mha.gov.in*, http://tinyurl.com/yfycz39m. Accessed on 6 September 2023.

24 Dikotter, Frank, *The Construction of Racial Identities in China and Japan*, Hurst Publishers, 1997.

25 Cartwright, Mark, 'The Dragon in Ancient China', *World History Encyclopedia*, 29 September 2017, http://tinyurl.com/bxtea67n. Accessed on 6 September 2023.

26 Xinjian, Xu, 'The Chinese Identity in Question: "Descendants of the Dragon" and "The Wolf Totem"', *Revue de littérature compare*, Vol. 337, 2011.

27 Mayor, Adrienne, *The First Fossil Hunters: Dinosaurs, Mammoths, and Myth in Greek and Roman Times*, Princeton University Press, 2011.

28 Barrow, Mandy, 'The Legend of Saint George and the Dragon', *Project Britain*, http://tinyurl.com/5n6mbf5c. Accessed on 6 September 2023.

29 'Nagas in Hindu Mythology', *India Netzone*, http://tinyurl.com/bddncy8v. Accessed on 8 February 2023.

30 'Naga Myth: Unveiling the Serpentine Legends and Folklore from Asia', *Old World Gods*, http://tinyurl.com/mvzezy68. Accessed on 8 February 2024.

Chapter 1: Geography: The Destiny of Nations

1. Nitkoski, Matthew, 'From West to East: The Charged Challenge of Delivering Electricity', *China Business Review*, 7 April 2021, http://tinyurl.com/ms82wc3c. Accessed on 6 September 2023.

2. 'Giant China Project Leads the Rise of Renewable Mega-Hubs', *The Economic Times*, 14 October 2021, http://tinyurl.com/34v5pkwe. Accessed on 6 September 2023.

3. O'Neill, Aaron, 'Largest Countries in the World by Area', *statista*, 2 February 2024, http://tinyurl.com/u9sfk2fm. Accessed on 7 February 2024.

4. Kurus, 'Heihe – Tengchong Line', *Indian Politics*, http://tinyurl.com/yvr4ess3. Accessed on 7 February 2024.

Chapter 2: Culture: Shaping Identities

1   Mente, Boye De, *The Chinese Mind: Understanding Traditional Chinese Beliefs and Their Influence on Contemporary Culture*, Tuttle Publishing, 2011.

2   Allison, Graham, Robert D. Blackwill, and Ali Wyne, *Lee Kuan Yew: The Grand Master's Insights on China, the United States, and the World*, MIT Press, 2012.

3   Jing Tsu, *Kingdom of Characters: The Language Revolution that made China Modern*, Penguin Publishing Group, 2022.

4   'Education in China: Statistics, Literacy, Women and Test Score Successes', *Facts and Details*, http://tinyurl.com/46dbmwzw. Accessed on 7 February 2024.

5   'Literacy Rate in China (2018 - 2021, %)', *GlobalData*, http://tinyurl.com/4um6fun4. Accessed on 7 February 2024.

6   Violatti, Cristian, 'Brahmi Script', *World History Encyclopedia*, 14 November 2016, http://tinyurl.com/msmjf6mf. Accessed on 6 September 2023.

7   Kumar, Anu, 'Thomas Macaulay Won the Debate on How to Shape Indian Education. So Who Were the Losers?', *Scroll.in*, 4 February 2017, http://tinyurl.com/4dzstunj. Accessed on 6 September 2023.

8   Tiwari, Saket, 'Independence Day 2023: India Then and Now in Terms of Population, Health, Literacy, and Economy', *News Nine*, 12 August 2023, http://tinyurl.com/yhvznz7f. Accessed on 7 February 2024.

9   Sharma, Sanjay, 'International Literacy Day 2022 Theme, Significance & History', *The Times of India*, 8 September 2022, http://tinyurl.com/8krhswx8. Accessed on 7 February 2024.

10   'Chinese Religions and Philosophies', *National Geographic*, http://tinyurl.com/33pe4wtj. Accessed on 6 September 2023.

11   Kautilya, *The Arthashastra*, L.N.Rangarajan (trans.), Penguin Books India, 1992.

12   Albert, Eleanor, and Lindsay Maizland, 'Religion in China', *Council for Foreign Relations*, 25 September 2020, http://tinyurl.com/38w9hzu2. Accessed on 6 September 2023.

13   Ibid.

14   Sunchu, Prakash S., 'Yin and Yang, Shiv and Shakti – Dual Forces in Singularity', *Indian Philosopher*, 6 December 2018, http://tinyurl.com/yhyvr85x. Accessed on 6 September 2023.

15   Babones, Salvatore, 'Zhongguo and Tianxia: The Central State and the Chinese World', *OUPblog*, 25 February 2018, http://tinyurl.com/mr87eu5s. Accessed on 6 September 2023.

16   Majumdar, R.C., *The History and Culture of the Indian People: The Maratha supremacy*, G. Allen & Unwin, 1951.

17   Chattopadhyay, R.K., and Arkaprava Sarkar, 'The Early Concept of Bharatavarsha', *National Security*, Vol. 4, No. 1, 2021.

18   Fei Xiaotong, *From the Soil: The Foundations of Chinese Society*, University of California Press, 1992.

19   Hsu Dau-Lin, 'The Myth of the "Five Human Relations" of Confucius', *Monumenta Serica*, Vol. 29, 1970.

20 Goh, Anthony, and Matthew Sullivan, 'The Most Misunderstood Business Concept in China', *Business Insider*, 24 February 2011, http://tinyurl.com/25x5nj7t. Accessed on 6 September 2023.

21 A series of debates held between court administrators and scholars between 86–81 BCE that initially focussed on the usefulness of government monopolies in the salt, iron and alcohol industries, and subsequently, as a broader debate on the role of the state in managing the economy and the ruler's right to do so; Hayward, Tyler, 'Discourses on Salt and Iron', *China Hands*, 30 October 2022, http://tinyurl.com/5vr4nw6s. Accessed on 7 February 2024.

22 Weber, Isabella, *How China Escaped Shock Therapy: The Market Reform Debate*, Routledge, 2021.

Chapter 3: History and Political Economy: The Past in the Present

1   Tharoor, Shashi, 'The Partition: The British Game of "Divide and Rule"', *Aljazeera*, 10 August 2017, http://tinyurl.com/5n8sdjs7. Accessed on 6 September 2023.

2   'Qin Shi Huang', *Britannica*, 5 January 2024, http://tinyurl.com/4tjs4aex. Accessed on 16 February 2024.

3   'Puyi', *Britannica*, 3 February 2024, http://tinyurl.com/bdz44wfs. Accessed on 16 February 2024.

4   'History of China', *China Education Center*, http://tinyurl.com/3bjznann. Accessed on 6 September 2023.

5   'The Yuan Dynasty in China (1279–1368)', *Britannica*, http://tinyurl.com/mpk7n67r. Accessed on 6 September 2023.

6   'Qing Dynasty', *Britannica*, 25 December 2023, http://tinyurl.com/2atcwvpe. Accessed on 6 September 2023.

7   'The Mughal Empire, 1526–1761', *Britannica*, http://tinyurl.com/ydcfkx5k. Accessed on 6 September 2023.

8   'Qing Dynasty', *Britannica*, 25 December 2023, http://tinyurl.com/2atcwvpe. Accessed on 16 February 2024.

9   'Factbox-Key Takeaways from China's 2020 Population Census', *Reuters*, 11 May 2021, http://tinyurl.com/3buhd6pk. Accessed on 6 September 2023.

10 Rowe, William T., *China's Last Empire: The Great Qing*, Harvard University Press, 2009.

11 Muhlhahn, Klaus, *Making China Modern: From the Great Qing to Xi Jinping*, Harvard University Press, 2019.

12 Tischler, Mark, 'China's "Never Again" Mentality', *The Diplomat*, 18 August 2020, http://tinyurl.com/43nfm9k5. Accessed on 6 September 2023.

13 Under China's hukou permit system, each citizen is required to register in one and only one place of (permanent) residence. An individual's hukou status defines his or her rights and eligibility for social welfare and various services, including public education and housing, in that specific administrative unit only. The hukou permit system thus restricts movement of citizens and strips illegal rural migrants to China's cities of rights to even basic housing, social and welfare services.

14   Xiaoyuan Liu, *Reins of Liberation: An Entangled History of Mongolian Independence, Chinese Territoriality, and Great Power Hegemony, 1911-1950*, Woodrow Wilson Center Press, 2006.

15   Lattimore, Owen, *Pivot of Asia: Sinkiang and the Inner Asian Frontiers of China and Russia*, Little & Brown, 1950.

16   Hobsbawm. E.J., *Nations and Nationalism Since 1780: Programme, Myth, Reality*, Cambridge University Press, 1990.

17   Sharma, Rishabh, 'Bothering Border: Tracing Origin of Lines Dividing India, China', *India Today*, http://tinyurl.com/2dtpc4k9. Accessed on 8 February 2024.

18   Chan, Alfred L., *Mao's Crusade: Politics and Policy Implementation in China's Great Leap Forward*, Oxford University Press, 2001.

19   Smil, Vaclav, 'China's Great Famine: 40 Years Later', *BMJ*, Vol. 319, No. 7225, 1999.

20   Walder, Andrew G., *Agents of Disorder: Inside China's Cultural Revolution*, Harvard University Press, 2019.

21   Jaffrelot, Christophe, and Anil Pratinav, *India's First Dictatorship: The Emergency, 1975-77*, Harper Collins, 2021.

22   Badhwar, Inderjit, 'Decision to Implement Mandal Commission Report Threatens to Tear India's Fabric Apart', *India Today*, 1 October 2013, http://tinyurl.com/yjb5k6td. Accessed on 6 September 2023.

23   Agrawal, S.P., and J.C. Aggarwal, *Educational and Social Uplift of Backward Classes: At What Cost and How: Mandal Commission and After*, Concept Publishing Company, 1991.

24   Frankel, Francine, *India's Political Economy, 1947-2004: The Gradual Revolution*, Oxford University Press, 2005.

25   Chakrabarty, Bidyut, and Bhuwan Kumar Jha, *Hindu Nationalism in India: Ideology and Politics*, Taylor & Francis, 2019.

26   Schram, Stuart R., 'Mao Tse-Tung and the Theory of the Permanent Revolution, 1958-69', *The China Quarterly*, Vol. 46, 1971.

27   'How Many Political Parties Are There in China? - China Law in One Minute', *China Justice Observer*, 30 November 2020, http://tinyurl.com/ymrcvhyu. Accessed on 6 September 2023.

Chapter 4: Leadership

1   Vogel, Ezra, *Deng Xiaoping and the Transformation of China*, Harvard University Press, 2013.

2   'The Great Pragmatist: Deng Xiaoping', *The Guardian*, 18 December 2008, http://tinyurl.com/4n7674s2. Accessed on 6 September 2023.

3   Liu Chunsheng, '"Cross the river by feeling the stone": A Valuable Lesson After 40 Years', *CGTN*, 18 December 2018, http://tinyurl.com/ykwfzt6p. Accessed on 6 September 2023.

4   Cheng Jin, *An Economic Analysis of the Rise and Decline of Chinese Township and Village Enterprises*, Springer International Publishing, 2017.

Chapter 5: Federalism

1   Shang Yang, *The Book of Lord Shang: Apologetics of State Power in Early China*, Yuri Pines (trans.), Columbia University Press, 2017.

2   Watson, Burton (trans.), *Han Feizi: Basic Writings*, Columbia University Press, 2003.

3   Heilmann, Sebastian, *Red Swan: How Unorthodox Policy Making Facilitated China's Rise*, Chinese University Press, 2018.

4   Montinola, Gabriella, Yingyi Qian, and Barry R. Weingast, 'Federalism, Chinese Style: The Political Basis for Economic Success in China', *World Politics*, Vol. 48, No. 1, 1995.

Chapter 6: Institutions and the Legal Framework

1   Dreyer, June, 'China's Minority Nationalities: Traditional and Party Elites', *Pacific Affairs*, Vol. 43, No. 4, 1970.

2   'Regional Autonomy for Ethnic Minorities in China', *China Daily*, http://tinyurl.com/bdfhxnxf. Accessed on 8 February 2024.

3   Rossabi, Morris (ed.), *Governing China's Multiethnic Frontiers*, University of Washington Press, 2004.

4   Cheng Li, 'China's New Politburo and Politburo Standing Committee', *Brookings*, 26 October 2017, http://tinyurl.com/yc5yvz7u. Accessed on 6 September 2023.

5   Lieberthal, Kenneth, *Governing China: From Revolution through Reform*, W. W. Norton, 2004.

6   Lampton, David M., and Kenneth G. Lieberthal, *Bureaucracy, Politics and Decision Making in Post-Mao China*, University of California Press, 2018.

7   Oud, Malin, 'Rule of Law', *China Media Project*, 20 May 2022, http://tinyurl.com/3ejvxnyb. Accessed on 16 February 2024.

8   Wo-Lap Lam, Willy, (ed.), *Routledge Handbook of the Chinese Communist Party*, Taylor & Francis, 2017.

9   Vakil, Raeesa, 'Constitutionalizing Administrative Law in the Indian Supreme Court: Natural Justice and Fundamental Rights', *International Journal of Constitutional Law*, Vol. 16, No. 2, 2018.

10 Ruskola, Teemu, 'Conceptualizing Corporations and Kinship: Comparative Law and Development Theory in a Chinese Perspective', *Stanford Law Review*, Vol. 52, No. 6, 2000.

11 Li, Bingqin, and David Piachaud, 'Urbanisation and Social Policy in China', *Asia-Pacific Development Journal*, Vol. 13, No. 1, June 2006.

12 Brown, Rajeswary Ampalavanar, *The Chinese and Indian Corporate Economies: A Comparative History of their Search for Economic Renaissance and Globalization*, Routledge, 2017.

Chapter 7: The First Yang: Agricultural Land Reforms and Markets

1   'Agriculture in Ancient Asia', *Britannica*, http://tinyurl.com/mwtm86u6. Accessed on 6 September 2023.

2   Legge, James (trans.), *The Works of Mencius*, Dover Publications, 2011.

3   Bray, Fransesca, *Science and Civilisation in China: Volume 6, Biology and Biological Technology; Part 2, Agriculture*, Cambridge University Press, 1984.

4   Lin, George C.S., and Samuel P.S. Ho, 'China's Land Resources and Land Use Change: Insights from the 1996 Land Survey', *Land Use Policy*, Vol. 20, No. 2, April 2003.

5   'Arable Land (Hectares per Person) – China', *The World Bank*, http://tinyurl.com/mr3hwr93. Accessed on 10 February 2024.

6   Parasara, H. V. Balkundi, and Y. L. Nene, *Krishi-Parashara*, Nalini Sadhale (trans.), Asian Agri-History Foundation, 1999.

7   'Marble Statue of Sage Parashara Established in the Premises of the First Agricultural University of the Country', *Organiser*, 21 June 2021, http://tinyurl.com/2wucbwtx. Accessed on 10 February 2024.

8   Nene, Y.L., 'Modern Agronomic Concepts and Practices Evident in Kautilya's Artha-Sastra (C. 300 BC)', *Research Gate*, January 2002, http://tinyurl.com/bdh7pfx9. Accessed on 6 September 2023.

9   Fuller, Dorian, 'Finding Plant Domestication in the Indian Subcontinent', *The University of Chicago Press Journals*.

10 Zhou Li, *Reform and Development of Agriculture in China*, Springer Nature Singapore, 2017.

11 'FAO in China', *Food and Agricultural Organization of the United Nations*, http://tinyurl.com/2s4kuwnu. Accessed on 10 February 2024.

12 Appu, P.S., *Land Reforms in India: A Survey of Policy, Legislation and Implementation*, Vikas Publishing House, 1996.

13 Frankel, Francine, *India's Political Economy, 1947-2004: The Gradual Revolution*, Oxford University Press, 2005.

14 Kishore, Roshan, 'What India Can Learn from Chinese Agriculture', *mint*, 9 June 2015, http://tinyurl.com/55cwcbj7. Accessed on 6 September 2023.

15 Jikun Huang, and Hengyun Ma, *Capital Formation and Agriculture Development in China*, 2010, http://tinyurl.com/3z82es95. Accessed on 6 September 2023.

16 Shenggen Fan, and Ashok Gulati, 'The Dragon and the Elephant: Learning from Agricultural and Rural Reforms in China and India', *Economic and Political Weekly*, 28 June 2008, http://tinyurl.com/28ka9djy. Accessed on 6 September 2023.

17 Ibid.

18. Ibid.

Chapter 8: The Second Yang: Special Economic Zones

1   'Learn All About Special Economic Zones in China', *FDI China*, 26 October 2020, http://tinyurl.com/3k2zbbwj. Accessed on 6 September 2023.

2   'China's Special Economic Zones', *World Bank*, http://tinyurl.com/yc3f2du7. Accessed on 6 September 2023.

3   Naughton, Barry, *The Chinese Economy: Transitions and Growth*, MIT Press, 2007.

4   Ibid.

5   Leong, Chee Kian, 'Special Economic Zones and Growth in China and India: An Empirical Investigation', *International Economics and Economic Policy*, Vol. 10, No. 4, 2013.

6   Mukherjee, Arpita, et al., *Special Economic Zones in India: Status, Issues and Potential*, Springer, 2016.

7   Naughton, Barry, *The Chinese Economy: Transitions and Growth*, MIT Press, 2007.

8   Digby, Simon, 'The Maritime Trade of India', *The Cambridge Economic History of India*, Tapan Raychaudhuri and Irfan Habib (eds), Cambridge University Press, 1982.

9   Zhuang Guotu, 'The Overseas Chinese: A Long History', *UNESCO*, 21 September 2021, http://tinyurl.com/2ckd6y9e. Accessed on 6 September 2023.

10   Santos, Nina dos, 'China Operating over 100 Police Stations across the World with the Help of Some Host Nations, Report Claims', *CNN*, 4 December 2022, http://tinyurl.com/mr286bvm. Accessed on 6 September 2023.

11   Chee-Beng Tan (ed.), *Routledge Handbook of Chinese Diaspora*, Routledge, 2013.

12   Ibid.

13   Thuno, Mette, 'Reaching Out and Incorporating Chinese Overseas: The Transterritorial Scope of the PRC by the End of the 20th Century', *The China Quarterly*, 2001.

14   Chee-Beng Tan (ed.), *Routledge Handbook of Chinese Diaspora*, Routledge, 2013.

15   Ibid.

16   Ibid.

17   Ibid.

18   Ibid.

19   'International Migration 2020 Highlights', *United Nations: Department of Economic and Social Affairs*, http://tinyurl.com/35wh8e4d. Accessed on 6 September 2023.

20   Bates, Crispin, and Marina Carter, 'Kala Pani Revisited: Indian Labour Migrants and the Sea Crossing', *Journal of Indentureship and Its Legacies*, September 2021.

21   Agarwala, Rina, 'Transnational Diaspora Organisations and India's Development', *Routledge Handbook of the Indian Diaspora*, Radha Hegde and Ajaya Sahoo (eds), Routledge, 2017.

22   Ibid.

23   Naujoks, Daniel, 'Paradigms, Policies, and Patterns of Indian Diaspora Investments', *Routledge Handbook of Indian Diaspora*, Radha Hegde and Ajaya Sahoo (eds), Routledge, 2017.

24   Ibid.

Chapter 9: The Third Yang: Real Estate and Urbanization

1   McMahon, Dinny, *China's Great Wall of Debt: Shadow Banks, Ghost Cities, Massive Loans, and the End of the Chinese Miracle*, Houghton Mifflin Harcourt, 2018.

2   Batarags, Lina, 'China Has at Least 65 Million Empty Homes — Enough to House the Population of France. It Offers a Glimpse into the Country's Massive Housing-Market Problem', *Business Insider*, 14 October 2021, http://tinyurl.com/3kzcjktd. Accessed on 6 September 2023.

3   'China: Revised Land Administration Law Takes Effect', *Library of Congress*, 20 February 2020, http://tinyurl.com/4m4vwbjn. Accessed on 6 September 2023.

4   Mckinsey Global Institute, *The Rise and Rise of the Global Balance Sheet*, November 2021, http://tinyurl.com/27u7nxkk. Accessed on 6 September 2023.

5   'The Link between GDP Growth and the Real Estate Market', *Asia Green Real Estate*, http://tinyurl.com/mr3jf6vz. Accessed on 6 September 2023.

6   Rithmire, Meg E., 'Land Institutions and Chinese Political Economy: Institutional Complementarities and Macroeconomic Management', *Politics & Society*, Vol. 45, No. 1, 2017.

7   Smith, Elliot, 'China's Property Market Debt Could Weigh on the Country for Years, Economist George Magnus Warns', *CNBC*, 9 November 2021, http://tinyurl.com/5472955f. Accessed on 6 September 2023.

8   Magnus, George, 'End to China's Real Estate Boom Could Spell Trouble for the Economy', *The Guardian*, 15 October 2021, http://tinyurl.com/43s8wrx4. Accessed on 6 September 2023.

9   Rithmire, Meg. E., *Land Bargains and Chinese Capitalism: The Politics of Property Rights under Reform*, Cambridge University Press, 2015.

10   Ibid.

11   Rithmire, Meg. E., 'Rule by Market: The Chinese State in Factor Markets', *Harvard Business School*, March 2023.

12   Rithmire, Meg. E., *Land Bargains and Chinese Capitalism: The Politics of Property Rights under Reform*, Cambridge University Press, 2015.

13   Rithmire, Meg E., 'Land Institutions and Chinese Political Economy: Institutional Complementarities and Macroeconomic Management', *Politics & Society*, Vol. 45, No. 1, 2017.

14   'The Fiscal Stimulus Programme and Public Governance Issues in China', *OECD Journal on Budgeting*, 2011.

15   McMahon, Dinny, *China's Great Wall of Debt: Shadow Banks, Ghost Cities, Massive Loans, and the End of the Chinese Miracle*, Houghton Mifflin Harcourt, 2018.

16   Xin Sun, 'Selective Enforcement of Land Regulations: Why Large-scale Violators Succeeded', *The China Journal*, Vol. 74, July 2015.

17   Li, Zhuoran, 'What doomed China's Much Anticipated Property Market Reform Plan?', *The Diplomat*, 17 March 2022, http://tinyurl.com/y6frdamn. Accessed on 6 September 2023.

18   Wahi, Namita, 'Indian Courts Clogged with Land Disputes Because Laws Keep
      Conflicting Each Other', *The Print*, 26 June 2019, http://tinyurl.com/bj7usvyd.
      Accessed on 6 September 2023.

19   Sathe, Dhanamnjiri, *The Political Economy of Land Acquisition in India: How
      a Village Stops Being One*, Springer Nature Singapore, 2017.

20   Bhattacharyya, Dwaipayan, *Government as Practice: Democratic Left in a
      Transforming India*, Cambridge University Press, 2016.

21   Palit, Amitendu, and Subhomoy Bhattacharjee, *Special Economic Zones in India:
      Myths and Realities*, Anthem South Asian Studies, 2008.

22   Mahapatra, Dhananjay, 'Singur Rerun? 90% of SEZ Land Lying Unused, Should
      Be Returned, Says PIL', *The Times of India*, 10 January 2017, http://tinyurl.
      com/26ysc6d9. Accessed on 6 September 2023.

23   Ahluwalia, Isher Judge, Ravi Kanbur and P. K. Mohanty (eds), *Urbanisation in
      India: Challenges, Opportunities and the Way Forward*, Sage India, 2014.

24   Ibid.

25   Ibid.

26   Mehta, Meera, Dinesh Mehta and Dhruv Bhavsar, 'India's Cities Drive Economic
      Growth but are Short on Resources. How Can the Gap Be Bridged?', *Scroll.in*,
      25 September 2020, http://tinyurl.com/atpn9mjm. Accessed on 6 September
      2023.

Chapter 10: The Fourth Yang: Policy and Infrastructure

1   Kim, M. Julie, and Rita Nangia, 'Infrastructure Development in India and
      China—A Comparative Analysis', August 2008.

2   Ibid.

3   *The Story of Shenzhen: Its Economic, Social and Environmental Transformation*,
      United Nations Human Settlements Program, 2019.

4   GSMA Intelligence, *The Mobile Economy: China 2021*, 2021.

5   Jones, Ben, 'Past, Present and Future: The Evolution of China's Incredible
      High-Speed Rail Network', *CNN Travel*, 9 February 2022, http://tinyurl.com/
      mr3ppz3e. Accessed on 10 February 2024.

6   Ibid.

7   Ibid.

8   Ibid.

9   Lawrence, Martha, Richard Bullock and Ziming Liu, *China's High-Speed Rail
      Development*, World Bank Group, 2019.

10   Ahmed, Aroosa, 'Mumbai to Ahmedabad Bullet Train Project May Miss 2023
      Deadline', *Hindustan Times*, 8 September 2021, http://tinyurl.com/328nsh7h.
      Accessed on 6 September 2023.

11   'Delhi-Varanasi, Mumbai-Nagpur among 7 New Bullet Train Projects, to Cost Rs
      10 Lakh Crore', *Business Today*, 14 September 2020, http://tinyurl.com/4fy4f9h3.
      Accessed on 10 February 2024.

12   Ollivier, Gerald, Jitendra Sondhi and Nanyan Zhou, 'High-Speed Railways in

China: A Look at Construction Costs', *World Bank*, July 2014, http://tinyurl. com/4x2nmwcf. Accessed on 20 February 2024.

13   Sweet, Rod, 'Why China Can Build High-Speed Rail So Cheaply', *Global Construction Review*, 14 July 2014, http://tinyurl.com/bdh5dmzk. Accessed on 6 September 2023.

14   Rapoza, Kenneth, 'How China's Solar Industry Is Set to Be the New Green OPEC', *Forbes*, March 2021, http://tinyurl.com/yck5m8yk. Accessed on 12 February 2024.

Chapter 11: The Fifth Yang: Entrepreneurship

1   North, Douglass C., *Understanding the Process of Economic Change*, Princeton University Press, 9 May 2010.

2   Yang, Keming, *Entrepreneurship in China*, Routledge, 2007.

3   Ibid.

4   Keming Yang, *Entrepreneurship in China*, Routledge, 2007.

5   Ibid.

6   Ibid.

7   Julie Zhu, and Kane Wu, 'Jack Ma and Donald Trump: What led to China's crackdown on Alibaba?', *mint*, 5 November 2021, http://tinyurl.com/mspvk3zx. Accessed on 6 September 2023.

8   Yeh, Nadya, 'Has Beijing Signaled an Ease to the Tech Crackdown?', *The China Project*, 16 March 2022, http://tinyurl.com/yxu4jfwf. Accessed on 6 September 2023.

9   Tiwary, Deeptiman, 'What Coal Blocks Cases Are Ed, CBI Investigating, and What Is Their Status?', *The Indian Express*, http://tinyurl.com/52wh7uvv. Accessed on 12 February 2024.

10 Reddy, Rahul Karan, 'China's Anti-Corruption Campaign: Tigers, Flies, and Everything in Between', *The Diplomat*, 12 May 2022, http://tinyurl.com/5d48x44p. Accessed on 12 February 2024.

Chapter 12: The First Yin: Debt

1   Yen Nee Lee, 'These Charts Show the Dramatic Increase in China's Debt', *CNBC*, 28 June 2021, http://tinyurl.com/2s3fnjt8. Accessed on 6 September 2023.

2   Apostolou, A., Alexander Al-Haschimi and Martino Ricci, 'Financial Risks in China's Corporate Sector: Real Estate and Beyond', *European Central Bank*, http://tinyurl.com/ywvb6b25. Accessed on 12 February 2024.

3   Chunlin Zhang, 'How Much Do State-Owned Enterprises Contribute to China's GDP and Employment', *World Bank*, 2019.

4   Molnar, Margit, and Jiangyuan Lu, 'State-Owned Firms behind China's Corporate Debt', *OECD*, 7 February 2019.

5   S&P Global, *China's SOEs Are Stuck in a Debt Trap Ratings*, 20 September 2022, http://tinyurl.com/mr5h482c. Accessed on 12 February 2024.

6   Molnar, Margit, and Jiangyuan Lu, 'State-Owned Firms behind China's Corporate Debt', *OECD*, 7 February 2019.

7   He, Laura, 'China's Real Estate Crisis Is Coming for Its Massive Shadow Banks', *CNN*, 7 December 2023, http://tinyurl.com/yc7vs8f3. Accessed on 12 February 2024.

8   Chang, Evelyn, 'What Is Shadow Banking? Unpacking the Risks for China', *CNBC*, 13 September 2023, http://tinyurl.com/2498v4mb. Accessed on 12 February 2024.

9   Blum, Jeremy, 'A Dog Could Run China's Banking System, Says Former Statistics Bureau Spokesman', *South China Morning Post*, 24 December 2013, http://tinyurl.com/3bwhd42d. Accessed on 6 September 2023.

10   'China to Deepen Financial Reform, Open to More Foreign Investment', *Reuters*, 4 March 2023, http://tinyurl.com/2r5f25e7. Accessed on 6 September 2023.

Chapter 13: The Second Yin: Corruption

1   Fewsmith, Joseph, 'Can Fighting Corruption Save The Party?', *The China Questions: Critical Insights into a Rising Power*, Jennifer Rudolph and Michael Szonyi (eds), Harvard University Press, 2018.

2   Ibid.

3   Hu Zhongyue, 'The Symptoms, Damages, and Lessons of Historical Nihilism in the Communist Party of the Soviet Union', *CSIS*, 20 December 2019, http://tinyurl.com/5cxs2kyp. Accessed on 20 February 2024.

4   Holmes, Leslie, *Corruption: A Very Short Introduction*, Oxford University Press, 2015.

5   OECD, *Issues Paper on Corruption and Economic Growth*, http://tinyurl.com/mvsw48em. Accessed on 13 February 2024.

6   Yeun Yeun Ang, *China's Gilded Age*, Cambridge University Press, 2020.

7   'India More Corrupt than China, Better than Pak: Transparency', *The Economic Times*, 22 February 2018, http://tinyurl.com/97htzxrr. Accessed on 13 February 2024.

8   'People and Corruption: Asia Pacific – Global Corruption Barometer', *Transparency International*, 7 March 2017, http://tinyurl.com/b86m9has. Accessed on 20 February 2024.

9   Yeun Yeun Ang, *China's Gilded Age*, Cambridge University Press, 2020.

10   Jun Mai, 'China Plans New Law to Restrict Business Activities of Civil Servants', *South China Morning Post*, 16 January 2023, http://tinyurl.com/4dsx6ppd. Accessed on 13 February 2024.

11   Shum, Desmond, *Red Roulette: An Insider's Story of Wealth, Power, Corruption, and Vengeance in Today's China*, Scribner, 2021.

Chapter 14: The Third Yin: Geopolitics

1   'Ch'ien Lung, (Qianlong) Letter to George III (1792)', http://tinyurl.
    com/2j4n9eb7. Accessed on 6 September 2023.
2   Paranjpe, V.V., 'Panchsheel: The Untold Story', *Hindustan Times*, 26 June 2004,
    http://tinyurl.com/mwetssuj. Accessed on 6 September 2023.
3   *Jawaharlal Nehru's Speeches*, Ministry of Information and Broadcasting, 1958.
4   Shambaugh, David, *China and the World*, Oxford University Press, 2020.
5   Swaine, Michael D., 'Perceptions of an Assertive China', *China Leadership
    Monitor*.
6   Shambaugh, David, *China and the World*, Oxford University Press, 2020.
7   Cai Fang, and Lu Yang, 'A New Age of Chinese Growth', *East Asia Forum*, 12
    April 2015, http://tinyurl.com/ya2bsxjs. Accessed on 13 February 2024.
8   Berger, Brett, and Robert F. Martin, 'The Growth of Chinese Exports: An
    Examination of the Detailed Trade Data', *Board of Governors of the Federal
    Reserve System, International Finance Discussion Papers*, November 2011, http://
    tinyurl.com/47ryeyv2. Accessed on 20 February 2024.
9   Pettis, Michael, 'How China Trapped Itself: The CCP's Economic Model Has
    Left It with Only Bad Choices', *Foreign Affairs*, 5 October 2022, http://tinyurl.
    com/bdhrb2w5. Accessed on 13 February 2024.
10 Noughton, Barry, 'China's Global Economic Interactions', *China and the World*,
    David Shambaugh (ed.), Oxford University Press, 2020.
11 'Gross Fixed Capital Formation (% of GDP) – China', *The World Bank*, http://
    tinyurl.com/3xv7ew7h. Accessed on 26 February 2024.
12 Ibid.
13 Noughton, Barry, 'China's Global Economic Interactions', *China and the World*,
    David Shambaugh (ed.), Oxford University Press, 2020.
14 Gupta, Shishir, 'Was Cash Strapped Sri Lanka Duped by China in Hambantota
    Port?', *Hindustan Times*, 26 June 2022, http://tinyurl.com/2x4m82af. Accessed
    on 6 September 2023.
15 'A Chinese Ship at Hambantota: A Reality Check for India – Sri Lanka Relations',
    mint, 18 August 2022, http://tinyurl.com/2y9f8fcm. Accessed on 6 September
    2023.
16 'Galwan Valley: A Year after the Violent Clash', *The Indian Express*, 14 June
    2021, http://tinyurl.com/4trn7538. Accessed on 6 September 2023.
17 Poling, Gregory B., et el., *Pulling Back the Curtain on China's Maritime
    Militia*, CSIS, 18 November 2021, http://tinyurl.com/9kc69mrx. Accessed on
    6 September 2023.
18 'UK Police Identify Offences Committed in Chinese Consulate Incident', *Reuters*,
    21 November 2022, http://tinyurl.com/387zf92w. Accessed on 6 September 2023.
19 'China Removes 6 Diplomats After Manchester Consulate Violence: UK',
    Aljazeera, 14 December 2022, http://tinyurl.com/4nj88vh6. Accessed on 6
    September 2023.
20 Clarence-Smith, Louisa, 'Ban on Chinese Institutes at UK Universities Drawn

up after Rishi Sunak's Pledge to Scrap Them', *The Telegraph*, 25 October 2022, http://tinyurl.com/3vcjf3tm. Accessed on 6 September 2023.

21 Zhiqun Zhu, 'Interpreting China's "Wolf-Warrior Diplomacy"', *The Diplomat*, 15 May 2020, http://tinyurl.com/32e8fysh. Accessed on 6 September 2023.

22 Ibid.

23 Westad, Odd Arne, 'Legacies of the Past', *China and the World*, David Shambaugh (ed.), Oxford University Press, 2020.

24 Mosca, Matthew W., *From Frontier Policy to Foreign Policy: The Question of India and the Transformation of Geopolitics in Qing China*, Stanford University Press, 2013.

25 Menon, Shivshankar, *India and Asian Geopolitics: The Past, Present*, Brookings Institution Press, 2021.

26 Sattar, Saba, 'Pakistan on Brink of Ceding More Territory to China as Beijing Gains Momentum on China-Pak Economic Corridor', *The EurAsian Times*, 31 January 2022, http://tinyurl.com/4sjx34tu. Accessed on 6 September 2023.

27 Mattoo, Shashank, and Subhash Narayan, 'India, Iran Set to Ink Long-Term Deal on Chabahar Port', *mint*, 28 July 2023, http://tinyurl.com/4x6c43ys. Accessed on 6 September 2023.

28 Menon, Shivshankar, *India and Asian Geopolitics: The Past, Present*, Brookings Institution Press, 2021.

Chapter 15: The Fourth Yin: Demographics

1 'India's Population Has Already Overtaken China's, Analysts Estimate', *businessline*, 18 January 2023, http://tinyurl.com/2zzdjuj2. Accessed on 13 February 2024.

2 Biswas, Sayantani, '1.4 Billion and Counting: How Did India's Population "Explode" and Get So Big?', *mint*, 30 April 2023, http://tinyurl.com/2ubjbv35. Accessed on 13 February 2024.

3 Rai, Dipu, 'India vs China: What Changes in Population Structures Mean for Both Countries, and the World', *India Today*, 20 January 2023, http://tinyurl.com/28y4tbt2. Accessed on 6 September 2023.

4 Zhihe Wang, et el., 'Ending an Era of Population Control in China: Was the One-Child Policy Ever Needed', *The American Journal of Economics and Sociology*, Vol. 75, No. 4, 6 September 2016.

5 Patranobis, Sutirtho, 'Chinese Population Is Ageing Rapidly, Says Top Health Official', *Hindustan Times*, 20 September 2022, http://tinyurl.com/m54x2avr. Accessed on 6 September 2023.

6 Xinran, *Buy Me the Sky: The Remarkable Truth of China's One-Child Generations*, Ebury Digital, 2015.

7 Shenshen Cai, *Television Drama in Contemporary China: Political, Social and Cultural Phenomena*, Routledge, 2017.

8 Zhihe Wang, et el., 'Ending an Era of Population Control in China: Was the One-Child Policy Ever Needed?', *The American Journal of Economics and Sociology*, Vol. 75, No. 4, September 2016.

9   Young, Scott, *China's Hukou System: Markets, Migrants and Institutional Change*, Palgrave Macmillan, 2013.

10   'Migrant Workers and Their Children', *China Labour Bulletin*, 6 September 2023, http://tinyurl.com/jrau82wz. Accessed on 20 February 2024.

11   Jane Cai, and He Huifeng, 'China's Army of Retirees Seek Return to Work as Economic Toll on Their Families Mounts', *South China Morning Post*, 12 December 2022, http://tinyurl.com/mr3kmpt4. Accessed on 13 February 2024.

12   'Migrant Workers and Their Children', *China Labour Bulletin*, 6 September 2023, http://tinyurl.com/jrau82wz. Accessed on 20 February 2024.

13   *Statista*, http://tinyurl.com/2znnpewn, Accessed on 29 February 2024.

14   Chen, Sharon, 'China Has a Huge Wealth-Gap Problem – and It's Getting Worse', *Bloomberg*, 24 December 2020, http://tinyurl.com/bdejw6fm. Accessed on 6 September 2023.

15   Hui, Mary, 'Will China Be as Unequal as the US Is by 2025?', *Quartz*, 9 November 2021, http://tinyurl.com/mr3fa2su. Accessed on 6 September 2023.

16   Ke Long, 'Can China Avoid the Middle-Income Trap?', *Nippon*, 16 June 2022, http://tinyurl.com/bdzjzrwe. Accessed on 6 September 2023.

Chapter 16: The Fifth Yin: Environment

1   'World Population by Year', *Worldometer*, http://tinyurl.com/4mxrd5b6. Accessed on 6 September 2023.

2   'Urban Development', *The World Bank*, http://tinyurl.com/2p82679y. Accessed on 13 February 2024.

3   'Living Planet Report 2022', *WWF*, http://tinyurl.com/4vvkww6b. Accessed on 6 September 2023.

4   'Land and Geography of China', *Facts and Details*, http://tinyurl.com/wdkzchze. Accessed on 13 February 2024.

5   Elvin, Mark, *The Retreat of the Elephants: An Environmental History of China*, Yale University Press, 2004.

6   Shapiro, Judith, *Mao's War against Nature: Politics and the Environment in Revolutionary China*, Cambridge University Press, 2001.

7   Steinfeld, J., 'China's Deadly Science Lesson: How an Ill-Conceived Campaign against Sparrows Contributed to One of the Worst Famines in History', *Index on Censorship*, Vol. 47, No. 3, 2018.

8   Shapiro, Judith, *China's Environmental Challenges*, Wiley, 2016.

9   Yifei Li, and Judith Shapiro, *China Goes Green: Coercive Environmentalism for a Troubled Planet*, Polity, 2020.

10   Ibid.

11   'China Steps Up Its Push into Clean Energy', *Bloomberg*, 26 September 2018, http://tinyurl.com/mfpfm4ua. Accessed on 13 February 2024.

12   'China Allocates 8.8 Bln Yuan for Weather Modification Program', *reliefweb*, 21 September 2017, http://tinyurl.com/mrxapypy. Accessed on 13 February 2024.

13 Yifei Li, and Judith Shapiro, *China Goes Green: Coercive Environmentalism for a Troubled Planet*, Polity, 2020.

14 Watts, Jonathan, 'China Plans Rapid Expansion of "Weather Modification" Efforts', *The Guardian*, 3 December 2020, http://tinyurl.com/3jfj462d. Accessed on 6 September 2023.

15 'China Plans to Use Water as a Weapon: Report', *The Economic Times*, 1 February 2023, http://tinyurl.com/44sac4b9. Accessed on 6 September 2023.

16 Donnellon-May, Genevieve, 'China's Super Hydropower Dam and Fears of Sino-Indian Water Wars', *The Diplomat*, 9 December 2022, http://tinyurl.com/5hb8k42n. Accessed on 6 September 2023.

17 '1985: Narmada Bachao Andolan', *Frontline*, 15 August 2022, http://tinyurl.com/49hw9uft. Accessed on 6 September 2023.

18 Seetharaman, G., 'The Story of One of the Biggest Land Conflicts: No Mine Now but Is It All Fine in Niyamgiri?', *The Economic Times*, 18 April 2018, http://tinyurl.com/mswtmjas. Accessed on 6 September 2023.

Chapter 17: Understanding the Differential

1 Duara, Prasenjit, and Elizabeth J. Perry (eds), *Beyond Regimes: China and India Compared*, Harvard University Press, 2018.

2 Ibid.

3 'Problems of War and Strategy', *Selected Works of Mao Tse-tung*, 6 November 1938.

4 Tao Xie, 'Is President XI Jinping's Chinese Dream Fantasy or Reality?', *CNN*, 14 March 2014, http://tinyurl.com/bdd4h69r. Accessed on 6 September 2023.

5 Kuhn, Robert Lawrence, 'Xi Jinping's Chinese Dream', *The New York Times*, 4 June 2014, http://tinyurl.com/2zpzr62c. Accessed on 6 September 2023.

Chapter 18: Influence of Culture

1 Harrison, Lawrence E., and Samuel P. Huntington (eds), *Culture Matters: How Values Shape Human Progress*, Basic Books, 2001.

2 Spence, Jonathan, *The Search for Modern China*, W.W. Norton & Co, 1999.

3 Huntington, Samuel P., *The Clash of Civilisations and the Remaking of World Order*, Simon & Schuster, 1996.

4 Weber, Max, *The Protestant Ethic and the Spirit of Capitalism*, 1904.

5 Landes, David, 'Culture Makes Almost All the Difference', *Culture Matters: How Values Shape Human Progress*, Lawrence E. Harrison and Samuel P. Huntington (eds), Basic Books, 2000.

6 Tiwari, Lalan, *Democracy and Dissent (A Case Study of the Bihar Movement, 1974-75)*, Mittal Publications, 1987.

7 Mukhopadhyay, Nilanjan, *The Demolition and The Verdict: Ayodhya and the Project to Reconfigure India*, Speaking Tiger, 2021.

Chapter 19: Democracy with Indian Characteristics

1   Jun Mai, 'China Deletes 2 Million Online Posts for "Historical Nihilism" as Communist Party Centenary Nears', *South China Morning Post*, 11 May 2021, http://tinyurl.com/5cfwfj6f. Accessed on 6 September 2023.

2   Singh, Tripurdaman, 'How India's Founding Fathers Built an "Eastminster-Style" Democracy', *The Times of India*, 22 January 2022, http://tinyurl.com/56eaadk3. Accessed on 6 September 2023.

3   Khosla, Madhav, *India's Founding Moment: The Constitution of a Most Surprising Democracy*, Harvard University Press, 2020.

4   Stasavage, David, *The Decline and Rise of Democracy: A Global History from Antiquity to Today*, Princeton University Press, 2020.

5   Basu, Kaushik, *Republic of Beliefs: A New Approach to Law and Economics*, Princeton University Press, 2018.

6   Ramani, Srinivasan, and Vignesh Radhakrishnan, 'World within a Country: The Size of India's Electorate in Four Charts', *The Hindu*, 12 March 2019, http://tinyurl.com/mruzx5b8. Accessed on 6 September 2023.

Chapter 20: Institutional Reforms

1   Montinola, Gabriella, Yingyi Qian and Barry R. Weingast, 'Federalism, Chinese Style: The Political Basis for Economic Success in China', *World Politics*, Vol. 48, No. 1, 1995.

2   Das, Gurcharan, *India Grows at Night: A Liberal Case for a Strong State*, Penguin India, 2012.

3   Kapur, Devesh, Milan Vaishnav and Pratap Bhanu Mehta (eds), *Rethinking Public Institutions in India*, Oxford University Press, 2017.

4   Joshi, Sandeep, 'Elders Clear Bill to Set up Judicial Appointments Commission', *The Hindu*, 5 September 2013, http://tinyurl.com/2s4a53ue. Accessed on 6 September 2023.

5   Kapur, Devesh, and Madhav Khosla (eds), *Regulation in India: Design, Capacity, Performance*, Bloomsbury Publishing, 2019.

6   Bhattacharya, Saugata, and Urjit R. Patel, 'New Regulatory Institutions in India: White Knights or Trojan Horses', *Public Institutions in India: Performance and Design*, Devesh Kapur and Pratap Bhanu Mehta (eds), Oxford University Press, 2017.

Chapter 21: Local Government

1   Grindle, Merilee S., *Going Local: Decentralization, Democratization, and the Promise of Good Governance*, Princeton University Press, 2007.

2   Chaudhari, Shubham, 'What Difference Does a Constitutional Amendment Make? The 1994 Panchayati Raj Act and the Attempt to Revitalize Rural Local Government in India', 2006.

3   'Centre Approves Rs. 56,415 Crore to 16 States for Capital Investment under "Special Assistance to States for Capital Investment 2023-24" Scheme for Giving Timely Boost to Capital Spending by States', *Press Information Bureau*, 26 June 2023, http://tinyurl.com/yck329r4. Accessed on 21 February 2024.

Chapter 22: Land and Agricultural Market Reforms

1   Wahi, Namita, 'Indian Courts Clogged with Land Disputes Because Laws Keep Conflicting Each Other', *The Print*, 26 June 2019, http://tinyurl.com/yc47n85v. Accessed on 6 September 2023.

In Conclusion: Parrots and Tea Leaves

1   Stella Yifan Xie, Yoko Kubota and Cao Li, 'China's Cities Struggle Under Trillions of Dollars of Debt', *The Wall Street Journal*, 6 March 2023, http://tinyurl.com/ypzwxnw6. Accessed on 6 September 2023.

2   Siracusa, Joseph M., 'Xi Jinping in "Use It or Lose It" Territory amid CCP's "Pathological Obsession" with Avoiding the Fate of Communist Russia', *Skynews*, 13 March 2023, http://tinyurl.com/2m52um25. Accessed on 6 September 2023.

3   'Summary of the Economic Survey 2022-23', *Press Information Bureau*, 31 January 2023, http://tinyurl.com/ypy9uspx. Accessed on 20 February 2024.

Bibliography

'China and India: Partners and Rivals', *USC US-China Institute*, 18 April 2022, http://tinyurl.com/vxzksb3n. Accessed on 13 February 2024.

'Economic Outlook for Southeast Asia, China, and India', *OECD*, 2020.

'Explained: Why China's Crumbling Real Estate Sector Has the World on Edge', *The Economic Times*, 23 July 2022, http://tinyurl.com/bdhaufsc. Accessed on 29 February 2024.

Adam Y. Liu, Jean C. Oi and Yi Zhang, 'China's Local Government Debt: The Grand Bargain', *The China Journal*, Vol. 87, 2022.

Agrawal, S.P., and J.P. Aggarwal, *Educational and Social Uplift of Backward Classes: At What Cost and How: Mandal Commission and After*, Concept Publishing Company, 1991.

Ahluwalia, Isher, Ravi Kanbur and P. K. Mohanty (eds), *Urbanisation in India: Challenges, Opportunities and the Way Forward*, Sage India, 2014.

Allison, Graham, *Destined for War: Can America and China Escape Thucydides' Trap?*, Houghton Mifflin Harcourt, 2017.

Allison, Graham, Robert D. Blackwill and Ali Wyne, *Lee Kuan Yew: The Grand Master's Insights on China, the United States, and the World*, MIT Press, 2012.

Amstad, Marlene, Guofeng Sun and Wei Xiong (eds), *The Handbook of China's Financial System*, Princeton University Press, 2020.

Andrews-Speed, Philip, and Sufang Zhang, *China as a Global Clean Energy Champion: Lifting the Veil*, Palgrave Macmillan, 2019.

Ang, Yuen Yuen, *China's Gilded Age: The Paradox of Economic Boom and Vast Corruption*, Cambridge University Press, 2020.

Appu, P.S., *Land Reforms in India: A Survey of Policy, Legislation and Implementation*, Vikas Publishing House, 1996.

Armstrong-Taylor, Paul, *Debt and Distortion: Risks and Reforms in the Chinese Financial System*, Palgrave Macmillan, 2016.

Ascher, William, and Corinne Krupp (eds), *Physical Infrastructure Development: Balancing the Growth, Equity, and Environmental Imperatives*, Palgrave Macmillan, 2010.

Babones, Salvatore, 'Zhongguo and Tianxia: The Central Sstate and the Chinese World', *OUPblog*, 25 February 2018, http://tinyurl.com/mr87eu5s. Accessed on 22 February 2024.

Bardhan, Pranab, and Dilip Mookherjee (eds), *Decentralisation and Local Governance in Developing Countries: A Comparative Perspective*, MIT Press, 2006.

Basu, Kaushik, *Republic of Beliefs: A New Approach to Law and Economics*, Princeton University Press, 2018.

Bekkevold, Jo Inge, and S. Kalyanaraman, S. (eds), *India's Great Power Politics: Managing China's Rise*, Routledge, 2020.

Berger, Brett, and Robert F. Martin, *The Growth of Chinese Exports: An Examination of the Detailed Trade Data*, November 2011, http://tinyurl.com/47ryeyv2. Accessed on 20 February 2024.

Bernier, François, *Travels in the Mogul Empire*, Irving Brock (trans.), London, W. Pickering, 1826.

Bhagat-Ganguly, Varsha (ed.), *Land Rights in India: Policies, Mmovements and Cchallenges*, Routledge, 2016.

Bhandari, Laveesh, and Bibek Debroy, *Corruption in India – The DNA and the RNA*, Konark Publishers, 2011.

Bhattacharyya, Dwaipayan, 'Implosion: Singur, Nandigram', *Government as Practice: Democratic Left in a Transforming India*, Cambridge University Press, 2016.

Boer, Roland, *Socialism with Chinese Characteristics: A Guide for Foreigners*, Springer Nature Singapore, 2021.

Bolesta, Andrzej, *China and Post-Socialist Development*, Bristol University Press, 2014.

Bray, Fransesca, *Science and Civilisation in China: Volume 6, Biology and Biological Technology; Part 2, Agriculture*, Cambridge University Press, 1984.

Brown, Rajeswary Ampalavanar, *The Chinese and Indian Corporate Economies: A Comparative History of their Search for Economic Renaissance and Globalisation*, Routledge, 2017.

Cai Fang, and Lu Yang, 'A New Age of Chinese Growth', *East Asia Forum*, 12 April 2015, http://tinyurl.com/ya2bsxjs. Accessed on 13 February 2024.

Cai Fang, *China's Economic Growth Prospects: From Demographic Dividend to Reform Dividend*, Edward Elgar Publishing, 2016.

Cai, Sheshen, *Television Drama in Contemporary China: Political, Social and Cultural Phenomena*, Routledge, 2017.

Cartwright, Mark, 'The Dragon in Ancient China', *World History Encyclopedia*, September 2017, http://tinyurl.com/bxtea67n. Accessed on 22 February 2024.

Chakrabarty, Bidyut, and Bhuwan Jha, *Hindu Nationalism in India: Ideoalogy and Politics*, Taylor & Francis, 2020.

Chan, Alfred L., *Mao's Crusade: Politics and Policy in China's Great Leap Forward*, Oxford University Press, 2001.

Chattopadhyay, Rupendra Kumar and Arkaprava Sarkar, 'The Early Concept of Bharatavarsha', *National Security*, Vol. 4, No. 1.

Chau, Adam Yuet, *Religion in China: Ties that Bind*, John Wiley & Sons, 2019.

Chee-Beng Tan (ed.), *Routledge Handbook of the Chinese Diaspora*, Routledge, 2013.

Cheng Jin, *An Economic Analysis of the Rise and Decline of Chinese Township and Village Enterprises*, Springer International Publishing, 2017.

Chi Hung Kwan, 'The Debate over Constitutionalism: Political Reforms at a Crossroads', *Research Institute of Economy, Trade and Industry*, http://tinyurl.com/3wcp4nbf. Accessed on 29 January 2024.

Clarke, Michael E., *Xinjiang and China's Rise in Central Asia – A History*, Routledge, 2011.

Croll, Elisabeth, Delia Davin and Penny Kane (eds), *China's One-Child Family Policy*, Macmillan, 1985.

Dai Shuanping, and Markus Taube, *China's Quest for Innovation: Institutions and Ecosystems*, Routledge, 2020.

Das, Gurcharan, *India Grows at Night: A Liberal Case for a Strong State*, Penguin India, 2012.

Das, Gurcharan, *India Unbound: From Independence to the Global Information Age*, Penguin India, 2012.

De Mente, Boye, *The Chinese Mind: Understanding Traditional Chinese Beliefs and Their Influence on Contemporary Culture*, Tuttle Publishing, 2009.

Debroy, Bibek, Sanjay Chadha and Vidya Krishnamurthi, *Indian Railways: The Weaving of a National Tapestry*, Portfolio Penguin, 2017.

Dhar, Biswajit, 'The Ultimate Captive Market', *DNA*, January 2019, http://tinyurl.com/5cs6rmh3. Accessed on 22 February 2024.

Dikotter, Frank (ed.), *The Construction of Racial Identities in China and Japan*, C., Hurst & Company, 1997.

Donnellon-May, Genevieve, 'China's Super Hydropower Dam and Fears of Sino-Indian Water Wars', *The Diplomat*, 9 December 2022, http://tinyurl.com/5hb8k42n. Accessed on 6 September 2023.

Dreyer, June, 'China's Minority Nationalities: Traditional and Party Elites', *Pacific Affairs*, Vol. 43, No. 4, 1970–71.

Duara, Prasenjit, and Elizabeth J. Perry (eds), *Beyond Regimes: China and India Compared*, Harvard University Press, 2018.

DuBois, Thomas, and Huaiyin Li (eds), *Agricultural Reform and Rural Transformation in China since 1949*, Brill, 2016.

Elman, Benjamin A., and Sheldon Pollock (eds), *What China and India Once Were: The Pasts That May Shape the Global Future*, Columbia University Press, 2018.

Elvin, Mark, *The Retreat of the Elephants: An Environmental History of China*, Yale University Press, 2004.

Fei Xiaotong, *From the Soil: The Foundations of Chinese Society*, University of California Press, 1992.

Fenby, Jonathan, *The Penguin History of Modern China: The Fall and Rise of a Great Power, 1850 to the Present*, Penguin Books, 2013.

Fogel, Joshua A., *The Cultural Dimensions of Sino-Japanese Relations: Essays on the Nineteenth and Twentieth Centuries*, Routledge, 1995.

Frankel, Francine, *India's Green Revolution: Economic Gains and Political Costs*, Princeton University Press, 2015.

Frankel, Francine, *India's Political Economy, 1947-2004: The Gradual Revolution*, Oxford University Press, 2005.

Gandhi, Ajay, et el. (eds), *Rethinking Markets in Modern India: Embedded Exchange and Contested Jurisdiction*, Cambridge University Press, 2020.

Gandhi, Supriya, *The Emperor Who Never Was: Dara Shukoh in Mughal India*, Harvard University Press, 2020.

Gardner, Kyle J., *The Frontier Complex: Geopolitics and the Making of the India-China Border, 1846-1962*, Cambridge University Press, 2021.

Golley, Jane, and Rodney Tyers, 'Demographic Dividends, Dependencies, and Economic Growth in China and India', *Asian Economic Papers*, Vol. 11, No. 3, 2012.

Goswami, Binoy, Madhurjya Prasad Bezbaruah and Raju Mandal (eds), *Indian*

Agriculture after the Green Revolution: Changes and Challenges, Routledge, 2018.

Greenhalgh, Susan, *Just One Child: Science and Policy in Deng's China*, University of California Press, 2008.

Grindle, Merilee S., *Going Local: Decentralization, Democratization, and the Promise of Good Governance*, Princeton University Press, 2007.

Guilmoto, Christophe Z., and Gavin W. Jones (eds), *Contemporary Demographic Transformations in China, India, and Indonesia*, Springer, 2016.

Gulati, Ashok, and Shenggen Fan (eds), *The Dragon and the Elephant: Agricultural and Rural Reforms in China and India*, Johns Hopkins University Press, 2007.

Gulati, Ashok, Ranjana Roy and Shweta Saini, *Revitalizing Indian Agriculture and Boosting Farmer Incomes*, Springer, 2021.

Harrison, Lawrence E., and Samuel P. Huntington (eds), *Culture Matters: How Values Shape Human Progress*, Basic Books, 2001.

Hegde, Radha, and Ajaya Sahoo (eds), *Routledge Handbook of the Indian Diaspora*, Routledge, 2017.

Heilmann, Sebastian, *Red Swan: How Unorthodox Policy Making Facilitated China's Rise*, Chinese University Press, 2018.

Hillman, Jonathan E., *The Emperor's New Road: China and The Project of the Century*, Yale University Press, 2020.

Hobsbawm. E.J., *Nations and Nationalism Since 1780: Programme, Myth, Reality*, Cambridge University Press, 1990.

Huang, Yasheng, *Capitalism with Chinese Characteristics: Entrepreneurship and the State*, Cambridge University Press, 2008.

Huntington, Samuel P., *The Clash of Civilisations and the Remaking of World Order*, Simon & Schuster, 1996.

Jaffrelot, Christophe, and Anil Pratinav, *India's First Dictatorship: The Emergency, 1975-77*, Harper Collins, 2021.

Jiang Qing, *A Confucian Constitutional Order: How China's Ancient Past Can Shape Its Political Future*, Princeton University Press, 2012.

Jing Tsu, *Kingdom of Characters: The Language Revolution that made China Modern*, Penguin Publishing Group, 2022.

Joe, William, Abhishek Kumar and Sunil Rajpal, 'Swimming against the Tide: Economic Growth and Demographic Dividend in India', *Asian Population Studies*, Vol. 14, No. 2, 2018.

Kapur, Devesh, and Madhav Khosla (eds), *Regulation in India: Design, Capacity, Performance*, Bloomsbury Publishing, 2019.

Kapur, Devesh, and Pratap Bhanu Mehta (eds), *Public Institutions in India: Performance and Design*, Oxford University Press, 2017.

Kapur, Devesh, Milan Vaishnav and Pratap Bhanu Mehta (eds), *Rethinking Public Institutions in India*, Oxford University Press, 2017.

Kattakayam, Jiby J., 'An NRI Businessman's Suicide, a Destructive Political Culture', *The Times of India*, 27 June 2019, http://tinyurl.com/4rtn8yba. Accessed on 29 February 2024.

Kautilya, *The Arthashastra*, L.N.Rangarajan (trans.), Penguin Books India, 1992.

Khosla, Madhav, *India's Founding Moment: The Constitution of a Most Surprising Democracy*, Harvard University Press, 2020.

Kim, M. Julie, and Rita Nangia, 'Infrastructure Development in India and China—A Comparative Analysis', August 2008.

Klein, Matthew C., and Michael, Pettis, *Trade Wars Are Class Wars: How Rising Inequality Distorts the Global Economy and Threatens International Peace*, Yale University Press, 2020.

Kosuke Inoue, and Iori Kawate, 'China Overtakes U.S. In National Net Worth to Grab Top Spot', *NIKKEI Asia*, 19 December 2021, http://tinyurl.com/yscmdf3c. Accessed on 6 September 2023.

Krishnan, Ananth, 'India's Imports from China Reach Record High in 2022, Trade Deficit Surges beyond $100 Billion', *The Hindu*, 13 January 2023, http://tinyurl.com/y9yaze8e. Accessed on 6 September 2023.

Krishnan, Ananth, *India's China Challenge: A Journey through China's Rise and What It Means for India*, HarperCollins India, 2020.

Kroeber, Arthur R., *China's Economy: What Everyone Needs to Know*, Oxford University Press, 2016.

Krueger, Anne O., *China and the Sovereign-Debt Bomb*, Project Syndicate, January 2023, http://tinyurl.com/hvdswk3t. Accessed on 22 February 2024.

Kumar, Anu, 'Thomas Macaulay Won the Debate on How to Shape Indian Education. So Who Were the Losers?', *Scroll.in*, 4 February 2017, http://tinyurl.com/4dzstunj. Accessed on 6 September 2023.

Kumar, Dharma, and Tapan Raychaudhuri (eds), *The Cambridge Economic History of India*, Cambridge University Press, 1983.

Landes, David S., *The Wealth and Poverty of Nations: Why Some Are So Rich and Some So Poor*, W.W. Norton & Co, 1999.

Lardy, Nicholas R., and Kenneth Lieberthal (eds), *Chen Yun's Strategy for China's Development: A Non-Maoist Alternative*, Routledge, 1983.

Lawrence, Martha, Richard Bullock and Ziming Liu, *China's High-Speed Rail Development*, World Bank Group, 2019.

Legge, James (trans.), The Works of Mencius, Dover Publications, 2011.

Leong, Chee Kian, 'Special Economic Zones and Growth in China and India: An Empirical Investigation', *International Economics and Economic Policy*, Vol. 10, No. 4, 2013.

Levi, Scott C., *Caravans: Indian Merchants on the Silk Road*, Penguin Books Limited, 2015.

Li, Bingqin, and David Piachaud, 'Urbanisation and Social Policy in China', *Asia-Pacific Development Journal*, Vol. 13, No. 1, June 2006.

Li, Yifei, and Judith Shapiro, *China Goes Green: Coercive Environmentalism for a Troubled Planet*, Polity, 2020.

Li, Zhenfa, Fulong Wu and Fangzhu Zhang, *The Political Economy of China's Local Debt*, Cambridge University Press, 2003.

Li, Zhou, *Reform and Development of Agriculture in China*, Springer Nature Singapore, 2017.

Li, Zhouran, 'What Doomed China's Much-Anticipated Property Market Reform Plan?', *The Diplomat*, 17 March 2022, http://tinyurl.com/9anef6vv. Accessed on 22 February 2024.

Lo, Vai lo, *Law and Society in China*, Edward Elgar Publishing, 2020.

Luo, Guoliang, Jiahai Yuan, and Jianguo Chen, *Renewable Energy in China*, Nova Science Publishers, 2014.

MacFarquhar, Roderick, and Michael Schoenhals, *Mao's Last Revolution*, Belknap Press of Harvard University Press, 2006

'Macroeconomic Management', *Politics & Society*, Vol. 45, No. 1, 2017.

Magnus, George, *Red Flags: Why Xi's China is in Jeopardy*, Yale University Press, 2018.

Mahapatra, Dhananjay, 'Singur Rerun? 90% of SEZ Land Lying Unused, Should Be Returned, Says PIL', *The Times of India*, 10 January 2017, http://tinyurl.com/2eh7y88h, Accessed on 29 February 2024.

Majumdar, R.C., *The History and Culture of the Indian People: The Maratha Supremacy*, G. Allen & Unwin, 1951.

Marcus, Lilit, 'China Debuts World's Fastest Train', *CNN Travel*, 21 July 2021, http://tinyurl.com/33yhtjzp. Accessed on 6 September 2023.

Marshall, Tim, *Prisoners of Geography: Ten Maps That Will Tell You Everything You Need to Know About Global Politics*, Elliott and Thompson Limited, 2015.

Mayor, Adrienne, *The First Fossil Hunters: Dinosaurs, Mammoths, and Myth in Greek and Roman Times*, Princeton University Press, 2011.

McMahon, Dinny, *China's Great Wall of Debt: Shadow Banks, Ghost Cities, Massive Loans, and the End of the Chinese Miracle*, Houghton Mifflin Harcourt, 2018.

Menon, Shivshankar, *India and Asian Geopolitics: The Past, Present*, Brookings Institution Press, 2021.

Miller, Tom, *China's Asian Dream: Empire Building along the New Silk Road*, Zed Books, 2017.

Montinola, Gabriella, Yingyi Qian and Barry R. Weingast, 'Federalism, Chinese Style: The Political Basis for Economic Success in China', *World Politics*, Vol. 48, No. 1, 1995.

Morris, Ian, *The Measure of Civilization: How Social Development Decides the Fate of Nations*, Princeton University Press, 2014.

Mosca, Matthew W., *From Frontier Policy to Foreign Policy: The Question of India and the Transformation of Geopolitics in Qing China*, Stanford University Press, 2013.

Moser, David, *A Billion Voices: China's Search for a Common Language*, Penguin, 2016.

Muhlhahn, Klaus, *Making China Modern: From the Great Qing to Xi Jinping*, Harvard University Press, 2019.

Mukherjee, Arpita, et al., *Special Economic Zones in India: Status, Issues and Potential*, Springer, 2016.

Mukhopadhyay, Nilanjan, *The Demolition and The Verdict: Ayodhya and the Project to Reconfigure India*, Speaking Tiger, 2021.

Mukund, Kanakalatha, *The World of the Tamil Merchant: Pioneers of International Trade*, Penguin Portfolio, 2015.

Naughton, Barry, *The Chinese Economy: Transitions and Growth*, MIT Press, 2007.

Nitkoski, Matthew, 'From West to East: The Charged Challenge of Delivering Electricity', *China Business Review*, 7 April 2021, http://tinyurl.com/ms82wc3c. Accessed on 6 September 2023.

Orlik, Thomas M., *China: The Bubble that Never Pops*, Oxford University Press, 2020.

Palit, Amitendu, and Subhomoy Bhattacharjee, *Special Economic Zones in India: Myths and Realities*, Anthem Press, 2008.

Pant, Vasudha, *Beginning of Agriculture and Domestication in India*, Pentagon Press, 2016.

Pettis, Michael, 'How China Trapped Itself: The CCP's Economic Model Has Left It with Only Bad Choices', *Foreign Affairs*, 5 October 2022, http://tinyurl.com/bdhrb2w5. Accessed on 13 February 2024.

Pettis, Michael, *Avoiding the Fall: China's Economic Restructuring*, Carnegie Endowment for International Peace, 2013.

Poling, Gregory B., Tabitha Grace Mallory, and Harrison Prétat, 'Pulling Back the Curtain on China's Maritime Militia', *CSIS*, 18 November 2021, http://tinyurl.com/9kc69mrx. Accessed on 6 September 2023.

Prabhupada, A.C.B.S., *Bhagavad-Gita as It Is*, Bhaktivedanta Book Trust, 1983.

Rangarajan, Mahesh, and Vasant K. Saberwal (eds), *Battles Over Nature Science and the Politics of Conservation*, Permanent Black, 2005.

Rangarajan, Mahesh, *Fencing the Forest: Conservation and Ecological Change in India's Central Provinces, 1860-1914*, Oxford University Press, 1996.

Raychaudhuri, Tapan, and Irfan Habib (eds), *The Cambridge Economic History of India: Volume 1, c.1200-c.1750*, Cambridge University Press, 1982.

Rickett, Allen W. (ed.), *Guanzi: Political, Economic, and Philosophical Essays from Early China*, Princeton University Press, 1998.

Rithmire, Meg. E., 'Land Institutions and Chinese Political Economy: Institutional Complementarities and Macroeconomic Management', *Politics & Society*, Vol. 45, No. 1, 2017.

Rithmire, Meg. E., *Land Bargains and Chinese Capitalism: The Politics of Property Rights under Reform*, Cambridge University Press, 2015.

Rossabi, Morris (ed.), *Governing China's Multiethnic Frontiers*, University of Washington Press, 2004.

Rowe, William T., *China's Last Empire: The Great Qing*, Harvard University Press, 2009.

Roy, Tirthankar, *A Business History of India*, Cambridge University Press, 2018.

Rozelle, Scott, and Natalie Hell, *Invisible China: How the Urban-Rural Divide Threatens China's Rise*, University of Chicago Press, 2020.

Rudolph, Jennifer, and Michael Szonyi (eds), *The China Questions: Critical Insights into a Rising Power*, Harvard University Press, 2018.

Sanyal, Sanjeev, *Land of the Seven Rivers: A Brief History of India's Geography*, Penguin India, 2013.

Sastry, Trilochan, *The Essentials of Hinduism: An Introduction to All the Sacred Texts*, Penguin Viking, 2022.

Sathe, Dhanamnjiri, *The Political Economy of Land Acquisition in India: How a Village Stops Being One*, Springer Nature Singapore, 2017.

Schram, Stuart R., 'Mao Zedong and the Theory of the Permanent Revolution 1958-69', *The China Quarterly*, No. 46, 1971.

Shambaugh, David (ed.), *China and the World*, Oxford University Press, 2020.

Shang Yang, *The Book of Lord Shang: Apologetics of State Power in Early China*, Yuri Pines (trans.), Columbia University Press, 2017.

Shapiro, Judith, *China's Environmental Challenges*, Wiley, 2016.

Shapiro, Judith, *Mao's War against Nature: Politics and the Environment in Revolutionary China*, Cambridge University Press, 2001.

Shirk, Susan L., *How China Derailed Its Peaceful Rise*, Oxford University Press, 2023.

Shum, Desmond, *Red Roulette: An Insider's Story of Wealth, Power, Corruption, and Vengeance in Today's China*, Scribner, 2021.

Singh, Tripurdaman, 'How India's Founding Fathers Built an "Eastminster-Style" Democracy', *The Times of India*, 22 January 2022, http://tinyurl.com/56eaadk3. Accessed on 6 September 2023.

Smil, Vaclav, 'China's Great Famine: 40 Years Later', *BMJ*, Vol. 319, No. 7225, 1999.

Spence, Jonathan, *The Search for Modern China*, W.W. Norton & Co, 1999.

Srivastava, V.C., Lallanji Gopal, *History of Agriculture in India Up to C.1200 AD*, Concept Publishing Company, 2008.

Stasavage, David, *The Decline and Rise of Democracy: A Global History from Antiquity to Today*, Princeton University Press, 2020.

Strange, Austin, *Chinese Global Infrastructure*, Cambridge University Press, 2023.

Sud, Nikita, *The Making of Land and The Making of India*, Oxford University Press, 2021.

Sunchu, Prakash S., 'Yin and Yang, Shiv and Shakti – Dual Forces in Singularity', *Indian Philosopher*, 6 December 2018, http://tinyurl.com/yhyvr85x. Accessed on 6 September 2023.

Sweet, Rod, 'Why China Can Build High-Speed Rail So Cheaply', *Global Construction Review*, 14 July 2014, http://tinyurl.com/bdh5dmzk. Accessed on 6 September 2023.

Timberg, Thomas A., *The Marwaris: From Jagat Seth to the Birlas*, Penguin Books Limited, 2015.

U.S.-China Economic and Security Review Commission, *2020 Report to Congress of the U.S.-China Economic and Security Review Commission*, December 2020, http://tinyurl.com/52u9wu6y. Accessed on 6 September 2023.

Vakil, Raeesa, 'Constitutionalizing Administrative Law in the Indian Supreme Court: Natural Justice and Fundamental Rights', *International Journal of Constitutional Law*, Vol. 16, No. 2, 2018.

Veeck, Gregory, et el., *China's Geography: Globalisation and the Dynamics of Political, Economic and Social Change*, Rowman & Littlefield, 2021.

Violatti, Cristian, 'Brahmi Script', *World History Encyclopedia*, 14 November 2016, http://tinyurl.com/msmjf6mf. Accessed on 6 September 2023.

Vittal, N., *Corruption in India: Overview, Detection and Prevention of 'Corruption in India'*, Academic Foundation, 2003.

Vogel, Ezra F., 'Chen Yun: His Life', *Journal of Contemporary China*, Vol. 14, No. 45, January 2007.

Vogel, Ezra F., *Deng Xiaoping and the Transformation of China*, Harvard University Press, 2013.

Walder, Andrew G., *Agents of Disorder: Inside China's Cultural Revolution*, Harvard University Press, 2019.

Walsh, Megan, *The Subplot: What China Is Reading and Why It Matters*, Columbia Global Reports, 2022.

Wang, Bing, and Tobias Just, *Understanding China's Real Estate Markets: Development, Finance, and Investment*, Springer, 2021.

Wang, Jingai, Shunlin Liang and Peijun Shi, *The Geography of Contemporary China*, Springer, 2003.

Wang, Zhihe, et el., 'Ending an Era of Population Control in China: Was the One-Child Policy Ever Needed', *The American Journal of Economics and Sociology*, Vol. 75, No. 4, 6 September 2016.

Watson, Burton (trans.), *Han Feizi: Basic Writings*, Columbia University Press, 2003.

Weber, Isabella, *How China Escaped Shock Therapy: The Market Reform Debate*, Routledge, 2021.

Weber, Max, *The Protestant Ethic and the Spirit of Capitalism*, 1904.

Willy Wo-Lap Lam (ed.), *Routledge Handbook of the Chinese Communist Party*, Taylor & Francis, 2017.

Xin Sun, 'Selective Enforcement of Land Regulations: Why Large Scale Violaters Succeed', *The China Journal*, Vol. 74, 2015.

Xinran, *Buy Me the Sky: The Remarkable Truth of China's One-Child Generations*, Ebury Digital, 2015.

Xinzhong Yao, *An Introduction to Confucianism*, Cambridge University Press, 2000.

Xu Xinjian, 'The Chinese Identity in Question: "Descendants of the Dragon" and "The Wolf Totem"', *Revue de littérature compare*, Vol. 337, 2011.

Yang, Keming, *Entrepreneurship in China*, Routledge, 2007.

Yang, Sunny L., *The War on Corruption in China: Local Reform and Innovation*, Routledge, 2023.

Ye, Sang Barme, and Geremie R., 'The Fate of the Confucious Temple, the Kong Mansion and Kong Cemetery', *China Heritage Quarterly*, 2009.

Yi-Fu Tuan, *A Historical Geography of China*, Routledge, 2008.

Yitao Tao, and Zhiguo Lu, *Special Economic Zones and China's Development Path*, Springer, 2013.

Young, Scott, *China's Hukou System: Markets, Migrants and Institutional Change*, Palgrave Macmillan, 2013.

Zhang, Xiaoling, and Yongnian Zheng (eds), *China's Information and Communications Technology Revolution: Social Changes and State Responses*, Routledge, 2009.

Zhenhua Chen, et el., *High Speed Rail and China's New Economic Geography*, Edward Elgar Publishing, 2019.

Zhu, Zhiqun, 'Interpreting China's "Wolf-Warrior Diplomacy"', *The Diplomat*, 15 May 2020, http://tinyurl.com/32e8fysh. Accessed on 6 September 2023.

Index

5G, 139, 145

access money, 184, 185, 186, 189, 269
Afghanistan, 9, 98, 214, 215, 216
Africa, xvi, 99, 103, 104, 105, 106,
    169, 194, 198, 204, 217, 283
agricultural reforms, 81, 86, 87, 249
Ahluwalia, Montek, 56
Ahmedabad, 135, 143
Akhand Bharat, 33
Aksai Chin, 215
Alstom, 141
American hegemony, 13
Anglo-Saxon, 24, 29, 34, 64
Anhui, 79, 151
Ant Group, 153, 154, 249
Anthropocene, 229
anti-imperialist, 214
Appu, P.S., 82
Arabian Sea, 97, 216
Arabs, 98
Arthashastra, 17, 26, 76
Asia, xvi, 3, 8, 90, 91, 92, 93, 95, 97,
    98, 99, 102, 103, 104, 105, 112, 114,
    169, 194, 198, 204, 208, 212, 213,
    214, 216, 217, 241, 242, 251, 252,
    280, 283
Asian Century, xiv, xv, 285
Asian Infrastructure Investment Bank
    (AIIB), 205, 284
Atharvaveda, 76
Atmanirbhar Bharat, 282
AUKUS, xii
Aurangzeb, 28, 29, 30
Australia, 99, 105, 144, 199, 206, 207,
    208
authoritarianism, xix, 27, 64, 194, 211,
    233, 236, 244, 250, 258

autocratic, 61, 186, 260
Ayodhya, 255

Ba Shusong, 111
Baihetan Dam, 6
Bandar Abbas, 216
Bangalore, 96
Bangladesh, 9, 215
Bangladesh–Myanmar border, 9
banking, xxi, xxvi, 163, 164, 165, 166,
    167, 168, 170, 172, 173, 174, 175,
    281, 284
Battle of Plassey, 212
Bay of Bengal, 7
Beihai, 93
Beijing Consensus, xvi
Beijing Gas Group Company Limited,
    237
Beijing, xii, xvi, 32, 74, 142, 154, 176,
    177, 190, 199, 215, 216, 233, 237,
    239, 241, 269
Beijing–Tianjin–Hebei, 237
Belgian, 154
Belt and Road Initiative (BRI), xi, 142,
    143, 169, 203, 204, 205, 211
Bengal, 7, 76, 104, 126, 127, 128, 129,
    130, 131, 133, 157, 212, 272
Berlin, 90
Bhagavad Gita, 256
Bharatavarsha, 20, 21
Bharatiya Janata Party (BJP), 37, 38
Bhattacharjee, Buddhadeb, 128
Bhutan, 213, 214
Big Bang reform, 26, 46
Bihar, 7, 76, 188, 272
Bo Xilai, 176, 177, 178, 179
Bo Yibo, 177
Bombardier, 141

Bombay, xvii, 8, 94
boom–bust cycles, 123
Boxer Rebellion, 192
Brahmaputra, 241, 242
Brahmi script, 14
Brazil, 134
Bretton Woods, 217
Brezhnev Doctrine, 195
bribery, 184, 185, 186, 187, 188
Britain, xv, 34, 35, 92, 94, 208, 214, 216
British common law, 66
British Commonwealth, 214
British Guyana, 104
British India, 8, 213, 214
Buddhism, xxv, 15, 17, 18
Buddhist, 18, 21, 98, 99, 193, 231
Bush, George W., 198

Calcutta, 8, 94
Cambodia, 8, 99
Cantonese, 4, 12, 14, 92, 155
capitalism, 13, 36, 129, 145, 153, 155, 159, 252
Central Asia, 97, 213, 214, 216
Central Bureau of Investigation, 55, 157
Central China, xii, 119
Central Military Commission, 45, 60, 211, 248
Central Party History Research Office, 181
Central Vigilance Commission, 55
century of humiliation, 6, 20, 31, 32, 35, 89, 191, 212
Ceylon, 98
Chabahar Port, 216
Chairman, 33, 43, 137, 211
Chanakya, 17, 26
Chandigarh, 131
Chandil, 124
Chaxugeju, 21, 22
checks and balances, xvi, xx, 39, 59,

69, 156, 185, 186, 189, 243, 250, 258, 263, 280
chemical fertilizers, xxiii, 229, 242
Chen Yun, 26, 46, 78, 86
Chengdu, 176
Chennai, iv, 8, 95, 96, 143
Chhattisgarh, 157
Chiang Kai-shek, 33, 192
Chidambaram, P., 57
Chief Minister (CM), 128, 129, 130, 188
China Dream, 178, 210, 218, 248, 253
China Mobile, 139
China model, 135
China Plus One strategy, 167, 277
China Question, xvi
China Sea, 4, 74, 98, 199, 206, 207, 212
China Telecom, 139
China Unicom, 139
China's GDP, xiv, xxii, 89, 94, 115, 119, 165, 178, 201
China-centric, 99
Chinalco, 199
China–Pakistan Economic Corridor (CPEC), 205, 216
Chinese Civil War, 33, 113, 192
Chinese diaspora, 24, 99, 101
Chinese economic miracle, xv, xxi, 4
Chinese emigrants, 100, 101
Chinese Emperor, 211
Chinese financial system, 170, 171
Chinese model of development, 204
Chinese New Year, 238
Chinese policymakers, 86, 87, 201, 202, 204, 212
CHIPS Act, 278
Chola kingdom, 98
Chongqing, 176, 177
Christian, xxv, 18, 192
clean energy, 9, 234, 283
Climate change, 229, 242
Clinton, Bill, 198

coal scam, 56, 156, 189
coastal China, 89, 92, 97, 163, 225
Cochin, 95
Cold War, 13, 192, 193, 195, 214, 215, 252
collateral-based model, 170
collectives, 78, 113, 114, 117
colonialism, 15, 247, 254
common prosperity, xxiii, 46, 69, 178, 182, 210, 227, 279
Communist Party of China (CPC), xiii, xx, xxii, 24, 26, 33, 34, 39, 43, 44, 45, 47, 49, 52, 54, 60, 61, 62, 63, 65, 67, 68, 69, 78, 79, 80, 109, 112, 113, 120, 148, 149, 150, 151, 153, 154, 155, 176, 177, 178, 179, 180, 181, 189, 192, 194, 196, 197, 199, 210, 211, 212, 220, 225, 233, 234, 239, 248, 249, 257, 258, 263, 280
Communist Party of India (Marxist), 126
Communist Party of Indonesia, 194
communist, xiv, xxii, xxiv, 16, 17, 18, 26, 30, 31, 35, 39, 52, 64, 113, 114, 122, 126, 127, 130, 146, 147, 151, 153, 163, 167, 176, 177, 178, 186, 187, 194, 195, 196, 197, 210, 220, 247, 248, 253, 257, 279
Comptroller and Auditor General of India (CAG), 55, 133, 157, 158
concurrent (joint) list, 54
Confucian, 16, 17, 18, 19, 22, 31, 64, 67, 191, 194, 195, 210, 220, 231, 251, 252, 253, 276
Confucianism, 15, 17, 18, 210
Confucius Institutes, 208
Confucius, 15, 16, 23, 208, 220
Constitution, 36, 65, 68, 113, 125, 180, 248, 258, 259, 261, 263, 266, 271
contract farming, xxi, 81, 85, 228, 274, 275

Copenhagen Climate Change Conference, 199
corruption perception index (CPI), 185
corruption, xix, xxiii, 32, 36, 49, 50, 56, 69, 85, 123, 134, 136, 145, 153, 159, 160, 172, 176, 177, 178, 179, 181, 182, 183, 184, 185, 186, 187, 188, 189, 196, 210, 269, 271
Country Garden, 166, 171
Covid-19, 208, 277
Cultural Revolution, 18, 23, 35, 43, 44, 47, 49, 50, 52, 61, 64, 69, 177, 180, 195, 210, 232, 248, 249, 251, 257, 279
culture, xiii, xv, xviii, xxiv, xxv, xxvi, 3, 8, 9, 11, 12, 13, 18, 19, 20, 23, 28, 29, 30, 35, 40, 60, 73, 74, 89, 92, 97, 98, 99, 146, 148, 173, 208, 214, 222, 251, 253, 254, 255, 258, 259, 264, 276, 280
current exchange rates, xiv
current population, 219
Czechoslovakia, 195

Dadri, 128
Dalian, 93
dam, xii, 6, 109, 124, 128, 240, 242, 243
Danjiangkou Reservoir, xii
debt, xi, xiii, xix, xxiii, xxvi, 50, 118, 119, 122, 163, 164, 165, 166, 167, 169, 171, 205, 276, 277, 281
Deccan Plateau, 7
decentralization, 36, 53, 58, 228, 263, 266, 269, 270, 271
Delhi–Mumbai Industrial Corridor (DMIC), xiv, 135
demand and supply, 26, 85
democracy, xvi, xix, 10, 15, 27, 34, 36, 40, 51, 68, 69, 82, 128, 132, 185, 189, 192, 196, 208, 217, 243, 247, 248, 254, 258, 259, 260, 262, 264,

271, 272, 280
demographic, xix, xxiii, 4, 7, 129, 219,
219, 220, 221, 222, 227, 228, 278,
282
Deng era, 46, 258
Deng Xiaoping, xi, xiii, xx, 34, 43,
44, 45, 49, 61, 63, 65, 67, 92, 93,
101, 102, 113, 149, 151, 195, 197,
221, 257
Denmark, 199
Department of Telecommunications
(DoT), 140
dependency ratio, 222
Direct Benefit Transfers (DBT), 85
divide and rule, 29, 215
Document no. 9, 180
domestic production, 86
Dragon Emperor, 29
dragon, xxiv, xxv
drought, xxiii, xxiv, 75, 230, 243
dual track, 47, 92, 152
Dujiangyan, 230
Duke Huan, 25
Durgapur Expressway, 126
Dutch East Indies, 90

earthquake, 75, 240, 241
ease of doing business, 160
East India, 9, 14, 29, 94, 98, 212
Eastern China, 3, 91, 92, 242
Eastern Dedicated Freight Corridor
(EDFC), 135
ecological civilization, 234, 241
economic growth, xiii, xiv, xvi, xvii,
xviii, xix, xxi, xxv, 5, 7, 9, 28, 43,
47, 50, 51, 53, 67, 68, 69, 86, 93,
94, 95, 100, 101, 110, 120, 122, 126,
128, 134, 137, 138, 146, 150, 153,
159, 163, 164, 167, 168, 171, 172,
175, 178, 182, 184, 186, 187, 189,
196, 202, 212, 217, 226, 227, 233,
234, 235, 243, 244, 248, 249, 252,
263, 264, 268, 269, 272, 273, 276,

277, 278, 279, 281, 282, 284
Ecuador, xi
Eight Elders, 48, 61
Emergency, 36, 48, 51, 156, 250, 255,
258, 266
English Channel, xiii
entrepreneurship, xix, 47, 146, 147,
149, 151, 152, 153, 154, 155, 159,
247
Eurasia, 230
European Union (EU), 198, 199
evangelization, 13, 14, 208
Evergrande, xiii, 111, 112, 166, 171
export processing zone (EPZ), 95
export-led manufacturing, 107, 163
extraterritoriality, 90, 92, 94, 205

factory of the world, xi, 89, 164, 209,
227, 276
Falta, 95
federalism, xix, 58
Fei Xiaotong, 22
feng shui, 17
Fidelity, 170
Fiji, 103, 104
financial sector, xvii, 57, 163, 164,
167, 168, 172, 173, 174
fiscal expenditure, 81
Five Principles of Peaceful
Coexistence, 193
Five-Year Plan, 35
flood, xxiii, xxiv, 5, 6, 75, 230, 240,
243
fodder scam, 188
Food and Agricultural Organization
(FAO), 82
Food Corporation of India, 84
food processing, 129
foreign direct investment (FDI), 89,
93, 95, 96, 103, 107, 204
foreign exchange rates, xxi
fourteenth Finance Commission, 272
French Indochina, 90

French, 89, 90, 94, 192, 254
Fujian, 47, 92
fundamental right, 125, 261
Fuzhou, 93

G7, 197
Galwan Valley, 206
Gandhi, Indira, xxi, 36, 38, 48, 50, 156, 255, 266
Gandhi, Mahatma, 33, 43, 106, 255, 271
Gandhi, Rajiv, 37, 38, 49
Gandhi, Sanjay, 49
Gandhian, 258
Gang of Four, 44, 61
Ganges Delta, 126
Garibi Hatao, 36
geography, xviii, xxvi, 3, 6, 8, 14, 33, 73, 89, 93, 258, 276
geopolitics, xv, xix, xx, xxiii, xxvi, 3, 13, 18, 21, 30, 31, 50, 167, 169, 195, 206, 212, 213, 217, 218, 277, 278
Germany, 120, 165, 259
Gilgit–Baltistan, 215
Gini coefficient, 226, 227
Glaciers, 241
Global Corruption Barometer (GCB), 185
global exports, 142
global financial crisis (GFC), 110, 111, 120, 164, 166, 168, 178, 199, 200, 201, 202, 204
global market, xx, 40, 198
Global South, xvi, 199
Godavari, 8, 76
Golden Quadrilateral, xiv, 135
Government of India, xvi, 59, 218
Grand Canal, 5, 6, 230
Grand Trunk Road, 9
Great Leap Forward (GLF), 35, 43, 45, 50, 61, 69, 79, 180, 221, 231, 232, 249, 252, 257, 279

Great Wall, xiii, 5, 20, 30, 35, 137
Greek, xxiv, 278
Green plots, 238
Green Revolution, 36, 76, 83, 273
gross domestic product (GDP), xiv, xxii, 4, 85, 89, 94, 95, 114, 115, 119, 120, 123, 134, 136, 164, 165, 178, 200, 202, 228, 249, 251, 277, 278
Growth Corridor, 135
Gu Kailai, 177
Guan Zhong, 25
Guangdong, 47, 92, 152
Guangzhou, 6, 89, 93, 111, 141, 177
Guanxi, 21, 23, 24, 121, 152
Guanzi, 25, 26, 46, 53, 88, 171
Gujarat, 104, 130, 133
Gulf countries, 105
Gurugram, 96, 131, 135
Gwadar, 216

Haldia, 127
Hambantota, 205
Han Fei, 60
Han, xxiv, 8, 13, 20, 23, 29, 30, 53, 60, 61, 211
Hanzi, 11, 12
Harappan civilization, 76
Harbin, 142
Haryana, 131, 188
hegemony, 13, 36, 47, 54, 55, 98, 156, 284
Heibei, 237
Heihe, 4
Heihe–Tengchong Line, 4
Heilmann, Sebastian, 53
Heywood, Neil, 176, 177
high-speed rail, 141, 142, 143, 204, 234, 282
Himalayan border, 33, 206
Himalayas, xiii, 3, 230, 241, 242
Hindu, 14, 19, 98, 99, 123, 254
Hindustani, 14

Hindutva, 37, 39, 254, 255
Hirakud Dam, 124, 128
historical nihilism, 180, 181, 234, 257
history, xi, xiii, xix, xviii, xxi, xxii,
    xxiii, xxiv, xxvi, 3, 5, 8, 9, 12, 14,
    22, 28, 29, 30, 31, 32, 40, 43, 45,
    48, 49, 51, 52, 61, 63, 74, 75, 77,
    79, 89, 94, 96, 97, 99, 100, 104,
    109, 112, 113, 114, 123, 156, 181,
    211, 212, 225, 230, 231, 248, 249,
    251, 252, 253, 254, 257, 276, 285
Hong Kong, 6, 52, 80, 89, 93, 94, 101,
    102, 103, 110, 155, 163, 196, 198,
    208
household responsibility system
    (HRS), 79, 80, 81, 85, 113
Hu Angang, 178
Hu Ming, 177
Hua Guofeng, 44, 79
Huai River, 4, 73
Huangdao, xii
Huawei, 139, 249
Hui Ka Yan, 111
hukou, 32, 114, 121, 122, 211, 225,
    226
hydropower, 240
hydroprojects, 241

illegal abortions, 222
immigration, 13, 100
Indentured labour, 105
Independence, xxi, xxii, 8, 27, 82, 83,
    94, 104, 105, 125, 131, 155, 156,
    214, 258, 260, 264
India Investment Centre (IIC), 105
Indian Administrative Service (IAS),
    55, 156, 265
Indian ambassador, 218
Indian Civil Service (ICS), 156
Indian Constitution, 65
Indian diaspora, 103, 105, 106, 107
Indian National Congress (INC), 34,
    36, 48, 54

Indian Ocean, 98, 216, 242
Indian Railways, 9
Indian start-ups, 107
Indian subcontinent, 3, 7, 17, 20, 21,
    24, 29, 30, 33, 76, 97, 212, 215,
    230, 240, 241, 254, 285
indicization, 28
individual ownership, 113
Indo-China border, 32, 206
Indo-China, xv, xvii, xviii, xxv, 28, 32,
    99, 206, 215, 216
Indo-Gangetic plains, 76
Indonesia, 8, 101, 126, 127, 134, 185,
    193, 194, 207, 214
Indus, 4, 7, 76, 241
Industrial Revolution, xi, 229, 283
infanticide, 222
inflation, 46, 77, 196, 201
information technology, 129
infrastructure, xi, xiv, xvi, xvii, xix,
    xxii, xxiii, 4, 5, 6, 7, 9, 56, 57, 83,
    109, 110, 111, 112, 113, 118, 119,
    120, 124, 125, 126, 129, 134, 135,
    136, 137, 138, 141, 142, 143, 144,
    146, 158, 159, 164, 172, 174, 175,
    178, 182, 202, 204, 205, 211, 216,
    227, 237, 238, 243, 249, 263, 267,
    269, 270, 273, 274, 275, 276, 277,
    279, 282, 283
Inner Mongolia, 14
International Monetary Fund (IMF),
    56, 57, 115
international trade, xxi, 8, 89, 94
Iran, 216

Jack Ma, 153, 154, 249
JAM trinity, 281
Jamaica, 104
Japan, 18, 20, 91, 92, 99, 141, 154,
    164, 197, 199, 201, 206, 207, 252,
    253
Jews, 98
Jharkhand, 157

Jiang Qing, 44
Jiang Zemin, 63, 198
Jiangsu, 141
Jiaozhou Bay Bridge, xii
Jinsha, 241
Jintao, Hu, 38, 63, 65, 199, 234
Junghar Mongols, 212
Jungharia, 212

Kabul, 9
kalapani, 104
Kalinganagar, 128
Kannur, 160
Karakoram Highway, 215, 216
Karakoram, 3, 215, 216
Karnataka, 133
Kartavya Path, 255
Kashmir, 215
Kautilya, 76
Kaveri, 8, 76
Kaveripattinam, 104
Ken-Betwa link, 175
Kharagpur, 130
Khrushchev, Nikita, 192, 257
Khunjerab Pass, 215
Kim II Sung, 194
King George III, 190
Kissinger, Henry, 195
Kolkata, iv, 8, 126, 131
Korea, 18, 20, 91, 194, 197, 199, 201,
    207, 251
Korean War, 194
Kozhikode, 160
Krishi-Parashara, 76
Krishna, 8, 76, 256
K-shaped recovery, 281
Kuomintang (KMT), 192, 220

labour-intensive, 75, 200, 201
Lama, Dalai, 199
Land Acquisition Act, 124
land acquisition, xxiii, 66, 107, 121,
    124, 125, 126, 127, 128, 135, 143,

145, 174, 243, 249, 274
Land Administration Law, 114, 117
land ceiling, 123
language, xviii, 11, 12, 13, 14, 15, 208,
    247, 254, 260
Lao Tsu, 17
Laos–China Railway, 142
large-scale migration, 105
Latin America, 198
Lee Kuan Yew, 13, 197
Li Keqiang, 122
Li Peng, 197
Lianyungang, 93, 141
liberalization, xiv, xvi, xxi, 10, 37, 65,
    86, 123, 124, 125, 126, 131, 155,
    156, 173, 174, 189, 204, 217, 243,
    266, 267, 280
Lieberthal, Kenneth, 63
Lin Biao, 43, 44, 49
liquified natural gas (LNG), 237
little emperors, 222
Liu Bang, xxiv
Liu Xiaobo, 199
local government financing vehicle
    (LGFV), xxiii, 119, 120, 166, 263
local governments, xxi, xxii, xxiii, 90,
    92, 102, 103, 109, 110, 111, 114,
    115, 116, 117, 119, 120, 121, 122,
    138, 169, 170, 182, 237, 249, 263,
    266, 269, 270, 271, 272, 273, 278
Loess Plateau, 231, 239, 240
London, 90
Look East policy, 217

M document, 56
Macartney, George, 190, 212
Macaulay, 15
Madras, 8, 94
Magna Carta, 254
Mahabharata, 20, 21
Maharashtra, 128, 133
Make in India, 95, 106
Malabar Coast, 8

Malacca Straits, 216
Malaya, 90
Malayalam, 14
Malthusian, 220
Manchu Qing, 30
Manchuria, 31, 32, 60, 74, 91, 92
Manchus, 20, 31
Mandal Commission, 37
Mandarin, 5, 12, 14
Mandate of Heaven, 35, 69, 73, 210,
    211, 248, 280
Mandela, Nelson, 43
Manusmriti, 123
Mao era, 64, 195, 196, 231, 239, 257
Mao Zedong Thought, 47, 210
Mao Zedong, xx, 33, 34, 43, 47, 210,
    257
market economy, xi, xxii, 16, 25, 47,
    67, 80, 87, 114, 164, 202, 257, 266
Marxism, 31
Marxist-Leninist, 34, 52, 67, 192, 253,
    257
Mauritius, 103, 104
Mekong, 241
Mencius, 220
Menon, Shivshankar, 217, 218
Middle Ages, xxv
Middle Kingdom, xii, 18, 19, 29
migration, 7, 99, 104, 105, 113, 121,
    122, 134, 225, 226, 247, 277
Ming dynasty, 30, 99
Minh, Viet, 194
minimum alternate tax (MAT), 133
minimum support prices (MSP), 83,
    88
Ministry of Agriculture, 82
Ministry of Information Industry, 139
Ministry of Land and Resources
    (MLR), 116
Ministry of Overseas Indian Affairs
    (MOIA), 106
Minute on Education, 15
miracle growth, 200, 201

Mitsubishi, 141
mixed economy, 35, 173
MNREGA, 84
Modi, Narendra, xxi, 38, 51, 217
Mohan, Rakesh, 56
monetization, xxi, xxii, 109, 110, 114,
    123, 136, 138, 169, 272, 273, 276,
    277
Mongol Yuan, 30
Mongolia, 14, 32, 73
Mongols, 20, 30, 212
monocultural unitary, 40
Monoculture, 239
Mukherjee, Pranab, 57
Muller, Max, 75
Multicultural diversity, 40
multiplier, xv, 7, 81, 87, 113, 114, 119,
    136, 169
Mumbai, iv, xiv, 8, 95, 131, 135, 143
Muslim, 18, 30
mythology, xxiv, xxv

Nagapattinam, 104
Nandigram, 126, 127, 128, 130
Nanjing, 192
Nanshan Lijing Holiday Hotel, 176
Nantong, 93
Narayan, Jayprakash, 255
Narmada Bachao Andolan, 124, 243
Narmada River, 124
Narmada, 7, 76, 124, 243
Narsimham Committee report, 173
Natal, 104
National Action Plan on Climate
    Change (NAPCC), 243
National Bureau of Statistics (NBS),
    118, 119, 219, 226
National Clean Air Programme
    (NCAP), 243
National Democratic Alliance (NDA),
    125
National Family Planning
    Commission, 225

National Green Tribunal Act, 243
National Highway programme, xiv
National Infrastructure Pipeline (NIP), 175
National Judicial Appointments Commission, 266
National Mission for Clean Ganga, 243
National River Conservation Plan (NRCP), 243
National Sample Survey Office (NSSO), 85
National Security Advisor (NSA), 218
nationalization, xvii, 173
natural resources, 66, 112, 140, 158, 186, 203, 221, 229
Naughton, Barry, 90, 93
Nawab of Bengal, 212
Nehru, 34, 35, 36, 38, 48, 124, 193, 214, 285
Neighbours First, 217
neo-colonialism, 254
neoliberal, 26, 27, 46, 56, 88
Neolithic, 75
Nepal, 213, 214
New Pension Scheme (NPS), 261
New York, 153, 259
New Zealand, 144
Nian Guangjiu, 149
nineteenth century, 6, 12, 20, 104
Ningbo, 93
Nixon, Richard, 195
Nobel Prize, 199
Noida, 95, 96, 135
non-agricultural reforms, 86
non-agricultural use clearance (NAC), 132
Non-Aligned Movement (NAM), 193, 214
non-elite exchange, 184
non-farm sector, 86
non-performing asset (NPA), 145, 159, 168, 172

non-resident Indian (NRI), 105, 106, 160
North India, 7, 8, 9
North Korea, 194
Northwest China, 46
Norway, 199

one-child policy, 220, 221, 222, 223, 224, 225
open economic zone, 93
Open Up the West, 119
Opium War, 20, 89, 97
Opposition, 36, 37, 127, 157
Orissa, 128, 131, 157
Outer Ring Road, 135
Overseas Citizenship of India (OCI), 106
Overseas Indian Facilitation Centre (OIFC), 106
Oxford, 56

Pakistan, 205, 215, 217
pancasila, 193
panchayat, 54, 129
Panchayati Raj, 255, 271
Panchsheel, 193, 194, 285
Paracel Islands, 206, 207
paramount leader, xx, 46, 48, 60, 61, 63, 64, 155, 257, 263
Parayil, Sajan, 160
Paris, 90
Parliament, xxi, 54, 59, 65, 126, 255
parliamentary democracy, 128, 247, 248, 259
Partition, 33
Patel, Sardar Vallabhbhai, 48, 50
Pearl River Delta, 6
Pearl River, 6, 73
Peking University, 177
Peninsular India, 76
People's Liberation Army (PLA), 60, 192, 248
People's Republic of China, xx, 31, 32,

33, 60, 93, 99, 113, 192, 195, 249
per capita GDP, xiv
Persian Gulf, 98, 216
Persian, 14, 98, 216
philosophy, xviii, 15, 17, 19, 28, 53, 192, 234, 254
Pir Panjal, 3
Planning Commission, 56, 225
point to surface, 46, 53, 88, 269
Politburo Standing Committee (PSC), 39, 46, 52, 63, 176
pollution, 6, 229, 233, 236, 237, 242
Pompeo, Mike, 208
Pong, 124
population, xiii, xxiv, 3, 4, 5, 7, 8, 9, 14, 15, 18, 30, 31, 32, 34, 60, 74, 75, 77, 78, 82, 83, 86, 93, 101, 103, 110, 112, 113, 120, 121, 123, 124, 126, 129, 133, 134, 139, 155, 167, 219, 220, 221, 222, 225, 226, 227, 228, 229, 230, 231, 232, 242, 264, 278, 281
Portuguese, 94
post-Cold War, 13, 252
post-Covid, 204, 205, 280, 281, 282
Post-Independence, 94
post-Keynesian economics, 164
post-liberalization, 65, 123, 126, 131
post-Mao China, 44
post-Mao era, 64
post-reform, xxv
post-Stalinist Soviet Union, 195
pre-colonial, 103, 123
pre-Independence, 8
Prime Minister (PM), xi, xxi, 13, 36, 38, 48, 49, 51, 56, 157, 158, 193, 214, 255, 266
princelings, 38, 49
privatization, 57, 111, 136, 146, 172
Procter & Gamble, 264
production linked incentive (PLI), 96, 228, 282
Property Law, 67

public distribution system (PDS), 83, 84
public infrastructure projects, 5, 124
public interest, 65, 140, 156, 158
public policy, 26, 56, 115, 140, 182
public–private partnership (PPP), 135, 175
Pudong New Area, 93
Punjab, 131, 133, 215
purchasing power parity (PPP), xi, xiv

Qi, 25
Qianlong Emperor, 190, 211, 212
Qiao Weiyue, 5
Qing dynasty, 14, 30, 32, 192, 212
Qing empire, 30, 32, 33, 90, 211, 212
Qing Zhong, 25, 26, 171
Qing zhong, 88
Qingdao, xii, 91, 93
Qinhuangdao, 93
Qinling, 4
Qinling–Huaihe (QH) Line, 4
Quadrilateral Security Dialogue, xi
Queen of Jordan, 154

Raigad, 128
railway lines, 204
Raj Path, 255
Raja Todar Mal's, 32
Rajya Sabha, 126
Ram Janmabhoomi, 255
Ram Rajya, 17
Ramesh, Jairam, 56
Rao, P.V. Narasimha, 49, 56
Rashtriya Swayamsevak Sangh, 254
real estate, xiii, xix, xxii, xxiii, 4, 7, 9, 10, 47, 67, 96, 111, 112, 113, 114, 115, 117, 118, 119, 120, 121, 122, 123, 132, 133, 134, 135, 136, 137, 138, 154, 163, 164, 165, 166, 167, 168, 169, 172, 178, 182, 184, 202, 276, 277
Red Guards, 44, 177, 210
Red Line Policy, xxiii

Red Line, xxiii, 116
reform and opening-up, xvi, 6, 26, 45,
    46, 51, 68, 89, 101, 109, 138, 148,
    152, 163, 171, 178, 181, 196, 210,
    221, 225, 226, 227, 233, 248, 251,
    253, 263
rehabilitation programme, 239
Restoration, Meiji, 252, 253
Revitalize Northeast China, 119
Right to Education, 265
Right to Information, 265
Right to Life, 261
Rigveda, 75, 76
Ring Fence policy, 213
Rio Tinto, 199
Rise of Central China Plan, 119
river systems, 3, 4, 7
Rogoff, Kenneth, 115
Roman, xxiv, 12, 15, 19, 97
Rudd, Kevin, xi
Rural migrant workers, 226
Russia, 87, 146, 198, 199, 212, 213,
    216, 217, 280
Russian Revolution, 34

Sagarmala project, xiv
Salim Group, 126, 127
Salt and Iron, 25, 46, 88
Sanskrit, 14, 20, 75, 76
Sarasvati River, 76
Sardar Sarovar, 124, 243
Savarkar, Vinayak Damodar, 254
Sayanacharya, 76
Second Judges Case, 266
Securities and Exchange Board of
    India (SEBI), 173
Senkaku Islands, 199
shadow banking, 164, 165, 166, 168,
    172
Shaksgam Valley, 215
Shang Yang, 53, 60
Shanghai International Settlement
    (SIS), 90

Shanghai, 6, 89, 90, 91, 92, 93, 117,
    154, 198, 238, 284
Shantou, 92, 102
Shanxi, 237
Shaoqi Liu, 43, 44, 49
Shenzhen, 80, 89, 92, 102, 117, 118,
    227
Shi Huangdi, xiii, 29, 137
Shikoh, Dara, 28, 30
Shinkansen, 141
Shum, Desmond, 189
Sichuan, 241
Silicon Valley, 107
Silk Route, 97, 98
Singapore, 13, 90, 101, 142, 197
Singh, Manmohan, 38, 56, 57, 157
single-party, xvi, 68
Singur, 125, 126, 127, 128, 130
Singur–Nandigram, 126
Sinocentric, 20, 191
Sino-Indian War, xv
Sino-Soviet relationship, 195
Sitadhakashya, 76
Sky River project, 240
small and medium enterprises
    (SMEs), 107
social imperialist, 195
socialism with Chinese characteristics,
    xiii, 16, 34, 63, 210, 253, 257
socialism, xiii, 16, 34, 82, 129, 150,
    210, 253, 257
sociocultural, 251, 256
socio-economic, 87, 127, 219, 227,
    249, 273, 275
sociologist, 22, 182, 251, 252
sociology, xviii, 151
soft-power, 218
soil structure, 240
South China Sea, 199, 206, 207, 212
South China tour, 151
South China, 4, 5, 67, 112, 151, 155,
    199, 206, 207, 212, 230
South India, 7, 8, 98

South Korea, 194, 197, 199, 207, 251
Southeast Asia, 90, 97, 98, 99, 102, 103, 104, 105
Southern Tour, xx, 93
South-to-North Water Diversion Project, xii, 109
Soviet Ambassador, 195
Soviet bloc, 195
Soviet Union, 34, 43, 87, 179, 181, 192, 194, 195, 196, 197, 198, 214, 217, 220, 257
Soviet Union's invasion, 195
Spain, 120, 141
special economic zone (SEZ), xii, xiv, xvii, xix, xxii, 4, 6, 9, 45, 47, 50, 53, 89, 92, 93, 95, 96, 102, 107, 108, 109, 125, 126, 128, 131, 132, 133, 137, 181, 196, 227, 269, 273, 274, 276
speed money, 184, 186, 187, 269
Sri Lanka, xi, 97, 98, 103, 205
Stalin, Joseph, 192
state monopoly, 77, 78, 81
state-controlled production, 81
state-owned banks, 145, 163, 165, 167, 173, 174
state-owned enterprises (SOE), 47, 54, 146, 147, 151, 155, 163, 169, 198, 200
state-owned firms, 165, 168
stock markets, 54, 173
stubble burning, 238, 242
subsidization, 175
subsistence agriculture, 77, 87
Suharto, 194, 214
Sukarno, 193, 194
Sun Yat-sen, 102, 112
Supreme Court, 59, 65, 66, 132, 156, 157, 158, 265, 266, 274
Surat, 8
surgical strike, 195
Suri, Sher Shah, 9
Suriname, 103, 104

Swachh Bharat Abhiyan, 243

Taiping Rebellion, 192
Taiwan, 31, 32, 50, 91, 93, 94, 101, 155, 163, 192, 196, 202
Tamil, 14, 98, 99, 104, 133
tantra, xix
Taoism (Daoism), 15, 17, 18
Tarim Basin, 98
Tata Group, 126, 127, 130
Tata Small Car Project, 127
technological innovations, 234
Tehri, 124
telecommunication, 50, 57, 137, 139, 140, 141, 144, 145, 158, 159, 189
Tengchong, 4
Terracotta Army, 29, 231
the Fool, 149, 151
The Great Game, 213, 216
the Philippines, 101, 199
theory of wild chickens, 147
Third Judges Case, 266
Thitu, 207
Three Gorges Dam, xii, 6, 109
Tiananmen Square protests, xx, 196
Tianjin, 91, 93, 237
tianxia, 19, 20, 21, 28, 191, 193, 194, 211
Tibet, 3, 14, 32, 33, 60, 73, 87, 102, 212, 213, 215, 241, 242
Tibetan Plateau, xiii, 3, 4, 230, 240, 241
tigers and flies, 159, 179, 182
Timurid Mughals, 30
Tito, Josip Broz, 214
total fertility rate, 221
totalitarian, 10, 24, 35, 36, 68, 82, 121, 146, 147, 172, 176, 195, 249, 280
trade deficit, xv
transportation, 5, 9, 104, 118, 129, 134, 135, 143, 204, 226
treaty ports, 6, 8, 9, 89, 90, 91, 94, 97, 108, 205, 276

Trinidad, 103, 104
Trump, Donald, 153, 208
Tungabhadra, 76
Turkey, 216
Turki, 14
Turkmenistan, 216
twentieth centuries, 104, 213
twenty-first century, 46, 141

Uganda, xi, 103, 105
Ukraine, 182
Ultra High Voltage Direct Current
    (UHVDC), 6
UN Security Council, 199
Union Budget, 272
Union Public Services Commission,
    55
United Kingdom (UK), 103, 110, 120,
    141, 177, 208
United Nations Convention Against
    Corruption (UNCAC), 182
United Nations, 82, 103, 154, 182, 196
United Progressive Alliance (UPA),
    125, 157, 158
United States (US), xiii, xxii, 13, 44,
    103, 107, 115, 141, 142, 144, 164,
    165, 176, 192, 195, 196, 199, 201,
    202, 203, 206, 207, 208, 209, 214,
    215, 217, 227, 259, 278
unity in diversity, 21, 36
universal adult franchise, 34
urbanization, xix, xxii, xxiii, 4, 7, 9,
    89, 110, 111, 112, 113, 121, 122,
    126, 132, 133, 134, 138, 143, 164,
    182, 219, 222, 227, 228, 242, 249,
    263, 269, 270, 273, 274, 275, 276,
    278, 282, 283
Urdu, 14
US military, 208
US treasury bills, 201, 203
US, xiii, xxii, 13, 44, 103, 107, 115,
    141, 142, 144, 164, 165, 176, 192,
    195, 196, 199, 201, 202, 203, 206,

207, 208, 209, 214, 215, 217, 227,
    259, 278
Ussuri River, 195
Uttar Pradesh, 7, 76, 128
Uttarapatha, 9
Uzbekistan, 216

Vande Bharat, 143, 282
Vanguard, 170
vastu shastra, 17
Vedas, 21, 76
Vedic, 37, 75
Venezuela, 204
Vientiane, 142
Vietnam, 8, 20, 96, 99, 185, 194, 206,
    207
Vindhya Range, 7
Vogel, Ezra, 45

Wakhjir Pass, 216
Wang Huning, 248
Wang Lijun, 176, 177
War against Nature, 231
War of Independence, 104
Washington Consensus, xvi
Washington, George, 43
Washington, xvi, 43, 195
water pollution, 6, 229, 242
wealth management products
    (WMPs), 170
Weber, Max, 252
Wei River valley, 73
Weihai, 93
Wen Jiabao, 176
Wenzhou, 93
West Bengal Industrial Development
    Corporation (WBIDC), 126, 127
Western Ghats, 7
Western neoclassical, 171
Western thought, 15, 192
Westphalian, 193, 194, 205
Whitsun Reef, 207
wildlife, 229, 232, 239

WIN/Gallup International, 182
wolf warrior diplomacy, 206, 207
Wolf Warrior, 206
working age population, 219, 228
World Bank, 56, 57, 101, 142, 143,
    240, 270, 284
World Religion Database, 17
World Trade Organization, xx, 67, 81,
    198, 276
World War II, 33, 90, 91, 92, 100,
    220, 253, 278
Wuhan, 208

xenophobic, 195
Xi Jinping Thought, 46, 63
Xi Jinping, xx, xxiii, 38, 39, 46, 48, 61,
    63, 64, 65, 69, 103, 122, 141, 153,
    154, 178, 179, 180, 189, 199, 200,
    204, 206, 209, 210, 211, 218, 227,
    234, 236, 248, 253, 257, 279, 280
Xi Zhongxun, 61
Xiamen, 92, 102, 118
Xiaogang, 79
Xinhai Revolution, 192
Xinhua, 118
Xinjiang, 14, 32, 33, 60, 87, 141, 212,
    215, 216, 241
Xuantong, 30
Xuzhou–Lianyungang line, 141

Yangde, 238
Yangtze Delta, 73
Yangtze River, 4, 5, 6, 73, 96

Yantai, 93
Yao Jiaxin, 223
Yao Jingyuan, 168
Yellow River, xii, 4, 5, 73, 74
yin-yang, xxiv, 18, 19, 26, 32, 277, 279
Yoga day, 218
yuan, 110, 119, 149, 151, 200, 201,
    203, 204, 249
Yuanchen Yang, 115
Yunnan, 74

Zahedan, 216
Zambia, xi
zamindari, 82
zero-COVID policy, 50
Zhang Xiangwen, 4
Zhanjiang, 93
Zhao Ziyang, 109, 196, 197
Zheng He, 97
Zhengzhou East-Guangzhou line, 141
Zhongguo, xii, 19, 20, 21, 22, 29, 30,
    137, 248
Zhongrong, 166
Zhou Enlai, 44, 193, 285
Zhou Li, 78
Zhou Ziyang, 47
Zhu Rongji, 188
Zhuhai, 92, 102
Zipingpu, 240
zombie firms, 165, 168, 169, 173, 276
Zoroastrians, 98
ZTE, 139

Made in the USA
Monee, IL
15 May 2026

96af1ee9-5490-452a-8696-6b6dbbbef0f5R01